Nietzsche

Nietzsche

Naturalism and Interpretation

Christoph Cox

UNIVERSITY OF CALIFORNIA PRESS
Berkeley · *Los Angeles* · *London*

University of California Press
Berkeley and Los Angeles, California

University of California Press, Ltd.
London, England

Library of Congress Cataloging-in-Publication Data

Cox, Christoph, 1965–
    Nietzsche : naturalism and interpretation / Christoph Cox.
        p.   cm.
    Includes bibliographical references and index.
    ISBN 0-520-21553-2 (alk. paper).
    1. Nietzsche, Friedrich Wilhelm, 1844–1900—
    Contributions in theory of knowledge.   2. Knowledge,
    Theory of.   3. Nietzsche, Friedrich Wilhelm, 1844–
    1900—Contributions in ontology.   4. Ontology.
    I. Title.
    B3318.K7C68   1999
    193—dc21   99-30107
                                                  CIP

Manufactured in the United States of America

08   07   06   05   04   03   02   01   00   99
10   9   8   7   6   5   4   3   2   1

The paper used in this publication meets the minimum
requirements of ANSI/NISO Z39.48-1992 (R 1997)
(*Permanence of Paper*).

To
David Hoy
without whom not

For
Molly Whalen
without whom nought

Contents

Acknowledgments

I have had the good fortune to work in a field well laid out by remarkable predecessors. My original attraction to Nietzsche came through the work of Michel Foucault, Jacques Derrida, and Gilles Deleuze, whose writings constantly allude to, and are deeply informed by, an interpretation of Nietzsche that, in some sense, I have tried to reconstruct here. In so doing, I have been greatly aided by the clarity and rigor of several American interpretations of Nietzsche, particularly those of Richard Schacht, Alexander Nehamas, David Hoy, and Alan Schrift. These interpreters demonstrated to me the value of presenting Nietzsche's radical conceptual and stylistic refigurations in a sober philosophical language and proved to me that this "bit of tyranny" (*BGE* 188) against Nietzsche and his poststructuralist heirs could have genuine heuristic value.

This book is the product of a long series of apprenticeships that began while I was an undergraduate. I thank my mentors at Brown University: Michael Silverman and Bennet Schaber for introducing me to contemporary critical theory and Martha Nussbaum for introducing me to Nietzsche. For supporting and guiding my project at the graduate level, I express my gratitude to a group of remarkable teachers and scholars at the University of California, Santa Cruz: Donna Haraway, Jocelyn Hoy, Marsh Leicester, Dick Terdiman, and Hayden White. For providing me with ongoing opportunities to present my work to an expert audience, I thank my colleagues in the North American Nietzsche Society, especially Daniel Conway, Kathleen Higgins, Kevin Hill, Bernd

Magnus, Richard Schacht, and Alan Schrift. Friends and colleagues at
Hamilton College, especially Katheryn Doran, Steve Teles, and Rick
Werner, offered generous support and rigorous criticism and provided a
wonderful place to teach and work. Helpful comments and criticism in
the book's later stages were provided by the members of the Workshop
in Continental Philosophy at the University of Chicago, and particularly Dan Smith.

To my editor at the University of California Press, Ed Dimendberg, I
owe special thanks for his steadfast support of this project and for his
kind patience and encouragement as one deadline after another passed
without the book's completion. I am also extremely grateful to Alan
Schrift and Richard Schacht, who, as readers for the Press, gave not
only their support but also exceptionally detailed criticisms and suggestions that made this a better book. David Severton offered loads of wise
suggestions that made my prose more clear and readable.

Deepest thanks are due to my family as well, especially to my parents,
Christa Cox and Jim Cox, without whose encouragement and support
this book, and so much else, would not have been possible. Few aca-
demics are blessed with such a family, in which love and generosity are
matched by intellectual intensity and vitality. I owe a special debt to my
older sister Valerie, who, on the Christmas Eve before her death, gave
me my first introduction to Nietzsche by boldly presenting the family
with a reading from *Thus Spoke Zarathustra*.

Finally, my most substantial debts of gratitude are owed to two
people. I thank David Hoy for the extraordinary guidance he gave me
as my dissertation advisor and for so much more. He has not only provided me with the finest example of how to be a "Continental" philosopher but has also given me a host of opportunities that have allowed me
to go some way toward becoming such a philosopher myself. He has
unfailingly supported me and my work and has campaigned on my behalf well beyond the call of duty. I owe no less to Molly Whalen, whose
love, friendship, encouragement, and critical acumen have allowed me
to see this work through. Though our countless discussions and debates
go undocumented in what follows, they sound in the spaces between
every word.

Portions of this book previously have appeared in print. Parts of chapters 1 and 2 were published as "Being and Its Others: Nietzsche's Revaluation of Truth" in *Man and World* 29, no. 1 (1996): 43–61. This
material is reprinted with kind permission from Kluwer Academic Pub-

lishers. Earlier presentations of chapter 2 and chapter 4 were published, respectively, as "Nietzsche, Naturalism, and Interpretation" in *International Studies in Philosophy* 27, no. 3 (1995): 3–18, and "Nietzsche's Heraclitus and the Doctrine of Becoming" in *International Studies in Philosophy* 30, no. 3 (1998): 49–63. I thank Leon Goldstein for allowing me to use this material in the book. A version of the first half of chapter 3 appeared as "The 'Subject' of Nietzsche's Perspectivism" in *Journal of the History of Philosophy* 35, no. 2 (April 1997): 269–91. Rudolf A. Makkreel kindly granted permission to reprint portions of this article.

Note on Sources

I have followed the North American Nietzsche Society's guidelines for citing Nietzsche's works, which are designated by the standard acronyms of their English translations followed by the appropriate section number(s), designated by Arabic numerals. Exceptions to this rule are listed in the bibliography under Nietzsche's published works. Nietzsche's Prefaces are indicated with a "P" after the book's acronym, followed by a colon and the section number from that preface.

Though I have largely relied on the English editions and translations listed below, I have occasionally modified these translations and assume final responsibility for the rendering into English of Nietzsche's German. Given that since Nietzsche often uses ellipsis as a stylistic device, I have indicated my ellipses by placing them in brackets; ellipses not bracketed are Nietzsche's.

Abbreviations

Abbreviations of Nietzsche's texts are as follows:

A   *The Antichrist*

AOM   *Assorted Opinions and Maxims*

BGE   *Beyond Good and Evil*

BT   *The Birth of Tragedy.* "SC" denotes the 1886 Preface, titled
            "Attempt at a Self-Criticism."

CW   *The Case of Wagner*

D   *Daybreak*

EH   *Ecce Homo.* The four major divisions of this text are in-
            dicated by abbreviations of their titles: "Wise," "Clever,"
            "Books," and "Destiny." The subsections of "Books" that
            discuss Nietzsche's individual writings are indicated by the
            acronyms of those writings provided here.

GM   *On the Genealogy of Morals.* Roman numerals indicate
            essay number.

GS   *The Gay Science* (Books I–IV, Book V)

HC   "Homer's Contest"

HH   *Human, All too Human,* Vol. I

HL	"On the Use and Disadvantage of History for Life." References to this text provide both section and page numbers from the edition listed in the bibliography.
KGW	*Kritische Gesamtausgabe*
KSA	*Kritische Studienausgabe*
PTA	*Philosophy in the Tragic Age of the Greeks*
SE	"Schopenhauer as Educator." References to this text provide both section and page numbers from the edition listed in the bibliography.
TI	*Twilight of the Idols.* The eleven major divisions of this text are indicated by abbreviations of their titles: "Maxims," "Socrates," "Reason," "World," "Morality," "Errors," "Improvers," "Germans," "Skirmishes," "Ancients," and "Hammer."
TL	"On Truth and Lies in a Nonmoral Sense"
WP	*The Will to Power*
WS	*The Wanderer and His Shadow*
Z	*Thus Spoke Zarathustra.* Arabic numerals indicate the part number, followed by the chapter title.

Introduction

0.1 NIETZSCHE AND POSTMODERN PHILOSOPHY

Nietzsche is commonly regarded as the grandfather of philosophical postmodernism. If, to cite its most prominent exponent, postmodernism is characterized by "incredulity toward metanarratives," a "delegitimation [of metanarratives] fueled by the demand for legitimation itself," Nietzsche's relevance is not difficult to see.[1] Such incredulity and delegitimation is precisely what Nietzsche reveals to be the defining feature of our intellectual-historical situation, one marked by what he calls the "death of God" and "nihilism"—the self-overcoming of theological and metaphysical world interpretations.[2]

Nietzsche's analysis of this situation over a century ago was certainly precocious (or, on his own account, "untimely"), given that only in the postwar period have these issues of postmodernism come to prominence in European and Anglo-American thought. It is no coincidence, then, that the past few decades have seen a remarkable "Nietzsche renaissance" throughout Europe, Great Britain, and the United States.

1. Jean-François Lyotard, *The Postmodern Condition: A Report on Knowledge*, trans. Geoff Bennington and Brian Massumi (Minneapolis: University of Minnesota Press, 1984), xxiv, 39.
2. "[W]hat does nihilism mean?—*that the highest values devaluate themselves*" (*WP* 2). See the *Nachlaß* notes on "European Nihilism," collected in *WP* Book One, and *GM* III:27. I discuss these ideas in chapter 1.

This renewed interest in Nietzsche has been most significant in France and the United States. Nietzsche's tremendous influence on postmodern French philosophy has been direct and well documented.[3] Beyond Hegel, Husserl, and Heidegger, and beyond Marx and Freud, it was Nietzsche who provided the central figures in contemporary French philosophy (Deleuze, Foucault, Derrida, Lyotard, and Irigaray) with their most basic problems and resources.[4] The Anglo-American Nietzsche renaissance has had a less direct effect on mainstream contemporary philosophy in the United States. Yet here, too, Nietzsche has arguably "prefigured" the moves made by "postmodern American philosophers" (e.g., Quine, Sellars, Goodman, Davidson, Rorty, and Kuhn) toward antirealism in ontology, antifoundationalism in epistemology, and antidualism in the philosophy of mind.[5] Nietzsche's philosophy, then, is not only of interest for the history of ideas but is of genuine relevance to contemporary philosophy.

It is in this context that I have written the present book. Nietzsche is taken here as an important antecedent for more recent attempts at formulating a postmetaphysical epistemology and ontology, as traversing the same philosophical territory as the hermeneutics of Heidegger and Gadamer, the poststructuralism of Foucault, Derrida, Deleuze, and Lyotard, the neo-pragmatism of Quine, Goodman, and Rorty, and the philosophy of science of Kuhn and Feyerabend. For the most part, these more recent figures remain in the background and the focus is on Nietzsche. But, throughout, my aim remains twofold: to make a contribution to Nietzsche studies by providing a systematic interpretation of his later epistemology and ontology; and to uncover Nietzsche's solutions to some current philosophical problems.

3. See, for example, Alan D. Schrift, *Nietzsche and the Question of Interpretation: Between Hermeneutics and Deconstruction* (New York: Routledge, 1990), and *Nietzsche's French Legacy: A Genealogy of Poststructuralism* (New York: Routledge, 1995).

4. Thus, for example, Michel Foucault captured the spirit of postwar French philosophy when, in 1966, he wrote, "Nietzsche, offering his future to us as both promise and task, marks the threshold beyond which contemporary philosophy can begin to think again; and he will no doubt continue for a long while to dominate its advance" (*The Order of Things: An Archaeology of the Human Sciences*, trans. Alan Sheridan [London: Tavistock, 1970], 342).

5. See Cornel West, "Nietzsche's Prefiguration of Postmodern American Philosophy," in *Why Nietzsche Now?* ed. Daniel O'Hara (Bloomington: Indiana University Press, 1985).

0.2 THE ARGUMENT

A particularly important contemporary problem animates this project. Critics have consistently identified in Nietzsche's work a difficulty that has also been said to plague more recent postmodern positions: the problem of how an antifoundationalist philosophy can avoid vicious relativism and legitimate its claim to provide a platform for the critique of arguments, practices, and institutions. In Nietzsche, the problem is that of reconciling his genealogy and perspectivism (which seem to reject the notion that there is a uniquely correct conception of the world) with his doctrines of becoming and will to power (which seem to present just such a normative—perhaps even metaphysical—conception). I argue that Nietzsche successfully navigates between relativism and dogmatism and offers a viable, indeed exemplary, postmetaphysical epistemological and ontological position. I show that Nietzsche accepts the scientific project's naturalistic critique of metaphysics and theology but maintains that a thoroughgoing naturalism must move beyond scientific reductionism to accept a central feature of aesthetic understanding: an acknowledgment of the primacy and irreducibility of interpretation. I argue that the apparent relativism of perspectivism is held in check by Nietzsche's naturalism (which offers the doctrines of becoming and will to power in place of all theological interpretations) and that the apparent dogmatism of these doctrines is mitigated by his perspectivism (which grants that these doctrines are themselves interpretations yet ones that are better by naturalistic standards).

The first two chapters present an overview of Nietzsche's project. Chapter 1 situates this project within a genealogy of European thought that begins with Platonist metaphysics, passes through Christian theology to positivistic science, and culminates in "the death of God." It shows that Nietzsche accepts this inheritance and takes upon himself the task of rigorously thinking through the consequences of the "death of God." This "event," he believes, requires an elimination of the theological posits that remain implicit in the scientific concern for presuppositionless truth. Thus, Nietzsche sees "God's death" as forcing a reconciliation between truth and its traditional opponents, becoming and appearance, and a reconciliation between science and its traditional adversary, art. Chapter 2 explores the consequences of the death of God for epistemology and ontology and introduces the book's guiding figures: naturalism and interpretation. It shows that Nietzsche's rejection of the traditional epistemological ideal of a "God's eye view" leads him to a thoroughly naturalistic conception of knowing and being. Yet it maintains that Nietzsche also comes to reject the corollary to the "God's eye view": the notion of an absolute ontology, the idea that there must be some one, true way that the world really is. Instead, Nietzsche comes to see ontologies as always relative to background interpretations and to claim that interpretations can be challenged only by other interpretations, not by recourse to brute facts. Nonetheless, Nietzsche's naturalism is seen as providing him with compelling, if not final, reasons for the assertion that some interpretations are better than others.

The remainder of the book calls on the twin notions of naturalism and interpretation to make sense of Nietzsche's central epistemological and ontological doctrines: perspectivism, becoming, and will to power. These chapters argue against prominent readings that hold that perspectivism assumes the existence of a pre-given world upon which there are perspectives, a world that becoming and will to power are taken to describe. Chapter 3 argues that Nietzsche's misleading language of "perspective" ought to be subsumed within his broader and richer language of "interpretation" and that "interpretations," for Nietzsche, are not construals of some primary ontological ground but rather reconstruals of world conceptions already on hand. It argues that Nietzsche's naturalism leads him to dissolve the traditional epistemological dualism of "subject" and "object" into a common field of "interpretation" in which "subject" and "object" are of a piece and boundaries between them are constantly shifting. Chapter 4 argues that, on the one hand, Nietzsche views "becoming" as a naturalistic doctrine that counters the metaphysical preoccupation with being, stasis, and eternity by foregrounding the empirically evident ubiquity of change in the natural world. On the other hand, "becoming" is also seen as describing the incessant shift of perspectives and interpretations necessitated by a world that lacks a grounding essence. In the final chapter, I provide a similar reading for the doctrine of will to power. On the one hand, I see will to power as the empirical theory at which Nietzsche arrives after the elimination of all theological posits from prevailing scientific accounts of the natural world. On the other hand, I argue that natural change essentially involves "interpretation" in Nietzsche's vastly extended sense, that is, as every entity's impulse to extend its domain and incorporate others in its environment.

0.3 QUESTIONS OF TERMINOLOGY

My use of some contemporary philosophical terminology calls for comment. Throughout the book, I describe Nietzsche's position as a kind of "naturalism," a term ubiquitous in recent Anglo-American discussions of epistemology and metaphysics. As David Papineau has recently written, "nearly everybody nowadays wants to be a 'naturalist,' but the aspirants to the term nevertheless disagree widely on substantial questions of philosophical doctrine." [6] Though the term has a long history, its current usage is associated with the work of W. V. Quine, for whom "naturalism" signifies the rejection of first philosophy, the priority of natural science, and the redescription of philosophy as continuous with science. [7] Though Nietzsche does not himself use the term, his consistent appeals to "nature" and "the natural" and his overall project of "de-deifying nature" and "naturalizing humanity" (GS 109) ally him with Quine and other recent proponents of philosophical naturalism. Nietzsche's "naturalism," too, rejects first philosophy, whether conceived as metaphysics or epistemology. It denies the existence of supernatural entities and explanatory principles and endorses a broadly scientific conception of the world.

Yet Nietzsche insists that a thoroughgoing "naturalism" cannot be a scientism; that is, it cannot accept the Quinean view that "[t]he world is as natural science says it is" and "[n]aturalism looks only to natural science [. . .] for an account of what there is and what what there is does." [8] Nietzsche's genealogy of European thought (presented

---

6. David Papineau, *Philosophical Naturalism* (Oxford: Blackwell, 1993), 1. This sentiment was echoed even more recently by Barry Stroud in his Presidential Address to the Pacific Division of the American Philosophical Association. "'Naturalism,'" Stroud remarked, "seems [. . .] rather like 'World Peace.' Almost everyone swears allegiance to it, and is willing to march under its banner. But disputes still can break out about what it is appropriate or acceptable to do under the name of that slogan" ("The Charm of Naturalism," *Proceedings and Addresses of the American Philosophical Association* 70 [1996]: 43).

7. See Roger F. Gibson, *Enlightened Empiricism: An Examination of W. V. Quine's Theory of Knowledge* (Tampa: University of South Florida Press, 1988), 23 ff., for a collection and analysis of Quine's statements of his naturalistic position.

8. W. V. Quine, "Structure and Nature," *Journal of Philosophy* 89 (1992): 9. For naturalist critiques of Quinean scientism see Richard Rorty, *Philosophy and the Mirror of Nature* (Princeton: Princeton University Press, 1979), 171 ff., 199 ff., "Pragmatism without Method," in *Objectivity, Relativism, and Truth: Philosophical Papers*, vol. 1 (Cambridge: Cambridge University Press, 1991), 65 ff., and "Is Natural Science a Natural Kind?" in *Objectivity, Relativism, and Truth;* and Kai Nielsen, *Naturalism without Foundations* (Amherst, N.Y.: Prometheus Books, 1996), 25–55, whose versions of naturalism have much in common with that of Nietzsche.

in chapter 1) uncovers a residual theology in the modern scientific project's claim to describe the way the world really is. He argues that, if one carries through the naturalistic program implicit in modern science, one will discover that science overcomes itself, giving way to another discourse that can claim to be more rigorously naturalistic and that reveals the scientific to be but one among many true accounts of the world. That discourse is the *aesthetic,* which affirms sensuousness, materiality, multiplicity, becoming, historicity, creativity, and the irreducibility of interpretation. The aesthetic cannot and does not claim to take the place of science as the one true theory. It justifies itself holistically, by reference to a genealogical story; and it challenges the very idea of a single, final account.

I describe Nietzsche's naturalism as "antimetaphysical" or "postmetaphysical." This usage, too, must be qualified, since "metaphysics" has a notoriously wide range of uses. I use the term in two related senses. The first of them is quite literal. In this sense, metaphysics refers to discourses about what is beyond, above, or outside *physis* or nature. "Naturalism," then, is antimetaphysical in an obvious sense: it denies the existence of super-natural entities (souls, Forms, God, etc.) and extranatural (disembodied, ahistorical, noncontextual, foundational, infallible) points of view. This does not rule out talk of theoretical entities or principles such as quarks, force-points, *différance,* or will to power. Such entities and principles are perfectly admissible, provided that they are taken as revisable posits whose role is to explain (aspects of) experience and nature and are acknowledged to be the productions of a particular natural creature with its own peculiar purposes and projects. I also occasionally use the term "metaphysics" in a more specific sense drawn from Heidegger and Derrida. In this sense, "metaphysics" names "the determination of Being as *presence,*" that is, the privilege of what is *given,* existing purely and simply—not contextually, holistically, or differentially.[9] In this sense, recourse to "the immediate facts of experience," to necessary and universal categories of the mind, to mental meanings, or to underlying substances and subjects (to name but a few examples) is "metaphysical." Indeed, Heidegger and Derrida often call this metaphysics "ontotheology," since God is the archetype of such entities: a being untouched by becoming, context, or

9. See Jacques Derrida, "Structure, Sign, and Play in the Discourse of the Human Sciences," in *Writing and Difference,* trans. Alan Bass (Chicago: University of Chicago Press, 1978), 279.

difference. A "naturalism" that repudiates not only God but also his "shadows" (*GS* 108) will have no place for such entities.

A final set of terms needs to be qualified. I often speak of Nietzsche's "epistemology" and "ontology." Yet in contemporary philosophy it is common to view "epistemology" as a transcendental, foundational discipline that assumes the preexistence of subjects and objects and attempts to explain how the former can adequately represent the latter. As such, the discipline has been repudiated by those who, like Nietzsche, wish to move toward an antifoundationalist, holist conception of knowledge.[10] Nietzsche rarely uses the term (in German, *Erkenntnistheorie*); and where he does, he, too, tends to treat with disdain the discipline it names (see *GS* 354; *BGE* 204; *TI* "Reason" 3; *WP* 253, 410, 462, 591). Yet the term can also be taken in a more literal and innocuous sense to refer to a "theory of knowledge," that is, a theory about what we know, what knowledge is, and how we arrive at this knowledge. In this sense, Nietzsche certainly has a "theory of knowledge," albeit a naturalistic, holistic, antifoundationalist one. Given the awkwardness of alternative terminology, I have opted to use the term "epistemology" in this latter sense. The same is true of "ontology," which can be taken to describe a metaphysical discipline dealing with "what ultimately, truly, or really exists." But, here too, the term has a broader and less metaphysical sense; in this sense, "ontology" describes "what there is" qualified however one likes (e.g., "what there is relative to a theory or interpretation"). Again, it is in this latter sense that I use the term.

0.4 QUESTIONS OF METHOD

It has become obligatory, in works on Nietzsche, to make explicit and to justify one's methodological decisions regarding which of his texts one has chosen to take into account. There are two such decisions, one concerning periodization (how one divides up Nietzsche's corpus and which texts one takes to represent the "mature" Nietzsche), the other concerning use of the *Nachlaß* (whether or not to make use of those texts and notes that Nietzsche left unpublished). With regard to periodization, I generally restrict myself to the later texts, by which I mean the texts from *The Gay Science* onward.[11] I do so for several reasons,

---

10. Most influential has been Rorty, *Philosophy and the Mirror of Nature.*

11. *The Gay Science* is often considered a "middle period" work, though, for the reasons given below, I think it can be considered the entry way into the "later" Nietzsche, a

most important of which is that in *The Gay Science* Nietzsche first proclaims the "death of God" and begins a concerted inquiry into issues of
truth, knowledge, and being that results in the doctrines of perspectivism, becoming, and will to power. This is not to say that Nietzsche is
unconcerned with these issues in earlier works, nor that his position on
these matters is markedly different in those earlier works. In the earlier
texts—particularly in "Homer's Contest," "On Truth and Lies in a
Nonmoral Sense," *Philosophy in the Tragic Age of the Greeks, Human,
All Too Human,* and *Daybreak*—one can find a host of claims, arguments, and analyses dealing with epistemological and ontological topics
that resonate richly with those found in the later texts. Because of this,
I occasionally quote or refer to these earlier texts in relation to issues
raised in the later texts. But there is also another reason I choose to con-
centrate on the later texts. While I think there are significant problems
with the standard tripartite periodization of Nietzsche's corpus—a
schema first proposed by Hans Vaihinger and prevalent ever since—
and with the more elaborate periodization of Nietzsche's epistemological and ontological writings more recently proposed by Maudemarie
Clark, my view on this issue is heterodox, and substantiation of it would
require a separate study.[12] Therefore, I opt for a fairly uncontroversial
restriction to the texts beginning with *The Gay Science,* which provide
sufficient material for the development and elaboration of my reading.
Only in chapter 4 do I undertake an extended reading of an early text,
Philosophy in the Tragic Age of the Greeks. I think the reasons for this
are made clear and that I have given sufficient indication of how fully
this text accords with the view of Heraclitus, becoming, and metaphysics Nietzsche articulates in his later work.

Among these later works, I refer to, but rarely quote or discuss at
length, Nietzsche's long prose-poem, *Thus Spoke Zarathustra.* This text
has much to offer on the issues that concern me. Yet the profusion of
voices, styles, and narrative situations one finds in that text makes it
especially difficult to quote and explicate in the sort of expository essay
I offer here. I also believe that the philosophical themes explored in

strategy also taken by Richard Schacht, *Nietzsche* (London: Routledge and Kegan Paul,
1983), xiii. Moreover, I make greatest use of the material in Book V, added in 1887, just
after the publication of *Beyond Good and Evil* and shortly before the publication of *On
the Genealogy of Morals,* both of which are generally regarded as "later" works.
    12. See Hans Vaihinger, *Nietzsche als Philosoph* (Berlin: Reuther und Reichard,
1902), 44ff., and Maudemarie Clark, *Nietzsche on Truth and Philosophy* (Cambridge:
Cambridge University Press, 1990), chap. 4.

Zarathustra are presented elsewhere in a style more amenable to my expository aims.

An explanation is also in order concerning my use of the *Nachlaß*, and especially *The Will to Power*. It can no longer be supposed that the set of notes compiled by Nietzsche's sister, Elisabeth Förster-Nietzsche, under the title *The Will to Power* represents what Heidegger called "the preliminary drafts and fragmentary elaborations" of "Nietzsche's chief philosophical work," "his planned *magnum opus*."[13] This view has been effectively discredited by the publication, under the editorship of Giorgio Colli and Mazzino Montinari, of the new critical edition of Nietzsche's works and correspondence. On the basis of this edition, several scholars have shown that neither the selection nor the arrangement of notes that appear as *The Will to Power* is Nietzsche's own and that, before composing his final books, Nietzsche had, in fact, abandoned the project of writing a book to be called *The Will to Power*.[14]

For decades, Nietzsche scholarship has been divided over whether or not the *Nachlaß* constitutes a legitimate source from which to draw in developing an interpretation of Nietzsche's philosophy.[15] And the recent discoveries concerning the construction of *The Will to Power* have sharpened the debate, leading some scholars to consider suspect any interpretation that makes substantial use of this collection.[16] Yet some of

13. Martin Heidegger, *Nietzsche,* vol. 1, *The Will to Power as Art,* trans. David F. Krell (San Francisco: Harper, 1979), 3, 7. In all fairness, however, it should be recalled that Heidegger himself expressed some reservations about the status of "Nietzsche's so-called major work." See Martin Heidegger, *Nietzsche,* vol. 3, *The Will to Power as Knowledge and as Metaphysics,* trans. Joan Stambaugh et al. (San Francisco: Harper, 1987), §2.

14. See Mazzino Montinari, "Nietzsche's Nachlaß 1885–1888 und der 'Wille zur Macht,'" *KSA* 14:383–400; Bernd Magnus, "Nietzsche's Philosophy in 1888: *The Will to Power* and the *Übermensch,*" *Journal of the History of Philosophy* 24 (1986): 85–93; and Wayne Klein, *Nietzsche and the Promise of Philosophy* (Albany: State University of New York Press, 1997), 181–99. Earlier worries about the status of *The Will to Power* were expressed by Karl Schlechta, who, in his 1954–56 edition of Nietzsche's works, scrambled *The Will to Power* into a series of notes arranged neither thematically nor chronologically. In his presentation of Nietzsche to an Anglophone audience, Walter Kaufmann also issued warnings about the inauthenticity of *The Will to Power*. See his *Nietzsche: Philosopher, Psychologist, Anti-Christ,* 4th ed. (Princeton: Princeton University Press, 1974), 6–9, and "Editor's Introduction" to Friedrich Nietzsche, *The Will to Power,* ed. Walter Kaufmann, trans. Walter Kaufmann and R. J. Hollingdale (New York: Vintage Books, 1967).

15. On this issue, see Magnus, "Nietzsche's Philosophy in 1888," 82–83, where Magnus divides Nietzsche scholars into two groups, "lumpers," "who regard the use of Nietzsche's *Nachlaß* as unproblematic," and "splitters," who "distinguish sharply between the published and unpublished writings."

16. See, e.g., Magnus, "Nietzsche's Philosophy in 1888," and Klein, *Nietzsche and the Promise of Philosophy,* 181–99.

the most influential and respected accounts of Nietzsche's philosophy
have been offered by those who draw freely from the *Nachlaß* and, especially, *The Will to Power*: for example, Jaspers, Heidegger, Kaufmann,
Deleuze, Danto, Müller-Lauter, Schacht, and Nehamas. These interpreters have provided a variety of justifications for continuing to make
use of this material.[17] On my view, the most persuasive of these was
offered recently by Richard Schacht, whose hermeneutical principles I
most fully share.[18] Schacht grants the general interpretive rule that priority should be given to what an author published or intended for publication. Yet, he argues, Nietzsche's case is unusual and presents special
considerations that warrant consultation of his unpublished material.
Nietzsche's collapse was abrupt and untimely, coming upon him at a
moment in his career when he had begun to publish with increasing
frequency. The notebooks were always the workshop for Nietzsche's
published writings; and the *Nachlaß* no doubt contains the seeds of
what would have been Nietzsche's future projects. Moreover, Nietzsche's published works do not differ significantly in form from the material left in the notebooks. Like the notebooks, the published works
contain relatively brief discussions and remarks that rarely, if ever, exhaust or provide Nietzsche's definitive view on any given issue. Instead,
as in his notebooks, Nietzsche's published work continually revisits earlier themes, issues, and problems, adding new insights and perspectives

17. Despite his reservations, Walter Kaufmann decided to publish an English translation of *The Will to Power*, arguing that it allows us "to look, as it were, into the workshop of a great thinker" and that it presents some of Nietzsche's most sustained treatments of, among other things, epistemological issues ("Editor's Introduction" to *The Will
to Power*, xvi, xiv–xv, and *Nietzsche*, 204–5). Though generally a "splitter" (see n. 15,
above), R. J. Hollingdale, co-translator of *The Will to Power*, concurs with Kaufmann on
this point in his *Nietzsche* (London: Routledge and Kegan Paul, 1973), 131. In similar
fashion, Richard Schacht (*Nietzsche*, xii) justifies his heavy reliance on *The Will to Power*
by stating that the "unpublished writings [. . .] contain much more of [Nietzsche's] expressed thinking on certain important matters than do his finished works" and that *The
Will to Power* is "sufficiently representative" of this unpublished material. Karl Jaspers
(*Nietzsche: An Introduction to the Understanding of His Philosophical Activity*, trans.
Charles F. Walraff and Frederick J. Schmitz [South Bend, Ind.: Regnery Gateway, 1979],
xii) contends that Nietzsche's posthumous notes are legitimate sources, because "none of
Nietzsche's forms of communication has a privileged character" and because "Nietzsche
himself is intelligible only when we gather everything together." According to Alexander
Nehamas (*Nietzsche: Life as Literature* [Cambridge: Harvard University Press, 1985], 9),
The Will to Power "has become, for better or worse, an integral part of Nietzsche's literary and philosophical work, and it has been instrumental in forming our reactions to him
over the past eighty years."
18. Richard Schacht, "Beyond Scholasticism: On Dealing with Nietzsche and His
Nachlaß," in *Making Sense of Nietzsche* (Urbana: University of Illinois Press, 1995),
117–25.

in piecemeal fashion. The large mass of material left in the notebooks provides a wealth of such insights and perspectives on which we can draw in constructing our interpretations of Nietzsche. And, while we can never be sure just how much or what parts of this material Nietzsche fully endorsed or intended for publication, responsible use of the notebooks as a supplement to Nietzsche's published work gives us a much broader and deeper view of his philosophical thinking than a purist restriction to the published texts alone could provide.

The same considerations support use of the material in *The Will to Power*. It is certainly true that, unlike *The Gay Science* or *Beyond Good and Evil*, *The Will to Power* cannot be read as a book, let alone as Nietzsche's *Hauptwerk*. But it is nevertheless a collection of notes that Nietzsche himself wrote and, moreover, the only such collection available in English translation. It is true that the editors of *The Will to Power* occasionally cut and splice Nietzsche's notes, instead of leaving them whole. But this occurs less frequently or egregiously than is claimed by critics of *The Will to Power*.[19] It is true that *The Will to Power* severs Nietzsche's notes from their original contexts and that a reconsideration of them in these contexts can be revealing. But we must remember that Nietzsche's notebooks are just that, books of notes rather than continuous works; that is, they are fragmentary and, hence, their original context is of somewhat less importance than it is in his fully composed books. Furthermore, just as in the treatment of Nietzsche's published works (which, after all, are composed of semiautonomous sections or aphorisms), it is often equally or even more revealing to consider these notes in other contexts, to consider them, for example, in relation to other notes or published passages that take up similar themes and issues. Because I aim to construct a general interpretation of Nietzsche's epistemological and ontological position rather than to present a reading of one or another of his books, this has been my interpretive practice: to read Nietzsche across his *œuvre*, "looking cautiously fore and aft" (D P:5).

For these reasons, I consider it not only legitimate but wise to draw on the *Nachlaß* and *The Will to Power* as supplements to Nietzsche's published work. Where I quote the published texts, I often refer the reader to notes in *The Will to Power* or the *Nachlaß* that correspond to or develop the issues under discussion in the quoted passage. And,

19. See, e.g., Klein, *Nietzsche and the Promise of Philosophy*, 187–98.

where I quote *The Will to Power* or the *Nachlaß*, I try to note passages in the published work that, I think, corroborate or significantly connect with the views presented in the notebook entry. For readers who wish to consult Nietzsche's original, or who want to consider the original context for any of these notes, I have provided, as an appendix, a concordance between *The Will to Power* notes to which I refer and corresponding entries in *Kritische Studienausgabe*.

PART ONE

Nietzsche's Philosophical Position

CHAPTER ONE

Being and Its Others

Nietzsche's Genealogy of European Thought

We know the way, we have found the exit
out of the labyrinth of thousands of years.
                    Nietzsche, The Antichrist § 1

1.1 INTERPRETING NIETZSCHE

In a late text, having declared himself to be the first German master of
the aphorism, Nietzsche writes, "it is my ambition to say in ten sentences what everyone else says in a book—what everyone else does *not*
say in a book" (*TI* "Skirmishes" 51). A year earlier he remarked in the
preface to *On the Genealogy of Morals* that "an aphorism, properly
stamped and molded, has not been 'deciphered' when it has simply
been read; rather, one has then to begin its *interpretation* [Auslegung],
for which is required an art of interpretation" (*GM* P:8). He goes on to
say that the third essay of the *Genealogy*—some seventy pages in the
standard German edition—is simply commentary upon an aphorism
drawn from his monumental prose-poem, *Thus Spoke Zarathustra*.
Nietzsche thus gives his interpreters an essential role: that of unpacking
his terse, rhetorically dense remarks and elaborating them into an explicit philosophical view.

This is certainly the case with Nietzsche's most famous aphorism:
"God is dead" (*GS* 125, 343). These words will be familiar to anyone
even casually acquainted with Nietzsche. Yet the meaning of this phrase
is by no means transparent. It can be, and has been, taken in any number of ways. On my reading, this audacious claim condenses an entire
genealogy of European thought that has profound consequences for
epistemology and ontology. To see this, however, we need to take Nietz-

sche's advice and read him "slowly, deeply, looking cautiously fore and
aft" (*D* P: 5). That is, we must trace this notion through the host of passages in which it appears, allowing each passage to elucidate the others
and attempting to draw out what they merely suggest.

1.2 THE "DEATH OF GOD" AS THE TURNING POINT OF EUROPEAN THOUGHT

The notion of "the death of God" first appears in 1882, in Book Three
of *The Gay Science*. In the following few years, it finds its way into several passages of *Thus Spoke Zarathustra*. But it is not until 1887, with
the composition of Book Five of *The Gay Science*, *On the Genealogy of
Morals*, and the *Nachlaß*[1] from this period, that Nietzsche makes clear
the full significance of the madman's cry: "God is dead. God remains
dead. And we have killed him" (*GS* 125).

In *Gay Science* §343, which opens Book Five, we discover that Nietzsche's announcement of the "death of God" is not at all a personal confession of atheism or loss of faith; nor is it so for the various characters
who make this proclamation (the madman, Zarathustra, the last pope,
the ugliest man, etc.).[2] Rather, it becomes evident that, for Nietzsche,
the "death of God" is *a cultural and historical event* ("a generally Eu-

---

1. See, for example, *The Will to Power*, Book I, titled "European Nihilism," which
collects a group of notes written primarily from late 1886–early 1888. Nietzsche refers to
this set of notes in *GM* III:27, where, discussing the "death of God" as "Europe's longest and bravest self-overcoming," he announces a future project that "shall probe these
things more thoroughly and severely [. . .] (under the title 'On the History of European
Nihilism' [. . .] contained in a work in progress: *The Will To Power: Attempt at a Revaluation of All Values*)." Though this project was later abandoned, it was still very much
alive as the *Genealogy* and Book Five of the *Gay Science* were being composed; and the
conception of "European nihilism" that Nietzsche presents in the notes from this period
clearly informs these published texts. On the history of Nietzsche's *Will to Power* project,
see Mazzino Montinari, "Nietzsche's Nachlaß 1885–1888 und der 'Wille zur Macht,'"
KSA 14:383–400; Bernd Magnus, "Nietzsche's Philosophy in 1888: The Will to Power
and the Übermensch," *Journal of the History of Philosophy* 24 (1986): 85–93; and
Wayne Klein, *Nietzsche and the Promise of Philosophy* (Albany: State University of New
York Press, 1997), 181–99.
2. This has been stressed by a number of Nietzsche's commentators. See, e.g., Karl
Jaspers, *Nietzsche: An Introduction to the Understanding of His Philosophical Activity*,
trans. Charles F. Walraff and Frederick J. Schmitz (South Bend, Ind.: Regnery Gateway,
1979), 242; Martin Heidegger, "The Word of Nietzsche: 'God is Dead,'" in *The Question Concerning Technology and Other Essays*, trans. William Lovitt (New York: Harper
and Row, 1977), 57ff.; George A. Morgan, *What Nietzsche Means* (New York: Harper and
Row, 1941), 37ff.; Walter Kaufmann, *Nietzsche: Philosopher, Psychologist, Anti-Christ*,
4th ed. (Princeton: Princeton University Press, 1974), 99ff.; and Maurice Blanchot, *The
Infinite Conversation*, trans. Susan Hanson (Minneapolis: University of Minnesota Press,
1993), 144–46.

ropean event," he calls it in §357). Thus the passage begins, "The greatest recent event—that 'God is dead,' that the belief in the Christian god has become unbelievable—is already beginning to cast its first shadows over Europe."

Furthermore, it becomes clear that this event concerns far more than theology and religion; that it is an *intellectual* event, a crucial moment in the history of European thinking in general. Thus, reiterating the madman's conclusion, Nietzsche goes on to write:

> The event is far too great, too distant, too remote from the multitude's capacity for comprehension even for the tidings of it to be thought of as having *arrived* as yet. Much less may one suppose that many people know as yet *what* this event really means—and how much must collapse now that this faith has been undermined because it was built upon this faith, propped up by it, grown into it; for example, the whole of our European morality. This long plenitude and sequence of breakdown, destruction, ruin, and cataclysm that is now impending—who could guess enough of it today to be compelled to play the teacher and advance proclaimer of this monstrous logic of terror, the prophet of a gloom and an eclipse of the sun whose like has probably never yet occurred on earth?

Here, we get an inkling of what Nietzsche will later make clear: that the "death of God" involves nothing less than a dismantling of the basic structures of belief and value upon which European thought has been founded. Moreover, we soon learn that this event is not brought about from the outside, by some external cataclysm; nor is it some chance occurrence. Rather, the "monstrous logic of terror" set in motion by the "death of God" is brought about from the inside, through a critique necessitated by the very presuppositions of European thought. In short, for Nietzsche, the "death of God" marks the beginning of a *self*-overcoming of the foundational structures of European thought.[3]

These themes are more thoroughly elaborated in §357 of *The Gay Science*, where Nietzsche writes:

> [T]he decline of the faith in the Christian god, the triumph of scientific atheism, is a generally European event in which all races had their share and for which all deserve credit and honor.[. . . U]nconditional and honest atheism [. . . is] a triumph achieved finally and with great difficulty by the European conscience, being the most fateful act of two thousand years of discipline

---

3. Recall Nietzsche's description of nihilism: "what does nihilism mean?—*that the highest values devaluate themselves*" (*WP* 2). This notion of "self-overcoming" appears frequently in the texts of 1887–88. See, e.g., *GS* 357; *GM* II:10, III:27; *EH* "Destiny" 3; *WP* P, 3, 5, 404–5.

for truth that in the end forbids itself the *lie* in faith in God. . . . You see *what* has really triumphed over the Christian god: Christian morality itself, the concept of truthfulness that was understood ever more rigorously, the father confessor's refinement of the Christian conscience, translated and sublimated into a scientific conscience, into intellectual cleanliness at any price. Looking at nature as if it were proof of the goodness and governance of a god; interpreting history in honor of some divine reason, as a continual testimony of a moral world order and ultimate moral purposes; interpreting one's own experiences as pious people have long enough interpreted theirs, as if everything were providential, a hint, designed and ordained for the sake of the salvation of the soul: that is all *over* now, that has man's conscience *against* it, that is considered indecent and dishonest by every more refined conscience—mendaciousness, feminism, weakness, and cowardice. In this severity, if anywhere, we are *good* Europeans and heirs of Europe's longest and most courageous self-overcoming [*Selbstüberwindung*].

After quoting this passage in the penultimate section of the *Genealogy of Morals,* Nietzsche continues:

All great things bring about their own destruction through an act of self-overcoming [*Selbstaufhebung*]: thus the law of life will have it, the law of the necessity of "self-overcoming" [*Selbstüberwindung*] in the nature of life— the lawgiver himself eventually receives the call: "*patere legem, quam ipse tulisti*" [submit to the law you yourself proposed]. In this way Christianity *as a dogma* was destroyed by its own morality; in the same way Christianity *as morality* must now perish too: we stand on the threshold of *this* event. After Christian truthfulness has drawn one inference after another, it must end by drawing its *most striking inference,* its inference *against* itself; this will happen, however, when it poses the question, "*what is the meaning of all will to truth?*" . . . And here I again touch on my problem, on our problem [. . .]: what meaning would our whole being possess if it were not this, that in us the will to truth becomes conscious of itself as a *problem?* . . . As the will to truth thus gains self-consciousness, from now on—there is no doubt about it—morality will go *to ruin* [geht . . . *zu Gründe*]: this is the great spectacle in a hundred acts reserved for the next two centuries in Europe— the most terrible, most questionable, and perhaps also the most hopeful of spectacles. . . . (*GM* III:27)

Taken together, these passages present a genealogy that is of utmost importance for understanding Nietzsche's later thought. In these passages, he attempts to explain both the sequence of events leading to the "death of God" and its inevitable consequences. This account is highly condensed and elusive, to be sure. But, fortunately, these passages do not stand alone. They form part of a network of texts, written in 1887 and constantly cross-referenced by Nietzsche. Following the various strands of this network, we can piece together a genealogy that

links "God" and "morality" with "truth" and shows that a "refinement" of the "European conscience" eventually leads to the "self-overcoming" of metaphysics, theology, morality, and science and to a "revaluation" of "truth."

1.3 FROM METAPHYSICS AND THEOLOGY TO SCIENCE

Like Hegel's "phenomenology of spirit," but with a very different motivation and trajectory, Nietzsche's genealogy is concerned with the quasi-
historical movement of European thought.[4] Like his heirs, Heidegger
and Derrida, Nietzsche considers all of Western thought—from Plato
through positivism—as forming a single epoch, the closure of which is
at hand. This epoch is characterized by the accordance of an absolute
value to "truth" conceived as the determination of "being" apart from
all "becoming" and "appearing" (or "seeming") (see, e.g., BGE P, 2,
34; GM III:24; TI "Reason" and "World").[5] Since the history of this
epoch is a history of self-overcoming, this self-overcoming will have
something to do with truth—more specifically, with a contradictory development of the concept of truth.

Since its inception, Nietzsche maintains, European thought has attempted rigorously to distinguish "what is" from "what merely seems
or appears to be," "what is not yet," and "what is no longer."[6] Yet the
earliest philosophers (e.g., the Eleatics) already noted that, within the
physical world in which we have bodily existence and sensuous experience, we nowhere encounter this "truth as being." On the contrary, as
physical, embodied creatures, we are continually confronted by a volatile
sensory experience in which things incessantly appear and disappear.
This experience repeatedly embroils us in deceptions, for what the eye
sees the hand may not feel, and what the eye sees from one point of view
it sees differently from another. Furthermore, every thing in this world,
including our own bodies, exists only for a relative duration, in which it

---

4. For further comparison of Hegel's "phenomenology" and Nietzsche's "genealogy,"
see §5.3.3, below.

5. Note that der Schein (semblance) and die Erscheinung (appearance) derive from a
common root and, while not identical, are often used interchangeably by Nietzsche in
contrast with "truth," "being," and "essence."

6. For a Nietzschean account of the traditional subordination of becoming and seeming to being, and the modern inversion of this hierarchy, see Gilles Deleuze, Difference
and Repetition, trans. Paul Patton (New York: Columbia University Press, 1994), 59–69,
and The Logic of Sense, ed. Constantin V. Boundas, trans. Mark Lester and Charles Stivale (New York: Columbia University Press, 1990), 253–66.

undergoes constant local movement and qualitative change. And within this world, each thing owes its existence to other things and to a sequence of events that stretches into an infinite past. In short, the world of which we are a part seems to be, in its entirety, a domain of temporal, spatial, contingent, and conditional particulars. If truth is being, it is not to be found within this domain. Convinced of the existence of truth and knowledge, the founders of the Western tradition thus resolved that truth resides in another, *meta*physical world, an eternal world of necessary, unconditioned, universal, and absolute being: for the Platonist, the world of the Forms; for the Christian, the kingdom of God.[7]

Yet Nietzsche remarks that the Platonic–Christian notion of truth subtly changes with the institutionalization of religion. With "the father confessor's refinement of the Christian conscience" (*GS* 357), truth comes to be formulated as the commandment not to lie, to tell the truth no matter how terrible and regardless of consequence. As such, truth is partially dislodged from its otherworldly residence. No longer strictly defined by the belief in and search for a "true world of being," the will to truth becomes the demand to tell the truth, to say, unconditionally, what is the case and what has occurred. With this development is born a key figure in Nietzsche's genealogy: what he variously calls "the European conscience," the "intellectual conscience" [*Gewissen*], "intellectual integrity" [*Rechtschaffenheit*], or "honesty" [*Redlichkeit*].[8] For Nietzsche, this "intellectual conscience" involves a "training in truthfulness" (*GM* III:27), the "discipline for truth," "the concept of truthfulness [. . .] understood ever more rigorously" as the demand for "intellectual cleanliness at any price" (*GS* 357; cf. *GM* III:24ff.). Further refined, the "father confessor's" demand for truth gives rise to a profound skepticism: the requirement that beliefs, convictions, and ideals

---

7. Note that Nietzsche considers Platonism and Christianity to be, in their basic orientation, the same, deeming Christianity "Platonism for 'the people'" (*BGE* P).

8. On "intellectual conscience," see *AOM* 26; *GS* 2, 99, 335; *BGE* 205, 230; *GM* III:24; *TI* "Skirmishes" 18; *A* P, 12. On "intellectual integrity," see *A* 36, 50, 53, 59; *WP* 460. On "honesty," see *D* 84, 111, 370, 456, 482; *GS* 107, 110, 114, 319, 335; *BGE* 5, 227; *Z*:4 "Retired"; *GM* III:26; *A* P, 12, 52; *EH* "Books" *CW*:3. One might add to this list Nietzsche's notion of "justice" [*Gerechtigkeit*], discussed more fully in chapter 3. The importance for Nietzsche of these philological virtues has been discussed by Jaspers, *Nietzsche*, 201–11; Kaufmann, *Nietzsche*, 354–61 and *passim*; Blanchot, *Infinite Conversation*, 138, 145; Jean-Luc Nancy, "'Our Probity!' On Truth in the Moral Sense in Nietzsche," in *Looking after Nietzsche*, ed. Laurence A. Rickels (Albany: State University of New York Press, 1990); Richard Schacht, *Nietzsche* (London: Routledge and Kegan Paul, 1983), 99ff.; and Alan D. Schrift, *Nietzsche and the Question of Interpretation: Between Hermeneutics and Deconstruction* (New York: Routledge, 1990), 165–67, 188–90. In what follows, I treat these notions as more or less interchangeable.

be tested rigorously to determine whether or not they are justified and certain.⁹

In fact, this development of the "intellectual conscience" leads to a questioning of the "true world" of Christianity and Platonism. It provokes the suspicion that the existence of God, of otherworldly being, and of innate ideas cannot adequately be demonstrated. It points out, in contrast, that so much else is perfectly clear and demonstrable, particularly the regularities of nature confirmed by repeated experimental observation. And with this, "the Christian conscience" is "translated and sublimated into the scientific conscience" (GS 357). No longer concerned with the unjustifiable claims of metaphysics and theology, science turns its attention to the natural world, which it aims to master through scrupulous empirical inquiry.

1.4 SCIENCE AS THEOLOGY BY OTHER MEANS

One might suppose that, with the triumph of science, Platonism and Christianity are finally overcome, that, within the scientific worldview, "God is dead" or at least forgotten. This certainly is what contemporary scientific culture believes, says Nietzsche. When the madman appears among the atheists in the marketplace crying "God is dead. [. . .] And we have killed him," they ridicule and taunt him. He finally leaves, muttering: "I have come too early [. . .], my time is not yet. This tremendous event is still on its way, still wandering: it has not yet reached the ears of men. [. . .] This deed is still more distant from them than the most distant stars—*and yet they have done it themselves*" (GS 125). A similar description is found in the *Genealogy of Morals*. It is said, Nietzsche writes, that modern culture has finally vanquished the otherworldly, this-world-denying "ascetic ideal,"

> that it has already conquered this ideal in all important respects: all of modern *science* is supposed to bear witness to that—modern science which, as a genuine philosophy of reality, [. . .] has up to now survived well enough without God, the beyond, and the virtues of denial. [. . . T]hese hard, severe, abstinent, heroic spirits who constitute the honor of our age; all these

9. Cf. *WP* 4–5 (*KSA* 12:5 [71]): "in sum: morality was the great *antidote* against practical and theoretical *nihilism*. But among the forces cultivated by morality was *truthfulness;* this eventually turned against morality [. . .] and now the *insight* into this inveterate mendaciousness that one despairs of shedding becomes a stimulant. To nihilism"; also *WP* 3 (*KSA* 12:10 [192]): "*Radical nihilism* [. . .] is a consequence of highly developed 'truthfulness': thus itself a consequence of the faith in morality."

pale atheists, anti-Christians, immoralists, nihilists; these skeptics, ephectics
[. . .]; these last idealists of knowledge in whom alone the intellectual conscience dwells and is incarnate today—they certainly believe they are as completely liberated from the ascetic ideal as possible [. . .] (GM III:23–24)

Yet they are mistaken, argues Nietzsche. Science does not represent the
triumph over God, the otherworldly, and the ascetic ideal. Though it
potentially prepares the way for that triumph, science itself represents,
rather, the "*kernel*" of the ascetic ideal, "this ideal itself in its strictest,
most spiritual formulation, esoteric through and through with all external additions abolished" (GM III:27). Nietzsche elaborates:

> No! this "modern science"—let us face this fact!—is the *best* ally the ascetic
> ideal has at present, and precisely because it is the most unconscious, invol-
> untary, hidden, and subterranean ally! [. . .] The ascetic ideal has decidedly
> not been conquered: if anything, it became stronger, which is to say, more
> elusive, more spiritual, more captious, as science remorselessly detached and
> broke off wall upon wall, external additions that had *coarsened* its appear-
> ance. (GM III:25)

This seems a rather odd claim. One might well ask how it is that modern science, which explicitly rejects metaphysics and theology, represents the inner essence of "the ascetic ideal." Nietzsche explains:

> [T]o disclose to them what they themselves cannot see—for they are too
> close to themselves: this ideal is precisely *their* ideal, too [. . .]—if I have
> guessed any riddles, I wish that this proposition might show it—They are
> far from being *free* spirits: *for they still have faith in truth* [. . .]; it is pre-
> cisely in their faith in truth that they are more rigid and unconditional than
> anyone. [. . .] That which constrains these men, however, this uncondi-
> tional will to truth, is *faith in the ascetic ideal itself,* even if as an uncon-
> scious imperative—don't be deceived about that—it is the faith in the *meta-
> physical* value, the value of *truth in itself* [*einen Werth* an sich der Wahrheit],
> sanctioned and guaranteed by this ideal alone (it stands or falls with this
> ideal). (GM III:24)

Modern science, that is, represents both the essence and consummation
of the ascetic ideal insofar as it strips that ideal of all external coverings
and reveals what is essential to it and, indeed, to the entirety of Western
thought, which has been predicated upon this ideal.[10] Having rejected
the Platonic Forms, the Christian God, and other representatives, modern science retains the one conviction with which Western thought com-

10. See GM III:24.

mences: faith in the absolute and unconditional value of truth. While it
may no longer believe that "God is the truth," science nonetheless still
believes that "truth is divine" (GS 344), that truth must govern every inquiry and serve as its incontestable goal. Nietzsche thus makes the striking assertion that the "death of God" has only derivatively to do with
theology and Christianity, that it primarily involves what Heidegger has
called a "fundamental structuring" of thought, based upon the accordance of an ultimate value to truth.[11] In this sense, according to Nietzsche, even the scientists and "godless anti-metaphysicians" (GS 344)
have yet fully to comprehend the meaning of the "death of God."

It might be objected that the "truth" sought after by science is quite
different from the "truth" desired by Platonism and Christianity. For
this latter pair, truth is something otherworldly, not to be found within
the natural world; while, for science, truth is entirely this-worldly, aim-
ing simply at the discovery of demonstrable, empirical "facts" about
the natural world. Nietzsche acknowledges this difference and, indeed,
often praises science for its this-worldliness.[12] Yet he points out that
science still retains the essence of the ascetic ideal insofar as it accords
truth *an absolute, unconditional value.* This conviction, Nietzsche insists, is nothing other than a "metaphysical" faith.

Again, one might ask how this is so. Science does indeed claim truth
as its ultimate goal. But the truth it demands is not metaphysical; it is,
rather, physical and empirical, available for all to see. To explain his
strange accusation, Nietzsche cites another passage from Book Five of
The Gay Science: §344, entitled "How We, Too, Are Still Pious." This
passage begins by praising science for its "intellectual conscience," for
its "mistrust" of "convictions" and its decision to demote them "to the
modesty of hypotheses, of a provisional experimental point of view, of a
regulative fiction." Yet he notes that, while the scientific method grants
admission only to such provisional, revisable hypotheses, the entire enterprise of science rests upon a prior conviction that it is unwilling to
relinquish:

> We see that science also rests on a faith; there is simply no "presupposition-
> less" science. The question whether *truth* is needed must not only have been
> affirmed in advance, but affirmed to such a degree that the principle, the

11. Heidegger, "Word of Nietzsche," 64–65.
12. See, especially, A 47–49, where, against the otherworldly "lies" of Christianity,
Nietzsche calls science "the 'wisdom of this world.'" See also GS 293, 355, 357, and TI
"Reason" 3.

faith, the conviction finds expression: "*Nothing* is needed more than *truth*, and in relation to it everything else has only second-rate value." (*GS* 344)

Nietzsche does not object to this conviction on the grounds that it is a "presupposition," because he denies the possibility of a "'presuppositionless' science."[13] What he does object to, however, is the dogmatic nature of this conviction, a dogmatism that proves to be metaphysical. This becomes apparent, Nietzsche argues, if we inquire into the motivations and reasons behind the conviction that truth is of ultimate value. He asks what justifies this conviction and considers two possible answers. Perhaps the justification is *pragmatic:* "One does not want to allow oneself to be deceived because one assumes that it is harmful, dangerous, calamitous to be deceived. In this sense, science would be a long-range prudence, a caution, a utility." Yet he argues that this explanation fails to justify the ultimacy of the will to truth, because, on pragmatic considerations, we can see that it is *not* unconditionally harmful to allow oneself to be deceived. While the will to truth certainly does serve the interests of life in important ways (e.g., by helping us to determine more or less accurately the conditions that obtain in the world so that we can respond accordingly), it is one of Nietzsche's recurrent insights that the opposite will, the will to ignorance, is equally beneficial for life.[14] He continually points out that human survival is predicated upon conceptual and linguistic abstractions that allow us to reify the ever-changing world and to simplify and select from our multifaceted experience. In this way, he argues, we "lie" in "an extramoral sense"; that is, we strategically, and often unconsciously, overlook and forget features of the world that are not relevant or crucial to our survival or to our particular purposes, interests, values, and goals. Furthermore, Nietzsche points out that, in art and dreams, we continually allow ourselves to be deceived and take pleasure in this deception. If not beneficial, such "lies" cannot be considered harmful, except to the most obstinate Platonist.[15] Hence, the ultimacy of the will to truth is not to be justified on pragmatic grounds.

13. See also *GM* III:24 and II:12. This notion is discussed more fully below.

14. For some instances of this line of thought, see *TL; HL* (on the "value for life" of "forgetting" and "the unhistorical"); *GS* 110–12, 354; *BGE* 1, 4, 9, 11, 24; *TI* "Reason," "World," "Errors"; *WP* 466–617. See also Alexander Nehamas, *Nietzsche: Life as Literature* (Cambridge: Harvard University Press, 1985), chap. 2. I discuss these issues further below (§1.5.2).

15. On the "deception" of dreams, see *TL*, 80. On the "deception" of art, see *BT* SC:5 and *GM* III:25.

If this will does not receive a naturalistic, conditional, pragmatic justification, from where does its justification come? If it is not justified by the role it plays in the actual process of inquiry and the actual exigencies of life, what justifies it? Nietzsche argues that it must rest on the *moral* prescription never to deceive, not even oneself. Science, then, would represent simply a "translation and sublimation" of the Christian commandment: "thou shalt not lie" (see *GS* 357). Were it to be strictly enforced, however, this unconditional proscription would be extremely harmful to natural life, which, in so many ways, requires the "extramoral lie." Nietzsche thus concludes that the absolute and unconditional value accorded the will to truth by science is antinatural, otherworldly, metaphysical:

> For you only have to ask yourself carefully, "Why do you not want to deceive?" especially if it should seem—and it does seem!—as if life rested upon semblance, I mean error, deception, simulation, delusion, self-delusion, and when the great sweep of life has actually always shown itself to be on the side of the most unscrupulous *polytropoi*. Charitably interpreted, such a resolve might perhaps be a quixotism, a minor slightly mad enthusiasm; but it might also be something more serious, namely a principle that is hostile to life and destructive. . . . "Will to truth"—that might be a concealed will to death.— Thus the question "Why science?" leads back to the moral problem: *Why have morality at all* when life, nature, and history are "unmoral"? No doubt, those who are truthful in that audacious and ultimate sense that is presupposed by the faith in science *thus affirm another world* than the world of life, nature, and history; and insofar as they affirm this "other world"— look, must they not by the same token negate its counterpart, this world, *our* world? . . . But you will have gathered what I am driving at, namely, that it is still a *metaphysical faith* upon which our faith in science rests—that even we seekers after knowledge today, we godless anti-metaphysicians still take *our* fire, too, from the flame lit by a faith [*Glaube*] that is thousands of years old, that Christian faith which was also the faith of Plato, that God is the truth, that truth is divine. . . . But what if this should become more and more incredible [*unglaubwürdig*], if nothing should prove to be divine any more unless it were error, blindness, the lie—if God himself should prove to be our most enduring lie?—(*GS* 344; cf. *WP* 1011)

Briefly put, Nietzsche argues that, while the "intellectual conscience" that animates modern science demands a rejection of every unconditional faith, science itself is "still unconditional on one point," regarding its belief in "the absolute value of truth" (*GM* III:24). This unconditional belief is not only unconscionably dogmatic but also unconscionably metaphysical, insofar as—against the requirements of "this world,

our world," "the world of life, nature, and history"—it receives its justification solely from the otherworldly domain of Christian morality.
The "intellectual conscience" thus demands that this final conviction be
put into question.

Yet this final conviction is not just one among many. Nietzsche takes
it to be *the* conviction upon which all of Western thought is based. A
questioning of this conviction, then, amounts to a questioning of Western thought itself. Nietzsche makes clear that this is just what the
"death of God" entails and just what the "intellectual conscience" requires. Impelled by the "intellectual conscience," science demands its
own self-overcoming. Insofar as science represents the kernel and esoteric form of the ascetic ideal, this self-overcoming of science is, at the
same time, a self-overcoming of the ascetic ideal:

> This pair, science and the ascetic ideal, both rest on the same foundation—I
> have already indicated it: on the same overestimation of truth (more exactly:
> on the same belief that truth is *in*estimable and *cannot* be criticized). There-
> fore they are *necessarily* allies, so that if they are to be fought they can only
> be fought and called in question together. A depreciation of the ascetic ideal
> unavoidably involves a depreciation of science: one must keep one's eyes and
> ears open to this fact! (*GM* III:25)

And this self-overcoming of the ascetic ideal points to the self-overcoming of the foundations of European thought:

> Consider on this question both the earliest and most recent philosophers:
> they are all oblivious of how much the will to truth itself first requires justifi-
> cation; here there is a lacuna in every philosophy—how did this come about?
> Because the ascetic ideal has hitherto *dominated* all philosophy, because
> truth was posited as being, as God, as the highest court of appeal—because
> truth was not *permitted* to be a problem at all. [. . .]—From the moment
> faith in the God of the ascetic ideal is denied, *a new problem arises:* that of
> the *value* of truth. The will to truth requires a critique—let us thus define
> our own task,—the value of truth must for once be experimentally *called
> into question.* (*GM* III:24; cf. *BGE* 1; *A* 8)

> [W]hat meaning would *our* whole being possess if it were not this, that in us
> the will to truth becomes conscious of itself as a *problem?* . . . As the will to
> truth thus gains self-consciousness, from now on—there can be no doubt
> about it—morality [read: the ascetic ideal and the otherworldly, generally]
> will go *to ruin:* this is the great spectacle in a hundred acts reserved for the
> next two centuries in Europe—the most terrible, most questionable, and
> perhaps the most hopeful of all spectacles. . . . (*GM* III:27)

With this, the trajectory of Western thought nears its end; or rather, it nears its midpoint, because, for Nietzsche, our modernity marks not the end of history but the inauguration of a new history, "a higher history than all history hitherto" (*GS* 125), not the "dusk" of infinite wisdom, but the innocence of "daybreak." Even so, that dawn is as yet merely announced. At present, we remain at "midnight," between the old day and the new. This dark night is characterized by "nihilism," the general malaise brought upon European culture by its recognition that "the highest values [i.e., truth, God, being] devaluate themselves" (*WP* 2). This nihilism, Nietzsche argues, still essentially belongs to the old day; it remains a "shadow of God" (*GS* 108). For, though the nihilist acknowledges that all absolute values have devaluated themselves, he or she still laments the loss, and what remains still appears valueless. The nihilist does not yet *affirm* the "death of God" and its consequences.

Nietzsche, however, urges us to push what is falling (see *Z:*3 "On Old and New Tablets"; *A* 2). Wishing to become "the first perfect nihilist of Europe who, however, has [. . .] lived through the whole of nihilism, to the end, leaving it behind, outside himself" (*WP* P:3), Nietzsche encourages an "active nihilism" (*WP* 22–23) that will bring the old epoch to a close. This is the momentous task toward which Nietzsche directs his energies; and the achievement of this task will bring us to the final phase of his genealogy of Western thought.

Thus far, we have seen that metaphysics and theology overcome themselves through science, and that science, too, ends in a self-overcoming. What follows this self-overcoming of science? To answer this question, and to move from science to its successor, we must first take up the task announced above, the initial phase of the revaluation of values: the revaluation of truth.

1.5 THE REVALUATION OF TRUTH I:
BEING, BECOMING, AND APPEARING

Nietzsche's genealogy of Western thought culminates in a "critique" of the "will to truth," a demand that "the value of truth [. . .] for once be experimentally *called into question*" (*GM* III:24). What does this critique entail? And what, for Nietzsche, remains of truth?

Nietzsche clearly considers the issue of truth to be of central philosophical and cultural importance. From the early essays through the final

notes, he constantly returns to this topic, offering remarks that are as
bold as they are elusive. These texts have recently attracted much attention, and the quantity of commentary on Nietzsche's discussions of truth
has grown rapidly over the past few decades.[16] For the most part, these
discussions have attempted to extract from Nietzsche's elusive comments
a "theory of truth." Yet no consensus has been reached. Indeed, every
major theory of truth (correspondence, pragmatic, coherence, semantic) has been attributed to Nietzsche by one commentator or another,[17]

16. See, e.g., Arthur Danto, *Nietzsche as Philosopher* (New York: Columbia Uni-
versity Press, 1965), *passim;* Jean Granier, "Perspectivism and Interpretation," in *The
New Nietzsche: Contemporary Styles of Interpretation,* ed. David B. Allison (Cambridge,
Mass.: MIT Press, 1977); Wolfgang Müller-Lauter, *Nietzsche: Seine Philosophie der
Gegensätze und die Gegensätze seiner Philosophie* (Berlin: Walter de Gruyter, 1971),
chap. 5; John T. Wilcox, *Truth and Value in Nietzsche: A Study of His Metaethics and
Epistemology* (Ann Arbor: University of Michigan Press, 1974), and "A Note on Corre-
spondence and Pragmatism in Nietzsche," *International Studies in Philosophy* 12 (1980):
77–80, and "Nietzsche's Epistemology: Recent American Discussions," *International
Studies in Philosophy* 15 (1983): 67–77, and "Nietzsche Scholarship and 'the Correspondence Theory of Truth': The Danto Case," *Nietzsche-Studien* 15 (1986): 337–57;
Mary Warnock, "Nietzsche's Conception of Truth," in *Nietzsche's Imagery and Thought:
A Collection of Essays,* ed. Malcolm Pasley (Berkeley: University of California Press,
1978); Jacques Derrida, *Spurs: Nietzsche's Styles,* trans. Barbara Harlow (Chicago: University of Chicago Press, 1978); Daniel Breazeale, "Introduction," in *Philosophy and
Truth: Selections from Nietzsche's Notebooks of the Early 1870's,* ed. and trans. Daniel
Breazeale (Atlantic Highlands, N.J.: Humanities Press, 1979); Bernd Magnus, "Nietzsche's Mitigated Skepticism," *Nietzsche-Studien* 9 (1980): 260–67; Lawrence M. Hinman, "Nietzsche, Metaphor, and Truth," *Philosophy and Phenomenological Research* 43
(1982): 179–99; Schacht, *Nietzsche,* chap. 2; Nancy, "'Our Probity!'"; Willard Mittelman, "Perspectivism, Becoming, and Truth in Nietzsche," *International Studies in Philosophy* 16 (1984): 3–22; Kenneth R. Westphal, "Nietzsche's Sting and the Possibility of
Good Philology," *International Studies in Philosophy* 16 (1984): 71–89; Alexander Nehamas, "Immanent and Transcendent Perspectivism in Nietzsche," *Nietzsche-Studien* 12
(1983): 473–94, and *Nietzsche: Life as Literature,* chap. 2, and "Will to Knowledge, Will
to Ignorance and Will to Power in *Beyond Good and Evil,*" in *Nietzsche as Affirmative
Thinker,* ed. Yirmiyahu Yovel (Dordrecht: Martinus Nijhoff, 1986); Steven G. Crowell,
"Nietzsche's View of Truth," *International Studies in Philosophy* 19 (1987): 3–18;
Robert Nola, "Nietzsche's Theory of Truth and Belief," *Philosophy and Phenomenological Research* 47 (1987): 525–62; Rüdiger Bittner, "Nietzsche's Begriff der Wahrheit,"
Nietzsche-Studien 16 (1987): 70–90; Maudemarie Clark, *Nietzsche on Truth and Philosophy* (Cambridge: Cambridge University Press, 1990); Schrift, *Nietzsche and the Question of Interpretation,* chap. 6; Ken Gemes, "Nietzsche's Critique of Truth," *Philosophy
and Phenomenological Research* 52 (1992): 47–65; Steven D. Hales and Robert C.
Welshon, "Truth, Paradox, and Nietzschean Perspectivism," *History of Philosophy Quarterly* 11 (1994): 101–19.

17. The correspondence theory of truth holds that a statement or belief is true if and
only if it accurately represents "reality," "the world," "states of affairs," or "the facts."
Versions of the correspondence theory of truth are explicitly attributed to Nietzsche by
Westphal, "Nietzsche's Sting"; Nola, "Nietzsche's Theory of Truth and Belief"; and Clark,
Nietzsche on Truth and Philosophy, chaps. 2, 4, and *passim.* A "metaphysical" version of
the correspondence theory of truth is implicitly attributed to Nietzsche by many writers

while still others have argued that Nietzsche does not provide a theory of truth and is not interested in doing so.[18]

Oddly enough, I think each of these views is, in some respect, right; and later I will give some indication of why I think this is so (see §1.6.3). However, the debate over which theory of truth to attribute to Nietzsche seems to me improperly framed, so I will not enter into it directly here. Rather, I want to suggest that we arrive at a better sense of Nietzsche's conception of truth by examining what he himself takes to be the crucial consideration: the question of "the *value* of truth," or rather, how truth is to be *revalued* in light of his genealogy of European thought.

---

who argue that Nietzsche conceives of the ultimate nature of reality as "becoming," "chaos," or "will to power," whether or not we can adequately think or communicate the character of the world as such. See, e.g., Danto, *Nietzsche as Philosopher*, 80, 96–97; Granier, "Perspectivism and Interpretation"; Wilcox, *Truth and Value in Nietzsche*, 132–33; Rüdiger Grimm, *Nietzsche's Theory of Knowledge* (Berlin: Walter de Gruyter, 1977), 30 and *passim*; and Mittelman, "Perspectivism, Becoming, and Truth." A version of the correspondence theory also seems implicit in many writers' emphasis upon Nietzsche's language of "honesty," "aptness," and "justice." See, e.g., Jaspers, *Nietzsche*, 201–11; Kaufmann, *Nietzsche*, 354–61; Schacht, *Nietzsche*, 63, 66, 95–117; and Schrift, *Nietzsche and the Question of Interpretation*, 155, 188ff. The pragmatic theory of truth holds that a statement or belief is true if and only if it is, in some respect, useful. This theory is attributed to Nietzsche by Danto, *Nietzsche as Philosopher*, chap. 3; Grimm, *Nietzsche's Theory of Knowledge*, chap. 2 and *passim*, and "Circularity and Self-Reference in Nietzsche," *Metaphilosophy* 10 (1979): 289–305; and George Stack, "Kant, Lange, and Nietzsche: Critique of Knowledge," in *Nietzsche and Modern German Thought*, ed. Keith Ansell-Pearson (London: Routledge, 1991), 36, and "Nietzsche's Evolutionary Epistemology," *Dialogos* 59 (1992): 77. Other commentators argue that Nietzsche affirms the pragmatic theory of truth on at least one level within a multileveled theory of truth. See Granier, "Perspectivism and Interpretation," 198–99; Warnock, "Nietzsche's Conception of Truth," 49, 51ff.; Schacht, *Nietzsche*, 71ff.; and Nola, "Nietzsche's Theory of Truth and Belief." The coherence theory of truth holds that a statement or belief is true if and only if it coheres or fits within the system of connected statements and beliefs that constitutes our knowledge. Schacht (*Nietzsche*, 63, 66ff.) and Magnus (*Nietzsche's Existential Imperative* [Bloomington: Indiana University Press, 1978], 29, 201, and "Nietzsche's Mitigated Skepticism," 265) argue that Nietzsche's theory of truth is, at least in part, a coherence theory. The semantic theory of truth, formulated by Alfred Tarski decades after Nietzsche's death, holds that a sentence is true, in a given language, if it satisfies the rules by which sentences in the language and objects are picked out and correlated with one another. (It is of some debate, among Nietzsche scholars and philosophers generally, to what degree this theory is a correspondence theory). This conception of truth is attributed to Nietzsche by Nola, "Nietzsche's Theory of Truth and Belief," 538ff.; and Clark, *Nietzsche on Truth and Philosophy*, 32, 38–40, 61, 135. It should be noted that many commentators attribute to Nietzsche a hybrid or multileveled theory of truth that combines several of the theories described above.

18. See Nehamas, *Nietzsche: Life as Literature*, 54–55; and Gemes, "Nietzsche's Critique of Truth," 48.

1.5.1 TRUTH, BEING, AND BECOMING

This revaluation obviously presupposes some preliminary characterization of truth. For Nietzsche, such characterization is provided by the history of metaphysics, which, he argues, retains essentially the same conception of truth from Plato through positivism: truth considered as the absolute priority of determining "what is" apart from "what becomes" and "what merely seems or appears to be."

With regard to this conception of truth, as we have seen, the advent of modern experimental science represents, for Nietzsche, a decisive step in the history of metaphysics. Science turns its attention away from the Platonic-Christian "world of being" toward the "world of becoming"— the spatiotemporal, physical, natural, and empirical world. Moreover, as it develops, science casts off its residual ties with theology, gradually rejecting the deism to which it was initially wedded.[19] The scientific revolution, then, brings us closer to an affirmation of what Nietzsche calls "a pure, newly discovered, newly redeemed nature" (GS 109) and a restoration of what he terms the "innocence of becoming" (TI "Errors" 8).

Yet Nietzsche argues that the dominant scientific theories and methods of the nineteenth century—mechanism, evolutionism, and positivism—still harbor a residual theology that corrupts the "innocence of becoming": they still attempt to discover a "world of being" as the ground and essence of the "world of becoming." The "necessity," "law," "atomism," and "equilibrium" central to mechanistic physics, the "struggle for preservation" and inherent teleology of evolutionary theory, and the "facts" and "disinterested observation" desired by positivism—all of these, according to Nietzsche, are but further attempts to place becoming in the service of being, to claim that becoming and change are always governed by, tend toward, or are reducible to some static, enduring, and isolable thing or state.

Nietzsche's arguments against these various scientific theories are manifold and complex; and a discussion of his philosophy of science and nature would take us too far afield.[20] But his general point is fairly simple. Nietzsche does not object to these or any other scientific theo-

---

19. See GS 357, quoted above on pp. 17–18. Cf. BGE 209: "science has most happily rid itself of theology, whose 'handmaid' it was too long."
20. I discuss these theories further below (§§1.5.2, 2.3.1, 5.2.1, and 5.2.3). On mechanism, see GS 109, 373; BGE 21, 22, 36, 213; GM II:12; WP 618–19, 634–35, 689, 708, 712, 1066. On evolutionary theory, see TL; HL; GS 349; GM II:12–13; WP 647–

ries on the basis of their pragmatic aims—their desire to select, simplify, quantify, and map relative tendencies and to hierarchize appearances for the purposes of increasing our ability to cope with our environment. What he objects to is the scientific propensity to *forget* that these are indeed pragmatic constructions and the consequent claim simply to have sketched from reality itself this picture of a simple and stable world. Nietzsche writes:

> One should not understand this *compulsion* to construct species, forms, purposes, laws—"*a world of identical cases*"—as if they enabled us to fix the *true world;* but as a compulsion to arrange a world for ourselves in which *our existence* is made possible—we thereby create a world which is calculable, simplified, comprehensible, etc., for us. (*WP* 521; cf. *BGE* 14)

What is objectionable and ultimately indemonstrable, for Nietzsche, is the idea that the world follows some grand plan that involves a resolution of becoming into being, into some terminal state or thing. Once we give up faith in the "true world" of the Platonists and Christians, we should come to see our world in a new light: as a becoming without beginning, end, origin, purpose, goal, or privileged aspect (see *GS* 109; *BGE* 22; *TI* "Errors" 8; *WP* 708, 711, 1062–67). While, within this becoming, we may be able to isolate some tendencies, regularities, and solidities, we should remember that, in doing so, we are only marking *relative* movements, regularities, durabilities, and phenomena that, considered within a different perspective or framework (e.g., from different points in the universe, over much larger or smaller time spans, with keener faculties of perception) would appear otherwise (i.e., as having other modes of individuation, as ongoing processes rather than stable states, as moving in contrary directions, etc.).[21] Nietzsche writes in a note from 1887:

> Duration, identity with itself, being are inherent neither in that which is called subject nor in that which is called object; they are complexes of events apparently durable in comparison with other complexes—e.g., through the difference in tempo of the event (rest-movement, firm-loose: oppositions that

---

50, 684–85, 709, 881. On positivism, see *GS* 347, 373; *BGE* 10, 204, 210; *GM* III:24; *WP* 1, 120, 481.

21. See, e.g., *D* 117: "If our eyes were a hundredfold sharper, man would appear to us tremendously tall; it is possible, indeed, to imagine organs by virtue of which he would be felt as immeasurable. On the other hand, organs could be so constituted that whole solar systems were viewed contracted and packed together like a single cell: and to beings of an opposite constitution a cell of the human body could present itself, in motion, construction and harmony, as a solar system." See also *GS* 228, 301–2.

do not exist in themselves and that actually express only *variations in degree* that from a certain perspective appear to be oppositions. There are no opposites: only from those of logic do we derive the concept of opposites—and falsely transfer it to things). (*WP* 552; cf. *GS* 110–12; *WP* 521, 523)

In short, Nietzsche maintains that, contrary to metaphysics, being and becoming are not opposed to one another. Rather, being is a mode of becoming—becoming conceived under a particular description, which, however, will always conflict with others and can claim no ultimate priority.

This re-orientation of the relationship between being and becoming also changes the character of truth. If, for metaphysics, truth consisted in the separation of being from all becoming, the result of Nietzsche's argument is that truth must now take its place within the world of becoming—within a world that is in constant movement and alteration, and which appears differently from every point (see *WP* 568). In this new guise, truth is concerned not with the determination of absolute and ultimate being, but with a specification of the perspectives and interpretations relative to which the world *appears* as being such and such.

1.5.2 TRUTH, BEING, AND APPEARING

This reorientation of truth points toward what can be considered the central concern in Nietzsche's discussions of truth and knowledge: the attempt to reconcile truth with its traditional arch enemy—semblance (*der Schein*) or appearance (*die Erscheinung*). Indeed, for Nietzsche, this reconciliation is already implied in the reconciliation of truth and being with becoming. For, following Heraclitus, Nietzsche conceives of the "world of becoming" not simply as a world of "constant change" but also as a world of "changing aspects," a world that takes on different appearances when considered within different frameworks.[22] To

22. According to Terence Irwin ("Plato's Heracleiteanism," *Philosophical Quarterly* 27 [1977]: 4–5), the notion of "becoming" or "flux," for Heraclitus, Plato, and Aristotle, involves not only "local movement" and "qualitative alteration"—what Irwin calls "self-change"—but also "aspect change," "things with compresent opposite properties [. . .] resulting from dependence on different situations." John Richardson has argued that "becoming" holds this sense for Nietzsche as well, helping to account for the doctrine of perspectivism. Thus, on Richardson's reading of Nietzsche, "to say that things become is to say that they 'come to be' one way from one point of view, and another way from another, and that some at least of these opposing perspectives are equally legitimate" ("Reply to Professor Robin Small," *International Studies in Philosophy* 21 [1989]: 136). These two conceptions of "becoming" are discussed more fully in chapter 4.

situate truth within the world of becoming, then, is also to situate it within the world of seeming and appearance; it is to say that "the 'apparent' [»*scheinbare*«] world is the only one" (*TI* "Reason" 2; cf. *BGE* 34; *TI* "Reason" 6; *WP* 566–68) and that, if there is to be truth, it must take its place within this "apparent" world.

Again, Nietzsche conceives of his task as a continuation and radicalization of the project of modern science, which turned the intellect's attention away from the otherworldly claims of Platonism and Christianity toward the earthly domain of nature and becoming. Following the lead of science, and having rejected the otherworldly conception of truth and knowledge as the attempt to achieve absolute certainty and to grasp unconditional, necessary, and eternal entities, Nietzsche attempts to resituate truth and knowledge within what he calls "the world of life, nature, and history" (*GS* 344). Yet in this same passage, he tells us that "life aim[s] at semblance, meaning error, deception, simulation, delusion, self-delusion [Anschein, . . . Irrthum, Betrug, Verstellung, Blendung, Selbstverblendung]" (*GS* 344), or, as he puts it in the 1886 preface to *The Birth of Tragedy,* "all of life is based on semblance, art, deception, points of view, and the necessity of perspectives and error [Schein, Kunst, Täuschung, Optik, Nothwendigkeit des Perspektivischen und des Irrthums]" (*BT* SC: 5).[23] If so, it seems unlikely that anything akin to truth will be discovered within the realm of "life."

This certainly was Plato's conclusion, and that of metaphysics ever since. Yet Nietzsche thinks otherwise. It is his contention that, when we investigate the actual conditions and processes of human knowledge and inquiry, we find that, as with truth and becoming, truth and semblance (i.e., "art, deception, points of view, and the necessity of perspectives and error") are not at all opposed but rather are constantly and necessarily intermingled with one another (see, e.g., *BGE* 2, 24, 34). The impulse to reject this supposition, he argues, merely betrays a "hostility to life," a metaphysical desire to negate "the world of life, nature, and history" in favor of "another world," which, however, remains "indemonstrable" (see *BT* SC: 5; *GS* 344; *TI* "Reason" 6; *GM* III: 28; *EH* "Destiny" 8).

The scientific rejection of metaphysics, according to Nietzsche, allows

23. Compare the 1886 preface to *Human, All Too Human* (1): "Enough, I am still living; and life is, after all, not a product of morality: it *wants* deception, it *lives* on deception . . . but there you are, I am already off again, am I not, and doing what I have always done, old immoralist and bird-catcher that I am—speaking unmorally, extramorally, 'beyond good and evil'?"

the emergence of a question that had thus far remained foreclosed: the question concerning the *value* of both truth and deception. Having repudiated morality as the ultimate tribunal, Nietzsche asserts that truth ought not to be determined in advance as unquestionably "good," nor ought deception to be determined in advance as unquestionably "evil." Rather, the respective values of truth and deception ought to be determined "experimentally" (see *GM* III: 24) through investigations carried out "beyond good and evil" (*BGE* 4, 2). The new tribunal, according to Nietzsche, is that of "life," which concerns the actual conditions for the existence, preservation, and flourishing of natural beings, human beings included (see *WP* 495). This change of tribunal means that the "will to truth" is no longer to be considered a divine gift or command, and neither are the "will to semblance" or "will to deception"[24] to be considered signs of immorality. Rather, both "wills" are to be viewed as natural, physico-psychological impulses developed within a particular species of life to help it to cope with its conditions of existence.

The results of Nietzsche's "experiments" concerning truth can be summarized as follows: (1) to the degree that it is satisfiable, the "will to truth"—the desire accurately to represent the world as it really is—is not necessarily what is most useful, beneficial, or of highest value for "life"; (2) the "will to deception"—the will consciously or unconsciously to select from, simplify, embellish, or ignore features of the world—[25] is not necessarily pernicious but, indeed, can be of tremendous value; (3) the "will to truth" and the "will to deception" can both be seen to affirm and to negate the interests of "life"; and (4) the "will to truth" and the "will to deception" can be seen to require and to supplement one another in even the most rigorous intellectual inquiry.

Nietzsche consistently makes the point that, in the actual practice of our everyday and scientific inquiry, truth is not solely what we are after. For instance, we are selective with regard to what concerns us. We do not make it our task to provide an infinitely detailed description of the state of everything in the universe at every given moment. Were it pos-

---

24. There is a close association between what Nietzsche calls "the will to semblance [*der Wille zum Schein*]" (*GS* 107), "the will to deception [*der Wille zur Täuschung*]" (*BGE* 2; *GM* III: 25), and "the will to ignorance [*der Wille zum Nicht-wissen* or *Unwissen*]" (*BGE* 24). Nehamas discusses "the will to ignorance" in relation to "the will to knowledge [*der Wille zum Wissen*]" in *Nietzsche: Life as Literature*, chap. 2.

25. In the *Genealogy* (III: 24), Nietzsche names this "will to deception" "interpretation" (*Interpretation*), which requires the "forcing, adjusting, abbreviating, omitting, padding, inventing, [and] falsifying" of particular features of the world in the service of "life."

sible, such a description would not only be too complex and full of
trivia but would also be too fleeting, requiring infinitely many such descriptions every second. Therefore, we make do with vastly simplified
representations of even the small portion of the universe with which we
are, for the most part, concerned (see *BGE* 230). We describe this limited domain using a host of generalizations that smooth over myriad
particularities, differences, irregularities, and anomalous cases to satisfy
cognitive interests other than that of precise description (see *TL* 83).
Weighing the demands of precision and scope against those of coherence, utility, clarity, and explanatory and predictive power, we try to
achieve a balance that describes as much as possible about the world
(or some part of it) with the greatest possible economy and systematicity.[26] We see the world as composed of subsistent, self-identical "beings,"
even though, examined closely, the world is always in flux and beings
are constantly becoming-other, either through spatial, temporal, physical, chemical, and biological changes, or through reconsideration within
new perspectives, modes of inquiry, and linguistic and conceptual sortings (see *GS* 110, 112, 121).[27] We subsume temporally diverse sensory
experiences under a single name, identifying them as composing the
"same" object or person (see *TL* 83; *GS* 335; *WP* 508ff.); and we view
the world in terms of species and kinds that are sorted by classifica-
tory schemes that determine features as "important" or "unimportant"
relative to our particular purposes (see *TL* 83, *WP* 521).[28] The more
successful these simplifications, selections, and classifications prove to
be for us, the more entrenched they become, and the more "real" and
"true" they are taken to be. In other words, rather than simply describ-

26. On economy of method, see *BGE* 13, 36. This point has been repeatedly made,
within the context of contemporary Anglo-American philosophy of science, by Nelson
Goodman. See Goodman, *Languages of Art*, 2d ed. (Indianapolis: Hackett, 1976),
262–65, and *Ways of Worldmaking* (Indianapolis: Hackett, 1978), 18, 120–21. See also
Nancy Cartwright, *How the Laws of Physics Lie* (Oxford: Oxford University Press,
1983), chap. 2, for an argument that the great explanatory power of the fundamental
laws of physics is proportional to their falsehood.

27. Note that Nietzsche joins company with more recent philosophers such as W. V.
Quine, who maintains that such things as "physical objects," "forces," and "the abstract
entities which are the substance of mathematics" are simply "myths," "posits comparable, epistemologically, to the gods of Homer," "Two Dogmas of Empiricism," in *From
a Logical Point of View* (Cambridge: Harvard University Press, 1961), 44–45.

28. For a similar point, see Catherine Z. Elgin, "The Relativity of Fact and the Objectivity of Value," in *Relativism: Interpretation and Confrontation*, ed. Michael Krausz
(Notre Dame: University of Notre Dame Press, 1989). Cf. Stephen Jay Gould's critique of
essentialist taxonomies in *The Flamingo's Smile: Reflections in Natural History* (New
York: W. W. Norton, 1985), 160ff., and *Full House: The Spread of Excellence from Plato
to Darwin* (New York: Harmony, 1996), 38–42.

ing the world as we find it, we as much fabricate it to suit our needs: we individuate, sort, select, classify, and weight features of the world so as to make it more comprehensible, calculable, predictable—in a word, more *habitable* for human beings (see *BGE* 14). "Science at its best," Nietzsche writes, "seeks most to keep us in this *simplified,* thoroughly artificial, suitably constructed and suitably falsified world—[. . .] it loves error, because, being alive, it loves life" (*BGE* 24).

Yet this is not to argue that truth is equivalent to utility or that Nietzsche supports a "pragmatist theory of truth." Nietzsche constantly reminds us that the demands for utility and for truth are quite often at odds with one another. He writes in *The Gay Science:* "We have arranged for ourselves a world in which we can live—by positing bodies, lines, planes, causes and effects, motion and rest, form and content: without these articles of faith nobody could now endure life. But that does not prove them. Life is no argument; the conditions of life might include error" (*GS* 121; cf. *BGE* 39; *EH* P:3; *WP* 493).

Even so, he is quick to add that this is no condemnation of the will to error and deception:

> The falseness of a judgment is not for us necessarily an objection to a judgment; in this respect our new language may sound strangest. The question is to what extent it is life-promoting, life-preserving, species-preserving, perhaps even species-cultivating. And we are fundamentally inclined to claim that the falsest judgments [. . .] are indispensable for us; [. . .] that renouncing the falsest judgments would mean renouncing life and a denial of life. To recognize untruth as a condition of life—that certainly means resisting accustomed value feelings in a dangerous way; and a philosophy that risks this would by that token alone place itself beyond good and evil. (*BGE* 4)

Each of these passages claims that, strictly speaking, the simplifications and categorizations taken for granted by our science and common sense are not "true," that, from some other perspective and by other criteria, they could be seen as "erroneous" or "false"; and yet these passages seem to point in opposite directions—one toward truth in spite of utility, the other toward utility in spite of truth. This is no inconsistency on Nietzsche's part. When these passages are read together, it becomes clear that Nietzsche does not want to condemn or celebrate either the "will to deception" or the "will to truth." While he aims to reveal the extent to which the "will to deception" is operative and highly useful in our everyday and scientific formulations of the world, he is also concerned to remind us that these formulations are artificial and relative to particular sets of interests and concerns.

We can see that, on both sides, Nietzsche's target is metaphysics and its kin, theology and morality, which claim that truth is of absolute value and that the will to truth leads to the disclosure of a "true world." On the one hand, Nietzsche argues that, contrary to demands of metaphysics, theology, and morality, our inquiry does not unconditionally strive for the truth—for the "plain facts"—but instead has constant recourse to useful fictions and artificial constructions. On the other hand—and this point is crucial—he argues that a recognition of this artificiality should tempt us away from the essentialist view that science (or any other discourse) discovers a "real" and "true" world. Indeed, for Nietzsche, the conviction that there exists such a "true world" is simply a metaphysical faith (see *BGE* 2, 3, 34; *TI* "Reason" 2, 6, "World"; *WP* 566–67). Hence, a recognition of the artificiality and contingency (what Nietzsche hyperbolically calls the "falsehood") of a particular construction of the world is simply *a recognition that it could be constructed otherwise* and that what resists such novel construction is not "the way the world really is" but the inertia of established conceptions of the world.[29] Thus, in a telling passage, he writes:

> [W]*hat things are called* is incomparably more important than what they are. The reputation, name, and appearance [*Anschein*], the usual measure and weight of a thing, what it counts for—originally almost always erroneous [*ein Irrthum*] and arbitrary, thrown over things like a dress and altogether foreign to their essence [*Wesen*] and even their skin—all this develops from generation to generation, merely because people believe in it, until it gradually grows onto and into the thing and becomes its very body. What at first was semblance [*Schein*] becomes at last, almost invariably, the essence [*Wesen*], and *functions* [*wirkt*] as essence. How foolish it would be to suppose that one only needs to point out this origin and misty shroud of delusion in order to *destroy* the world that counts for real, so-called "*reality*" [»*Wirklichkeit*«]. We can destroy only as creators!—But let us not forget this either: it is enough to create new names and estimations and probabilities in order to create in the long run new "things." (*GS* 58)

Initially, this passage seems to maintain an opposition between essence and appearance; yet as it proceeds, this distinction is undercut. Retrospectively, we come to see that even those "original essences" were once constructions or "semblances" that gradually established themselves and came to "count for real." Thus, Nietzsche regards the dis-

---

29. See *GS* 110: "the *strength* of knowledge does not depend on its degree of truth, but on its age, on the degree to which it has been incorporated, on its character as a condition of life."

tinction between "essence" and "appearance" as one of degree, not one
of kind. "What is" has become so through its articulation within an interpretation that has managed to secure itself (see *GM* II:12). To see
things otherwise is to have created a new interpretation that individu-
ates things differently and ascribes to them different origins, ends, and
purposes. And for this new, "wrong," interpretation to become "right,"
for this "semblance" to become "essence," one must campaign on its
behalf until it comes to be taken for granted.[30]

I will return to these issues below. For the present discussion, the important point is that we are never concerned with a world of "truth"
and "being" (in the strict, metaphysical senses) but always with a world
of "seeming" and "appearance": a world that seems or appears to be
such and such for a particular perspective or interpretation.[31] "Let at
least this much be admitted," writes Nietzsche, "there would be no life
at all if not on the basis of perspective estimates and appearances; and
if, with the virtuous enthusiasm and clumsiness of some philosophers,
one wanted to abolish the 'apparent world' altogether—well, supposing *you* could do that, at least nothing would be left of your 'truth'
either" (*BGE* 34; cf. *WP* 567).

Nietzsche recognizes and affirms that it is a constitutive feature of
natural creatures that they construe the world from a particular perspective and cannot avoid doing so. Such creatures are always situated

30. My reading of this passage thus differs significantly from the skeptical reading
offered by Stephen Houlgate, who argues that the passage's apparent collapse of the
opposition between essence and appearance actually presupposes that very opposition.
Houlgate reads Nietzsche as beginning from the presupposition that there was once a legitimate distinction between essence and appearance but that this distinction is now impossible to discern, because alien appearances have veiled and, by now, fused with
essences to such a degree that the latter are no longer distinguishable or knowable ("Kant,
Nietzsche, and the 'Thing in itself,'" *Nietzsche-Studien* 22 [1993]: 118, 141–42, 145–
46). I maintain, on the contrary, that Nietzsche rejects the very notion that the distinction
between essence and appearance is one of kind, arguing instead that it is simply one of degree—that essences are simply established appearances. Several other passages support
my antiskeptical reading, e.g., *HL* (3, p. 77), where Nietzsche notes that every "first nature was once a second nature and [. . .] every victorious second nature will become a
first," and *GS* 290, which offers a similar conception of the interpretive construction of
"first natures" out of "second natures." (See also the account of "things" and their role in
"interpretations" given in *GM* II:12, which is discussed at length in chapter 3.) Note that
the scenario in *GS* 58 also recalls the famous passage from "On Truth and Lies," where
Nietzsche describes truth as an ever-shifting system in which the strange and new has become the familiar and taken for granted, and those passages in Nietzsche's later work
where he argues that "knowledge" consists simply in the reduction of the strange to the
familiar (see, e.g., *GS* 355; *TI* "Errors" 5; *WP* 499, 501, 551).
31. Here, I treat these notions as more or less equivalent. The relation between these
two notions in Nietzsche's work is discussed more fully in chapter 3.

at a particular time and place and relate to their environment in ways shaped by their prior development and their current capacities, habits, and skills. This is no less the case for human beings. Each of us sees from a particular point of view, defined as much by what it excludes as by what it includes. Theorists of film and photography note that the camera image is defined by a host of exclusions: by what lies outside the four sides of the frame, beyond its depth of field, and behind the position of the camera; by what has gone into the composition of the image before the shot was taken; and by one's previous training in the various semiotic codes that allow one to see the image as representing such and such.[32] The same is true of human vision itself, which not only has a spatially limited purview but also functions as part of an organism with a range of biological, cultural, and individual needs and desires that determine in advance horizons of significance.[33]

This analysis can be further extended to "perspectives" in the broader sense that Nietzsche has in mind: that is, to "disciplines," "methodologies," "styles," "worldviews," and "ideologies." Each such "perspective" marks out a field of concern on the basis of particular presuppositions, needs, desires, goals, aims, and objects of inquiry. And, while it may be relatively easy to take up different visual perspectives, it is considerably more difficult to master different "disciplines," "methodologies," and "styles" and notoriously more difficult still to take up different "worldviews" and "ideologies." Moreover, simply combining all these different perspectives will not yield a total view, because each will be in conflict with many others with regard to prominent presuppositions, methods, aims, and conclusions.[34]

"Truth" and "knowledge," then, always take their place within the world of "perspective" and "interpretation"—that is, within the world of "appearance" and "semblance." We should note that this is not a mere reversal of the metaphysical view, according to which the "will to

32. See, e.g., Kaja Silverman, *The Subject of Semiotics* (New York: Oxford University Press, 1983), 201–22, and Stephen Heath, *Questions of Cinema* (Bloomington: Indiana University Press, 1981), chap. 2 and *passim*.

33. Cf. Marx's poignant comment that "[t]he development of the five senses is a labor of the whole previous history of the world" (*Economic and Philosophical Manuscripts*, in *Marx: Selections*, ed. Allen W. Wood [New York: Macmillan, 1988], 59). Also cf. Goodman, *Languages of Art*, 3–19.

34. Nehamas (*Nietzsche: Life as Literature*, 51) points out the impossibility of such conjunction through a poignant aesthetic example: "the understanding of everything would be like a painting that incorporates all styles or that is painted in no style at all—a true chimera, both impossible and monstrous."

truth" and the "will to deception" are, respectively, good and evil. That is, Nietzsche is not arguing for a rejection of every notion of truth in favor of semblance, error, and deception. Among other difficulties, such a move would maintain the "faith in opposite values" that Nietzsche deems "the fundamental faith of the metaphysicians" (*BGE* 2). On the contrary, Nietzsche's "experimental" antimetaphysical investigation, which situates itself "beyond good and evil," must renounce this faith and instead recognize that nature, life, and history countenance no "opposites" but "only degrees and many subtleties of gradation" (*BGE* 24; cf. *HH* 1; *WS* 67; *GS* 1, 375; *BGE* 2, 3; *WP* 37, 552). Thus, Nietzsche comes to reject the supposition "that there is an essential opposition of the 'true' and 'false'" and discovers instead that there are only "degrees of apparentness [*Scheinbarkeit*] and, as it were, lighter and darker shadows and shades of appearance—different *valeurs* [values], to use the language of painters" (*BGE* 34). Rather than seeing them in opposition, then, Nietzsche comes to see that, at their best, the "will to truth" and the "will to deception" supplement one another, that they are not opposites but "refinement[s]" of one another (*BGE* 34).

Accordingly, Nietzsche does not argue for an unqualified indulgence in the "will to deception." Rather, he contends that, on the chromatic spectrum of "truth" and "deception," both extremes are to be avoided. Having noted the dangers of "the unconditional will to truth," and having reinstated "semblance," "appearance," "error," "deception," and "perspective" to their rightful place within "the general economy of life" (*BGE* 23), Nietzsche is also concerned to show that the "will to deception" can be put to use against the interests of "life."

The most egregious case is that of the "believers," the metaphysicians and theologians who "lie" in an objectionable, *moral* sense. According to Nietzsche, these "believers" have not yet made the scientific turn and are thus out of step with the "intellectual conscience" of the age. They do not adequately scrutinize their convictions and beliefs but instead claim them to be exempt from consideration by the mistrustful gaze of science, which demands a restraint of the "will to deception" and an attention to both reason and sense-evidence.[35] Thus, Nietzsche writes:

35. Note that, while Nietzsche often criticizes the ability of sense-evidence to deliver unqualified "facts" about the world (see, e.g., *GS* 114; *BGE* 14; *WP* 516), he nonetheless considers its testimony an important criterion (see, e.g., *BGE* 134; *TI* "Reason" 3); and while Nietzsche often criticizes reason for its opposition to the natural world of becoming (see, e.g., *TI* "Reason"), he nonetheless often praises reason as that which demands "hon-

One sort of honesty [*Redlichkeit*] has been alien to all founders of religions and their kind:—they have never made their experiences a matter of conscience for knowledge. "What have I actually experienced? What happened in me and around me at that time? Was my reason bright enough? Was my will opposed to all deceits [*Betrügereien*] of the senses and bold in resisting the fantastic?"—none of them has asked such questions, nor do any of our dear religious people ask them even now: rather, they thirst after things that are *contrary to reason,* and they do not wish to make it too hard for themselves to satisfy it,—so they experience "miracles" and "rebirths" and hear the voices of little angels! But we, we others who thirst after reason, are determined to scrutinize our experiences as severely as a scientific experiment, hour after hour, day after day. We ourselves wish to be our own experiments and guinea pigs. (*GS* 319)

In a number of passages that resonate with this one, Nietzsche argues against taking as the only criterion of truth what he calls "the proof of strength": the notion that beliefs are to be held true solely on the basis of the *strength* of our belief in them or the *beneficial effects* of such belief (see *HH* 120; *GS* 347; *BGE* 210; *GM* III:24; *TI* "Errors" 5; *A* 12, 50; *WP* 171–72, 452). Nietzsche suggests that this crude pragmatist conception of truth has biblical origins[36] and easily accommodates the otherworldly agendas of metaphysics and theology. He writes:

We "knowers" [*Erkennenden*] have gradually come to mistrust believers [*Gläubige*] of all kinds; our mistrust has gradually brought us to make inferences the reverse of those of former days: wherever the strength of a faith [*Glaubens*] is very prominently displayed, we infer a certain weakness of demonstrability [*Beweisbarkeit*], even the *improbability* of what is believed [*Geglaubten*]. We, too, do not deny that faith [*Glaube*] "makes blessed": that is precisely *why* we deny that faith *proves* [*beweist*] anything,—a strong faith that makes blessed raises suspicion against that which is believed; it does not establish "truth," it establishes a certain probability—of *deception.* (*GM* III:24; cf. *HH* 484; *BGE* 210; *WP* 456, 459)

In these and other passages, Nietzsche argues against the "deceptions" of the "believers" in favor of the "honesty" of the "intellectual con-

esty" and "intellectual conscience" (see *GS* 319, cited immediately below; *A* 12). The notions of "honesty" and "intellectual conscience" are discussed below.

36. In his note to *GS* 347, Walter Kaufmann writes: "the reference is to I Corinthians 2:4, where the King James Bible has 'in demonstration of the Spirit and of power' and Luther '*in Beweisung des Geistes und der Kraft.*' In theological and homiletical quotations the old-fashioned *Beweisung* gave way to *Beweis* (proof—the word Nietzsche uses) during the nineteenth-century. Since Schleiermacher this passage became very popular, and the parallelism of *Geist* and *Kraft* was replaced by either *Geist* or, as in Nietzsche's case, *Kraft.*"

science." The latter refuses to accept the former, which seeks to exempt itself from rigorous scrutiny and refuses to enter the space of questions and reasons, demonstration and proofs. It is precisely this that Nietzsche finds "contemptible" and that leads him to reject all claims regarding transcendent entities.

Yet, having endorsed the "will to deception," how is Nietzsche to challenge this ignoble form of it? What differentiates this "bad" deception from the other "good" deception? If Nietzsche wants to accept the latter, must he not accept the former as well? Two related criteria distinguish these varieties of deception and justify Nietzsche's attitude toward them. Whereas moral-metaphysical deceptions are both unconditional and otherworldly, practical-vital deceptions are conditional and this-worldly. The former claim for themselves an absolute and ultimate status. As such, they plead exemption from scientific inquiry and affirm the existence of a prior science (a meta-physics) and a super-natural realm. Yet Nietzsche argues not only that the supposedly unconditional and otherworldly posits of metaphysics and morality are explicable in naturalistic terms but also that such explanation reveals these posits to be pernicious and contemptible. He diagnoses these deceptions as products of an irrational self-hatred: a hatred of "the world of nature, life, and history" (in all its sensuousness, physicality, conditionality, and contingency) on the part of a natural, living being—"fundamentally, life's nausea and disgust with life" (*BT* SC: 5). Posits such as "God," the "Forms," and the "thing in itself," he insists, are simply ideal projections that betray a human desire to be other-than-human, a desire for self-negation or annihilation.[37] Seen in this light, moral-metaphysical deceptions turn out to be not only *superfluous,* because they can be given an "internal" account, but also *deplorable,* because they deny the most palpable features of natural life in favor of indemonstrable claims and because they rest upon psychological motives that are, by all accounts, odious.

Practical-vital deceptions, on the other hand, are both conditional and worldly. Such deceptions always justify themselves with regard to particular aims and goals that, in the final analysis, serve to increase the ability of human beings to preserve or enhance themselves as individuals, as groups, or as a species. In relation to other ends, or for other

---

37. Such arguments were, of course, a central feature of nineteenth-century German thought. Forms of this argument against religion had previously been asserted by Hegel and the Young Hegelians, particularly Feuerbach, Bauer, and Marx; and such a theory of projection was later elaborated by Freud and his followers.

individuals, groups, or species, such deceptions might certainly be inadequate or counterproductive. And while, in our hubris, we sometimes forget the relative, conditional, and pragmatic origins and aims of these useful fictions, recognition of their fictional status does nothing to destroy their value. This, then, is a primary difference between the two sorts of deceptions: recognition of the fictional nature of metaphysical-moral deceptions destroys them, since absolute being and unconditional value is of their essence. The world in which we live, however, is contingent and conditional through and through. It countenances neither absolute entities nor absolute values. On the contrary, every entity in the natural world is enmeshed in a web of contingent relations and enjoys only a temporary existence. Such entities have limited, relative, and conditional horizons and posit for themselves limited, relative, and conditional goals. Such is "life"; and only those interpretations that affirm this conditionality, contingency, and relativity will affirm life. And it is precisely on this account that metaphysical-moral deceptions are found wanting, while practical-vital deceptions pass the test.

The "will to deception," then, is justified by Nietzsche only insofar as it places itself in the service of "life." This is also the case with the "will to truth." We have seen that Nietzsche rejects the "unconditional will to truth," which desires the eradication of every form of semblance and deception and thus ends up willing the eradication of "life"—because "life rest[s] upon semblance, [. . .] error, deception, simulation," etc. (GS 344). Any search for "the true world" betrays this other-worldly, antiworldly desire, for it is nothing other than a desire for the absolute, the unconditional, and the genuinely certain, which are not to be found within "the world of life, nature, and history" (see GS 344, 373; GM III:23–28).

It is precisely this "unconditional will to truth" that Nietzsche still finds in science and that, despite his praise of scientific method, is the crux of his frequent criticisms of science. He argues that science has not yet broken from theology and metaphysics insofar as it retains "a *metaphysical faith*" (GS 344), namely, faith in the unconditional value of truth. Nietzsche's prime target here is positivism, the scientific and philosophical project that aims to discover simple, presuppositionless "facts" and to ground all knowledge on these primitives.[38] According

38. Though Nietzsche's target is positivism in its nineteenth-century incarnation—the tradition of Comte, Mill, and Spencer—I think this critique applies equally well to its major twentieth-century manifestation, logical positivism. Nietzsche's response to nineteenth-century positivism, i.e., his development of a holistic empiricism (see chap. 2), has

to Nietzsche, this remains a metaphysical desire; for, no less than Platonism or Christianity, positivism is motivated by the demand for ultimate foundations and for a knowledge that excludes every form of semblance and deception.[39]

This attempt to eliminate all perspective and interpretation in order to get at "the facts" is, once again, not only impossible but deplorable; for, in essence, it is nothing but a rejection of nature and life, for which all knowledge is perspectival or interpretive and thus involves the kinds of "extramoral" deceptions discussed above. In a passage from the *Genealogy of Morals,* Nietzsche makes just this point. With philosophical and scientific positivism clearly in mind, he writes:

> [T]hat *desire* to halt before the factual, the *factum brutum,* [. . .] through which French scholarship [*Wissenschaft*] nowadays tries to establish a sort of moral superiority over German scholarship; that general renunciation of all interpretation (of forcing, adjusting, abbreviating, omitting, padding, inventing, falsifying, and whatever else is of the *essence* of interpreting)—all this expresses, broadly speaking, as much ascetic virtue as any denial of sensuality (it is at bottom only a particular mode of this denial). That which *constrains* these men, however, this unconditional will to truth, is *faith in the ascetic ideal itself,* even if as an unconscious imperative—don't be deceived about that—it is the faith in a *metaphysical* value, the value of *truth in itself,* sanctioned and guaranteed by this ideal alone (it stands or falls with this ideal). There is, strictly speaking, no such "presuppositionless" science, the thought of such a thing is unthinkable, paralogical: a philosophy, a "faith," must always first be there to give science a direction, a meaning, a limit, a method, a *right* to exist. (Whoever has the opposite notion, whoever tries, for example, to place philosophy "on a strictly scientific basis," first needs to stand not only philosophy but also truth *on its head* [. . .]). (*GM* III:24)

In short, we must reject not only *a priori* but also empirical attempts to provide perspectiveless, ultimate foundations for our knowledge. Science, facts, and truth are possible only within the framework of one or another interpretation, each of which construes the world according to a set of presuppositions that receive only relative, conditional justifica-

---

much in common with the responses to logical positivism offered by Heidegger and Gadamer, Quine and Davidson.

39. On positivism as the demand for ultimate foundations, see *GS* 347; on positivism as the demand for knowledge without distortion and deception, see *GM* III:24, cited below. For other critiques of positivism, see *BGE* 204, 210; *WP* 1 and 481.

tion.[40] There is no such thing as absolute or unconditional truth.[41] Thus, as with "the will to deception," Nietzsche sanctions "the will to truth" only insofar as it acknowledges its conditionality and contingency— only, that is, insofar as it takes its place within the actual conditions of existence and inquiry of living beings.

1.6 THE REVALUATION OF TRUTH II: TRUTH AND THE "INTELLECTUAL CONSCIENCE"

What, then, remains of "the will to truth," and what sort of "truth" does it "will"? The answer lies in Nietzsche's conception of "honesty" and "intellectual conscience." These terms, however, are easily misunderstood, and their Nietzschean significance eludes a casual reading. Before offering an account of how these terms ought to be understood, then, I first want to indicate how they ought *not* to be understood.

1.6.1 UTILITY, CORRESPONDENCE, AND THE "INTELLECTUAL CONSCIENCE"

In several of the passages in which Nietzsche speaks of "intellectual conscience," "intellectual integrity," and "honesty," he tells us that these philological virtues are characterized by *"the demand for certainty"* (GS 2) and the demand that everything be surrendered in the service of truth (A 50). This has led prominent commentators such as Walter Kaufmann to argue that Nietzsche's consistent calls for "intellectual integrity" and the like manifest his rejection of the notion of truth as utility and his unwillingness to give up reason's desire for truth as correspondence, despite the recognition that this desire is destructive of life.[42] On the other side, Arthur Danto has taken issue with Kaufmann's

40. See WP 481: "Against positivism, which halts at phenomena—'There are only facts'—I would say: No, facts is precisely what there is not, only interpretations."

41. Through analyses of the "Preface" to *Beyond Good and Evil*, both Wolfgang Müller-Lauter, in "On Associating with Nietzsche," trans. R. J. Hollingdale, *Journal of Nietzsche Studies* 4–5 (1992–93): 28ff., and Derrida, in *Spurs*, make this point. Derrida more explicitly argues that truth, for Nietzsche, must take its place within the world of semblance.

42. Kaufmann, *Nietzsche*, 359–61. Admittedly, Kaufmann makes no explicit reference to "the correspondence theory of truth." Yet something like it is clearly what he has in mind. For, according to Kaufmann, Nietzsche conceives of truth as a heroic resistance to every illusion and all considerations of utility or pleasure so as to be able to state simply what is the case. This is corroborated by Mary Warnock ("Nietzsche's Conception of

view. Without offering an alternative account of the notions of "honesty" and "intellectual conscience," Danto argues that Nietzsche's discussions of the life-negating results of "the will to truth" provide sufficient evidence that Nietzsche does indeed relinquish the desire for truth as correspondence and instead sanctions useful fictions insofar as they are life-promoting.[43]

This debate has become a centerpiece in the literature on Nietzsche, and each side has attracted a number of advocates.[44] Indeed, it has been suggested that, with regard to Nietzsche, "the distinction between correspondence truth and pragmatic truth. [. . .] deserves to be called The Official Distinction."[45] Yet, again, I think the debate is improperly framed and that, contrary to both sides, Nietzsche identifies truth neither with utility nor with correspondence. A reconsideration of the passages concerning "honesty" and "intellectual conscience" bears this out.

Kaufmann is certainly right to point out that, in these and other passages, Nietzsche argues against the notion that truth is equivalent to utility of belief. Indeed, Nietzsche seems to argue that "intellectual integrity" consists precisely in a constant "doubt," "mistrust," and "skepticism" with regard to convictions, faiths, and beliefs, especially those one holds dearest (see *BGE* 34, 39; *GM* I:1, III:24; *A* P, 12–13, 54). Yet Nietzsche does not reject pragmatic criteria altogether. He simply claims that utility of belief is *insufficient* for the determination of truth and that, *unchecked by other criteria,* the pragmatic criterion of truth quickly becomes dogmatic and deceptive (see *GS* 113; *GM* III:24; *A* 50; *WP* 456). We have seen that, taken as the sole criterion of truth, the pragmatic conception can support even the wildest metaphysical beliefs. By establishing a domain that in principle excludes every other criterion, metaphysics and morality come to sanction beliefs solely because of the strength that accrues to them due to their benefit for the believer.

Truth," 57–58 and *passim*), who both expresses agreement with Kaufmann's interpretation of Nietzsche's view of truth and argues that the conception of truth ultimately presupposed by Nietzsche is a correspondence theory. Also see n. 47, below.

43. Danto, *Nietzsche as Philosopher,* 72, 99, 191ff.

44. See n. 16 above. An interesting variant of this debate can be seen in the exchange between Jean Granier, *Le problème de la vérité dans la philosophie de Nietzsche* (Paris: Éditions du Seuil, 1966), 303–36, and Sarah Kofman, "Appendix: Genealogy, Interpretation, Text," in *Nietzsche and Metaphor,* trans. Duncan Large (Stanford: Stanford University Press, 1993), discussed by David C. Hoy in "Philosophy as Rigorous Philology? Nietzsche and Poststructuralism," *New York Literary Forum* 8–9 (1981): 178–80, and Schrift in *Nietzsche and the Question of Interpretation,* 166–68.

45. John T. Wilcox, "Nietzsche's Epistemology: Recent American Discussions," *International Studies in Philosophy* 15 (1983): 67–77, 72.

Thus, in several passages that take up this issue, Nietzsche inveighs against Christianity and Kantianism, both of which maintain that, ultimately, reason must yield to faith (see *D* P:3; *GS* 335; *GM* III:12; *TI* "World" 2–3; *A* 10, 12, 50, 54). It is this that the "intellectual conscience" finds contemptible:

> All these great enthusiasts and prodigies behave like our little females: they consider "beautiful sentiments" adequate arguments, regard a heaving bosom as the bellows of the deity, and conviction a *criterion* of truth. In the end, Kant tried, with "German" innocence, to give this corruption, this lack of any intellectual conscience, scientific status with his notion of "practical reason": he invented a special kind of reason for cases in which one need not bother with reason—that is, when morality, when the sublime command "thou shalt," raises its voice. (*A* 12)

> What does it mean, after all, to have *integrity* in matters of the spirit? That one is severe against one's heart, that one despises "beautiful sentiments," that one makes of every Yes and No a matter of conscience. Faith makes blessed: consequently it lies. (*A* 50)

The strength and utility of a belief, then, cannot be the only criterion of its truth. "Making unhappy and evil are no counterarguments," Nietzsche writes. "Something might be true, while being harmful and dangerous in the highest degree" (*BGE* 39). Those who accept the pragmatic criterion of truth, he concludes, show themselves to be "unaware of the most basic requirements of intellectual honesty" (*A* 12).[46]

But this is not to argue for a notion of truth as "correspondence with the way the world really is." In fact, Nietzsche argues that the correspondence conception of truth bears a fundamental affinity with the pragmatic conception—that, like the latter, the former achieves its force by a "proof of strength." In §347 of *The Gay Science*, having ridiculed the pragmatic "proof of strength," Nietzsche goes on to argue that—no less than pragmatist "believers," who deem their dearest beliefs "true"—the "scientific-positivistic" "demand for certainty" is simply the strong belief "that something should be firm [. . .] the demand for a support, a prop [. . .] the *need* for a faith, a support, a backbone, something to fall back on," which is then deemed "actual," "real," and "true." That is, for Nietzsche, the conviction that there is some absolute foundation—that there are indisputable "facts," or

---

46. Cf. *WP* 172: "That it does not matter *whether a thing is true,* but only what *effect* it produces—*absolute lack of intellectual integrity.* Everything is justified, lies, slander, the most shameless forgery."

some final "way that the world really is"—is nothing but a *need* that has been transformed into a *belief* or *faith*, which, because of its necessity and strength, comes to be considered *truth itself*:

> Here, the sudden feeling of power that an idea arouses in its originator is everywhere counted proof of its *value*:—and since one knows no way of honoring an idea other than by calling it true, the first predicate with which it is honored is the predicate *true*. . . . How otherwise could it be so effective? [. . .] [I]f it were not real it could not be effective. [. . .] An idea that such a decadent is unable to resist, to which he completely succumbs, is thus "proved" *to be true*!!! (*WP* 171)

Of course, nowhere in these or any other passages does Nietzsche directly mention the correspondence theory of truth.[47] Yet this realist con-

---

47. In a number of articles, John Wilcox ("Note on Correspondence and Pragmatism in Nietzsche"; "Nietzsche's Epistemology," 72–74; "Nietzsche Scholarship and 'the Correspondence Theory of Truth'") takes issue with the notion of the "correspondence theory of truth" in general and in Nietzsche. Wilcox argues, first, that there does not seem to be any such thing as "*the* correspondence theory of truth." "*Too many* philosophers have used the word 'correspondence,'" he writes ("Nietzsche's Epistemology," 73), and each of them has "construed that relation in different ways—indeed, to some extent they *had to*, since the relata were so different" ("Nietzsche Scholarship and 'the Correspondence Theory of Truth,'" 340). Second, he argues that "there is not much in Nietzsche's writings that might plausibly be translated as 'correspond' or 'correspondence'" ("Nietzsche Scholarship and 'the Correspondence Theory of Truth,'" 339). With regard to the first issue, I grant that there is no single, canonical, and unequivocal formulation of "the correspondence theory of truth." Nevertheless, I think the phrase is still a useful label for realist theories that hold that a statement or belief is true if and only if it matches up with some antecedent, extralinguistic, extraconceptual reality or a piece thereof. While I believe that such a view is incoherent, one can still find philosophers who hold it; and so the phrase allows one to distinguish such philosophers from those who hold other theories of truth, e.g., those according to which the criterion of truth lies in the consistency or coherence of beliefs or statements with one another or in the utility of beliefs. (Of course, such theories can themselves be realist and thus, in the final analysis, "correspondence," theories if they argue that coherence or utility is ultimately only an index of a belief's correspondence with a pregiven world.) With regard to the second issue, I note that Nietzsche does, at times, refer disparagingly to a canonical form of the "correspondence" theory of truth, namely the Scholastic notion of truth as an "adequation" between things and thought: *Veritas est adaequatio rei et intellectus* (see A. N. Prior, "Correspondence Theory of Truth," in *Encyclopedia of Philosophy*, vol. 2, ed. Paul Edwards [New York: Macmillan, 1967], 224). So, for instance, in "On Truth and Lies," Nietzsche asks: "Are designations congruent with things? Is language the adequate expression of reality? [decken sich die Bezeichnungen und die Dinge? Ist die Sprache der adäquate Ausdruck aller Realitäten?]" (p. 81, cf. p. 82) and concludes that "what would be called the adequate expression of the object in the subject [. . .] is a contradictory absurdity [das würde heissen der adäquate Ausdruck eines Objekts im Subjekt [. . .] ein widerspruchsvolles Unding]" (p. 86). Similarly, in a note from 1887–88, he writes: "That a sort of adequate relationship subsists between subject and object [. . .] is a well-meant invention which, I think, has had its day [Daß zwischen Subjekt und Objekt eine Art adäquater Relation stattfinde [. . .] ist eine gutmüthige Erfindung, die, wie ich denke, ihre Zeit gehabt hat]" (*WP* 474). This notion is somewhat more obliquely criticized in *The Gay Science* (373), where Nietzsche ridicules the scientific realist's "faith in a world that is supposed to have its equiv-

ception of truth is clearly one of his targets. For he is arguing against the very notion that truth could be *found*, that the "true world" *is there* somewhere awaiting adequate representation by thought or language. It is this belief that motivates both the metaphysician and the positivistic scientist. But this belief betrays an *"instinct of weakness,"* a *"disease of the will"*(GS 347), because, for Nietzsche, truth is not something *given* that might be *found* but something that must be perpetually *constructed* and *reconstructed*.[48]

> Will to truth is a *making*-firm, a *making*-true and -durable [. . .]. Truth is therefore not something there, that might be found or discovered—but something that *is to be created* and that gives a name to a *process,* or rather to a will to overcome that has no end—introducing truth, as a *processus in infinitum,* an *active determining*—*not* a becoming-conscious of something that is "in itself" firm and determined. (WP 552)

Those who hold that truth is "already there" waiting to be discovered simply prove to be not up for this creative task. Instead of undertaking the difficult and endless job of constructing interpretations and campaigning for their truth, such realists put their faith in an established construction, which they take to be given in the nature of things:

> Faith is always coveted most and needed most urgently where will is lacking; for will, as the affect of command, is the decisive sign of sovereignty and strength. In other words, the less one knows how to command, the more urgently one covets someone who commands—a god, prince, class, physician, father confessor, dogma, or party conscience. [. . .] Once a human being reaches the fundamental conviction that he *must* be commanded, he becomes "a believer." (GS 347)

> The affect of *laziness* now takes the side of "truth" [. . .] it is more comfortable to obey than to *examine* . . . it is more flattering to think "I possess the truth" than to see darkness all around one—above all: it is reassuring, it gives confidence, it alleviates life—it improves the *character,* to the extent that it *lessens mistrust.* "Peace of soul," "a quiet conscience": all inventions made possible by the presupposition that *truth has been found* [or: that

---

alent and measure [*Äquivalent und Maass*] in human thought and human valuations—a 'world of truth' that can be mastered completely and forever with the aid of our square little reason." See also WP 4, 625. Of course, Nietzsche never explicitly speaks of "the correspondence theory of truth" or, for that matter, of "the pragmatic theory," "the coherence theory," or any other theory of truth. But that does not mean that such theories cannot be attributed to him. Nietzsche characterizes truth in many different ways and on many different levels; and the attempt to sort out those ways and levels in terms of present-day terminology is, I think, of real value.

48. See GS 58 and the discussion of it above. See also BGE 210. This notion is discussed further below.

truth is *there* (*daß die* Wahrheit da *ist*)].—[. . .] This is the proof of strength. (*WP* 452; cf. *WP* 279)

The scientific realist, then, is just as much a "believer" as the pragmatist: both elevate their most strongly held beliefs and desires to the status of "truth." Indeed, lacking the self-consciousness of a more enlightened pragmatism, scientific realism shows itself to be the mirror image of metaphysics and theology. It, too, is inspired by a need for foundations, for what is ultimately real; and it, too, claims to have found this true world. In a section entitled " 'Science' as Prejudice," Nietzsche writes:

> It is no different with the faith with which so many materialistic investigators of nature rest content nowadays, the faith in a world that is supposed to have its equivalent and its measure in human thought and human valuations—a "world of truth" that can be mastered completely and forever with the aid of our square little reason. [. . .] That the only justifiable interpretation of the world should be one in which *you* are justified because one can continue to work and do research scientifically in *your* sense [. . .]—an interpretation that permits counting, calculating, weighing, seeing, and touching, and nothing more—that is a crudity and a naiveté, assuming that it is not a mental illness, an idiocy. (*GS* 373)

Here, we see that what is objectionable about scientific realism, for Nietzsche, is precisely what is objectionable about unchecked pragmatism, metaphysics, and theology: namely, its *dogmatism*.[49] And what is objectionable about dogmatism, Nietzsche argues, is that it "castrates the intellect" (*GM* III:12).

> The claim that *truth is found* [or: that *truth is there* (*daß die* Wahrheit da sei)] and that ignorance and error are at an end is one of the most potent seductions there is. Supposing it is believed, then the will to examination, investigation, caution, experiment [der Wille zur Prüfung, Forschung, Vorsicht, Versuchung] is paralyzed: it can even count as sinful, namely as *doubt* concerning truth. . . . "Truth" is therefore more fateful than error and ignorance, because it cuts off the forces that work toward enlightenment and knowledge [*Aufklärung und Erkenntnis*]. (*WP* 452)[50]

49. On the dogmatism of metaphysics and morality, see, e.g., *A* 9, 54.

50. Cf. *WP* 457: "The words '*conviction*,' '*faith*,' the pride of martyrdom—these are the least favorable states for the advancement of knowledge." On the "sinfulness," "wickedness," and "evil" of doubt, see also *GS* 4; *BGE* 212, 229–30; *A* 52; *WP* 459. Cf. also *HH* 630: "Conviction is the belief that on some particular point of knowledge one is in possession of the absolute [*unbedingten*] truth. This belief presupposes that absolute truths exist; likewise that perfect methods of attaining to them have been discovered; finally, that everyone who possesses convictions avails himself of these perfect methods. All

Dogmatism cuts off all further inquiry and questioning—and this the "intellectual conscience" cannot tolerate:

> [T]o stand in the midst of this *rerum concordia discors* and of this whole marvelous uncertainty and interpretive multiplicity of existence [der ganzen wundervollen Ungewissheit und Vieldeutigkeit des Daseins][51] *and not question,* not tremble with the craving and the rapture of such questioning [. . .]—that is what I feel to be *contemptible.* (GS 2)

Here Nietzsche hints at the most important reason why dogmatism is intolerable and why further inquiry must always be promoted: that "the interpretive multiplicity of existence" cannot be successfully captured within a single interpretive framework. Dogmatism is reductionist; and this reductionism, according to Nietzsche, is ascetic and antinatural, because it denies the multiplicity, struggle, and change that are constantly manifested in the world of our experience (see WP 470, 600, 655, 881, 933). ("Everything simple [*einfach*] is merely imaginary, is not 'true,'" Nietzsche writes. "But whatever is real, whatever is true, is neither one [*Eins*] nor even reducible to one [*Eins*]" [WP 536]).[52] One ceases to be a genuine inquirer when one becomes a "fanatic," whose inquiry is limited by "a sort of hypnotism of the whole system of the senses and the intellect for the benefit of an excessive nourishment (hypertrophy) of a single point of view" (GS 347).[53] Again referring to the dogmatism of the natural scientists, Nietzsche writes:

> What? Do we really want to permit existence to be degraded for us like this—reduced to a mere exercise for a calculator and an indoor diversion for mathematicians? Above all, one should not wish to divest existence of its

---

three assertions demonstrate at once that the man of convictions is not the man of scientific thought"; and HH 483: "Convictions are more dangerous enemies of truth than lies."

51. Here Nietzsche uses the term *Vieldeutigkeit* and, in GS 373, the term *vieldeutigen,* both of which Kaufmann renders as "rich ambiguity" and which I render, respectively, as "interpretive multiplicity" and "multiply interpretable." Whereas, in both English and German, "ambiguity" often means "unclear" or "having a double meaning" (*zweideutig, doppeldeutig*), my translations serve to emphasize that Nietzsche speaks not of two (*zwei-, doppel-*) but of many (*viel-*), that, unlike "ambiguity," this sort of multiplicity does not seem to call for a resolution or clarification, and that this "multiplicity" has to do with interpretation: *deuten.* The point, then, is that existence, for Nietzsche, is not unclear or equivocal but rather capable of supporting many different interpretations.

52. This text appears in the *Nachlaß* within a series of aphorisms titled "Maxims of a Hyperborean." It is immediately preceded by an aphorism that also appears in the "Maxims and Arrows" section that begins *Twilight of the Idols:* "'All truth is simple [*einfach*].'—Is that not doubly [*zwiefach*] a lie?" (TI "Maxims" 4; cf. KSA 13:15 [118]).

53. For more on this dogmatic reduction to a single perspective, see BGE P; A 9, 54. See also the discussion of "inverse cripples" in Z:2 "On Redemption."

multiply interpretable character [*seines vieldeutigen Charakters*]: that is a dictate of good taste, gentlemen, the taste of reverence for everything that lies beyond your horizon. (*GS* 373)

He then continues, offering a simple case in point: "Assuming that one estimated the value of a piece of music according to how much of it could be counted, calculated, and expressed in formulas: how absurd would such a 'scientific' estimation of music be! What would one have comprehended, understood, grasped of it? Nothing, really nothing of what is 'music' in it!" (*GS* 373).

That the "exact sciences" are plainly irrelevant for an understanding of the aesthetic, historical, cultural, and social aspects of music, Nietzsche suggests, should make it clear that the world of our experience cannot be suitably explained through a single interpretive framework. Indeed, a consideration of such examples, Nietzsche feels, should even tempt us in the opposite direction: toward a recognition of the endless variety of interpretive possibilities: "I should think that today we are at least far from the ridiculous immodesty that would be involved in decreeing from our corner that perspectives are permitted only from this corner. Rather has the world become 'infinite' for us all over again, inasmuch as we cannot reject the possibility that it may include infinite interpretations" (*GS* 374).[54]

Nietzsche thus pledges "to take leave of all faith and every wish for certainty" (*GS* 347), to have done with "a will to truth [. . .] that ultimately prefer[s] even a handful of 'certainty' to a whole carload of beautiful possibilities" (*BGE* 10). Leaving the land behind, he sets out

54. Nehamas, "Immanent and Transcendent Perspectivism," 475ff., and David Hoy, "Nietzsche, Hume, and the Genealogical Method," in *Nietzsche as Affirmative Thinker,* ed. Yirmiyahu Yovel (Dordrecht: Martinus Nijhoff, 1986), 24ff., have raised legitimate concerns about the claims of this section of *The Gay Science.* Nehamas focuses on the ways in which this section seems to sanction a sort of "species solipsism," insofar as "our corner" is meant to refer to "the human intellect" and the possibility of "infinite interpretations" to the possibility of "other kinds of intellects and perspectives" to which "the world" would appear fundamentally different. Hoy focuses on the ways in which this section seems to commit Nietzsche to a problematic metaphysical ontology about which Nietzsche claims knowledge while at the same time arguing that it is unavailable to us. These readings are persuasive and point to real problems in Nietzsche's language, if not his conception. However, as both Nehamas and Hoy go on to argue, Nietzsche elsewhere sanctions a different view of perspectivism, according to which there exist multiple, equally legitimate interpretive frameworks, to each of which we have access in principle and none of which is reducible to another. While acknowledging the aforementioned problems with the language of this section, I cite a portion of it above in support of this latter version of perspectivism.

onto the dangerous, open seas of interpretation in search of a new kind of knowledge (see *GS* 124, 283, 289, 343; *BGE* 23).

1.6.2 DOGMATISM, PLURALISM, CERTAINTY, AND "INTELLECTUAL CONSCIENCE"

The "intellectual conscience" thus consists neither in the will to truth as utility nor in the will to truth as correspondence. How, then, are we to characterize this elusive kernel of Nietzschean inquiry? We have already gone some way toward answering this question. We have discovered, for instance, that the "intellectual conscience" is relentlessly antidogmatic, antireductionist, antifoundationalist, and ever in search of new interpretations. Given such a characterization, however, the "intellectual conscience" appears to endorse a relativism that bears little resemblance to what we would usually consider "intellectual integrity" or concern for "truth." Yet Nietzsche aims to show that the actual conditions of our existence and the actual process of our inquiry necessitate such a view and that such inquiry results in "truths" that, though never absolute or ultimate, deliver all that we actually need from truth and, in any case, all we can ever have of it.

In the famous preface to *Beyond Good and Evil,* Nietzsche likens truth to a woman who will not allow herself to be won by any dogmatic suitor. This assessment of the dogmatist is reiterated in *The Antichrist,* where Nietzsche writes: "*Not* to see many things, to be impartial at no point, to be party through and through, to have a strict and necessary perspective in all questions of value—this alone makes it possible for this kind of being to exist at all. But with this they are the opposite, the *antagonists,* of truthfulness—of truth" (*A* 54).[55]

Thus, it is precisely a concern for "truth" that inspires the vigilant antidogmatism and antireductionism of the "intellectual conscience." An examination of these negative traits will perhaps give us a clearer sense of both the "intellectual conscience" and its "truth."

Indeed, Nietzsche primarily characterizes the "intellectual conscience" in such oppositional terms. Wherever the notion appears, we

---

55. Cf. *BGE* 43: "Are these coming philosophers new friends of truth? That is probable enough, for all philosophers so far have loved their truths. But they will certainly not be dogmatists." See also *BT* SC: 1, SC: 5, for an argument to the effect that the dogmatism of science and morality is contrary to "truth" and "life."

are told that it involves "mistrust," "skepticism," "suspicion," "severity," "hardness," "evil," "scrutiny," "caution," and "questioning" with
regard to all "faiths," "convictions," and "presuppositions" (see *HH*
631, 633, 635; *GS* 2, 4, 113, 293, 319, 344, 346, 357; *Z*:3 "On Old
and New Tablets"; *BGE* 25, 34, 39, 209–10, 212, 230; *GM* III:24; *A*
12–13, 47, 50, 54; *WP* 452). Yet we should be clear that this is not a
call for "presuppositionless" inquiry; because, as we have seen, Nietzsche denies that any such thing is possible. "There is, strictly speaking,
no such thing as science 'without presuppositions,'" he writes; "the
thought of such a thing is unthinkable"; because "a philosophy, a 'faith,'
must always first be there to give science a direction, a meaning, a limit,
a method, a *right* to exist" (*GM* III:24; cf. *GS* 344). Elsewhere he writes
that "'contemplation without interest'" is "a nonsensical absurdity,"
because it demands "that we should think of an eye that is completely
unthinkable, an eye turned in no particular direction, in which the active and interpreting forces through which alone seeing becomes seeing
something, are supposed to be lacking" (*GM* III:12). He then concludes,
"There is *only* a perspective seeing, *only* a perspective 'knowing'; and
the *more* affects we allow to speak about a thing [*eine Sache*], the *more*
eyes, different eyes we can use to observe a thing, the more complete
will our 'concept' of this thing, our 'objectivity,' be" (*GM* III:12).

Here we witness an interesting transformation. Instead of the skeptical relativism that might seem to result from such a perspectival thesis,
Nietzsche tells us that "knowledge" and "objectivity" are still possible,
provided that we understand them differently. Rather than conceiving
of "knowledge" and "objectivity" as "contemplation without interest,"
Nietzsche proposes that we understand them as "the ability to have one's
For and Against *under control* and to engage and disengage them, so
that one knows how to employ a *variety* of perspectives and affective
interpretations in the service of knowledge" (*GM* III:12).

With this, we begin to see the cognitive value of Nietzsche's interpretive pluralism.[56] It is the role of the "intellectual conscience" relentlessly
to question the "faiths," "convictions," and "presuppositions" of any
particular evaluative or interpretive framework. Such questioning of
presuppositions surely presupposes something against which to measure individual interpretations. Having rejected the notion of a presup-

56. See also Schrift, *Nietzsche and the Question of Interpretation*, 181–94, for a
valuable discussion of Nietzsche's "interpretive pluralism."

positionless standpoint, Nietzsche maintains that interpretations can only be measured against other interpretations and perspectives.[57] A proliferation of such interpretations, he suggests, will not only provide us with many different ways to construe the world but will also give us multiple criteria against which to measure any given interpretation. In Nietzsche's usage, then, "honesty," "intellectual conscience," and "intellectual integrity" are not only *compatible with* the necessarily perspectival character of all knowledge; they even *require* such a condition.[58] For they involve relationships *among* perspectives, namely the constant weighing and measuring of interpretations against one another—of existing interpretations against other existing interpretations, of new interpretations against old interpretations, and old interpretations against new interpretations. Refusing unquestioningly to endorse the dominant interpretations, no matter how "useful" or "necessary" they appear to be, the "intellectual conscience" constantly affirms the "evil" instincts that question existing frameworks and experiment with new or forgotten ones:

> The strongest and most evil spirits have so far done the most to advance humanity: again and again they have rekindled the passions that were going to sleep—all ordered society puts the passions to sleep—and *they reawakened again and again the sense of comparison, of contradiction,* of the pleasure in what is new, daring, untried; *they compelled man to pit opinion against opinion, model against model.* (GS 4, my emphasis; cf. GS 34)

This weighing and measuring of interpretations against one another serves a number of critical and heuristic purposes. First, it demonstrates the partiality of any one interpretation or perspective. It thus prevents

---

57. A similar sort of epistemological relativism has more recently been articulated by W. V. Quine ("Ontological Relativity," in *Ontological Relativity and Other Essays* [New York: Columbia University Press, 1969], 50), who writes, "The relativistic thesis to which we have come is this, to repeat: it makes no sense to say what the objects of a theory are, beyond saying how to interpret or reinterpret that theory in another." This position has also been developed by Nelson Goodman, e.g., "The Way the World Is," in *Realism with a Human Face* (Cambridge, Mass.: Harvard University Press, 1990), and *Ways of Worldmaking*; Hilary Putnam, e.g., "Realism and Reason," *Proceedings and Addresses of the American Philosophical Association* 50 (1977): 483–98, and *Reason, Truth, and History* (London: Cambridge University Press, 1981), chap. 3; and Rorty, e.g., "Inquiry as Recontextualization: An Anti-Dualist Account of Interpretation," in *Objectivity, Relativism, and Truth: Philosophical Papers,* vol. 1 (Cambridge: Cambridge University Press, 1991), differences between these philosophers notwithstanding.

58. Thus, the "antinomy" Jean Granier sees in Nietzsche's commitment to both perspectivism and philological probity turns out to be no antinomy at all. See Granier, "Perspectivism and Interpretation," 197–99.

any interpretation from taking itself to be uniquely correct and opens it up to critique and scrutiny from without. Second, this procedure calls attention to the rules of formation of interpretations and the different sets of these that govern different interpretations, thus highlighting the decisions in favor of one or more of the many criteria that compete for satisfaction in the composition of any interpretation. Thus, entrenchment is weighed against innovation; habit against novelty; simplicity, coherence, utility, and explanatory power against comprehensiveness and precise description, and so on. Third—and highly important for Nietzsche—a consideration of the dominant interpretations of an individual or group produces a whole symptomatology and genealogy of the dispositions and values that motivate these choices, revealing the affirmative or negative, healthy or sickly, active or reactive, noble or base states of being that underlie decisions in favor of a particular interpretation or set of interpretations.[59] Last, such recognition of the plurality of interpretations and their irreducibility to a single base reveals what Nietzsche calls "the whole marvelous uncertainty and interpretive multiplicity of existence" (GS 2) and thus affirms the world of becoming, change, and semblance (see GS 373; WP 600).

This construal of the "intellectual conscience" as a reciprocal calibration of interpretations also allows us to account for Nietzsche's apparently contradictory remarks concerning "the demand for certainty." In *Gay Science* §2, Nietzsche writes that one who has intellectual integrity will "account *the desire for certainty* [Verlangen nach Gewissheit] as his inmost craving and deepest distress—as that which separates the higher human beings from the lower." Yet in §347 of the same text, he argues that "that impetuous *desire for certainty* [Verlangen nach Gewissheit] that today discharges itself in scientific-positivistic form" betrays an "*instinct of weakness*" and "*disease of the will.*" There are

---

59. It should be noted that this procedure is not, for Nietzsche, a simple calculus but a complex symptomatology. Thus, for instance, while Plato is criticized for his hatred of becoming and semblance, he is praised for his "sharpened senses" and his "noble resistance to obvious sense evidence"; while Christianity is criticized for its repression of the active impulses, it is praised for its development of subtlety, depth, and cunning; while science is criticized for its residual metaphysics, it is praised for its development of skepticism, mistrust, and critical acumen; and while art and artists generally receive the highest praise from Nietzsche, he also argues that—in the case of Wagner, for instance—the artistic enterprise can be motivated by and can harbor the most objectionable metaphysical-moral dispositions and values. On this symptomatology, see Gilles Deleuze, *Nietzsche and Philosophy*, trans. Hugh Tomlinson (New York: Columbia University Press, 1983), chap. 2; Nehamas, *Nietzsche: Life as Literature*, 127ff.; and Schrift, *Nietzsche and the Question of Interpretation*, 171ff.

clearly two different conceptions of "certainty" at work here. The latter type, as we have seen, consists in the desire for an indubitable ground, for a final determination of "the way the world is." Such a desire is reprehensible to Nietzsche in that it wishes to deny the necessarily perspectival character of all knowledge and the "interpretive multiplicity of existence" in favor of some otherworldly standpoint and some simple, unchanging world. The "desire for certainty" affirmed in §2, however, is something else entirely. There Nietzsche makes clear that he has in mind simply the requirement that, in coming to rest on a particular interpretation, one has taken alternatives into account and has made explicit to oneself the reasons for, and the consequences of, one's decision. In this sense, the will to "certainty" is directed against those who tolerate "slack feelings in [their] faith and judgments," those who do not "consider it contemptible to believe this or that and to live accordingly, without first having given themselves an account of the most certain reasons for and against" (GS 2; cf. BGE 5). Against the blind acceptance of one's judgments and values, it asks that one scrutinize them to determine precisely why one holds on to them (see GS 335; HH 630).[60] And such scrutiny, as we have seen, can only come from serious consideration of counterinterpretations. Rather than sanctioning the desire for truth as correspondence, then, the "desire for certainty" that Nietzsche considers so central to the "intellectual conscience" achieves its force only within an interpretive pluralism that refuses to grant the ultimacy of any particular world-picture. It is not a demand that the world be rendered "the way it really is" but rather a demand for "honesty" regarding the presuppositions, inclusions, exclusions, aims, and goals that motivate any given perspective.[61]

60. In his note to GS 347, Walter Kaufmann makes a similar point.
61. Both Hoy, "Philosophy as Rigorous Philology?" 180, and Schrift, Nietzsche and the Question of Interpretation, 222, have rightly noted that Nietzsche's interpretive pluralism bears a certain resemblance to the "principle of proliferation" and "pluralistic methodology" more recently advocated by Paul Feyerabend in Against Method (London: Verso, 1978). Yet both Hoy and Schrift go on to criticize Feyerabend's slogan, "anything goes," as endorsing a problematic relativism. But I think Feyerabend is close to Nietzsche here, too. First, the relativism or pluralism advocated by both Nietzsche and Feyerabend is primarily methodological rather than substantive. (Feyerabend explicitly advocates the adoption of "a pluralistic methodology" [Against Method, 30].) That is, it does not claim that every individual interpretation is as good as any other but rather that no interpretation is final and that every interpretation must be rigorously tested from the point of view of other interpretations (p. 30). While both Nietzsche and Feyerabend grant that there will always be more than one valid interpretation (i.e., in different domains, given different interests and goals, etc.), neither argues that every interpretation is valid. (Both, for instance, reject theological interpretations; and, while Feyerabend rejects antidemo-

1.6.3 "INTELLECTUAL CONSCIENCE," TRUTH, AND METHOD

We now have a better sense of what the "intellectual conscience" is, for Nietzsche. One important issue, however, remains outstanding. We know that the "intellectual conscience" is concerned with truth; but we still do not know precisely what truth is, for Nietzsche. To answer this question, I want to return to a remark made above. At the outset of this discussion, I noted that every major theory of truth has been attributed to Nietzsche by one commentator or another, while some commentators have argued that Nietzsche neither provides nor is interested in providing any theory of truth at all. I went on to suggest that each of these views is, in some respect, correct. We are now in a position to see why this is so.

We have seen that Nietzsche rejects the notion that truth is simply utility of belief. Yet, clearly, he does not reject pragmatic criteria entirely. There is no such thing as "contemplation without interest," he claims; and "to eliminate the will altogether" would be "to *castrate* the intellect" (*GM* III:12). That is to say, truth is relative to our interests and goals—not, perhaps, to any particular interest, but certainly to the interests of inquiry in general. Truth is the answer to our questions; it is what fulfills our epistemological projects and satisfies our will to know. The truth *matters* to us; it *makes a difference*. At least in part, it is what allows us to predict or manage the world in which we find ourselves. That said, it is still not the case that every expedient belief must be counted as true. There remain truths that are useless, trivial, inexpedient, or even dangerous and beliefs that might be useful but are nevertheless false.

Nietzsche's attitude toward the criterion of coherence is similarly

---

cratic interpretations, Nietzsche rejects democratic ones). Second, neither Nietzsche nor Feyerabend advocates relativism or antidogmatism for its own sake. Rather, for both, relativism and pluralism is endorsed because of its *heuristic* and *critical* value. (Feyerabend, for instance, puts interpretive pluralism in the service of "progress" [23 and passim] and "objective knowledge" [46]). I have argued above (and continue to argue below) that Nietzsche advocates a perspectival pluralism *"in the service of knowledge" and "objectivity"* (*GM* III:12, my emphasis). Such too is the aim of Feyerabend's pluralism. "Knowledge so conceived," he writes, "is not a series of self-consistent theories that converges towards an ideal view; it is not a gradual approach to the truth. It is rather an ever increasing *ocean of mutually incompatible (and perhaps even incommensurable) alternatives,* each single theory, each fairy tale, each myth that is part of the collection *forcing the others into greater articulation* [my emphasis] and all of them *contributing via this process of competition, to the development of our consciousness* [my emphasis] [. . .] Variety of opinion is necessary for objective knowledge" (*Against Method,* 30, 46).

equivocal. While the coherence theory of truth does not figure explicitly in his texts, the criterion of coherence is nevertheless at work in Nietzsche's discussions of epistemological issues. He notoriously rejects the notions of "facts in themselves" and "things in themselves," arguing that there are "facts" and "things" only within the context of an interpretation or from the point of view of a particular perspective (see GM II:12, III:12, III:24; WP 481, 553–69). That is to say, what is known is so only insofar as it is part of a system or epistemological framework; and what is true is so only insofar as it "coheres" with the other terms of that system or framework. Furthermore, Nietzsche often remarks that new discoveries necessarily take place against the background of our previous knowledge and that they are accorded a place within our system of beliefs only once they have accommodated themselves to that system or once that system has modified itself to accommodate them (see GS 57, 114, 355; BGE 230; TI "Errors" 5; WP 499–501). Nonetheless, Nietzsche argues that some interpretations (e.g., moral and metaphysical ones) are false regardless of their coherence or systematicity while other highly systematic interpretations (e.g., those of logic and mathematics) are too skeletal and abstract to be considered unequivocally true. Moreover, he argues that the previous knowledge that grounds our current system of beliefs is no final guarantor of truth, because systems of belief often include central tenets that are later shown to be false or founded on narrow prejudice.

Even with regard to the correspondence theory of truth Nietzsche's attitude is not unequivocal. He frequently rejects the notion that truth consists in the correspondence between thought or language and a pre-given world. There are no "bare facts" or "pre-given things," he argues; there are "facts" only within the context of some interpretation. Nevertheless, one might justly say that, within a given interpretation, or relative to a particular description, one speaks truly when one speaks of the things and facts countenanced by that interpretation or description and falsely when one speaks otherwise.[62] Thus, from the viewpoint of everyday, practical discourse, we have no trouble judging the truth or falsity of statements like "it is raining" by observing whether or not it is, "in

62. Thus Nietzsche writes, in "On Truth and Lies," (p. 81) that, within the context of a system of valid designations, "the liar" is one "who misuses fixed conventions by means of arbitrary substitutions or even reversals of names." Schacht, *Nietzsche*, 60–71, discusses in further detail how Nietzsche seems to sanction this sort of internal, or "discourse-relative," correspondence conception of truth.

fact," raining.[63] Nevertheless, on a broader and more theoretical level, Nietzsche follows many contemporary philosophers in rejecting the correspondence theory of truth.

Nietzsche's ambivalent relationship to each of these major theories of truth is just the reason why I think some commentators have been right to argue that "Nietzsche is not ultimately interested in (theories of) truth." [64] In the end, neither utility, coherence, correspondence, nor any other single criterion serves, for Nietzsche, as the determinant of truth. Rather, the truth of a statement or belief is the more or less stable result of its having been relativized to a particular theory or interpretation that itself has been found viable according to at least some of the most rigorous criteria of justification available.[65] There are many such criteria, and no interpretation will fulfill all of them. Different criteria will be considered appropriate to different domains of knowledge and inquiry; and competing interpretations within a particular domain will take different criteria as dominant. But neither these domains and interpretations nor these rules of inclusion and exclusion are fixed and final. Like everything else, for Nietzsche, interpretations and their "truths" *become*,[66] and this becoming is a matter of struggle and power—not, as some have argued, a matter of what the strongest decree, or of what gives a particular individual the greatest feeling of power,[67] but of what

---

63. This conception of correspondence seems similar to that delineated within the semantic theory of truth and perhaps accounts for some commentators' attribution of that theory to Nietzsche. See n. 17, above.

64. Gemes, "Nietzsche's Critique of Truth," 48. Cf. Nehamas: "Nietzsche . . . is not interested in providing a theory of truth" (*Nietzsche: Life as Literature*, 55).

65. Here, Nietzsche is in agreement with Richard Rorty ("Solidarity or Objectivity?" in *Objectivity, Relativism, and Truth: Philosophical Papers*, vol. 1 [Cambridge: Cambridge University Press, 1991], 23), who writes that "there is nothing to be said about either truth or rationality apart from descriptions of the familiar procedures of justification which a given society—*ours*—uses in one or another area of inquiry." Note that, while Rorty is perhaps the most prominent heir to the pragmatist tradition, he does not accept the pragmatic theory of truth. Rather, following Donald Davidson, he endorses a conception of truth that makes use of various aspects of the pragmatic, coherence, and correspondence theories, but that, ultimately, endorses none of these, preferring to consider truth the result of successful inquiry and interpretation rather than something that might be measured according to a single criterion. For a discussion of Rorty and Davidson on truth, see Donald Davidson, "Afterthoughts, 1987," in *Reading Rorty*, ed. Alan R. Malachowski (Oxford: Blackwell, 1990). Cf. also Samuel C. Wheeler, "True Figures: Metaphor, Social Relations, and the Sorites," in *The Interpretive Turn: Philosophy, Science, Culture*, ed. David R. Hiley et al. (Ithaca: Cornell University Press, 1991).

66. See *HH* 2: "But everything has become: there are *no eternal facts*, just as there are no absolute truths. Consequently what is needed from now on is *historical philosophizing*, and with it the virtue of modesty."

67. See Grimm, *Nietzsche's Theory of Knowledge*, 17ff.

rules of formation and criteria of justification *prevail* or *hold sway* in a particular discourse at a specific cultural and historical moment.[68]

Nietzsche is not interested in providing a theory of truth, then, because truth is not something that admits of final determination by a fixed set of criteria. Truth is the fleeting calm between battles within a war that has no preordained or final victor. What *does* interest Nietzsche, however, is ensuring that the struggle continue and that inquiry not come to an end with the enforced peace of dogmatism. Toward that end, he seeks to proliferate and sharpen the weapons to be used in this battle. Those weapons, Nietzsche tells us, are "methods."[69] He writes:

> Truth, that is to say, the scientific method, was grasped and promoted by those who divined in it a weapon of war—an instrument of *destruction*. (*WP* 457)[70]

> [W]e *ourselves,* we free spirits, are nothing less than a "revaluation of all values," an *incarnate* declaration of war and triumph over all the old conceptions of "true" and "untrue." The most valuable insights are developed last; but the most valuable insights are the *methods. All* the methods, *all* the presuppositions of our current scientificity, were opposed for thousands of years with the most profound contempt. [. . .] We have had the whole pathos of mankind against us—their conception of what truth *ought* to be, of what the service of the truth *ought* to be: every "thou shalt" has hitherto been aimed against us. Our objectives, our practice, our quiet, cautious, mistrustful manner—all these were considered utterly unworthy and contemptible. (*A* 13; cf. *WP* 469)

> All the presuppositions for a scholarly culture, all the scientific *methods,* were already there [in the ancient world]; the great, the incomparable art of reading well had already been established—that presupposition for the tradition of culture, for the unity of science. [. . .] Everything *essential* had been found, so that the work could be begun: the methods, one must say it ten times, *are* what is essential, also what is most difficult, also what is for the

---

68. In *BGE* 211, Nietzsche speaks of "former *positings* of value, creations of value which have become dominant and are for a time called 'truths'." See also *WP* 552, cited above, and *BGE* 210.

69. For more on this, see Jaspers, *Nietzsche,* 172ff.

70. Cf. *WP* 455: "The methods of truth were not invented from motives of truth, but from motives of power, of wanting to be superior." It should be said that Nietzsche goes on to say, "But that is a prejudice: a sign that truth is not involved at all." He thus seems to endorse a pure will to truth against the notion of truth as motivated by considerations of power. Yet this contradicts so many of his texts on truth (from *TL* to *GS* 344 and *GM* III:23–28), which generally argue that the notion of "disinterested truth" is absurd and impossible. I suggest that what Nietzsche condemns is not the notion that the will to truth is a will to power but that the obsession with power can make one a "fanatic" and thus can "prolong [. . .] the dominion of antiscientific methods." See *HH* 629–38 for Nietzsche's affirmation of the "struggle" and "conflict" that drive the will to truth.

longest time opposed by habits and laziness. What we today have again conquered with immeasurable self-mastery [. . .]—the free eye before reality,
the cautious hand, patience and seriousness in the smallest matters, the whole
integrity in knowledge—that had already been there once before! (*A* 59)

In these passages, Nietzsche lauds "scientific methods" and argues that
they constitute a "declaration of war and triumph" against the faiths
and convictions of metaphysics, theology, and morality (see also *HH*
629–38). This triumph, however, does not lie in securing some truth
that was covered over by the adversaries of scientific method; rather, it
lies in the latter's "*integrity* in knowledge," its attempt to satisfy all our
cognitive demands. What is "essential" is not the *result* of scientific inquiry but its *methods*, which are praised for their "quiet, cautious, mistrustful manner," for their scrutiny of faiths and convictions in the
service of knowledge. Indeed, in *Human, All Too Human,* Nietzsche
writes: "[T]he pathos that one *has* the truth now counts for very little in
comparison with that other, gentler and less noisy pathos of *seeking*
truth that never wearies of learning and examining anew . . . for the scientific spirit rests upon an insight into *method,* and if every method
were lost all the *results* of science together would not suffice to prevent
a restoration of superstition and nonsense" (633, 635, my emphasis).

But this praise of "method," then, is nothing but a reiteration of
Nietzsche's praise of the "intellectual conscience." Here as well as there,
Nietzsche advocates the creation of a multiplicity of tests to determine
the value of values and systems of belief.[71] Against the "habits and laziness" manifested in the dogmatic notion that truth is simply to be found,
Nietzsche argues that "the spirit of all severe, of all profoundly inclined,
spirits teaches *the reverse*. At every step one has to *wrestle* for truth" (*A*
50, latter emphasis mine). Recalling his discussion of the Greek *agon,*
which never allows or admits a final victor (*HC*), Nietzsche encourages
a notion of inquiry as perpetual struggle, in which truth exists only while
the victor is uncontested.[72] Thus, in a section from *Daybreak* entitled

71. See *HH* 637: "Opinions grow out of *passions; inertia of the spirit* lets them stiffen
into *convictions.*—He, however, whose spirit is *free* and restlessly alive can prevent this
stiffening through continual change. [. . . W]e advance from opinion to opinion, through
one party after another, as noble *traitors* to all things that can in any way be betrayed—
and yet we feel no sense of guilt." Cf. *GS* 295.

72. Or, as another writer has recently put it: "truth is the momentary balance of
power in a many-sided war among various guerrilla bands" (Wheeler, "True Figures,"
217). This Nietzschean conception of truth and inquiry as a perpetual "agonistics"
has been advocated by Michel Foucault, "Truth and Power," trans. Colin Gordon, in
Power/Knowledge: Selected Interviews and Other Writings, 1972–1977, ed. by Colin
Gordon (New York: Pantheon, 1980), 144 and *passim;* and Jean-François Lyotard, *The*

"To What Extent the Thinker Loves His Enemy," Nietzsche writes: "Never keep back or bury in silence that which can be thought against your thoughts! Give it praise! It is among the foremost requirements of honesty of thought. Every day you must conduct your campaign also against yourself. A victory and a conquered fortress are no longer your concern, your concern is truth—but your defeat is no longer your concern, either!" (370).[73]

Finally, with this, we have perhaps also unraveled the aphorism that heads Nietzsche's examination of truth and the ascetic ideal in the *Genealogy of Morals:* "Unconcerned, mocking, violent—thus wisdom wants *us:* she is a woman and always loves only a warrior." Having spurned the dogmatist, truth and wisdom find their proper suitors in the warrior, who despises peace and settles for no final victory (see also *Z:1* "On War and Warriors").

1.7 ART AS SUCCESSOR TO SCIENCE

We can now return to and complete Nietzsche's genealogy of European thought. Where we left off, Nietzsche had described the self-overcoming of metaphysics and theology in science and then the self-overcoming of science itself. This last event finally accomplished "the death of God," for it signaled the end of the metaphysical-theological conception of truth as an otherworldly ideal—as "divine"—and ushered in a "revaluation of truth." Yet, as I remarked above, if Nietzsche's genealogy is a story of sunrise and sunset, it is one that covers more than a single day. At the end of the metaphysical day, Nietzsche offers a forecast of the day to come. Having outlined the rudiments of Nietzsche's "revaluation

Postmodern Condition: A Report on Knowledge, trans. Geoff Bennington and Brian Massumi (Minneapolis: University of Minnesota Press, 1984), 10 and *passim.* Without reference to martial metaphors, Jean-Luc Nancy offers another characterization of the point I want to make here. He writes ("'Our Probity!'" 72) that Nietzsche "turns this *Redlichkeit* into a strange probity that would in some way precede the truth of which it ought to be the guarantor or the witness, and which would precede or defer indefinitely the *reference* of its truthfulness."

73. Cf. *GS* 283, in which Nietzsche looks forward to an "age that will carry heroism into the search for knowledge and that will *wage wars* for the sake of ideas and their consequences"; and *GS* 285, in which Nietzsche tells the postmetaphysical thinker: "You will never pray again, never adore again, never again rest in endless trust; you do not permit yourself to stop before any ultimate wisdom [. . .]; no resting place is open any longer to your heart, where it needs to find and no longer seek; you resist any ultimate peace; you will the eternal recurrence of war and peace." Cf. also *HH* 638: "He who has attained only some degree of freedom of mind cannot feel other than as a wanderer on the earth—though not as a wanderer *to* a final destination: for this destination does not exist."

of truth," we are now in a position to present that forecast, with which his genealogy ends.

Again, this genealogy is impelled by a constant process of self-overcoming, the gradual accumulation and exacerbation of tensions that eventually lead to a takeover by an element that had thus far been subordinate. The changes it describes are not radical breaks but significant reconfigurations that nonetheless maintain much of the old order in the new.[74] Thus science comes into existence through a "translation and sublimation" of the father confessor's demand for truth at any price (see *GS* 357; *GM* III: 27); and thus, too, does science's successor retain something of science itself.

Metaphysics and theology are overcome through an internal tension (the demand for faith vs. the requirement of truth-telling); and such, too, is the fate of science. As we have seen, Nietzsche criticizes science for its residual metaphysics—its refusal to question the absolute value of truth and its attempt to discover a "true world" of "facts" that disregards all becoming, seeming, perspective, and interpretation. Yet he also praises science for its development of a contrary drive that ultimately clashes with and overwhelms the desire for unconditional truth. This triumphant drive manifests itself in science's relentless "mistrust," "suspicion," "scrutiny," and "questioning" of all faiths, convictions, and presuppositions—a tendency that leads not to the valorization of presuppositionless inquiry but to the proliferation of interpretations and "methods" with which to test any given interpretation. This movement is succinctly summarized in two texts from 1888. In an unpublished note, Nietzsche writes, "It is not the victory of science that distinguishes our nineteenth century, but the victory of scientific method over science" (*WP* 466); and, in *The Antichrist,* "The most valuable insights are discovered last; but the most valuable insights are the *methods*" (13). That is, the greatest legacy of science is not its *ends* or *results,* its discovery of truths, but its *means* or *methods,* its questioning of all truths and its construction of alternative frameworks within which the world can be viewed differently.

Yet science is not ultimately the discourse that most fully affirms this

---

74. As Gilles Deleuze (*Nietzsche and Philosophy,* 5) puts it, "a new force can only appear and appropriate an object by first of all putting on the mask of the forces which are already in possession of the object." Deleuze refers to Nietzsche's discussion, in *GM* III: 10, of the way in which philosophy established itself only by taking into itself central features of religious asceticism.

project. Indeed, according to Nietzsche, a thoroughgoing movement in this direction would lead to the self-overcoming of science and its passage into another discourse—that of *art*. Hence, in the *Genealogy of Morals,* Nietzsche writes:

> Art—to say it in advance, for I shall some day return to this subject at greater length—art, in which precisely the *lie* is sanctified and the *will to deception* has a good conscience, is much more fundamentally opposed to the ascetic ideal than is science: this was instinctively sensed by Plato, the greatest enemy of art Europe has yet produced. Plato *versus* Homer: that is the complete, the genuine antagonism—there the sincerest advocate of the "beyond," the great slanderer of life; here the instinctive deifier, the *golden* nature. (III:25)

Taken in the broadest sense, art (or, the aesthetic)[75] affirms everything to which Nietzsche's genealogy has directed us. Against the otherworldly claims of metaphysics and theology, art affirms this-worldly sensuousness and materiality. It counteracts the ascetic demand for desensualization and extirpation of the passions by indulging the senses and passions and encouraging their multiplication and cultivation.[76] Yet, contrary to the scientific hypertrophy of the receptive faculties, art also affirms the active powers of creation and transformation. Within the aesthetic, discovery and creation go hand in hand: every act of sensation is also a construction of the world according to a particular perspective and interpretation (see *GS* 57, 114; *WP* 500, 505, 520). Indeed, Nietzsche maintains that a denial of perspective and interpretation would mean the denial of sensuality itself and, by extension, an ascetic denial of life (see *GM* III:24).

---

75. Mark Warren, *Nietzsche and Political Thought* (Cambridge, Mass.: MIT Press, 1988), 179, rightly states that "Nietzsche understands art not as a set of artifacts and works, but rather as an archetype of practice; he is interested in the process more than the products." To this one might add: more than the products and works of the artist, Nietzsche is interested in the artist's *values* and *affirmations,* specifically, the affirmation of appearance, perspective, and interpretation. This is what I focus on here.

76. Nietzsche's notion of the aesthetic no doubt draws upon the original Greek sense of *aisthesis* (sense perception). See *WP* 820: "In the main, I agree more with the artists than with any philosopher hitherto: they have not lost the scent of life, they have loved the things of 'this world'—they have loved their senses. To strive for 'desensualization': that seems to me a misunderstanding or an illness or a cure, where it is not merely a hypocrisy or self-deception. I desire for myself and for all who live, *may* live, without being tormented by a puritanical conscience, an ever-greater spiritualization and multiplication of the senses; indeed, we should be grateful to the senses for their subtlety, plenitude and power and offer them in return the best we have in the way of spirit [. . .]: it is a sign that one has turned out well when, like Goethe, one clings with ever-greater pleasure and warmth to the 'things of this world.'" See also *WP* 800, 809–10.

This brings us to what is perhaps most important about art for Nietzsche: its affirmation of appearance, semblance, perspective, and interpretation and, consequently, its affirmation of life—"for all of life rests upon semblance, art, deception, points of view, and the necessity of perspectives and error" (*BT* SC: 5; cf. *GS* 54; *BGE* 2, 34). Once again, this is not an unqualified rejection of truth and reality in favor of falsehood and lies. Nietzsche's use of the terms "lie," "deception," and "error" is clearly polemical, directed against Platonists and positivists who search for absolute truth and for whom art is at best a diversion and at worst a seduction to untruth. Against this view, Nietzsche asserts that

> there would be no life at all if not on the basis of perspective estimates and appearances; and if, with the virtuous enthusiasm and clumsiness of some philosophers, one wanted to abolish the "apparent world" altogether—well, supposing *you* could do that, at least nothing would be left of your "truth" either. Indeed, what forces us at all to suppose that there is an essential opposition of "true" and "false"? Is it not sufficient to assume degrees of apparentness and, as it were, lighter and darker shadows and shades of appearance—different *valeurs* [values], to use the language of painters? (*BGE* 34)

The aesthetic analogy is important, here (as is the move from a moral to an aesthetic conception of "value"). Nietzsche points out that we are inextricably bound to perspective and interpretation and that the world presents itself to us as a kaleidoscopic array of appearances. This is instinctively realized and affirmed by the artist, who acknowledges the impossibility of capturing the "interpretive multiplicity of existence" within a single work and is content to construct reality from within a particular perspective and style, which inevitably requires a focus or emphasis on certain aspects and a deemphasis or omission of others.[77] Such limitation, Nietzsche remarks, is necessary for any sort of creative activity (see *BGE* 188). Yet, while the artist acknowledges the necessity of limitation, he or she also recognizes it *as* a limitation; and this recognition serves as a further impetus to activity, spurring the artist to further creation. Indeed, more so than any other discourse, the aesthetic prizes experimentation and innovation and thus affirms change and becoming. In this way, too, art affirms life as an endless process of destruction and creation, becoming and overcoming. Moreover, though it is in some sense cumulative, this becoming is not teleological. The

77. This and related aesthetic themes are nicely formulated by Nehamas, *Nietzsche: Life as Literature*, chap. 2.

aesthetic shows little tolerance for absolute standards of style or interpretation and does not seem to sanction the notion of progress as convergence toward a final or totalizing viewpoint.[78] The history of art
countenances a multiplicity of different styles and interpretations, a few
of which may be dominant at a particular moment, but none of which
forever reigns supreme. It thus grants that there are "truths" but denies
that there is any "Truth": "There are many kinds of eyes [. . .] and
consequently there are many kinds of 'truths,' and consequently there is
no Truth" (WP 540).

But Nietzsche is not interested in art for art's sake (see WP 298). His
principle interest in art is philosophical. More specifically, he wants to
encourage the development of a new type of philosopher: the artist-
philosopher, an "artistic Socrates" (BT 14) who says "yes" to becoming,
semblance, perspective, and interpretation and sees these as an incite-
ment, rather than an impediment, to inquiry.[79] Such a philosopher will
find in "art [. . .] a necessary correlative of, and supplement for science"
(BT 14) and will combine the scientist's relentless questioning and search
for knowledge with the artist's affirmation of appearance and search
for ever-new perspectives and interpretations. Of course, this requires a
new conception of truth and knowledge; and the philosopher-artist will
be able to appear only after the "revaluation of truth," which, we have
seen, results in a conception of truth as relative to particular interpretive frameworks and a conception of knowledge as the accumulation of
a plurality of such interpretations under the administration of a practical wisdom that dispenses them appropriately.[80]

The new philosopher's goal, then, is not the discovery of absolute
truth but the cultivation of a broad-based and flexible understanding
through the incorporation and integration of a number of natural drives,
some of them "scientific," others "aesthetic." The development of this

78. Of course, Nietzsche himself does not hold back from asserting bold aesthetic
standards. His repeated criticisms of Romanticism are a case in point. Yet those judgments are based upon how fully an artist, artistic attitude, or work affirms its aesthetic nature, that is, affirms becoming, semblance, appearance, perspective, and interpretation.
Just as, for Nietzsche, the ascetic ideal constitutes a paradoxical "life against life itself,"
"nature against something that is also nature," "will against all willing," he sees Roman-
tic art as a sort of "art against art." See GS 370 and GM III: 2–4.
     79. This point was tirelessly advocated by Walter Kaufmann. See, e.g., BT "Transla-
tor's Introduction," 3; Nietzsche, 395; and Kaufmann's comments in Paul de Mán, "Nietzsche's Theory of Rhetoric," Symposium (Spring 1974): 48.
     80. This seems to me to be the main point of the highly important passage GM III: 12,
discussed briefly above and more fully in chapter 3. Cf. BGE 212; WP 259 and 928.

scientific-aesthetic synthesis is nicely summarized in a passage from *The Gay Science* entitled "On the Doctrine of Poisons." Nietzsche writes:

> So many things have to come together for scientific thinking to originate; and all these necessary strengths had to be invented, practiced, and cultivated separately. As long as they were still separate, however, they frequently had an altogether different effect than they do now that they are integrated into scientific thinking and hold each other in check. Their effect was that of poisons; for example, that of the impulse to doubt, to negate, to wait, to collect, to dissolve. Many hecatombs of human beings were sacrificed before these impulses learned to comprehend their coexistence and to feel that they were all functions of one organizing force within one human being. And even now the time seems remote when artistic energies and the practical wisdom of life will join with scientific thinking to form a higher organic system in relation to which scholars, physicians, artists, and legislators—as we know them at present—would have to look like paltry relics of ancient times. (113)

The development of this "synthetic human being" (*WP* 881, 883), Nietzsche suggests, is slow, and its realization still a long way off. Despite the fact that "God is dead," there remain many "shadows of God" (*GS* 108) that must still be "vanquished" before such a being and such a worldview can take root and flourish. This preparatory task Nietzsche makes his own; and it is to this that I turn in the following chapter.

CHAPTER TWO

Naturalism and Interpretation

Nietzsche's Conception of Epistemology and Ontology

> We laugh as soon as we encounter the juxtaposition of
> "man *and* world," separated by the sublime presumption
> of the little word "and"!
>
> *Nietzsche, The Gay Science §346*

2.1 THE "DEATH OF GOD" AND THE NATURALIST PROJECT

In the previous chapter, I argued that Nietzsche's notorious claim, "God is dead," condenses an elaborate genealogy of Western thought, a sequence of worldviews stretching from metaphysics and theology through science and art. The "recent event" of "God's death," I maintained, marks a turning point in that genealogy, ushering in a "revaluation" of all the "values" that have hitherto reigned supreme. Foremost among those values is the value of truth; and, thus, we saw that "God's death" immediately calls for a revaluation of truth. In this chapter, I want to continue this exploration of Nietzsche's "revaluation of values" as it concerns broader issues of epistemology and ontology.

We have seen that the "death of God" leads to a sort of *naturalism*, that is, to a rejection of all other- or unworldly frameworks and posits, and to a resituation of knowing and being within "the world of life, nature, and history" (GS 344).[1] In what follows, I elaborate on this idea,

1. Again, "naturalism," in contemporary philosophy, is often associated with scientism; and we have seen that Nietzsche is critical of science's ability to give a full account of human experience. This seems to be the reason for Heidegger's suggestion that the term "naturalism" poorly characterizes the project of Nietzsche's later philosophy (see *Nietzsche*, vol. 2, *The Eternal Recurrence of the Same,* trans. David F. Krell [San Francisco: Harper, 1984], 93–94). However, I argue that Nietzsche accepts a broadly scientific view of the world and only criticizes science for its residual theology, its claim to describe pure

showing that Nietzsche's naturalism leads him to replace metaphysical and transcendental explanatory principles and entities with a naturalized epistemology and ontology.[2] Yet we will see that, rigorously pursued, naturalism demands a rejection of both the epistemological ideal of a "God's-eye view" and the ontological ideal of a "pre-given world," leading Nietzsche to a holistic or hermeneutic position that accepts the primacy and irreducibility of interpretation.[3] Nevertheless, I will argue that Nietzsche's naturalism constrains the potential relativism of this position, allowing him to claim that some interpretations (namely naturalistic ones) are better than others. Indeed I suggest that Nietzsche's conception of the world as "will to power" or "innocent becoming" is an example of such an interpretation—one that cannot and does not claim to be uniquely correct but that still has reasonable grounds for claiming to be better than rival interpretations.

I take my departure from §108 of *The Gay Science,* where Nietzsche

---

and unmediated "facts" about the world. I aim to show that Nietzsche's "de-deification of nature" leads to a rejection of this claim and instead forces upon science a feature commonly associated with the aesthetic: the irreducibility of interpretation. Thus, as I suggested at the end of chapter 1, Nietzsche holds that the naturalistic discourse par excellence would be one in which science and art were inextricably intertwined. For this reason, I support neither the aestheticist, antinaturalist reading of Nietzsche offered by Allan Megill, *Prophets of Extremity: Nietzsche, Heidegger, Foucault, Derrida* (Berkeley: University of California Press, 1985), 29–35, nor the naturalist, antiaestheticist reading offered by Brian Leiter, "Nietzsche and Aestheticism," *Journal of the History of Philosophy* 30 (1992): 275–88. For other discussions of Nietzsche's naturalism, see Walter Kaufmann, *Nietzsche: Philosopher, Psychologist, Anti-Christ,* 4th ed. (Princeton: Princeton University Press, 1974), 102; Eugen Fink, "Nietzsche's New Experience of the World," trans. Michael A. Gillespie, in *Nietzsche's New Seas: Explorations in Philosophy, Aesthetics, and Politics,* ed. Michael A. Gillespie and Tracy B. Strong (Chicago: University of Chicago Press, 1988), 206; Richard Schacht, "Nietzsche's *Gay Science,* Or, How to Naturalize Cheerfully," in *Reading Nietzsche,* ed. Robert Solomon and Kathleen Higgins (New York: Oxford University Press, 1988), 68–86; and David C. Hoy, "Two Conflicting Conceptions of How to Naturalize Philosophy: Foucault versus Habermas," in *Metaphysik nach Kant?* ed. Dieter Henrich and Rolf-Peter Horstmann (Stuttgart: Klett-Cotta, 1988), 743–66.

2. Following Kant's usage, I call "metaphysical" or "transcendent" those features that are dogmatically claimed to exist, though their existence cannot be empirically demonstrated; and I call "transcendental" those nonempirical features the existence of which is said to be established through a deduction that shows them to be the necessary conditions for the empirical.

3. This distinguishes my construal of Nietzsche's naturalism from the more realist version offered by Brian Leiter in "Nietzsche and Aestheticism." Leiter argues that, for Nietzsche, the natural, organic world is a "fact of the matter," the ground and basis of all interpretation, and that the will to power is the most faithful, least distorting construal of this world. Contrary to this view, I argue that Nietzsche's thoroughgoing naturalism leads him to reject such primitive "facts." As I noted above, instead of *rejecting* aestheticism, as Leiter would have it, Nietzsche's naturalism indeed *demands* a sort of aestheticism, though not, perhaps, of the Nehamasian sort Leiter criticizes.

first announces the "death of God" and the concomitant demand that all the remaining "shadows" of God be "vanquished." He writes: "*New struggles.*—After Buddha was dead, his shadow was still shown for centuries in a cave—a tremendous, gruesome shadow. God is dead; but given the way of humanity, there may still be caves for thousands of years in which his shadow will still be shown.—And we—we still have to vanquish his shadow, too!"

In §109, Nietzsche informs us that the struggle against these "shadows" must take place on two fronts, requiring both a "naturalization of humanity" and a "de-deification of nature." Having rejected a host of theological worldviews, Nietzsche asks rhetorically: "When will all these shadows of God cease to darken us? When will we complete our de-deification of nature? When may we begin to *naturalize* humanity in terms of a pure, newly discovered, newly redeemed nature?" (*GS* 109).

I argue that the "naturalization of humanity" foregrounds Nietzsche's commitment to a thoroughgoing naturalism in epistemology and ontology, while the "de-deification of nature" foregrounds his commitment to the view that there is no "pre-given world" but only ever perspectives (or interpretations) and the entities internal to them.

2.2 THE "NATURALIZATION OF HUMANITY"

2.2.1 NATURALISM VERSUS METAPHYSICS

The "death of God" leads to a devaluation of all super- or extra-natural posits and explanatory principles. In the wake of this "death," Nietzsche calls for a revaluation of all those features of natural life previously maligned by theology and metaphysics: sensation, instinct, and affect; change, temporality, and history; contingency and conditionality; procreation, nutrition, growth, decay, and death; psychology, physiology, biology, and sociology; and so forth. Nietzsche's attempt to "naturalize humanity" is guided by the conviction that these characteristics of "the world of life, nature, and history" can give us a full account of being, knowing, and valuing that does without the superfluous and mendacious claims of the super-natural.

As a philosophical program, this naturalism is directed against metaphysics (or first philosophy, or transcendental philosophy), which Nietzsche suspects of doing theology even when it forgoes explicit talk of God. A discourse is metaphysical, for Nietzsche, if it maintains a strict division between the natural (the empirical, affective, physical, apparent, contingent, transitory, etc.) and the extra-natural (the rational, moral, mental, essential, necessary, eternal, etc.) and grants to the latter an ontological and epistemological superiority and priority. Metaphysics, he argues, attempts to avoid any contamination of the extra-natural by the natural and is thus led to the supposition that its two realms have entirely separate origins. Hence, he writes in *Human, All Too Human:*

> Almost all the problems of philosophy once again pose the same form of question as they did two thousand years ago: how can something originate out of its opposite, for example rationality in irrationality, the sentient in the dead, logic in unlogic, disinterested contemplation in covetous desire, living for others in egoism, truth in error? Metaphysical philosophy has hitherto surmounted this difficulty by denying that the one originates out of the other and assuming for the more highly valued thing a miraculous source in the very kernel and being of the "thing in itself." (1)

This line of thought is taken up again in the second section of *Beyond Good and Evil*, where Nietzsche parodies this dualism and its hierarchy, attacking that "fundamental faith of the metaphysicians [. . .] *the faith in opposite values*":

> "How *could* anything originate out of its opposite? for example, truth out of error? or the will to truth out of the will to deception? or selfless deeds out of selfishness? or the pure and sunlike gaze of the sage out of lust? Such origins are impossible; whoever dreams of them is a fool, indeed worse; the things of the highest value must have another, *peculiar* origin—they cannot be derived from this transitory, seductive, deceptive, paltry world, from this turmoil of delusion and lust. Rather from the lap of Being, the intransitory, the hidden god, the 'thing in itself'—*there* must be their basis, and nowhere else." This way of judging constitutes the typical prejudgment and prejudice which give away the metaphysicians of all ages. (cf. *TI* "Reason" 4)

And in *The Twilight of the Idols,* Nietzsche continues this parody of metaphysical dualism, elaborating on its degradation of the "world of life, nature and history":

> You ask me which of the philosophers' traits are really idiosyncrasies? For example, their lack of historical sense, their hatred of the very idea of becoming. They think that they show their *respect* for a subject when they dehistoricize it, *sub specie aeterni*—when they turn it into a mummy. All that philosophers have handled for thousands of years have been concept-mummies; nothing real escaped their grasp alive. [. . .] Death, change, old age, as well as procreation and growth, are to their minds objections—even

refutations. Whatever is does not *become;* whatever becomes *is* not. . . . Now they all believe, desperately even, in what has being. But since they never grasp it, they search for reasons why it is kept from them. "There must be mere appearance [*Schein*], there must be some deception which prevents us from perceiving that which has being: where is the deceiver?— We have found him," they cry ecstatically; "it is the senses! These senses, *which are so immoral in other ways too,* deceive us concerning the *true* world." Moral: let us free ourselves from the deception of the senses, from becoming, from history, from lies;—history is nothing but faith in the senses, faith in lies. Moral: let us say No to all who have faith in the senses, to all the rest of humanity; they are all "plebs" [*Volk*]. Let us be philosophers! Let us be mummies! Let us represent monotono-theism by adopting the expression of a gravedigger! And above all, away with the *body,* this wretched *idée fixe* of the senses, disfigured by all the fallacies of logic, refuted, even impossible, although it is impudent enough to behave as if it were real!" ("Reason" 1; cf. *HH* 2)

Against the perverse and extravagant claims of metaphysics, which embroils itself in this host of dualisms and degrades the very world with which we are most intimately acquainted, Nietzsche argues that "conscience of *method*" (*BGE* 36) and "economy of principles" (*BGE* 13)[4] demand that we question these dualisms and attempt to provide an account of all phenomena on the basis of "this world, *our* world," "the world of life, nature, and history" (*GS* 344). That is, he seeks to explain the binary oppositions erected by metaphysics as responses to the contingent needs and desires of natural beings. He comes to reject the metaphysical notion that there exist essential differences in kind, revealing instead that these represent nothing more than differences of degree within the natural. Thus, *Human, All Too Human* §1 continues:

Historical philosophy [. . .] which can no longer be separated from natural science, the youngest of all philosophical methods, has discovered in individual cases (and this will probably be the result in every case) that there are no opposites, except in the customary exaggeration of popular or metaphysical interpretations, and that a mistake in reasoning lies at the bottom of this antithesis: [. . . opposites] are only sublimations, in which a basic element seems almost to have dispersed and reveals itself only under the most pains-

4. This phrase appears within a discussion of the hypothesis of "will to power," but it applies equally well to Nietzsche's broader naturalistic project; for, as we will see, the notion of will to power is, for Nietzsche, the naturalistic interpretation par excellence, one that envisions the natural domain as a continuum in which the inorganic, the organic, the animal, and the human represent merely differences of degree but not of kind.

taking observation. All we require, and what can be given us only now that the individual sciences have attained their present level, is a *chemistry* of the moral, religious and aesthetic conceptions and sensations, likewise of all the agitations we experience within ourselves in cultural and social intercourse, and indeed even when we are alone: what if chemistry would end up by revealing that in this domain too the most glorious colors are derived from base, indeed from despised materials? [5]

If the problem with metaphysics, then, is its otherworldly dualism, the solution, Nietzsche proposes, is a this-worldly antidualism. The means for realizing this solution lie in Nietzsche's "genealogical" method, which plays a double role: on the one hand, it criticizes "the highest concepts" (*TI* "Reason" 4) by offering counterinterpretations that reveal their probable *pudenda origo;* on the other hand, it constructs new interpretations that replace these metaphysical dualisms with a thoroughly naturalized ontology and epistemology. Rejecting the notion that there exist fundamental divisions between the natural world and humanity, or between humanity and God, Nietzsche argues that the "death of God" serves to place human beings squarely within the natural world as creatures like any other and without special ontological status. Rejecting the "peculiar" origins and functions of such features as reason, morality, logic, and language, Nietzsche instead attempts

---

5. This critique of opposites and the dissolution of differences-in-kind into differences-of-degree is a central feature of Nietzsche's philosophy. He writes, e.g.: "between good and evil actions there is no difference in kind, but at the most of degree" (*HH* 107); "The general imprecise way of observing sees everywhere in nature opposites (as e.g., 'warm and cold') where there are only differences of degree" (*WS* 67); "Let us beware of saying that death is opposed to life. The living is merely a type of what is dead, and a very rare type" (*GS* 109); "Cause and effect: such a duality probably never exists; in truth we are confronted by a continuum out of which we isolate a couple of pieces" (*GS* 112); "It might even be possible that what constitutes the value of these good and revered things is precisely that they are insidiously related, tied to, and involved with these wicked, seemingly opposite things—maybe even one with them in essence" (*BGE* 2); "'being conscious' is not in any decisive sense the *opposite* of what is instinctive" (*BGE* 3); "Even if language, here as elsewhere will not get over its awkwardness, and will continue to talk of opposites where there are only degrees and many subtleties of gradation" (*BGE* 24); "what forces us at all to suppose that there is an essential opposition of 'true' and 'false'? Is it not sufficient to assume degrees of apparentness" (*BGE* 34); "*Health* and *sickness* are not essentially different. [. . .] In fact, there are only differences in degree between these two kinds of existence: the exaggeration, the disproportion, the nonharmony of the normal phenomena constitute the pathological state" (*WP* 47; cf. *WP* 812); "rest—motion, firm—loose: opposites that do not exist in themselves and that actually express only *variations in degree* that from a certain perspective appear to be opposites. There are no opposites: only from those of logic do we derive the concept of opposites—and falsely transfer it to things" (*WP* 552).

to provide hypothetical, contingent, and pragmatic explanations of their origins and functions that draw upon the resources of physiology, psychology, history, sociology, philology, and evolutionary theory.

2.2.2 NIETZSCHE'S NATURALIZED ONTOLOGY

To translate man back into nature, to become master over the many vain and overly enthusiastic interpretations and connotations that have so far been scrawled and painted over that eternal basic text of *homo natura;* to see to it that the human being henceforth stands before human beings as even today, hardened in the discipline of science, he stands before the *rest* of nature, with intrepid Oedipus eyes and sealed Odysseus ears, deaf to the siren songs of old metaphysical bird catchers who have been piping at him all too long, "you are more, you are higher, you are of a different origin"—that may be a strange and insane task, but it is a *task*—who would deny that? (*BGE* 230)

Nietzsche makes this task his own. He argues that with the repudiation of God (and the otherworldly in general) must come a repudiation of the metaphysical and theological notion that human beings are "higher" and "of a different origin" compared to the rest of the natural world. For Nietzsche, the human being "has become an *animal,* literally and without reservation and qualification, he who was according to his old faith, almost God ('child of God,' 'God-man')" (*GM* III:25). "We no longer derive the human from 'the spirit' or 'the deity,'" he writes, "we have placed him back among the animals" (*A* 14; cf. *HL* 9 and *D* 49).

Such statements no doubt reveal the influence of Darwin (see §§5.2.3–5.2.4, below). With the broad acceptance of evolutionary theory in the twentieth century, they may seem uncontroversial and commonplace to us today. Yet Nietzsche goes further, attacking more persistent philosophical and scientific notions that, he feels, ought to go the way of creationism. Prominent among these is the notion that human beings possess something extra-natural (whether consciousness, mind, spirit, rationality, language, or morality) that sets them apart from, and places them above, other natural creatures. While granting that there are certainly significant differences between human beings and insects, for example, Nietzsche argues that this difference is not hierarchical. On his view, the allegedly extra-natural features of human beings are simply "the means by which weaker, less robust individuals preserve themselves—since they have been denied the chance to wage the struggle for existence with horns or the sharp teeth of beasts of prey" (*TL* p. 80).

"Man is by no means the crown of creation," he writes; "every living being stands beside him on the same level of perfection" (*A* 14).[6]

Metaphysics has always conceived of human beings as divided creatures: half-beast and half-God, at once animal and rational, natural and super-natural. As natural beings, humans are said to be endowed with the animal capacities of sensation, perception, and desire; and it is by virtue of these capacities that they are contingently bound up with the rest of the natural world. Yet, as rational beings, humans are said to be endowed with the capacities for logical thought, language, and morality; and it is by virtue of these capacities that they confer necessity upon their actions and the world. Such capacities, it is said, allow human beings, at least partially, to extricate themselves from the contingencies of nature and ascend to a rational world of freedom.[7]

Against this conception, Nietzsche submits all the putatively transcendent or transcendental faculties and capacities to a deflationary critique. Detailed discussion of these critiques would take us too far afield; but a general characterization should suffice for the project at hand: to reveal Nietzsche's commitment to a thoroughly naturalized ontology. Against the description of human beings as divided between reason and nature, mind and body, consciousness and instinct, Nietzsche argues that the former terms are explicable on the basis of the latter. He writes that "'being conscious' is not in any decisive sense the *opposite* of what is instinctive" (*BGE* 3), that it "is actually nothing but a *certain behavior of the instincts toward one another*" (*GS* 333), that "thinking is merely a relation of [. . .] drives to each other" (*BGE* 36), and that "reason"

6. Cf. *GS* 115, where Nietzsche writes that one of the "four errors" of "man" is that "he placed himself in a false order of rank in relation to animals and nature." Cf. also *WP* 684: "man as a species does not represent any progress compared with any other animal. The whole animal and vegetable kingdom does not evolve from the lower to the higher— but all at the same time, in utter disorder, over and against each other." Cf. Stephen Jay Gould: "much as we may love ourselves, *Homo sapiens* is not representative, or symbolic, of life as a whole. We are not surrogates for arthropods (more than 80 percent of animal species), or exemplars of anything either particular or typical. We are the possessors of one extraordinary evolutionary invention called consciousness—the factor that permits us, rather than any other species, to ruminate about such matters (or, rather, cows ruminate and we cogitate). But how can this invention be viewed as the distillation of life's primary thrust or direction when 80 percent of multicellularity (the phylum Arthropoda) enjoys such evolutionary success and displays no trend toward neurological complexity through time—and when our own neural elaboration may just as well end up destroying us as sparking a move to any other state that we could designate as 'higher'?" (*Full House: The Spread of Excellence from Plato to Darwin* [New York: Harmony, 1996], 15).
7. Aristotle's *Nicomachean Ethics* (books I, VI, and X) offers an early version of this account, one that continues to inform the history of philosophy through Kant and beyond.

is "rather a system of relations between various passions and desires" (WP 387). Elsewhere, he writes, "body am I entirely, and nothing else; and soul is only a word for something about the body" (Z:1 "On the Despisers of the Body");[8] "the 'pure spirit' is a pure stupidity; if we subtract the nervous system and the senses—the 'mortal shroud'—*then we miscalculate*—that is all!" (A 14).[9]

These terse formulations condense a theory of consciousness as simply an extension of bodily instinct, impulse, passion, and desire.[10] According to Nietzsche, consciousness is not what directs the body and its instincts but is only a residuum of the body's instinctual processes. He conceives of the body as a host of competing instincts, drives, desires, and passions, some of which join together in an alliance so as to dominate, control, and subordinate the others. In "higher creatures," the result of this struggle "enters consciousness," which provides a vastly simplified picture of the myriad "unconscious" instinctual processes and allows these creatures to perceive themselves as a unity.[11] This supplemental consciousness has a specific evolutionary function: "*consciousness has developed only under the pressure of the need for communication*" (GS 354; cf. BGE 268). That is, the result of the struggle among the instincts enters consciousness only insofar as human beings, "the most endangered animal," need to be able to express their conditions to others, to make their needs felt, so as to make others sympathize and come to their aid. "The development of language and the development of consciousness," then, "go hand and hand" (GS 354). In brief, for Nietzsche, consciousness and language do not set human beings apart from nature but have developed merely as tools aiding a particular natural creature that is otherwise poorly endowed.

Hence, "rational animals," on Nietzsche's view, turn out to be simply animals with particular capacities and not others. But Nietzsche goes even further than this. His suspicion of metaphysical dualism leads him to suspect that the same prejudice that separates the rational from

8. Cf. BGE 230: "actually 'the spirit' is relatively most similar to a stomach."
9. Cf. WP 526: "there is no ground whatsoever for ascribing to spirit the properties of organization and systematization. The nervous system has a much more extensive domain; the world of consciousness is added to it. Consciousness plays no role in the total process of adaptation and systematization."
10. This theory can be gleaned from such texts and passages as TL; GS P: 2, 111, 333, 354; BGE 19; Z:1 "On the Despisers of the Body"; A 14; WP 504–5, 523–30. In chapter 3, I discuss in further detail Nietzsche's theory of affects and the body.
11. See GS 333: "the greater part of our spirit's activity remains unconscious and unfelt."

the nonrational also separates the organic from the inorganic; and so he comes to wonder whether there is any essential difference between these latter. Indeed, in the same passage in which he first calls for a naturalization of humanity, Nietzsche suggests that "the organic" is simply a "derivative, late, rare, accidental" extension of the inorganic and concludes that we must "beware of saying that death is opposed to life. The living is merely a type of what is dead, and a very rare type" (*GS* 109).

This view foreshadows Nietzsche's bold and often misunderstood supposition that all natural entities, whether animal, vegetable, or mineral, are "'will to power' and nothing besides" (*BGE* 36; cf. *WP* 1067). Generalizing from his theory of the body as a complex of drives and affects, each of which seeks to dominate and assimilate the others, Nietzsche decides "to make the experiment and to ask the question whether [our world of desires and passions] would not be *sufficient* for also understanding on the basis of this kind of thing the so-called mechanistic (or 'material') world." "In the end," he concludes, "not only is it permitted to make this experiment; the conscience of *method* demands" that we "determine all efficient force univocally as—*will to power.*"

In chapter 5, I explore this difficult and enigmatic doctrine in greater detail. For the present discussion, we need only see that this theory is developed as an attempt to construct a naturalized ontology that accepts no essential differences of kind in the natural world. Seen in this light, the doctrine of will to power is not an a priori account of the universe as a whole but rather an empirical hypothesis that pushes to its limits Nietzsche's rejection of the metaphysician's "faith in opposite values." The doctrine becomes less mysterious once we consider it as incorporating and extending certain basic scientific insights. Chemistry, for example, shows us that every known entity is simply a certain combination and arrangement of a limited number of materials and forces. Organic chemistry teaches us that the organic differs from the inorganic only by the structural incorporation of carbon compounds. Chemical analysis of both inorganic and organic matter also reveals that some compounds are more stable than others, that certain forces or the presence of particular materials can cause these compounds to break down and form new compounds, and that, in the course of these reactions, these elements and compounds are attracted to some elements or compounds and repelled by others. Nietzsche suggests that there is no fundamental difference between these sorts of chemical reactions and the biological phenomena of procreation, growth, and extension of influence that we witness from the level of the protoplasm to that of the human being. Reversing the direction of this analysis, he suggests that the human activity of "interpretation" (which, he argues, involves assimilating, adapting, taking over, transforming, subduing, forcing, adjusting, abbreviating, omitting, padding, inventing, and falsifying)[12] is discernible throughout the natural world, from the scholarly activities of human beings to the nutritive and procreative activities of the amoeba and the actions and reactions of inorganic chemical compounds.

Thus, despite significant differences between these various levels and kinds of activities, Nietzsche comes to construe the natural world, via the doctrine of will to power, as a continuum with many differentiations but no radical breaks. Gone are the "God-like" capacities that served to separate human beings from animals and the miraculous *pneuma* that brought dead matter to life. Instead, Nietzsche argues for a thoroughly naturalized ontology, one that explains all entities on a single model, as assemblages of "dynamic quanta," the incessant change and transformation of which is the result of successful and unsuccessful attempts by each assemblage to extend its control over environing assemblages.

2.2.3 NIETZSCHE'S NATURALIZED EPISTEMOLOGY

No less does Nietzsche attempt to naturalize epistemology.[13] Against metaphysical accounts that claim to reveal the indubitable, extranatural, and extra-empirical conceptual foundations for knowledge and experience, Nietzsche offers an alternative account that explains from within "the world of life, nature, and history" the origins and functions of these alleged transcendent or transcendental foundations. This account turns out to be, broadly speaking, evolutionary—or, in more Nietzschean terms, "genealogical."

12. This catalogue is culled from two important later texts on "interpretation," *GM* II:12 and III:24. Cf. also *BGE* 230, which attributes these operations to "everything that lives, grows, and multiplies." For more on this issue, see §5.3, below.

13. Nietzsche's naturalized epistemology has also recently been discussed by George Stack, "Kant, Lange, and Nietzsche: Critique of Knowledge," in *Nietzsche and Modern German Thought*, ed. Keith Ansell-Pearson (London: Routledge, 1991), and "Nietzsche's Evolutionary Epistemology," *Dialogos* 59 (1992): 75–101. I disagree with Stack that Nietzsche's evolutionary version of Kant's transcendental deduction commits Nietzsche to a Kantian skepticism or agnosticism. Nietzsche makes clear that what such tools of knowledge as language, logic, and the categories "falsify" is not an unknowable world in itself but rather a realm of experience that is available to us through science and ordinary perception (see, e.g., *HH* 16, 18, 19; *GS* 110, 112) and the senses (see, e.g., *TI* "Reason" 2). I discuss this idea in §2.2.4 and in chapter 4.

As we have seen, Nietzsche accepts the basic tenets of evolutionary theory, rejecting only the progressivist, teleological assumptions that construe the course of evolution as a process of development resulting in the survival of the most perfect individuals and species.[14] Genealogy dispenses with these assumptions and instead considers evolution to be a continual struggle for power, the movement of which is not a steady climb along an ascending line but a series of irregular displacements within a field of forces:

> [T]he entire history of a "thing," an organ, a custom [. . . is] a continual sign-chain of ever new interpretations and adaptations whose causes do not even have to be related to one another but, on the contrary, in some cases succeed and alternate with one another in purely chance fashion. The "evolution" of a thing, a custom, an organ, is by no means its *progressus* toward a goal, even less a logical *progressus* by the shortest route and with the smallest expenditure of force—but a succession of more or less profound, more or less mutually independent processes of subduing, plus the resistances they encounter, the attempts at transformation for the purpose of defense and reaction, and the results of successful counteractions. (*GM* II:12)

The "evolution" of knowledge and its faculties, according to Nietzsche, is no different. The framework of our knowledge has no extra-empirical or extra-natural source; nor is the development of our cognitive faculties evidence of progress toward perfection. Rather, these faculties and capacities are only chance endowments that have happened to aid human beings in their struggles with other natural creatures and forces.

Genealogical accounts of this sort can be found throughout the Nietzschean corpus (e.g., *TL*; *HH* Part I; *GS* 110–12, 344, 354–55; *BGE* 268; *TI* "Reason" and "Errors"; *WP* 466–617). The early essay "On Truth and Lies in a Nonmoral Sense," for example, explains the origin of the human conceptual and linguistic apparatus as the attempt of physically ill-equipped creatures to secure survival by controlling their environment through cunning and strategic alliance. Bombarded by sensory stimuli, Nietzsche explains, the human intellect learns to se-

---

14. Nietzsche's attitude toward evolutionary theory is explored more fully in chapter 5. Like his heirs, Deleuze and Guattari, Nietzsche criticizes the traditional notion of "evolution" for its subordination of "becoming" to "being" and attempts to reconceive the notion as a "becoming" without origin, destination, or purpose. See Gilles Deleuze and Félix Guattari, *A Thousand Plateaus*, trans. Brian Massumi (Minneapolis: University of Minnesota Press, 1987), 238ff. For more on Nietzsche's own evolutionary model, see *TL*; *HL* 9 and *passim*; *BGE* 13, 262; *GM* I:1–4, II:12–13; *A* 4; *WP* 90, 647–50, 684–85. Also, see Hoy, "Two Conflicting Conceptions," 745–51, and Stack, "Kant, Lange, and Nietzsche" and "Nietzsche's Evolutionary Epistemology."

lect a set of these salient to its survival and to encourage a forgetting of the rest. Toward the same end, these feeble creatures form herds and develop language as "a uniformly valid and binding designation [. . .] for things" that serves "to banish from [their] world at least the most flagrant *bellum omni contra omnes*" (*TL* p. 81; cf. *GS* 354).

This naturalistic story also accounts for the origin of metaphysics. It explains the evolutionary benefit involved in the move from sensation to concept and concept to word, showing that the conceptual and linguistic framework provides human beings with a theory of nature that simplifies and codifies their sensuous experience so as to make it manageable, predictable, and communicable. Yet Nietzsche argues that the *evolutionary* primacy of the repression or demotion of a whole range of experiences, along with the promotion of a simplified and stable world, comes to be transmuted into a *metaphysical* primacy, that the *pragmatic* "necessity" of this late-born conceptual and linguistic framework gets taken for a stronger, *metaphysical* necessity given in the structure of the world: "This awakens the [Platonic] idea that, in addition to leaves, there exists in nature the 'leaf': the original model according to which all the leaves were perhaps woven, sketched, colored, curled, and painted—but by incompetent hands, so that no specimen has turned out to be a correct, trustworthy, and faithful likeness of the original" (p. 83). Or, in a more critical moment, this a posteriori "necessity" awakens the (Kantian) idea that the conceptual and linguistic apparatus must be more than merely contingent, that it must be a priori, given in the structure of the human mind "—as though the world's axis turned within it" (p. 79).

Against these "arrogant" and "mendacious" suppositions, Nietzsche suggests that "the human intellect [. . .] has no additional mission which would lead it beyond human life" (p. 79), that it is merely a device for securing human survival. Moreover, it is only a means for securing *a particular sort* of human life. Thus, alongside the "rational man" Nietzsche imagines the "intuitive man" who (though he lives a more precarious and uncertain existence) sees the world as "eternally new" and constantly reveals the contingent, conditional, pragmatic, and sensuous origins of the conceptual edifice reified and elevated by his more conservative and secure opponent (*TL* pp. 89–91).[15]

---

15. This praise of the fleeting exceptions appears throughout Nietzsche's work. A characteristic passage from *Beyond Good and Evil* runs: "The human beings who are more similar, more ordinary, have had, and always have, an advantage; those more select,

This naturalistic account of the development of our cognitive faculties is expanded in part 1 of *Human, All Too Human,* the first section of which, we have seen, urges the replacement of "metaphysical philosophy" with "historical philosophy." "Lack of historical sense," Nietzsche writes, "is the family failing of all philosophers" (2). With Kantian transcendental philosophy clearly in mind, he explains that philosophers "take the most recent manifestation of man [. . .] as the fixed form from which one has to start out. They will not learn that man has become, that the faculty of cognition [*das Erkenntnissvermögen*] has become; while some of them would have it that the whole world is spun out of this faculty of cognition" (2).

Continuing this critique several sections later, Nietzsche writes:

> Philosophers are accustomed to station themselves before life and experience—before that which they call the world of appearance—as before a painting that has been unrolled once and for all and unchangeably depicts the same scene: this scene, they believe, has to be correctly interpreted, so as to draw a conclusion as to the nature of the being that produced the picture: that is to say, as to the nature of the thing in itself.

Yet this is to "overlook the possibility that this painting—that which we humans call life and experience—has gradually *become,* is indeed still fully in course of *becoming,* and should thus not be regarded as a fixed object on the basis of which a conclusion as to the nature of its originator [. . .] may either be drawn or pronounced undrawable" (16).

Against this sort of transcendental account of human experience and the cognitive faculties, Nietzsche advocates the development of "a *history of the genesis of thought*" (16), which would replace "metaphysical explanations" with "physical and historical explanations" (17), those having to do with "the physiology and history of the evolution of organisms and concepts" (10).[16]

Putting this methodological recommendation into practice, Nietz-

---

subtle, strange, and difficult to understand, easily remain alone, succumb to accidents, being isolated, and rarely propagate. One must invoke tremendous counter-forces in order to cross this natural, all too natural *progressus in simile,* the continual development of man toward the similar, ordinary, average, herdlike—*common!*" (268). Similarly, in a note from 1888, Nietzsche laments "the elimination of the lucky strokes, the uselessness of the more highly developed types, the inevitable dominion of the average" and remarks that "strange though it may sound, one always has to defend the strong against the weak" (*WP* 685). Cf. also *HL* 9; *Z* (on "the last men"); *BGE* 269; *GM* I: 8–9; *WP* 684.

16. Cf. *GS* 354, where Nietzsche argues that "the problem of consciousness" is now explicable via "physiology and the history of animals."

sche proceeds to a task that would occupy him throughout his career: that of providing naturalistic, evolutionary explanations for the existence and operation of all the so-called transcendental faculties of human knowledge: language, logic, mathematics, and the "categories of reason." [17] Without engaging in an extensive examination of these critiques (which, though frequent, are often tersely formulated and thus call for careful explication), we can provide an overview that should suffice to give a sense of their role in Nietzsche's more general project of developing a naturalized epistemology.

One notices at the outset that Nietzsche often blurs the lines of distinction between the operations of language, logic, mathematics, and the categories. That is because he sees them as thoroughly bound up with one another and serving, in slightly different ways, the same basic evolutionary role. All four are functions of consciousness (which we have seen to be a late-born and superficial extension of the sensuous, affective animal); and, as such, each of these forms serves to simplify and schematize the sensuous manifold into a calculable and communicable system. Logic and mathematics are said to have the basic role of equalization: the reduction of sensuous differences and similarities to cognitive identities (on logic, see *HH* 18; *GS* 111; *TI* "Reason" 3; *WP* 508–22, 554; on mathematics, see *HH* 11, 19; *GS* 112, 355; *TI* "Reason" 3; *WP* 516, 530, 554). The categories are said to have the role of individuating the sensuous manifold and subsuming it under a small set of cognitive forms (see *TL* p. 83; *GS* 110, 112; *TI* "Reason," "Errors"). Finally, language is said to make manifest and communicable this simplified and schematized cognitive world (see *GS* 354; *BGE* 268). Words, Nietzsche writes, unify groups of sensations and apply to these groups general designations that allow quick and abbreviated reference (see *TL* p. 83; *BGE* 268). Grammar serves the equalizing function through the copula "is" and reverses the genetic sequence by placing the conceptual and logical abstractions ("subjects," "substances," "causes") syntactically before the different manifestations ("actions," "accidents," "effects") from which they are, in actuality, derived (see *BGE* 17; *GM* I:13; *TI* "Reason").

17. Nietzsche's language here is imprecise. At times, he refers individually to the various categories (causality, substance, etc.), while at other times he simply uses the general notion of the "concepts," "categories of reason," or "presuppositions of reason." In each of these instances, however, Nietzsche seems to have in mind something like the Kantian a priori concepts or categories of the understanding.

From his earliest to his last writings, Nietzsche is keen to point out the specific role that these "transcendental" forms play within the overall conditions of human life.[18] As with consciousness, of which they are a function, he characterizes logic, language, and the categories of reason as simply products of natural selection that have aided human beings in the "struggle for existence" (see *TL* p. 80; cf. *GS* 354). He assures us that they are entirely contingent, stemming from "the earthly kingdom of desires" (*WP* 509) rather than from some inherent and necessary faculty or other nonempirical source. "All our *categories-of-reason* are of sensual origin: derived from the empirical world" (*WP* 488), he writes. Elsewhere he argues that

> The inventive force that invented categories labored in the service of our needs, namely of our need for security, for quick understanding on the basis of signs and sounds, for the means of abbreviation:—"substance," "subject," "object," "being," "becoming" have nothing to do with metaphysical truths. (*WP* 513)
>
> In the formation of reason, logic, the categories, it was need that was authoritative: the need, not to "know," but to subsume, to schematize for the purposes of calculation . . . the development of reason is adjustment, invention, with the aim of making similar, equal—the same process that every sense impression goes through! Here, there was no pre-existing "idea" at work, but rather the utilitarian fact [*die Nützlichkeit*] that only when we see things coarsely and made equal do they become calculable and usable to us [. . .] life miscarries with any other kinds of reason, to which there is a continual impulse—it becomes difficult to survey—too unequal—. (*WP* 515)

As we have seen with regard to consciousness in general, logic and language deal only in superficialities and superfluities and do not evidence any deep, rational core. Our categories, logic, and language, and eventually our senses, "merely glide over the surface of things and see 'forms.' [. . .] We obtain the concept, as we do the form, by overlooking what is individual and actual; whereas nature is acquainted with no forms and no concepts, and likewise with no species." (*TL* pp. 82, 83)

> Every word instantly becomes a concept precisely insofar as it is not supposed to serve as a reminder of the unique and entirely individual original experience to which it owes its origin; but rather, a word becomes a concept precisely insofar as it simultaneously has to fit countless more or less similar

---

18. We find such empirical deductions of logic and language throughout Nietzsche's work, and with a remarkable consistency of argument. From "On Truth and Lies" through Book Five of *The Gay Science* (e.g., 354) and the later *Nachlaß* (e.g., *WP* 508–22), Nietzsche's genealogies of logic and language are nearly identical.

cases—which means, purely and simply, cases which are never equal and thus altogether unequal. Every concept arises from the equation of unequal things. Just as it is certain that one leaf is never totally the same as another, so it is certain that the concept of "leaf" is formed by arbitrarily discarding these individual differences and by forgetting the distinguishing aspects. (*TL* p. 83)

Logic is said to arise due to the same practical necessity of overlooking particulars or reducing them to generalities and identities:

> Logic is bound to the condition: *assume there are identical cases.* In fact, to make possible logical thinking and inferences, this condition *must* first be treated fictitiously as fulfilled. (*WP* 512)

> On the *origin of logic.* The fundamental inclination *to posit as equal, to see things as equal.* [. . .] This whole process corresponds exactly to that external, mechanical process (which is its symbol) by which *protoplasm* makes what it appropriates equal to itself and fits it into its own forms and files. (*WP* 510; cf. *WP* 501)

This last analogy is important. Having externalized logic and language—revealing them as trading in superficialities rather than pointing toward some deep structure of thought—Nietzsche here makes the further claim that the seemingly immaterial operations of logic are really no different in kind from such a basely physical and material process as ingestion, the incorporation and conversion of matter into a form that is usable for a particular body's nourishment and sustenance. Elaborating on this analogy in another note, Nietzsche claims that it is not some special a priori determination that governs the categorization of our sense impressions but rather simply the historical embeddedness of a primeval physiological need: "The same equalizing and ordering force that rules in the idioplasma, rules also in the incorporation of the outer world: our sense perceptions are already the *result* of this *assimilation* and *equalization* in regard to *all* the past in us; they do not follow directly upon the 'impression'" (*WP* 500).

For Nietzsche, then, logic, language, and the categories cannot be derived from anything but the contingent development of human beings as natural creatures. Reasoning and speaking are perhaps peculiar to a certain species of animal, but this "rational animal" is not different from other animals by virtue of some extra-natural faculty. Rather, it is different only due to the means it has developed to relate its peculiar constitution to its particular environing conditions. In considering our dealings with the environing world, Nietzsche argues, we should be careful not to posit, in the manner of Plato and Kant, two realms—a realm of logic, language, and reason and a realm of the sensual or empirical—because, according to Nietzsche, language and logic are themselves thoroughly empirical in origin and function and are no less bound up with our contingent existence than are such patently noncognitive features of animal life as ingestion and growth.

2.2.4 NIETZSCHE'S EMPIRICISM AND NOMINALISM

While Nietzsche is concerned to show the evolutionary "necessity" of the so-called transcendental forms of human cognition, he also notoriously refers to them as "the fundamental errors of mankind" (*HH* 18), our "erroneous articles of faith" (*GS* 110), or the "lies" and "prejudices" of reason (*TI* "Reason" 2, 5). Such claims reveal the basic empiricism and nominalism that is at the root of Nietzsche's epistemology.

All of our knowledge, Nietzsche theorizes, originates in sense experience and ends in our various attempts to codify past and present experience so as to predict future experience. Such codification, as we have seen, entails the grouping of items in terms of unity and identity. Yet Nietzsche points out that something is lost or forgotten in this movement from sensation to concept. While sense evidence reveals to us a multiplicity of individuals, conceptual knowledge delivers over a world arranged according to a relatively small number of generalizations and abstractions. Thus, we read in "On Truth and Lies" (p. 83) that words and concepts derive from "unique and entirely individual experience[s]," that they equalize "cases which are never equal and thus altogether unequal," and that they "overlook [. . .] what is individual and actual," since "nature is acquainted with no forms and no concepts and likewise with no species." A similar critique of the Platonizing tendency of language and thought is presented in the first part of *Human, All Too Human*, where Nietzsche writes:

> The significance of language for the evolution of culture lies in this, that in language mankind set up beside the world a separate world, a place it took to be so firmly set that, standing upon it, it could lift the rest of the world off its hinges and make itself master of it. To the extent that man has for long ages believed in the concepts and names of things as in *aeternae veritates* he has appropriated to himself that pride by which he raised himself above the animal: he really thought that in language he possessed knowledge of the world. The sculptor of language was not so modest as to believe that he was only giving things designations, he conceived rather that with words he was expressing supreme knowledge of things. [. . .] A great deal later—only

now—it dawns on men that in their belief in language they have propagated a tremendous error. (11)[19]

And, in a note from fall 1887, Nietzsche reiterates this nominalist view:

> The *form* counts as something enduring and therefore more valuable; but the form has merely been invented by us; and however often "the same form is attained," it does not mean that it *is* the *same* form—*rather, what appears is always something new,* and it is only we who are always comparing, who include the new, to the extent that it is similar to the old, in the unity of the "form." As if a *type* should be attained and, as it were, was intended and inherent in the process of formation. *Form, species, law, idea, purpose*—in all these cases the same error is made of giving a false reality to a fiction. [. . .] One should not understand this *compulsion* to construct concepts, species, forms, purposes, laws—"*a world of identical cases*"—as if they enabled us to fix the *true world;* but rather as a compulsion to arrange a world for ourselves in which *our existence* is made possible. (*WP* 521)[20]

In these and other passages, Nietzsche argues that words and concepts make unities and identities out of what are really multiplicities and similarities. Since everything is similar to everything else in infinitely many respects,[21] Nietzsche implicitly asks why some groups of things are called "unities" and "identities" while others are not. Of course, he himself provides the answer to this question: such presumed unities and identities have aided human beings in their struggle for survival.[22] Yet, for several reasons, Nietzsche is reluctant to rest with this answer.

First, as we have already seen, the evolutionary establishment of these unities and identities has tended to lead to a Platonistic reification of words and concepts such that they become not only independently existing *entities* but even *the ultimately real entities* from which all sensuous particulars are derived. In this way, a reversal occurs whereby the "actual" world—the only world with which we are acquainted: the sensuous world of particulars—gets taken as the "world of mere appearance," derived from the "true" world of forms, concepts, laws, and

---

19. Cf. *TI* "Reason" 5: "'Reason' in language—oh, what an old deceptive female she is! I am afraid we are not rid of God because we still have faith in grammar."

20. See also *HH* 19 ("in fact nothing is identical to anything else") and *GS* 354 ("all our actions are altogether incomparably personal, unique, and infinitely individual; there is no doubt of that").

21. A poignant remark made by Hilary Putnam, *Reason, Truth, and History* (London: Cambridge University Press, 1981), 64.

22. See *GS* 110–11. This evolutionary answer has been more recently proposed by W. V. Quine, "Natural Kinds," in *Ontological Relativity and Other Essays.* (New York: Columbia University Press, 1969), 126ff. Stack, "Nietzsche's Evolutionary Epistemology," 88ff., discusses the similarities between Nietzsche's and Quine's views on this matter.

so on: "the leaf" becomes "the cause of leaves" (*TL* p. 83).[23] Nietzsche's talk of the "errors" of reason and knowledge serves, then, to set this reversal aright by reminding us of the actual derivation of the "true world" from the "world of appearance": "The reasons for which 'this' world has been characterized as 'apparent' are the very reasons which indicate its reality; any other kind of reality is absolutely indemonstrable" (*TI* "Reason" 6). And again, "The 'apparent' world is the only one: the 'true' world is merely *added by a lie*" (*TI* "Reason" 2).[24]

The primacy of this "apparent world" of sensuous particulars, Nietzsche thinks, can be shown through "scientific" inquiry, by which he seems to mean the macroscopic view afforded by historical, philological, and evolutionary research and the microscopic observation of biological, chemical, and physical phenomena. "Rigorous science," he contends, "can quite gradually and step by step, illuminate the history of the genesis of this world as idea [itself 'the outcome of a host of errors and fantasies'] and, for brief periods of time at any rate, lift us out of the entire proceeding" (*HH* 16). "Knowledge educated in the highest scientificality," he writes, "contradicts [. . .] the belief that there are *identical things*" (*HH* 18). Scrupulous scientific observation, he says elsewhere, uncovers "a manifold one-after-another [*ein vielfaches Nacheinander*] where the naive man and inquirer of older cultures saw only two separate things" (*GS* 112). The passage continues:

> Cause and effect: such a duality probably never exists—in truth we are confronted by a continuum [*ein continuum*] out of which we isolate a couple of pieces. [. . .] An intellect that could see cause and effect as a continuum and a flux of occurrences [*Fluss des Geschehens*] and not, as we do, in terms of an arbitrary division and dismemberment, would repudiate the concept of cause and effect.

Such conclusions, Nietzsche sometimes claims, are even available to attentive ordinary sense perception, which, he argues, is confronted by an

23. Wittgenstein (*The Blue and Brown Books* [New York: Harper and Row, 1958], 17–18) uses the same example in a very similar analysis of the "metaphysics" and "philosophical confusion" caused by "our craving for generality." Wittgenstein's warnings about "the bewitchment of our intelligence by means of language" (*Philosophical Investigations,* trans. G. E. M. Anscombe [Oxford: Basil Blackwell, 1953], §109) bear comparison with Nietzsche's critique of "the basic presuppositions of the metaphysics of language" (*TI* "Reason" 5). For some comparison between these two thinkers, see Erich Heller, "Wittgenstein and Nietzsche," in *The Importance of Nietzsche: Ten Essays* (Chicago: University of Chicago Press, 1988), and Tracy B. Strong, *Friedrich Nietzsche and the Politics of Transfiguration,* exp. ed. (Berkeley: University of California Press, 1988), 78–86.

24. Cf. *EH* "Destiny" 8: "The concept of the 'beyond,' the 'true world' invented in order to devaluate the only world there is [. . .] our earthly reality!"

ever-changing array of appearances. In praise of Heraclitus, Nietzsche writes in *Twilight of the Idols:*

> When the rest of the philosophic folk rejected the testimony of the senses because they showed multiplicity and change, he rejected their testimony because they showed things as if they had permanence and unity. Heraclitus too did the senses an injustice. They lie neither in the way the Eleatics believed, nor as he believed—they do not lie at all. What we *make* of their testimony, that alone introduces lies; for example, the lie of unity, the lie of thinghood, of substance, of permanence . . . "Reason" is the cause of our falsification of the testimony of the senses. Insofar as the senses show becoming, passing away, and change, they do not lie. ("Reason" 2)

Besides reminding us of the sensuous basis of all our knowledge, Nietzsche refers to the truths of logic, language, and the categories as "errors" for another reason. The evolutionary scenario tends toward a reification and ossification of words and concepts, Nietzsche thinks, because it is essentially conservative; its basic aim is the *preservation* of the species. To this end, it forbids any tampering with the established conceptual framework and discourages novel sortings of appearances. The process of reification aids this prohibition by encouraging the view that the established unities and identities not only are useful fictions but indeed are given in the nature of things.

Nietzsche, however, continually argues that "the wish to preserve oneself is a symptom of a condition of distress, of a limitation of the really fundamental instinct of life, which aims at *the expansion of power* and, wishing for that, frequently risks and even sacrifices self-preservation" (*GS* 349).[25] In a note from the same period, he reiterates this view:

> "Useful" in the sense of Darwinist biology means: proved advantageous in the struggle with others. But it seems to me that the *feeling of increase,* the feeling of *becoming-stronger,* is itself, quite apart from any usefulness in the struggle, the real *progress* [Fortschritt]: only from this feeling does there arise the will to struggle. (*WP* 649)

These claims have important consequences for a consideration of Nietzsche's epistemology; for, if self-preservation is not the sole or ultimate goal of our cognitive processes, the way is opened for a consideration of

---

25. Cf. *BGE* 13: "Physiologists should think before putting down the instinct of self-preservation as the cardinal instinct of organic being. A living thing seeks above all to *discharge* its strength—life itself is *will to power;* self-preservation is only one of the indirect and most frequent *results.*" Cf. also *WP* 649–51.

other possible sortings of appearances. These, in turn, provide us with foils that help to expose the contingent nature of our established conceptual framework.

Hence, having reminded us of the sensuous origins of our ordinary conceptual scheme, Nietzsche goes on to remind us of its artistic, "metaphoric" origins, which have been lost or sublimated into the literal truths of scientific fact. This artistic drive, or "intellectual play impulse" (*GS* 110), according to Nietzsche, is not only the real *origin* but also the real *end* of human activity. As with life in general, human beings ultimately seek not to preserve themselves but to become more, better, different; and this requires constant innovation, novel sortings, new interpretations. Intellectual endeavors begin in art and they end in art—which is to say that they do not end at all, because art, for Nietzsche, consists in ceaseless transformation. He writes:

> The drive toward the formation of metaphors is the fundamental human drive, which one cannot for a single instant dispense with in thought, for one would thereby dispense with man himself. This drive is not truly vanquished and scarcely subdued by the fact that a regular and rigid new world is constructed as its prison from its own ephemeral products, the concepts. It seeks a new realm and another channel for its activity, and it finds this in *myth* and in *art* generally. This drive continually confuses the conceptual categories and cells by bringing forward new transferences, metaphors, and metonymies. [. . .] That immense framework and planking of concepts to which the needy man clings his whole life in order to preserve himself is nothing but a scaffolding and toy for the audacious feats of the most liberated intellect. And when it smashes this framework to pieces, throws it into confusion, and puts it back together in an ironic fashion, pairing the most alien things and separating the closest, it is demonstrating that it has no need of these makeshifts of indigence and that it will now be guided by intuitions rather than concepts. There is no regular path which leads from these intuitions into the ghostly land of schemata, the land of abstractions. (*TL* pp. 88–90)

Years later, Nietzsche again voices this view, arguing that

> [w]here need and distress have forced men for a long time to communicate and understand each other quickly and subtly, the ultimate result is an excess of this strength and art of communication—as it were, a capacity that has gradually been accumulated and now waits for an heir who might squander it. (Those who are called artists are these heirs [. . .]—all of them people who come at the end of a long chain, "late born" every one of them in the best sense of the word and, as I have said, by their nature squanderers.) (*GS* 354)

Thus, as we saw in the previous chapter, Nietzsche ultimately sides with the artistic or "intuitive man" rather than with the scientific or "rational man." Unlike the latter, the former "do not lie at all" (in the metaphysical sense). They do not try to pass off words and concepts as entities or conditions for experience; rather, they affirm that all knowledge originates in the sense experience of particulars and that words and concepts are simply groupings of these toward various ends, self-preservation being neither the only nor the ultimate of those ends.

2.3 THE DE-DEIFICATION OF NATURE

In his attempt to naturalize epistemology, then, Nietzsche endorses a basic form of empiricism. Against the Platonic and Kantian priority given to the conceptual, Nietzsche warns of "confusing the last with the first" by placing "the most general, the emptiest concepts, the last smoke of evaporating reality, in the beginning, *as* the beginning" (*TI* "Reason" 4). Instead, he argues, "all credibility, all good conscience, all evidence of truth come only from the senses" (*BGE* 134).

Yet Nietzsche is not uncritical of empiricism, traditionally conceived. Anyone who would characterize him as a straightforward empiricist must confront prominent passages in which he decries "the coarse sensualistic prejudice that sensations teach us truths about things" (*WP* 516) and scoffs at "the eternally popular sensualism" according to which "what is clear, what is 'explained,'" is "only what can be seen and felt" (*BGE* 14). These and neighboring passages affirm Copernicus's and Boscovich's "triumph over the senses" (*BGE* 12) and "the Platonic way of thinking," which, contrary to the "fundamentally plebeian tastes" of the sensualists, he calls "a noble way of thinking [that] consisted precisely in a *resistance* to obvious sense evidence" (*BGE* 14; cf. *GS* 372). How are we to reconcile such claims with the positive revaluation of the sensual called for by Nietzsche's naturalism? The answer, I think, can be found in the second part of the project to eliminate the "shadows of God": namely, the "de-deification of nature."

We have seen that the "naturalization of humanity" (the first part of the project to eliminate the "shadows of God") requires a rejection of the notion that human beings possess some divine feature that separates them from, and raises them above, the natural world. It thus rejects the ideal of knowledge as providing a God's-eye view on the world that could secure necessary, unconditional, and objective truths. We saw Nietzsche oppose metaphysical epistemology and ontology with a naturalism that firmly resituates human beings within the contingent, sensuous world and refigures human reason as one more device aiding the struggle for survival and flourishing. Thus, Nietzsche argues that knowledge is always contingent and conditional, relative to some interest, purpose, or perspective.

The "de-deification of nature" (the second part of the project to eliminate the "shadows of God") itself has two aspects. On the one hand, it is a corollary of the first part of the project. It maintains that, if we want to get rid of all the "shadows of God," we must reject the notion of a pre-given world—the world "as it really is," as it would be given to a God's-eye view. The "death of God," Nietzsche argues, enjoins us to reject *both* the notion that there is an absolute *perspective* from which the world could be viewed "as it really is" *and* the notion that there *is* such an absolute world. Instead, it asks us to refigure knowing as relative to some perspective, theory, or interpretation [26] and being as relative to the ontological commitments of a particular perspective.[27] On the other hand, the "de-deification of nature" also leads Nietzsche to privilege a certain set of perspectives and interpretations: namely, naturalistic ones that withdraw from our conception of nature all theological posits. Once we have done so, Nietzsche thinks we will come to see the world as an "innocent becoming" or as "will to power."

2.3.1 NIETZSCHE'S HOLISM: THE PRIMACY AND IRREDUCIBILITY OF INTERPRETATION

If Nietzsche's epistemology supports an empiricism, it is not what more recently has been called a "reductionist" empiricism, which holds that

26. I make little differentiation, here, among the terms "perspective," "interpretation," and "theory." "Perspective" and "interpretation" are quite often found together in Nietzsche's writing and are never sharply differentiated, a point I discuss at the beginning of chapter 3. I also see little difference between what Nietzsche calls "perspective" or "interpretation" and what contemporary philosophers call "theory"—namely, a more or less systematic web of beliefs that arranges and makes sense of the world (or a portion of it) according to a set of purposes and desires.

27. This view can be gleaned from Nietzsche's critique of positivism. He argues that the positivist belief in pre-given facts about the world is an ascetic, ultimately theological belief that attempts to get beyond the conditionality and contingency of interpretation and perspective toward some "true world of being" (*GM* III:24). Against this view, Nietzsche claims that there are no essences-, facts-, or meanings-in-themselves; that, on the contrary, there are only "definitions," "facts" and "meanings" within an interpretation, which answers from a particular perspective the question "what is that?" (see *WP* 556, 481). For a brief but poignant discussion of this antirealism in Nietzsche and Hegel, see Robert C. Solomon, *In the Spirit of Hegel* (New York: Oxford University Press, 1983), 328–29 n 15.

all knowledge and experience is reducible to immediate observations that deliver a unique and full meaning.[28] In a passage partially cited above, Nietzsche shows his contempt for this kind of empiricism:

> It is perhaps dawning on five or six minds that physics, too, is only a world-interpretation and -exegesis [*eine Welt-Auslegung und -Zurechtlegung*] (to suit us, if I may say so!) and *not* a world-explanation [*eine Welt-Erklärung*]; but insofar as it is based on belief in the senses, it is regarded as more, and for a long time to come must be regarded as more—namely, as an explanation. Eyes and fingers speak in its favor, visual evidence and palpableness do, too; this strikes an age with fundamentally plebeian tastes as fascinating, persuasive, *convincing*—after all, it follows instinctively the canon of truth of eternally popular sensualism. What is clear, what is "explained"? [*Was is klar, was »erklärt«?*] Only what can be seen and felt—every problem has to be pursued to that point. (*BGE* 14)

This passage appears in *Beyond Good and Evil*, part 1, entitled "On the Prejudices of the Philosophers." Neighboring passages make clear that prominent among these "prejudices" is a "myth of the given," what Nietzsche calls the belief in "immediate certainties" (16, 17, 34). This myth encompasses the beliefs of rationalists and empiricists alike: the Cartesian *cogito* ("as though knowledge here got hold of its object purely and nakedly" [16])[29] as well as "Locke's superficiality regarding the origin of ideas" (20). In §12, Nietzsche presents a critique of materialistic atomism that celebrates Roger Boscovich's and Copernicus's "triumph over the senses." Boscovich in particular is credited with having criticized Newton's and Leibniz's conception of the atom as the ultimate unit of matter in favor of a relational notion of the atom as a quasi-material nodal point within a network of force.[30] In

---

28. The term "reductionist empiricism" is taken from W. V. Quine, "Two Dogmas of Empiricism," in *From a Logical Point of View* (Cambridge: Harvard University Press, 1961). One of the "two dogmas of empiricism," Quine writes, "radical reductionism" is the doctrine that "every meaningful statement is [. . .] translatable into a statement (true or false) about immediate experience" (p. 38). Though he is concerned to attack the theory as it survives in contemporary analytic philosophy, Quine argues that the doctrine "well antedates" analytic philosophy and can be found, for instance, in Locke and Hume (p. 38).

29. Nietzsche's critique of the Cartesian *cogito* continues in the following passage, *BGE* 17.

30. For further discussion of Boscovich's conception of the atom and Nietzsche's fascination with it, see §5.2.1, below; George Stack, "Nietzsche and Boscovich's Natural Philosophy," *Pacific Philosophical Quarterly* 62 (1981): 69–87, and *Lange and Nietzsche* (Berlin: Walter de Gruyter, 1983); Claudia Crawford, *The Beginnings of Nietzsche's Theory of Language* (Berlin: Walter de Gruyter, 1988), 87–89, 298–99: and Alistair Moles, *Nietzsche's Philosophy of Nature and Cosmology* (Berlin: Peter Lang, 1990), chap. 5.

each of these seemingly disparate cases, Nietzsche uncovers the myth of "immediate certainty," a basic conviction that there exists some foundational, simple, present item (whether it be the "I" of consciousness, immediate sense data, or the atom as the ultimate, indivisible unit of matter) that provides the basis of all knowing and being and is the goal of all inquiry.

Against these "immediate certainties," Nietzsche argues for a more complex, relational, and holistic conception of knowledge and its objects. Rejecting the Cartesian notion that the "I" is an irreducible, intuitive given, Nietzsche conceives of it as "a social structure," a complex of sensation, thought, and affect (*BGE* 19; see chapter 3, below). Contrary to the Schopenhauerian conception of "the will" as "something simple, a brute datum, underivable, and intelligible by itself" (*GS* 127), Nietzsche contends that "willing is above all something *complicated,* something that is a unit [*Einheit*] only as a word" (*BGE* 19). And, "by way of rejecting Locke's superficiality regarding the origin of ideas," Nietzsche explicitly puts forward the holistic view "[t]hat individual philosophical concepts are not anything capricious or autonomously evolving, but grow up in connection and relationship with each other; that, however suddenly and arbitrarily they seem to appear in the history of thought, they nevertheless belong just as much to a system as all the members of the fauna of a continent" (20).

Combining this conceptual holism, the evolutionary analogy that appears in this last phrase, and the claim that this section as a whole is meant as a rejection of Locke's reductionist empiricism, the passage can be read as arguing that perception is not pure and simple but rather is overdetermined by the other physiological, psychological, and intellectual functions that coexist with it in a complex organism whose constitution and activity has been shaped by a long evolutionary history.

These theses are presented much more explicitly in a passage from *The Gay Science* addressed "To the realists." Nietzsche writes:

> You sober people who feel well armed against passion and fantasy and would like to turn your emptiness into a matter of pride and an ornament: you call yourselves realists and hint that the world really is the way it appears to you. As if reality stood unveiled before you alone. [. . .] But in your unveiled state are not even you still very passionate and dark creatures compared to fish, and still far too similar to an artist in love? [. . .] You are still burdened with those estimates of things that have their origin in the passions and loves of former centuries. Your sobriety still contains a secret and inextinguishable drunkenness. Your love of "reality," for example—oh that is a primeval "love"! In every sensation and every sense impression there is a

piece of this old love; and some fantasy, some prejudice, some unreason, some ignorance, some fear, and ever so much else has woven it and worked on it. That mountain there! That cloud there! What is "real" in that? Subtract the phantasm and every human *ingredient* from it, you sober ones! If you *can!* If you can forget your descent, your past, your training—all of your humanity and animality. There is no "reality" for us—not for you either, you sober ones. (*GS* 57)

Here, Nietzsche states outright the twin theses (1) that there is no such thing as naked perception and (2) that what perception perceives is not a pre-given world. Rather, he argues, perception functions as part of the total human organism, and what it perceives is a world that is a palimpsest of previous interpretative construals. Perception and interpretation are inextricably intertwined.[31]

Nietzsche underscores these positions in his critique of a contemporary form of reductionist empiricism: the *positivism* that flourished in the latter half of the nineteenth century. A famous note from 1886–87 runs:

Against positivism, which halts at phenomena—"there are only facts"—I would say: no, facts is precisely what there are not, only interpretations [*Interpretationen*]. We cannot establish any fact "in itself": perhaps it is nonsense [*Unsinn*] to even want to do such a thing. [. . .] In so far as the word "knowledge" has any meaning [*Sinn*], the world is knowable: but it is *interpretable* [*deutbar*] otherwise, it has no meaning [*Sinn*] behind it, but countless meanings [*Sinne*]—"Perspectivism." (*WP* 481)[32]

This insight finds its way into the *Genealogy*, written shortly thereafter. Discussing the relationship of modern science to theology and metaphysics, Nietzsche asserts that the positivist's "renunciation of all interpretation" in the effort to discover unmediated "brute facts" constitutes

31. Cf. Nelson Goodman (*Languages of Art*, 2d ed. [Indianapolis: Hackett, 1976], 7–8): "The eye always comes ancient to its work, obsessed by its own past and by old and new insinuations of the ear, nose, tongue, fingers, heart, and brain. It functions not as an instrument self-empowered and alone, but as a dutiful member of a complex and capricious organism. Not only how but what it sees is regulated by need and prejudice. It selects, rejects, organizes, discriminates, associates, classifies, analyzes, and constructs. It does not so much mirror as take and make; and what it takes and makes it does not see bare, as items without attributes, but as things, as food, as people, as enemies, as stars, as weapons. Nothing is seen nakedly or naked. The myths of the innocent eye and of the absolute given are unholy accomplices. Both derive from and foster the idea of knowing as a processing of raw material received from the senses, and of this raw material as being discoverable either through purification rites or by methodical disinterpretation. But reception and interpretation are not separable operations; they are thoroughly interdependent."

32. Dated late 1886–spring 1887 (*KSA* 12:7[60]).

an "ascetic [. . .] denial of sensuality" (III:24, see §1.5.2, above). And, during the same period, in Book Five of *The Gay Science,* Nietzsche criticizes "that impetuous *demand for certainty* that today discharges itself among large numbers of people in a scientific-positivistic form. The demand that one *wants* by all means that something should be firm." No less than Christianity and metaphysics, he continues, "this, too, is still the demand for a support, a prop" (*GS* 347).

This group of passages makes clear what Nietzsche finds objectionable in the positivist project: its belief in the existence of, and its desire to represent, some given and certain ontological foundation for our knowledge—"the world as it really is." This belief and desire, Nietzsche contends, is simply "metaphysical" (*GM* III:24), for, as he argues in the first passage, "we cannot establish any fact 'in itself,'" "the world has no meaning behind it, but countless meanings." That is, the world we know is the world as constructed by one or another interpretation or perspective, of which there are many. The notion of the world "as it really is" or "as it is in itself" is simply fabricated through a *negation of,* a *desire to transcend,* the world we know (the world as it is constructed by the many interpretations/perspectives).[33] It is this metaphysical belief and desire that allows Nietzsche to say that positivism, which claims to be the most empirical doctrine, expresses an "ascetic" "denial of sensuality": in its desire for some firm, solid, "real" or "true" world, positivism disavows the actual conditions of our knowledge (the necessity and irreducibility of interpretation) and the world that this knowledge reveals (a world with "no meaning behind it, but countless meanings"). This putative "true" world, Nietzsche argues, is simply the world as it would be given to a God's-eye view. And having abandoned the notion of a God's-eye view, Nietzsche also abandons its correlate: the notion of a pre-given world.

Thus, Nietzsche criticizes every reductionist attempt to discover something "in itself," which always involves such ascetic "renunciation of interpretation."

> "Things that have a constitution in themselves"—a dogmatic idea with which one must break absolutely. (*WP* 559)

> That things possess a *constitution in themselves* totally apart from interpretation and subjectivity is *a totally futile hypothesis:* it presupposes that *inter-*

---

33. See *TI* "Reason" 6 and 2, quoted in §2.2.4, above.

pretation and subjective-being are not essential, that a thing freed from all relationships [i.e., all perspectival construal] would still be a thing. (*WP* 560)

A "thing in itself" just as perverse as a "sense in itself," a "meaning in itself." There are no "facts in themselves," *for a sense must always first be projected into them before there can be facts.* The "what is that?" is a *determination of meaning* [eine Sinn-Setzung] from some other viewpoint. *"Essence"* [*Die* »Essenz«], *"being"* [*die* »Wesenheit«] is something perspectival and already presupposes a multiplicity. At bottom there always lies "what is that for *me?*" (for us, for all that lives, etc.). A thing would be defined once all beings [*Wesen*] had asked "what is that?" and had answered their question. Supposing that one single being, with its own relationships and perspectives for all things, were missing, then the thing would not yet be "defined." In short, the being [*Wesen*] of a thing is always only an *opinion* [*Meinung*] about the "thing." Or rather: *"it is considered"* is the actual *"this is,"* the only "this is." (*WP* 556)

Against the very notion of the "in itself," Nietzsche advances a view akin to what more recent Anglo-American philosophers have called the doctrine of "ontological relativity," according to which (1) questions concerning "what there is" can only be answered relative to (what Nietzsche calls) an "interpretation" or "perspective"; (2) the only alternative to one "interpretation" is another; and (3) it is nonsense to ask (or answer) what things are absolutely, or "in themselves." [34]

Rejecting the notion of a pre-given world, then, Nietzsche's "dedeification of nature" requires that we revise our conception of empirical knowledge. We must give up the idea that sensation delivers some pure, unmediated content, that it mirrors a world with pre-given partitions and essences. This is not, however, to assert the Kantian, transcendental view that sensuous intuition can only ever appear to us already

34. The phrase "ontological relativity" is Quine's; but similar theses (deemed "irrealism," "internal realism," "antirealism," etc.) are found in the work of Goodman, Putnam, and others. Cf. Goodman ("The Way the World Is," in *Problems and Projects* [Indianapolis: Bobbs-Merrill, 1972], 31): "For me, there is no way that is the way the world is; and so of course no description can capture it. But there are many ways the world is; and every true description captures one of them. The difference between [the realist] and me is, in sum, the difference between absolutism and relativism"; Quine ("Ontological Relativity," in *Ontological Relativity and Other Essays* [New York: Columbia University Press, 1969], 50): "What makes sense is to say not what the objects of a theory are, absolutely speaking, but how one theory of objects is interpretable or reinterpretable in another"; and Putnam (*Reason, Truth, and History*, 49, 52): *"what objects does the world consist of?* is a question that it only makes sense to ask *within* a theory or description. [. . .] 'Objects' do not exist independently of conceptual schemes. We cut up the world into objects when we introduce one or another scheme of description." I discuss this idea more fully in §3.4.3.

shaped by the a priori forms of intuition and categories of the understanding.[35] Unlike Kant, Nietzsche does not separate cognition into
passive and active faculties. Having dismissed the very idea of the "in
itself," Nietzsche rejects the notion that sensation receives from "the
world" a raw material that is then processed by our various interpretative schemes. Sensation and interpretation, for Nietzsche, are insepa-
rable activities. "Our sense perceptions," he writes, "are already the
result of [. . .] *assimilation* and *equalization* with regard to *all* the past
in us; they do not follow directly upon the 'impression'" (*WP* 500).
That is, sense perception is not new and innocent every moment; rather,
what we experience each moment is the result of an entire evolutionary
history. Elsewhere, he argues that "all sense perceptions are permeated
with *value judgments*" (*WP* 505),[36] namely, interpretive decisions concerning what counts as "what there is."[37] Against both the reductionist
empiricist and the Kantian transcendentalist, then, Nietzsche advances
the naturalistic, evolutionary view that sense perception only functions
within an ongoing network of interpretations—within what he calls
an "already-created world, constructed out of nothing but appearances but become firm to the extent that this kind of appearance has
preserved life" (*WP* 520).[38]

According to Nietzsche, then, impressions, sensations, and perceptions do not offer any pure, simple, or unmediated picture of the world.
Yet neither do judgments or statements of fact. "There are no isolated
judgments!" Nietzsche writes: "An isolated judgment is never 'true,'

---

35. Babette Babich, *Nietzsche's Philosophy of Science: Reflecting Science on the
Ground of Art and Life* (Albany: State University of New York Press, 1994), 95 and
chap. 3 *passim*, attributes to Nietzsche this Kantian view.

36. Cf. *GS* 114: "*How far the moral sphere extends.*—As soon as we see a new
image, we immediately construct it with the aid of all our previous experiences [. . .]
All our experiences are moral [i.e., evaluative] experiences, even in the realm of sense
perception."

37. See *WP* 556, cited above, on how ontological ascriptions are judgments made
according to one perspective or another.

38. My interpretation here relies fairly heavily on the *Nachlaß*, where Nietzsche discusses epistemological issues more directly and extensively than anywhere else. Nevertheless, I find this interpretation entirely consistent with (and, indeed, helpful in making sense
of) much of the published material on these matters. Nietzsche's rejection of the "thing in
itself" can be found throughout his published work (see, e.g., *GS* 335, 354; *D* P:3; and
the other passages discussed in §4.3, below). Nietzsche's basic empiricism is stated fairly
plainly in *BGE* 134; *TI* "Reason" 1–3; and *A* 4 (and discussed in §2.2.4, above). His resistance to positivist or reductionist versions of empiricism is presented in such passages
as *BGE* 12, 14; *GS* 347; and *GM* III:24 (discussed in the present section). And his assertion of the primacy and irreducibility of interpretation can be found in such passages as
GS 57 and *GM* II:12, III:24 (also discussed in the present section).

never knowledge; only in the connection and relation of many judgments is there any surety" (*WP* 530). Thus, against a reductionist empiricism, Nietzsche espouses a holistic empiricism, which maintains that, while all knowledge is generated out of sensuous affection, the unit of empirical significance is neither the individual sensation nor the isolated statement of fact but the theory or interpretation as a whole in which sensations and statements are lodged.

This naturalistic, holistic view is not a skeptical view. It does not claim that human interests, desires, perspectives, and interpretations get in the way of some "true" knowledge that would reveal "the way the world really is." Nietzsche altogether dismisses the notion of a God's-eye view and, with it, the notion of a standard of truth transcending all contingent perspectives (see *GM* III:12). Yet this does not mean that there is no common measure for interpretations or perspectives. After all, Nietzsche holds that perspectives and interpretations are, in large part, developed to help us cope with our sensuous imbrication in the natural world. A basic standard for interpretations, then, is how well they do this. Considerations of entrenchment, simplicity, scope, coherence, utility, and novelty, as well as political considerations of ideology and power, will also figure significantly in the acceptance or rejection of interpretations.[39]

Despite these constraints, however, Nietzsche grants that the "de-deification of nature" permits a proliferation of interpretations.[40] There will be different interpretations over time, because no interpretation is immune from revision (see *GS* 58 and *WP* 616). And there will be different coexisting interpretations, because there are different purposes and goals in different areas of life and areas of life where several interests, purposes, and goals compete.[41] Yet Nietzsche also maintains that

---

39. Nietzsche emphasizes entrenchment, e.g., in *GS* 57–58, 110, and *BGE* 188. He emphasizes simplicity ("economy of principles" or "conscience of method") in *BGE* 13 and 36. Considerations of scope permeate his discussions of "will to power," which aim at giving a comprehensive account of all natural knowing and being, from the human to the inanimate (see, e.g., *BGE* 36). Coherence is stressed in such passages as *GS* 54; *BGE* 20; *WP* 530. Utility is stressed throughout Nietzsche's work (e.g., *BGE* 4; *WP* 493ff.). Novelty is stressed, e.g., in *TL* pp. 88–91 and *GS* 110. Finally, considerations of ideology and power fill his writings, particularly his analyses and critiques of Christianity and "slave morality."

40. The locus classicus for this view is *GS* 374 (partially quoted at the end of §1.6.1, above, where some of the critical problems with the passage are noted). See also *GS* 2, 347, and 373 (also quoted and discussed in §1.6.1) and *WP* 410, 470, 481, 600.

41. In *GS* 110, for example, Nietzsche shows how, in the area of truth and knowledge, two impulses come to compete with one another: on the one hand, an impulse to-

there will be different interpretations of "the same phenomena"; *and* that, because there is no pre-given world and no God's-eye view, there is no absolute fact of the matter as to which one is correct.[42]

In *Beyond Good and Evil* §22, Nietzsche provides a basic example. He argues that "the physicists'" notion of "nature's conformity to law" is a "bad mode of interpretation" motivated by the desire to show that the physical world conforms to the democratic values of modern European politics. Deeply suspicious of such ascriptions, Nietzsche offers a counterinterpretation. He claims that, "with opposite intentions and modes of interpretation," one "could read out of the same nature, and with regard to the same phenomena," a view of the world as "will to power," as "the tyrannically inconsiderate and relentless enforcement of claims of power"—an interpretation that, like the physicists' view, would also see the course of the world as "necessary" and "calculable" "*not* because laws obtain in it, but because they are absolutely *lacking*, and every power draws its ultimate consequences at every moment."

Bracketing, for now, the substantive view proposed in this passage, let us focus on its methodological point. Nietzsche prefaces and concludes his account of the "laws of nature" model with the claim that it is "no matter of fact" but rather an "interpretation." Yet things are no different, he grants, with his alternative model, following the proposal of which he writes: "Supposing that this also is only interpretation—and you will be eager enough to make this objection?—well, so much the better." The point of this concluding remark seems to be that, without a God's-eye view on a pre-given world, there are only interpretations with no absolute fact of the matter as to which one is correct. To challenge an existing view, one cannot simply present "the plain facts" but can only offer a counterinterpretation.[43] As Nietzsche puts it in *The*

---

ward self-preservation that strives to produce and maintain a simplified and selective version of the world and, on the other hand, an "intellectual play impulse" with a penchant for honesty and skepticism that delights in showing the contingency of the preservative "primeval errors."

42. Nietzsche's genealogies make clear his commitment to the notion that "the world [. . .] has no meaning behind it, but countless meanings" (*WP* 481). In the *Genealogy of Morals* and elsewhere, for example, Nietzsche maintains that, while both parties agree that affective life involves change, suffering, passion, pain, and pleasure, the strong, active person, who affirms affective life in its entirety, gives a wholly different interpretation to this "fact" than does the sickly ascetic, who rejects the sensuous world precisely on account of its changeability, pain, and suffering. See also *GM* II: 12–14, where Nietzsche catalogs the multiple interpretations of punishment, revealing how "one and the same procedure can be employed, interpreted, adapted to ends that differ fundamentally."

43. Contrary to the view of some Nietzsche scholars (e.g., Arthur Danto, *Nietzsche as Philosopher* [New York: Columbia University Press, 1965], 82ff.), Nietzsche is not a veri-

Gay Science: "We can destroy only as creators!—But let us not forget this either: it is enough to create new names and estimations and probabilities in order to create in the long run new 'things'" (*GS* 58).

2.3.2 WILL TO POWER AND THE INNOCENCE OF BECOMING

Yet this is not the end of the story. While Nietzsche's "de-deification of nature" allows for a proliferation of interpretations and admits that no interpretation could be uniquely correct, it does not concede that every interpretation is as good as any other. We saw, in the passage from *Beyond Good and Evil* quoted above, that Nietzsche deems the physicists' interpretation "bad 'philology,'" a "bad mode of interpretation." Conversely, everywhere that Nietzsche presents his own picture of a "de-deified world" (e.g., *GS* 109; *BGE* 13, 36; and *TI* "Errors" 8), he seems to want to promote it as a better interpretation. One might reasonably ask what criteria Nietzsche has for such an evaluation.

The answer is that naturalism itself provides the criterion. While the "death of God" leads to a rejection of all necessary, unconditional, or absolute perspectives and facts, we have seen that it also leads to a rejection of theological interpretations of nature, those that posit supernatural entities and explanatory principles. This is made particularly clear in the section of *The Gay Science* that immediately follows Nietzsche's first pronouncement of the "death of God"—a passage that bears quoting in full:

> *Let us beware!*—Let us beware of thinking that the world is a living being. Where should it expand? On what should it feed? How could it grow and multiply? We have some notion of the nature of the organic; and we should not reinterpret the exceedingly derivative, late, rare, accidental, that we perceive only on the crust of the earth and make of it something essential,

---

ficationist who can do away with metaphysical and theological beliefs simply by pointing to the lack of empirical evidence for them. On Nietzsche's view, as we have seen, interpretations can be criticized only on the basis of other interpretations, not by recourse to some bare, uninterpreted fact. Nietzsche's critique of metaphysics and theology, then, will have to be much more complex and hypothetical. Thus, it takes the form of *genealogy*, an elaborate attempt to retell the story of theology and metaphysics in a way that reveals them to be rooted in base and pathetic impulses. Nietzsche will argue not only that the supposedly unconditional and otherworldly posits of metaphysics and morality are explicable in naturalistic terms but also that such explanation reveals them to be pernicious and contemptible, generated through a psychological projection that sets up, as the antithesis of "the world of life, nature, and history," another world that allows us to escape life's sufferings and deceptions. The desire for the otherworldly, Nietzsche concludes, is nothing but "life's nausea and disgust with life" (*BT* SC:5; cf. *WP* 12).

universal, and eternal, which is what those people do who call the universe
an organism. This nauseates me. Let us even beware of believing that the
universe is a machine: it is certainly not constructed for one purpose, and
calling it a "machine" does it far too much honor. Let us beware of positing generally and everywhere anything as elegant as the cyclical movements
of our neighboring stars; even a glance into the Milky Way raises doubts
whether there are not far coarser and more contradictory movements there,
as well as stars with eternally linear paths, etc. The astral order in which we
live is an exception; this order and the relative duration that depends on it
have again made possible an exception of exceptions: the formation of the
organic. The total character of the world, however, is in all eternity chaos—
in the sense not of a lack of necessity but a lack of order, arrangement, form,
beauty, wisdom, and whatever other names there are for our aesthetic anthropomorphisms. Judged from the point of view of our reason, unsuccessful attempts are by all odds the rule, the exceptions are not the secret aim,
and the whole musical box repeats eternally its tune which may never be
called a melody—and ultimately even the phrase "unsuccessful attempt" is
too anthropomorphic and reproachful. But how could we reproach or praise
the universe? Let us beware of attributing to it heartlessness and unreason or
their opposites: it is neither perfect nor beautiful, nor noble, nor does it wish
to become any of these things; it does not by any means strive to imitate
man. None of our aesthetic and moral judgments apply to it. Nor does it
have any instinct for self-preservation or any other instinct; and it does not
observe any laws either. Let us beware of saying there are laws in nature.
There are only necessities: there is nobody who commands, nobody who
obeys, nobody who trespasses. Once you know that there are no purposes,
you also know that there is no accident; for it is only beside a world of purposes that the word "accident" has meaning. Let us beware of saying death
is opposed to life. The living is merely a type of what is dead, and a very rare
type.—Let us beware of thinking that the world eternally creates new things.
There are no eternally enduring substances: matter is as much of an error as
the God of the Eleatics. But when shall we ever be done with our caution
and care? When will all these shadows of God cease to darken our minds?
When will we complete our de-deification of nature? When may we begin to
naturalize humanity in terms of a pure, newly discovered, newly redeemed
nature? (*GS* 109; cf. *WP* 12)

This is a rich and difficult passage. For most of it, Nietzsche seems to be
arguing that none of our *human, anthropomorphic* conceptions provide
sustainable interpretations of the world. Yet the coda suddenly speaks
of these as "shadows of *God*" and calls for a "de-*deification*," rather
than a "de-*humanization*," of nature. In retrospect, we can see that
what Nietzsche has been urging all along is that we withdraw from the
world all those things that we have imagined God to have put there and
orchestrated: purpose, order, aim, form, beauty, wisdom, eternal nov-

elty, law, hierarchy, and so forth. What we are left with, Nietzsche tells us, is a world that is "in all eternity chaos."

This last remark has led some commentators to suppose that Nietzsche is committed to a form of metaphysical realism: to the view that the world "in itself" is a "chaos" that only appears to us, filtered through our "aesthetic anthropomorphisms," as ordered, arranged, or formed.[44] Yet we can and should read this passage otherwise (see also §4.7.1, below). Recall that *Beyond Good and Evil* §22 argued against the naive anthropomorphisms involved in the "physicists'" conception of "nature's conformity to law" and advocated instead a view of the world as a "tyrannical" and "inconsiderate" "will to power" with no laws or aims, expending itself fully at each moment. Such a world might approximate the "chaos" of the *Gay Science* passage. Indeed, having criticized a prevailing view, each passage advocates a view of the world as "necessary" yet lacking order, law, purpose, et cetera, one passage calling this "will to power," the other calling it "chaos." Recall, too, that Nietzsche conceded that his view of the world as "will to power" was "only interpretation" and not text or fact. Reading these passages together, then, we can see that the world as "chaos" is not offered as a fact—as what the world really is like before it is conceptualized by us—but as another, perhaps better (because atheological), interpretation. We can see that it is not a question of distinguishing the real from the apparent world but of distinguishing different ways of constructing apparent worlds. Seen in this light, Nietzsche is far from advocating metaphysical realism. Rather, he is seen consistently to hold the view that there is no fact of the matter that could be determined by a correct apprehension of the world in itself but only a host of competing interpretations.

As with the passage from *Beyond Good and Evil*, then, the one from *Gay Science* asserts Nietzsche's two-sided argument: on the one hand, there are only interpretations with no fact of the matter as to which one is absolutely correct; on the other hand, "better" interpretations are

44. Jean Granier, "Perspectivism and Interpretation" and "Nietzsche's Conception of Chaos," both in *The New Nietzsche: Contemporary Styles of Interpretation,* ed. David B. Allison (Cambridge, Mass.: MIT Press, 1977), and, at times, Martin Heidegger, *Nietzsche,* vol. 2, *The Eternal Recurrence of the Same,* trans. David F. Krell (San Francisco: Harper, 1984), 94–95, read Nietzsche this way. Despite her critique of Granier's reading, Sarah Kofman, *Nietzsche and Metaphor,* trans. Duncan Large (Stanford: Stanford University Press, 1993), 138–39, reads Nietzsche this way as well. I discuss Nietzsche's conception of "chaos" more fully below, in §§3.4.1 and 4.7.

those that attempt to eliminate all the "shadows of God." This elimination, Nietzsche contends, leaves a world without theological efficient causes (God as *causa prima*), formal causes (the world-as-organism, -cycle, -machine, -melody, -law abiding), final causes (equilibrium, progress, happiness), or material causes (materialistic atomism, pantheism).[45] The effort to imbue the world with such causes was an attempt to see the world from outside, to view its natural, internal features as representations of, or as guided by, some grander plan.[46] But this is just what Nietzsche's naturalism cannot allow. There is no "judging, measuring, comparing, or sentencing the whole" of life and nature (*TI* "Errors" 8; see also *TI* "Morality" 5), for that would require a position outside of life and nature, the possibility and intelligibility of which, Nietzsche points out, is not afforded living, natural creatures such as ourselves (and, of course, there are no creatures other than natural ones).[47]

Nietzsche urges us to give up the desire for such impossible and superfluous perspectives and instead to try to see the world "from inside." If we do so, he believes, we will come to see it as " 'will to power' and nothing besides" (*BGE* 36): a world without beginning, end, aim, purpose, foundation, or privileged aspect (see *GS* 109; *WP* 55, 1062–67). To see the world in this way is to restore "the innocence of becoming" (*TI* "Errors" 7–8). It is to see that there is no unique way the world is, that the world is capable of many formulations and transformations precisely because it has no essential character.[48] It is to see that there are

45. Against God as *causa prima*, see *TI* "Reason" 4–5, "Errors" 7–8; and *WP* 1066–67. Against the world as organism, etc., see *GS* 109, 357. Against the world as teleological, see *TI* "Errors" 8; *Z* Prologue and *passim* (on the last man); *WP* 55, 627, 708, 1062, 1066, 1067; and the discussion in §5.2.3, below. Against materialistic atomism, see *BGE* 12, 17; *WP* 624; and the discussion in §5.2.1, below. And against pantheism, see *GS* P:4 (the view that "God is everywhere" is precisely what the "de-deification of nature" sets out to reinterpret) and *WP* 55, 1062.

46. *GS* 357 makes this especially clear.

47. See *TI* "Socrates" 2: "Judgments, judgments of value, concerning life, for it or against it, can, in the end, never be true: in themselves such judgments are stupidities. One must by all means stretch out one's fingers and make the attempt to grasp this amazing finesse, *that the value of life cannot be estimated.* Not by the living, for they are an interested party, even a bone of contention, and not judges; not by the dead, for a different reason."

48. Nietzsche's advocacy of an interpretation in which "laws [. . .] are completely lacking" is, I think, nothing more than the advocacy of a thoroughly antiessentialist, antitheological view of the world and of ourselves. He asks only that we give up the strong, ontological notion of necessary laws inherent in nature or in the human mind, not that we give up the notion of "law" altogether. I do not see that he has trouble with the notion of "law" understood in a weaker sense, as describing a regularity or priority internal to a particular interpretation.

as many ways the world is as there are "perspectives and affective interpretations" (*GM* III:12). Even apparently antinaturalistic perspectives and interpretations are admissible, provided that they are reinterpreted as disguised naturalistic interpretations—as, for instance, expressions of an ascetic desire for the otherworldly.

2.4 THE CIRCLE OF NATURALISM AND INTERPRETATION

Let me summarize what I have argued thus far. The "death of God"—incredulity toward theological and metaphysical interpretations—enjoins us to give ourselves and our world a naturalistic reinterpretation. It asks that we stop seeing human beings as demi-Gods or as the center and goal of the universe and that we begin to see them as natural organisms who do not differ fundamentally from other natural organisms. It asks us to stop seeing human reason as a divine feature that provides access to the necessary, the universal, and the unconditional and to start thinking of it as a complex device for managing past, present, and future experience. The "death of God" also enjoins us to stop believing that there is some absolute point of view from which the world could be seen "as it really is." Instead, it tells us that "the way the world is" can only ever be determined by our various ongoing perspectives and interpretations, none of which is inherently unchangeable, and not all of which are of a piece or entirely consistent with one another. And it tells us that we can hope for no convergence of these perspectives, that no "absolute knowledge" is forthcoming. Finally, and coming full circle, Nietzsche's affirmation of the "death of God" asks that our interpretations do without theological entities and explanatory principles. It asks that we see ourselves as thoroughly enmeshed in a world that is contingent, conditional, temporal, and affective through and through, a world without absolute beginning, essence, purpose, or aim.

This naturalism yields Nietzsche's central epistemological and ontological doctrines: perspectivism, becoming, and will to power. With the doctrine of perspectivism, Nietzsche rejects the theological ideals of a God's-eye view and a pre-given world. He argues instead that there are only ever contingent perspectives (or interpretations) and the entities internal to them and that there is no absolute fact of the matter about which of these is uniquely correct. With the doctrines of becoming and will to power, however, Nietzsche gives his own naturalistic rendering

106   Nietzsche's Philosophical Position

of a world without the "shadows of God." Taken together, these doctrines tread between relativism and dogmatism without yielding to either extreme. The apparent relativism of perspectivism is held in check by Nietzsche's naturalism, which offers the doctrines of will to power and becoming in place of all theological interpretations; the apparent dogmatism of will to power and becoming is mitigated by perspectivism, which grants that will to power and becoming are themselves interpretations, yet ones that are better by naturalistic standards.

Of course Nietzsche grants that even his naturalism is an interpretation and not a matter of fact. He acknowledges that "God's death" is capable of being interpreted in a variety of ways (see GS 108, 125, 343; WP Book I).[49] Yet he maintains that his own naturalistic interpretation has "honesty" and "intellectual conscience" on its side, insofar as it takes up and pushes to the limit a centuries-old "will to truth" that finally forbids itself the lie involved in absolutist interpretations (see GS 344, 357; GM III:23–28; WP Book I). In short, Nietzsche grants that his view is itself an interpretation, which is all it could ever be; but he challenges objectors to come up with a better one. He is indeed committed to his naturalistic position yet well aware that it does not settle matters once and for all but only ushers in "new struggles" (GS 108)—which, like all struggles and contests, Nietzsche encouraged and relished.

Having presented this general picture of Nietzsche's epistemology and ontology, I can now provide a more thorough explication of his epistemological and ontological doctrines: perspectivism, becoming, and will to power.

---

49. For an elaboration of this point, see Gilles Deleuze, *Nietzsche and Philosophy,* trans. Hugh Tomlinson (New York: Columbia University Press, 1983), 152–59.

PART TWO

Nietzsche's Epistemological and Ontological Doctrines

CHAPTER THREE

Perspectivism

The Ubiquity Of Interpretation

Oh, the false oppositions: war *and* "**peace**"! reason and
passion! subject object!

> *Nietzsche, note from spring–fall 1881,*
> KSA 9:11[140]

3.1 IS THERE A DOCTRINE OF PERSPECTIVISM IN NIETZSCHE?

Any interpretation of Nietzsche's "perspectivism" confronts a peculiar
difficulty: the scarcity of explicit reference to the doctrine in Nietzsche's texts, published and unpublished. The term "perspectivism" appears in only a single passage in the published work: in *The Gay Science*
§354, where it is associated with "phenomenalism" but receives little
explanation and is not offered as a unique contribution. Even in the
large body of epistemological notes collected in *The Will to Power*—
where the German editors saw fit to employ the term in a section head-
ing (Third Book, I, d: "Biology of the Drive to Knowledge. Perspectivism")—"perspectivism" is mentioned only twice: in the oft-cited
§481 and in §636. Hence, one is led to wonder whether it is legitimate
to claim that perspectivism is a "doctrine" at all, let alone one central
to Nietzsche's work.

Despite this difficulty, I think there are good reasons for continuing to use the term "perspectivism" to describe a central feature of
Nietzsche's later work. There is, first of all, a strong critical precedent
for doing so: as already mentioned, the term was used as early as 1906
by the editors of *The Will to Power* to describe the later Nietzsche's
theory of knowledge; subsequently, it was taken up by Vaihinger in
1911, by Heidegger in the 1930s, by Morgan in the 1940s, by Danto in

the 1960s,[1] and by nearly every European and Anglo-American commentator since. More important, while Nietzsche rarely refers to "perspectivism" as a doctrine, the terms "perspective," "perspectival," and "perspectivity" do appear with considerable frequency in Nietzsche's later texts. Finally, and most significant, these terms appear in contexts that articulate something central and unique in the later Nietzsche: namely, the notion that all natural beings are inextricably caught up within a nexus of competing worldviews, each of which has its origin in particular physiological, psychological, historical, cultural, and political needs, desires, beliefs, and values.

In what follows, I explore this idea in detail. But a further proviso must still be added. While there are reasonable grounds for attributing to Nietzsche a "doctrine of perspectivism," this doctrine will always be a critical construct. That is, we must give up the desire, expressed by Daniel Conway, to distinguish between "Nietzsche's perspectivism" (the explication of "Nietzsche's position") and "Nietzschean perspectivism" (the delineation of "a position that he could [or should] have held in light of his other insights").[2] However one characterizes "Nietzsche's doctrine of perspectivism," that characterization will always be underdetermined by the textual evidence. All one can do is fill out the few comments concerning "perspectivism," "perspective," and "perspectivity" in light of their contexts and of Nietzsche's other central positions. Insofar as there are different conceptions of what those positions are and different interpretations of those contexts, there will also be different accounts of perspectivism.

This is not to say that all accounts of perspectivism will be equally valid or equally good. Indeed I will argue for an interpretation of perspectivism that I believe to be better than others. Nonetheless, it must be recognized that, in this situation, there are no "facts"—no transparent, doctrinal statements against which to measure interpretations. Interpretations of perspectivism can only be measured according to how well they articulate Nietzsche's remarks on "perspective" within a

1. Hans Vaihinger, "Nietzsche and His Doctrine of Conscious Illusion," in *Nietzsche: A Collection of Critical Essays,* ed. Robert C. Solomon (Notre Dame: University of Notre Dame Press, 1973), 94. Martin Heidegger, *Nietzsche,* vol. 3, *The Will to Power as Knowledge and as Metaphysics,* trans. Joan Stambaugh et al. (San Francisco: Harper, 1987), 199 and *passim.* George A. Morgan, *What Nietzsche Means* (New York: Harper and Row, 1941), 273 and *passim.* Arthur Danto, *Nietzsche as Philosopher* (New York: Columbia University Press, 1965), chap. 3.
2. Daniel W. Conway, "The Eyes Have It: Perspectives and Affective Investment," *International Studies in Philosophy* 23 (1991): 103.

whole that gives them a sense. As it turns out, this textual situation concerning perspectivism exemplifies what I take to be a central feature of the doctrine itself: the proposition that this holistic relationship of facts to interpretation, empirical evidence to system, part to whole obtains in every sphere of human inquiry—and beyond.

3.2 PERSPECTIVE AND AFFECTIVE INTERPRETATION

We have seen that foremost among Nietzsche's concerns is a naturalism, the epistemological and ontological consequences of which involve a rejection of the ideals of a God's-eye view and a pre-given world and a rejection of the distinction between appearance and the true world, reality, or the thing in itself. We must now try to offer an account of perspectivism that is faithful both to Nietzsche's explicit texts on the matter and to this thoroughgoing naturalism.

To begin this task, we must find some clue that connects Nietzsche's comments on "perspective" to this larger project. Such a clue appears, I think, in a notion that Nietzsche closely associates with "perspectivity": the notion of interpretation.[3] To indicate this connection, let us return to the famous passage on perspectivity from the *Genealogy of Morals,* paying close attention to the relationships between perspective and interpretation. Nietzsche writes:

> "[O]bjectivity" [ought to be] understood not as "contemplation without interest" (which is a nonsensical absurdity), but as the ability to have one's For and Against *under control* and to engage and disengage them, so that one knows how to employ a *variety* of perspectives and affective interpretations [*Perspectiven und Affect-Interpretationen*] in the service of knowledge. Henceforth, my dear philosophers, let us be on guard against the dangerous old conceptual fiction that posited a "pure, will-less, painless, timeless knowing subject"; let us guard against the snares of such contradictory concepts as "pure reason," "absolute spirit" [*«absolute Geistigkeit»*], "knowledge in itself": these always demand that we should think of an eye that is completely unthinkable, an eye turned in no particular direction, in which the active and interpreting forces [*die aktiven und interpretirenden Kräfte*], through which alone seeing becomes a seeing-something, are supposed to be

3. Nietzsche employs a variety of terms for "interpretation"/"to interpret." The most frequently used are *Interpretation/interpretieren* and *Auslegung/auslegen,* though *Ausdeutung/ausdeuten* and *Deutung/deuten* are relatively common, and *Umdeutung/umdeuten* ("reinterpretation"/"to reinterpret") is occasionally used as well. Yet Nietzsche does not appear to draw any significant denotative or connotative distinctions among these various terms. Different terms are used in strikingly similar contexts, often in the same passage. The choice of terminology appears to be stylistic rather than semantic.

lacking; these always demand of the eye an absurdity and a nonsense. There is *only* a perspective seeing [*ein perspektivisches Sehen*], *only* a perspective "knowing" [*ein perspektivisches «Erkennen»*]; and the *more* affects we allow to speak about a thing, the *more* eyes, different eyes, we can lend to the thing, the more complete will our "concept" of this thing, our "objectivity," be. But to eliminate the will altogether, to suspend each and every affect, supposing we were capable of this—what would that mean but to *castrate* the intellect? (III:12)

Here Nietzsche entwines the notion of "perspective" with the notion of "affective interpretation." He claims that a perspective is constituted and directed by a matrix of "active and interpreting forces" that allow something to appear *as* a particular something. A "perspective," then, would seem to be an ontological and evaluative horizon opened up by the operation of a particular "affective interpretation."[4]

Sifting through the various texts on perspectivity, one finds a number of passages in which the language of perspective is closely associated with the language of interpretation (e.g., GS 357, 374; WP 5, 556, 565, 590, 616, 617, 678, 804). In §357 of *The Gay Science,* for instance, Nietzsche alternately speaks of "the Christian interpretation" and "those Christian-ascetic moral perspectives." In §374 of the same text, he alternates between "perspective" and "interpretation" without differentiating between the two, at one point speaking of "the perspective character of existence," at another of "all existence" as "essentially an *interpreting* existence"; here of the possibility of many different "perspectives," there of the possibility of "*infinite interpretations.*" In a note from 1885–86, Nietzsche writes that "previous interpretations have been perspective evaluations by virtue of which we can survive in life" (*WP* 616). In a note from 1886–87, he refers, at one point, to "our perspective 'truths' which belong to us alone" and, at another, to "our human interpretations and values" (*WP* 565). Finally, in another note from 1886–87, the terms are so imbricated as to become indissociable:

> Whether the origin of our apparent "knowledge" is not to be sought solely in *older evaluations* which have become so much a part of us that they belong to our basic constitution? So that what really happens is only that *younger* needs grapple with the *results of the oldest needs?* The world seen, felt, interpreted [*ausgelegt*] as thus and thus so that organic life may preserve

4. See WP 616: "that every *elevation of man* brings with it the overcoming of narrower interpretations; that every strengthening and increase of power opens up new perspectives and means believing in new horizons—this idea permeates my writings." On the relation between horizons and perspectives, see Heidegger, *Nietzsche,* vol. 3, §§13, 19.

itself in this perspective of interpretation [*dieser Perspective von Auslegung*]. Man is *not* only a single individual but one particular line of the total organic world. That *he* endures proves that a species of interpretation [*eine Gattung von Interpretation*] (even though accretions are still being added) has also endured, that the system of interpretation [*das System von Interpretation*] has not changed. "Adaptation." Our "dissatisfaction," our "ideal," etc., is perhaps the *consequence* of this incorporated piece of interpretation, of our perspective point of view [*dieses einverleibten Stücks Interpretation, unseres perspektivischen Gesichtspunkts*]; perhaps organic life will in the end perish through it. (*WP* 678)

The evolutionary hypothesis proposed in this passage notwithstanding,[5] the close connection it draws between perspective and interpretation is highly important. The basic "needs" and "evaluations" of an organism are said to form an "incorporated" "system of interpretation" that gives the organism a particular "perspective point of view." "Perspectives," then, seem to be "outlooks" directed by "incorporated interpretations," which themselves are "systems of evaluation" made from the standpoint of particular "needs."

Indeed, one finds that the language of "interpretation" is more common and more significant in Nietzsche than the language of "perspective."[6] Virtually every sphere of human activity—from "morality," to "physics" and "natural science," to "rational thought" in general—is called, in one passage or another, an "interpretation."[7] Indeed, for Nietzsche, "interpretation" is present wherever there is "meaning" and "value" at all (see *GM* II:12; *WP* 590, 604–6, 616).

Given this, I want to suggest that commentators have been wrong to read Nietzsche's "perspective" language too rigidly (as describing the fixed bounds of a species' knowledge) and too literally or narrowly (as developing a simple analogy between seeing and knowing).[8] Instead,

5. Here, Nietzsche hypothesizes that the proper sphere of investigation concerning perspectives and interpretations is organic life as a whole. Elsewhere, he suggests that the proper sphere is that of the species (see *GS* 354, 374). Still elsewhere, he maintains that perspectives and interpretations are proper to intrahuman groups such as master and slave, Christian and Dionysian, etc. (see, e.g., *GM*). I will argue below that the best candidate is this third. For present purposes, suffice it to say that the passage under discussion is a hypothesis rather than a conclusion.

6. A search through the *KGW* CD-ROM reveals that "interpretation" terms (see n. 7) appear more than twice as often as "perspective" terms.

7. On morality as interpretation, see *GS* 357; *TI* "Improvers" 1; *WP* 1, 5, 114, 228, 254, 258, 270. On physics and natural science as interpretation, see *BGE* 14, 22; *WP* 682, 689. On rational thought as interpretation, see *WP* 522.

8. Heidegger and Mark Fowler also argue against the over-narrow construal of perspectivism as developing an ocular metaphor. Heidegger (*Nietzsche*, 3:197–98) writes:

I will argue that we should read Nietzsche's "perspective" language within the broader bounds of a general theory of interpretation.[9] Unlike the notion of "perspective"—which, literally construed, generates serious epistemological difficulties—[10] the notion of "interpretation" operates within a rich and increasingly important literary and philosophical tradition. Taking what has been called "the interpretive turn,"[11] philoso-

---

"The 'perspective' is never the mere angle of vision from which something is seen; rather, this perspectival vista looks toward 'conditions of preservation/enhancement.' As conditions, the 'viewpoints' posited in such 'seeing' are of such kind that they must be reckoned *on* and reckoned *with*. They take the form of 'numbers' and 'measures,' that is, values." Fowler ("Having a Perspective as Having a 'Will': Comment on Professor Conway's 'The Eyes Have It,'" *International Studies in Philosophy* 23 [1991]: 115) writes: "too often, Nietzsche's ocular metaphors continue to deceive if only by obscuring the centrality that affects have in his theory of perspectivism and, accordingly, what we need is a thorough reinvestigation of the question: What, on Nietzsche's theory, is a perspective?" Fowler goes on to suggest an account of "perspectivism" and "affect" that is very close to my own. See also Fowler, "Nietzschean Perspectivism: 'How Could Such a Philosophy Dominate?'" *Social Theory and Practice* 16 (1990): 119–62.

9. Alan D. Schrift, *Nietzsche and the Question of Interpretation: Between Hermeneutics and Deconstruction* (New York: Routledge, 1990), 145ff., also relates the notion of "perspective" to the notion of "interpretation" but draws a sharper distinction between the two notions and assigns them more definite roles. On Schrift's view, "perspectives" are relatively fixed physiological, instinctual, and sociohistorical outlooks, while "interpretations" are the various ways in which these "perspectives" can be organized and hierarchized. Nonetheless, Schrift grants that, "[o]n some level, this distinction will reveal itself to be merely heuristic" (p. 145).

10. David C. Hoy, "Philosophy as Rigorous Philology? Nietzsche and Poststructuralism," *New York Literary Forum* 8–9 (1981): 173, and "Nietzsche, Hume, and the Genealogical Method," in *Nietzsche as Affirmative Thinker*, ed. Yirmiyahu Yovel (Dordrecht: Martinus Nijhoff, 1986), 24ff., for instance, argues that Nietzsche's language of "perspective" runs into a host of problems and paradoxes and that it should be rejected in favor of the language of "interpretation." Narrowly and literally construed, the language of "perspective" is indeed problematic. However, I disagree with Hoy that Nietzsche's notion of "perspective" is to be taken in this literal sense and thus that the language of "perspective" is incompatible with the language of "interpretation." I am arguing here that Nietzsche construes the notion of "perspective" so broadly that it merges with the notion of "interpretation." Elsewhere, in an explication of Gadamer's hermeneutics, Hoy makes a connection between perspective and interpretation that is quite similar to the one I am urging with regard to Nietzsche. He writes (*The Critical Circle: Literature, History, and Philosophical Hermeneutics* [Berkeley: University of California Press, 1978], 51–52): "'Alles Verstehen ist Auslegung,' insists Gadamer repeatedly [. . .]; all understanding includes interpretation. This point follows from the necessary situatedness (*Situationsgebundenheit*) of understanding. Because an understanding is rooted in a situation, it represents a point of view, a perspective, on what it represents. There is no absolute, aperspectival standpoint [. . .] from which to see all possible perspectives."

11. On "the interpretive turn," see Paul Rabinow and William M. Sullivan, "The Interpretive Turn: Emergence of an Approach," in *Interpretive Social Science*, eds. Rabinow and Sullivan (Berkeley: University of California Press, 1979); David Hiley et al., eds., *The Interpretive Turn: Philosophy, Science, Culture* (Ithaca: Cornell University Press, 1991); and David C. Hoy, "Heidegger and the Hermeneutic Turn," in *The Cambridge Companion to Heidegger,* ed. Charles Guignon (Cambridge: Cambridge University Press, 1993). Prominent figures associated with this "turn" include Martin Heidegger, Hans-Georg

phers in both the "Continental" and "analytic" traditions have come to argue that our knowledge is not an edifice built upon a foundation of indubitable beliefs but rather an interpretive web of mutually supporting beliefs and desires that is constantly being rewoven.[12] These philosophers maintain that we are always already immersed in a world full of significances that we pre-theoretically understand and that the role of epistemology is to discover how particular sensory experiences, beliefs, and desires relate to our understanding as a whole, and vice versa.

I argued in the previous chapter that Nietzsche agrees with this turn from foundationalism to holism and the concomitant turn from first philosophy to naturalism. We have just seen that Nietzsche conceives of the understanding as always directed by one or another "interpretation," each of which opens up a particular horizon of meaning and value. He goes on to propose that the world in which we find ourselves is a world of struggle and that this struggle is among interpretations, each of which seeks to overwhelm [*überwältigen, überwinden*] others by incorporating their terms into its own and articulating these terms according to its own system. This is how "interpretation" is characterized in an important passage from the *Genealogy of Morals*. Discussing

---

Gadamer, Thomas Kuhn, W. V. Quine, Donald Davidson, Hilary Putnam, Richard Rorty, Charles Taylor, Jacques Derrida, Michel Foucault, and Paul Ricouer.

12. The most succinct statement of this view, articulated from a standpoint between hermeneutics and Quinean analytic philosophy, is Richard Rorty, "Inquiry as Recontextualization: An Anti-Dualist Account of Interpretation," in *Objectivity, Relativism, and Truth: Philosophical Papers*, vol. 1 (Cambridge: Cambridge University Press, 1991). Also see Heidegger, *Being and Time*, trans. John Macquarrie and Edward Robinson (New York: Harper and Row, 1962), esp. §§31–33: Hans-Georg Gadamer, *Truth and Method*, 2d ed., trans. John Cumming and Garrett Barden (New York: Continuum, 1989), esp. 345–66: W. V. Quine, *Word and Object* (Cambridge, Mass.: MIT Press, 1960), chap. 2, and "Ontological Relativity," in *Ontological Relativity and Other Essays* (New York: Columbia University Press, 1969); Donald Davidson, "Radical Interpretation," in *Inquiries into Truth and Interpretation* (Oxford: Clarendon Press, 1984); Nelson Goodman, *Languages of Art*, 2d ed. (Indianapolis: Hackett, 1976) and *Ways of Worldmaking* (Indianapolis, Hackett, 1978); and Goodman and Catherine Z. Elgin, *Reconceptions in Philosophy and Other Arts and Sciences* (Indianapolis: Hackett, 1988). On the connection between hermeneutics and the Quinean strand of analytic philosophy, see Richard Rorty, *Philosophy and the Mirror of Nature* (Princeton: Princeton University Press, 1979), chaps. 4–8; Richard J. Bernstein, *Beyond Objectivism and Relativism: Science, Hermeneutics, and Praxis* (Philadelphia: University of Pennsylvania Press, 1983); Joseph Rouse, *Knowledge and Power: Toward a Political Philosophy of Science* (Ithaca: Cornell University Press, 1987), chap. 3; Bjørn Ramberg, *Donald Davidson's Philosophy of Language: An Introduction* (Oxford: Basil Blackwell, 1989), chaps. 9–10; J. E. Malpas, *Donald Davidson and the Mirror of Meaning: Holism, Truth, Interpretation* (Cambridge: Cambridge University Press, 1992); and David C. Hoy, "Post-Cartesian Interpretation: Hans-Georg Gadamer and Donald Davidson," in *The Philosophy of Hans-Georg Gadamer*, ed. Lewis Hahn (La Salle, Ill.: Open Court, 1997).

the idea of punishment, Nietzsche pauses to "emphasize [a] major point of historical method"—to distinguish the *origin* of something from its current *purpose*. He writes:

> [T]he cause of the origin of a thing and its eventual utility, its actual employment and place in a system of purposes, lie worlds apart; whatever exists, having somehow come into being, is again and again reinterpreted to new ends [*auf neue Ansichten ausgelegt*], taken over, transformed, and redirected by some power superior to it; all events in the organic world are a *subduing, becoming master* [*ein* Überwältigen, Herrwerden], and all subduing and becoming master involves a fresh interpretation [*ein Neu-Interpretieren*], an adjustment through which any previous "meaning" and "purpose" are necessarily obscured or even obliterated. However well one has understood the *utility* of a physiological organ (or of a legal institution, a social custom, a political usage, a form in art or in a religious cult), this means nothing regarding its origin. [. . . P]urposes and utilities are only *signs* that a will to power has become master of something less powerful and imposed upon it the character of a function; and the entire history of a "thing," an organ, a custom can in this way be a continuous sign-chain of ever new interpretations [*Interpretationen*] and adaptations whose causes do not even have to be related to one another but, on the contrary, in some cases succeed and alternate with one another in purely chance fashion. The "evolution" of a thing, a custom, an organ is thus by no means its *progressus* toward a goal, even less a logical *progressus* by the shortest route and with the smallest expenditure of force—but the succession of more or less profound, more or less mutually independent processes of subduing [*Überwältigungsprozessen*], plus the resistances they encounter, the attempts at transformation for the purpose of defense and reaction, and the results of successful counteractions. The form is fluid, but the "meaning" is even more so. (*GM* II:12; cf. *GS* 58, *WP* 556, 604, 643, 616)

What is particularly striking in this passage is that what Nietzsche calls "interpretation" extends far beyond what the term ordinarily signifies. He claims that "all events in the organic world" and, indeed, "whatever exists" essentially involves interpretation and that this involvement concerns not only their *apprehension by subjects* but their *very constitution as objects or events*. At the end of the section from which this passage is cited, Nietzsche goes so far as to identify "interpretation" with "the essence of life, its *will to power*, [. . .] the essential priority of the spontaneous, aggressive, expansive, form-giving forces that give new interpretations and directions [*die . . . neu-ausgelegenden, neu-richtenden und gestaltenden Kräfte*]" (cf. *BGE* 259 and *WP* 643). Nietzsche is arguing that "thinghood," "eventhood," "history," "development," and "evolution" are, at bottom, only manifestations of "will to power," the incessant drive for interpretation and reinterpretation, forming and reforming; and that the very origin, history, and growth of "a 'thing'" (whether it be an object, practice, or institution) should be seen as the consequence of its role in a struggle among interpretations, each of which is "aggressive" and "expansive," seeking to increase power and control over its environment.

This same generalization and extension of meaning can also be found in Nietzsche's language of "perspective." Rather than functioning simply as an optical analog, Nietzsche calls upon the term "perspective" to characterize something about life in general—"the perspective optics *of life,*" he puts it in *Beyond Good and Evil* (11, my emphasis). Elsewhere in that text, he speaks of "perspective" as "the basic condition of all life" (preface), claiming that "there would be no life at all if not on the basis of perspective estimates and appearances" (34) and that "the *narrowing of our perspective* [. . . is] a condition of life and growth" (188).

We see, then, that Nietzsche's "perspective" language is quite peculiar and ought not to be taken at face value. Not only is the language of "perspective" subsumed under the broader language of "interpretation," but both "perspective" and "interpretation" are generalized far beyond their ordinary senses. "Perspective," for Nietzsche, comes to characterize a particular form of life's[13] directedness toward the conditions that preserve and enhance it, conditions that are codified in the "interpretation" that directs the perspective.[14]

This can serve as a rough characterization of the notions of "perspective" and "interpretation" as Nietzsche uses them. Yet many questions still remain. Two sets of questions, in particular, present them-

---

13. This Wittgensteinian phrase is felicitous precisely because of its flexibility. It is loose enough to capture the entire range of systems of valuation that Nietzsche considers important (e.g., active and reactive, ascending and descending, weakness and strength, master and slave, Dionysian and Christian, etc.) while refusing to identify perspectives with either the private points of view of individuals or the fixed physico-psychological schemas of biological species. I note that this phrase has circulated in previous discussions of Nietzsche's epistemology. See Tracy B. Strong, *Friedrich Nietzsche and the Politics of Transfiguration,* exp. ed. (Berkeley: University of California Press, 1988), 45, 79ff.; Richard Schacht, *Nietzsche* (London: Routledge and Kegan Paul, 1983), 63; and Alexander Nehamas, *Nietzsche: Life as Literature* (Cambridge, Mass.: Harvard University Press, 1985), 52. The term has also been employed by Bernd Magnus in a discussion of Nietzsche's *Übermensch,* "Nietzsche's Philosophy in 1888: *The Will to Power* and the *Übermensch,*" *Journal of the History of Philosophy* 24 (1986): 95.

14. For a somewhat similar assessment, see Martin Heidegger, "The Word of Nietzsche: 'God is Dead,'" *The Question Concerning Technology and Other Essays,* trans. William Lovitt (New York: Harper and Row, 1977), 71.

selves and demand answers. On the one hand, we are led to ask about
the *subject* of perspectives and interpretations: *who* or *what* is it that
has perspectives and interpretations? On the other hand, we are led to
ask about the *object* of perspectives and interpretations: what are these
interpretations *of* or perspectives *on*? Answering these questions will
allow us to fill out the schematic characterization of perspectivism
presented above. Before turning to Nietzsche's texts, I want first to
consider some previous and, I believe, inadequate answers to these
questions.

3.3 THE "SUBJECT" OF PERSPECTIVISM

3.3.1 TWO RECENT ACCOUNTS

It has become common, in Nietzsche scholarship, to view Nietzsche's
epistemological position as a modified version of Kant's.[15] According to
one such account (what, for reasons that will become clear, I call the
skeptical neo-Kantian account), Nietzsche accepts Kant's phenomenalism or idealism but gives it an evolutionary rather than a transcendental deduction. That is, what Kant takes to be logically and conceptually

---

15. This view was proposed early on by Vaihinger, "Nietzsche and His Doctrine of
Conscious Illusion," 84, and has gained currency in recent years. It has been suggested,
asserted, or argued for by Walter Kaufmann, *Nietzsche: Philosopher, Psychologist, Anti-
Christ*, 4th ed. (Princeton: Princeton University Press, 1974), 205ff.; Rüdiger Grimm,
Nietzsche's Theory of Knowledge (Berlin: Walter de Gruyter, 1977), 53 and *passim*;
George J. Stack, "Nietzsche's Critique of Things-in-Themselves," *Dialogos* 36 (1980): 48,
"Nietzsche and the Correspondence Theory of Truth," *Dialogos* 38 (1981): 108, "Nietz-
sche's Evolutionary Epistemology," *Dialogos* 59 (1992): 75–101; Bernd Magnus, "Nietz-
sche and the Project of Bringing Philosophy to an End," in *Nietzsche as Affirmative
Thinker*, ed. Yovel, 52; Schacht, *Nietzsche*, 62, 83, 139, "Nietzsche's *Gay Science*, Or,
How to Naturalize Cheerfully," in *Reading Nietzsche*, ed. Robert C. Solomon and Kath-
leen Higgins (New York: Oxford University Press, 1988), 79; Eric Blondel, *Nietzsche:
The Body and Culture*, trans. Seán Hand (Stanford: Stanford University Press, 1991),
98ff.; Steven G. Crowell, "Nietzsche's View of Truth." *International Studies in Philosophy* 19 (1987): 17 n. 2; Nicholas Davey, "Nietzsche and Hume on Self and Identity,"
Journal of the British Society for Phenomenology 18 (1987): 20–21; Daniel W. Conway,
"Beyond Realism: Nietzsche's New Infinite." *International Studies in Philosophy* 22
(1990): 99ff.; Maudemarie Clark, *Nietzsche on Truth and Philosophy* (Cambridge: Cambridge University Press, 1990), 121 and *passim*; Brian Leiter, "Perspectivism in Nietzsche's *Genealogy of Morals*," in *Nietzsche, Genealogy, Morality: Essays on Nietzsche's
Genealogy of Morals*, ed. Richard Schacht (Berkeley: University of California Press, 1994),
351; Stephen Houlgate, "Kant, Nietzsche, and the 'Thing in itself,'" *Nietzsche-Studien* 22
(1993): 132, 148, and *passim*; and Babette E. Babich, *Nietzsche's Philosophy of Science:
Reflecting Science on the Ground of Art and Life* (Albany: State University of New York
Press, 1994), 2–3, 77–78, 85, 90, 95. This view is also implicit, I think, in the distinction
between perspectival appearance and the unknowable world "in itself" assumed by Danto,
Nietzsche as Philosopher, 96, and Bernd Magnus, *Nietzsche's Existential Imperative*
(Bloomington: Indiana University Press, 1978), 26ff.

a priori, Nietzsche, following the neo-Kantian F. A. Lange, sees as having only an evolutionary priority. What Kant argues is necessary and universal for rational thought and experience, Nietzsche views as the contingent product of a particular "physico-psychological organization," itself a result of the natural selection of traits that have proven their practical value for the survival of the species.[16] Due to their different "physico-psychological" constitutions and organizations, different species can be supposed to have different "perspectives."[17] On this view, then, the proper subjects of perspectives are biological species.

It is certainly the case that Nietzsche's "perspective" language most frequently appears in contexts that discuss the conditions necessary for particular species (often, human beings) to preserve themselves and to enhance their power (see, e.g., BGE P, 11, 34, 188; WP 259, 293, 616, 678, 789, 904). Yet the interpretation of perspectivism generated by this account commits Nietzsche to a position that, I believe, he does not accept: the skeptical position that every species is in principle unable to apprehend the world as it is in itself and the world as it is apprehended by other species.[18] Nietzsche does not seem to believe, for example, that there is anything like a specifically *human* perspective, a unified and coherent totality rigorously differentiable from the "perspectives" of other species. First of all, Nietzsche's naturalism commits him to regard all living beings as, in fundamental respects, similar. He claims, for instance, that the human process of cognition is only a more complex and specialized form of the process of ingestion (or "incorporation" or "assimilation") found in the protoplasm (see WP 500, 501, 510, 511, 654, 666; also see §5.3, below). Indeed, a central theme of Nietzsche's later work is that knowledge is only a form of will to power, the drive to incorporate and subdue found in all organisms and species (see BGE 13, 36; GM II:12; WP 466–617). Second, Nietzsche argues that the human species itself does not have a unified worldview but rather is

16. See Stack, "Nietzsche's Critique of Things-in-Themselves," 33–35. This reading draws on passages such as GS 110, 354, and 374.

17. See Stack, "Kant, Lange, and Nietzsche: Critique of Knowledge," *Nietzsche and Modern German Thought,* ed. Keith Ansell-Pearson (London: Routledge, 1991), 44–45, and GS 374.

18. The more general Kantian metaphysical realism implicit in this account is rejected by Nietzsche's harsh critique of dualism and the notion of the thing in itself. See, e.g., GS 54, 354; TI "Socrates" 2, "Reason" 6, "World" 6; WP 552, 567. This argument against metaphysical realism is presented more fully in chapter 4, below. For a powerful argument against the species interpretation of perspectivism, see Alexander Nehamas, "Immanent and Transcendent Perspectivism in Nietzsche," *Nietzsche-Studien* 12 (1983): 473–94.

divided into a host of antagonistic "perspectives" or "interpretations": e.g., master and slave, Dionysian and Christian, Homeric and Platonic, Roman and Judaic, Goethean and Kantian, and various hybrids of these.[19] Such differences of perspective, for Nietzsche, are not simply minor differences of opinion; on the contrary, they designate significantly different modes of perception, desire, cognition, evaluation, and action that compose different forms of life.

Thus, rather than demarcating insurmountable divisions between species, perspectives mark both extra- and intraspecies differences and similarities. According to Nietzsche, the biological field is crossed by a continuum of perspectives, none of which is in principle disjoint from another but each of which can be shown to differ from others in important respects and to significant degrees.[20] The subject of perspectivism, then, must be something other than biological species.

This conclusion is shared by another recent interpretation (what I call the realist neo-Kantian account of perspectivism) that is explicitly "neo-Kantian" while rejecting the skepticism inherent in the species view.[21] Instead, it construes perspectivism as a doctrine limited to the description of human knowledge. Claiming that the doctrine simply draws an analogy between a commonsense conception of human vision and a commonsense conception of human knowing, this account maintains that the subject of perspectivism is simply the ordinary, individual, human viewer/knower.

Brian Leiter, for example, begins from the obvious premises that "necessarily, we see an object from a particular perspective: e.g., from a certain angle, from a certain distance, under certain conditions," and "the more perspectives we enjoy—the more angles we see the ob-

19. On master vs. slave, see *BGE* 260 and *GM* I. On Dionysian vs. Christian, see *EH* "Destiny" 9 and *WP* 1051 and 1052. On Homeric vs. Platonic, see *GM* III:25. On Roman vs. Judaic, see *GM* I:16. On Goethean and Kantian, see *TI* "Skirmishes" 49. On the various hybrids of these, see *GM* I:16 and *BGE* 260, and 200. In the oft-cited *GM* III:12, Nietzsche argues that we should learn to inhabit "a *variety* of perspectives and affective interpretations in the service of knowledge"—which certainly seems to argue against the view that we inhabit only some unified "human" perspective. See *WP* 339: "This mankind is not a whole: it is an inextricable multiplicity of ascending and descending life-processes [. . .] the strata are twisted and entwined together." Cf. Morgan, *What Nietzsche Means*, 261: "Nietzsche holds not only that there are countless varieties of perspectives for countless forms of living process, but also that we human beings inhabit, not one, but a veritable nest of perspectives."

20. For a more detailed argument to this effect, see Nehamas, "Immanent and Transcendent Perspectivism in Nietzsche," 476–77.

21. Prominent proponents of this view are Clark, *Nietzsche on Truth and Philosophy,* and Leiter, "Perspectivism in Nietzsche's *Genealogy of Morals.*"

ject from—the better our conception of what the object is actually like will be." [22] He goes on to argue by analogy that "necessarily, we know an object from a particular perspective: i.e. from the standpoint of particular interests and needs," and that "the more perspectives we enjoy— the more interests we employ in knowing the object—the better our conception of what the object is like will be." [23] His argument concludes that, contrary to an overzealous skepticism, "we do indeed have knowledge of the world, though it is never disinterested, never complete, and can always benefit from additional non-distorting [cognitive] perspectives." [24]

According to this account, then, just as there is no visual perspective that in principle is unavailable to us, so too is there no knowledge that in principle escapes our grasp. Unlike the skeptical account, this realist account has the merit of acknowledging Nietzsche's claim that we can and do have access to other perspectives. It suggests that, just as we can gain a new visual perspective on an object of vision by changing our position relative to it, so too can we gain different cognitive perspectives on an object of knowledge by bringing different sets of cognitive interests to bear upon it. Moreover, insofar as it grants the interest-ladenness of all inquiry, it suggests that we might come to appreciate and acknowledge the legitimacy of perspectival interests other than our own, even if we ourselves do not share them. [25]

Yet this construal of the subject of perspectivism also runs into difficulties. Foremost among these, I think, is its assumption of a *pre-given subject* who *has* perspectives or interpretations. According to the commonsense account of vision called upon by this realist interpretation, when I move around an object, there is a change of perspective but no change of subject; it is the *same I* that takes up *different perspectives*. Perspectives are cumulative and thus, too, is knowledge. While I cannot simultaneously inhabit different perspectives, I nonetheless can take up

22. Leiter, "Perspectivism in Nietzsche's *Genealogy of Morals*," 344. Leiter draws on Clark, whose presentation of this view is more fully elaborated. I draw on Leiter's presentation, because it is more concise and schematic yet, in important respects, the same as that of Clark.
23. Ibid., 345.
24. Ibid., 346. Cf. Clark, *Nietzsche on Truth and Philosophy*, 134–35.
25. Leiter ("Perspectivism in Nietzsche's *Genealogy of Morals*," 345–46) says that "there are an infinity of interpretive interests that could be brought to bear" on the object of knowledge. Similarly, Clark (*Nietzsche on Truth and Philosophy*, 135) writes: "We are, after all, finite creatures with a limited amount of time to discover truths, whereas there are surely an infinite number of truths to discover. We should therefore expect people with different interests to discover different truths."

consecutively a number of different perspectives on the same object and thus gain a richer visual sense of it. The situation is analogous in the cognitive case, according to the realist account. It holds that, although our knowledge is always "interested," we can bring a variety of "cognitive interests" to bear upon an object and thus come to know it better. Once again, across these different sets of "cognitive interests," there is a central, stable subject who consecutively occupies these different sets of interests and thus accumulates a more complete knowledge of the object on which these interests are brought to bear.

This view does, of course, receive some support from the passage privileged by its advocates. After all, in that passage, Nietzsche claims that "There is *only* a perspective seeing, *only* a perspective 'knowing'; and the *more* affects we allow to speak about a thing, the *more* eyes, different eyes, we can use to observe the thing, the more complete will our 'concept' of this thing, our 'objectivity,' be" (*GM* III:12).[26] This certainly lends some credence to the notion of perspective accumulation proposed by the realist account. Yet this account too narrowly focuses on this passage and, more specifically, on the optical analogy presented in it, to the neglect of more important features of the passage and Nietzsche's other central concerns. As I have indicated, it neglects to discuss the explicit connection between perspective and interpretation developed in this passage, a connection that we have seen to be fundamental to an understanding of perspectivism.[27] Furthermore—and more important for the present discussion—it fails to account for another central feature of Nietzsche's later work: his critique of the notion of a pre-given subject—what he calls "ego-substance" (*TI* "Reason" 5).

3.3.2 NIETZSCHE'S CRITIQUE OF "EGO-SUBSTANCE"

A critique of the notion of mental- or subject-substance is found throughout Nietzsche's later work. Though, like many of Nietzsche's

26. For Leiter ("Perspectivism in Nietzsche's *Genealogy of Morals*," 343), this is "[t]he primary text in [Nietzsche's] mature work in which he does offer a sustained discussion of [perspectives and perspectivism] in an epistemological context," while, for Clark (*Nietzsche on Truth and Philosophy*, 128), this passage is "the only statement of Nietzsche's perspectivism in [the mature works]."

27. Leiter ("Perspectivism in Nietzsche's *Genealogy of Morals*," 343) notes that "Nietzsche uses the language of 'interpretation' freely throughout the material published during his lifetime [while] discussions of 'perspectivism' and 'perspectives' are far less frequent." Yet Leiter proceeds to discuss perspectivism without reference to the notion of interpretation.

major ideas, it is never developed at length, this critique appears in much the same form in *Beyond Good and Evil*, the *Genealogy of Morals*, *Twilight of the Idols*, and the later *Nachlaß* (see, e.g., *BGE* 12, 16, 17, 19, 34, 54; *GM* I:13; *TI* "Reason" 5, "Errors" 3; *WP* 229, 370, 477, 481–92, 531, 545–53, 631–32). Not surprisingly, the critique of ego-substance is a result of Nietzsche naturalism, which is both antimetaphysical (against the posit of any otherworldly entity or explanatory principle) and holistic (against every absolute foundation or origin). Thus, Nietzsche considers theological the belief that there is some "being" or subject-substratum "behind doing, effecting, becoming" (*GM* I:13). To assume such a being is to posit an otherworldly entity that initiates or produces the happenings, effects, and appearances that constitute the natural world while remaining outside that world, unchanged by its contingencies and exigencies (see *TI* "Reason" 5, "Errors" 3; *WP* 487). The notion of ego-substance is also a form of the "myth of the given," what Nietzsche calls the myth of "immediate certainties," those simple, atomic unities that are supposed to serve as the absolute foundation of all being and knowing.[28] Nietzsche's naturalism rejects the idea that there is any entity that is not essentially dependent upon other entities for its genesis and continued existence and the idea that there is any fundamental, obvious "fact" that need not justify itself by relation to other "facts." For, according to Nietzsche, there are "facts" only against the background of a particular interpretation, and the only entities that exist are natural, that is, essentially relational and contingent, entities (see *WP* 481; *BGE* 34; and *GM* I:13). Thus, in rejecting the foundational presuppositions of "materialistic atomism," Nietzsche also rejects what he calls "*soul atomism* [. . .], the belief which regards the soul as something indestructible, eternal, indivisible, as a monad, as an *atomon*" (*BGE* 12). Such an idea, he claims, is not only super-natural but also fails to account satisfactorily for important features of human psychology, which reveals the human subject to be an amalgamation of competing impulses and drives rather than an atomic unity.[29]

As Nietzsche himself acknowledges, this critique of mental substance

28. See *BGE* 16, 17, 19, 34. Other "immediate certainties" repudiated by Nietzsche are God, the thing in itself, substance, and cause.

29. True to his naturalism, Nietzsche regards psychology as "the queen of the sciences," "the path to the fundamental problems" (*BGE* 23), against the Kantian view that claims this role for epistemology and metaphysics.

stems from the critique of that notion by Hume and Kant.[30] Following Hume, Kant argues that, because the subject or self is not discoverable among the contents of experience, some other justification must be sought for its postulation. Nietzsche takes up this line of thought in *Beyond Good and Evil* §54. For Nietzsche, as for Hume and Kant, we only ever experience discrete impressions, actions, and effects but never the "subject" that is supposed to have those impressions or initiate those actions and effects.[31] Yet whereas Kant came to regard the notion of the self as a formal requirement of reason and to posit the antinaturalistic notions of noumenal self and noumenal causality, Nietzsche comes to regard the self as merely a grammatical habit that supports a moral fiction. For the radically empiricist Nietzsche—who maintains neither Kant's distinctions between intuition, understanding, and reason nor Kant's conviction that practical reason must be taken for granted and its postulates deduced—we have justification only for belief in actions, effects, doings, becomings, and appearances; and it is only a "seduction of language" that leads us to posit a "'being' behind doing, effecting, becoming; 'the doer' is merely a fiction added to the deed—the deed is everything" (*GM* I:13).[32] Furthermore, this linguistic habit serves the Christian, moral purpose of making some isolable thing (i.e., a specific subject) *responsible* and *accountable* for these actions and deeds. The separation of doer from deed, the subsequent removal of this doer from the conditioned and contingent world of effects and happenings, and, finally, the ascription of a "free will" to this subject serve to isolate some being as responsible for every eventuality and to claim that this being was free to do otherwise.[33]

Of course Nietzsche also criticizes determinism, the notion of an "unfree will" (*BGE* 21). But this is not the place to delve into what

---

30. On Kant, see *BGE* 54. Hume is certainly the precursor to Nietzsche's critique of metaphysical conceptions of causality and the self, a fact that Nietzsche seems briefly to acknowledge in *WP* 550. For more comparison between Hume's and Nietzsche's critiques of the self, see Davey, "Nietzsche and Hume on Self and Identity." For a comparison between Nietzsche's and Kant's critiques of the self, see Schacht, *Nietzsche*, 138–40.

31. For Kant on the phenomenality of "inner sense," see *Critique of Pure Reason*, trans. Norman Kemp Smith (New York: St. Martin's Press, 1929), 87–88, 165–69; for Nietzsche on the "phenomenality of the inner world," see *WP* 477, 479.

32. For more on our metaphysical seduction by the subject-predicate form, see *BGE* 16, 17, 19, 34, 54; *TI* "Reason" 5; *WP* 482, 484.

33. See *BGE* 21, 219; *GM* I:13; *TI* "Reason" 5, "Morality" 6, "Errors" 3, 7–8. According to Nietzsche, human decisions and actions should not be viewed as the result of a detached "free will" possessed by every human being. Rather, they are to be seen as the results of a struggle among competing instincts, drives and desires. On this, see *A* 14.

would need to be a lengthy discussion of Nietzsche's philosophy of mind and moral theory. I simply want to indicate that a critique of the notion of a pre-given subject-substratum is basic to Nietzsche's naturalism. The point is that to assume the existence of a "free will" behind every action is to assert that the source of the contingent and the conditional is something given and unconditioned, in short, something unworldly. According to Nietzsche, this scenario "deprives becoming of its innocence"—and it is the primary goal of Nietzsche's naturalism to restore the "innocence of becoming." [34]

3.3.3 NIETZSCHE'S CONCEPTION OF SUBJECTIVITY: "THE SUBJECT AS MULTIPLICITY"

This does not mean, however, that we should alter the subject-predicate structure of our grammar or that we should completely do away with the notion of "subject" (or "soul" or "ego" or "will").[35] "Between ourselves," Nietzsche writes:

> it is not at all necessary to get rid of "the soul" [. . .] and thus to renounce one of the most ancient and venerable hypotheses—as happens frequently to many clumsy naturalists who can hardly touch on "the soul" without immediately losing it. But the way is open for new versions and refinements of the soul-hypothesis; and such conceptions as "mortal soul," "soul as subjective multiplicity," and "soul as social structure of the drives and affects," want henceforth to have citizens' rights in science. (*BGE* 12; cf. *AOM* 17; *D* 501; *WP* 490)

Thus, Nietzsche's rejection of the notion of subject as unmoved mover, *causa sui, causa prima,* or soul atom leads him to construct an alterna-

34. See Z:3 "Before Sunrise"; TI "Errors" 7–8; WP 552, 787. Nietzsche's relatively few, and always enigmatic, comments concerning free will and determinism might be further elaborated by comparing them with Heidegger's much more substantial discussion of being-in-the-world as a rejection of the Cartesian "worldless subject." See Heidegger's *Being and Time* and the discussion of these issues by Charles Guignon, *Heidegger and the Problem of Knowledge* (Indianapolis: Hackett, 1983), 85, and Hubert L. Dreyfus, *Being-in-the-World: A Commentary on* Being and Time, *Division I* (Cambridge, Mass.: MIT Press, 1990).

35. The terms "subject," "soul," "ego," and "will" are used more or less interchangeably by Nietzsche. He alternately speaks of the soul-atom (*BGE* 12), the subject-atom (*GM* I:13; *WP* 488, 636), and the ego-atom (*BGE* 17; *WP* 635), "the soul as subjective multiplicity" (*BGE* 12), and "the subject as multiplicity" (*WP* 490; cf. *WP* 492). In various passages, he identifies "soul" and "subject" (*WP* 485), the "I" and "the will" (*BGE* 19), "doer," "will," and "ego" (*TI* "Reason" 5), "subject," "ego," and "doer" (*WP* 488). It should be noted that what is often translated as "the ego" is, in German, simply *das Ich,* "the I."

tive theory of subjectivity. Following a recurrent strategy, he begins by reversing our common linguistic and philosophical habits, arguing that what is primary are actions, deeds, accidents, and becomings rather than subjects, doers, substances, or beings.[36] A naturalistic theory, Nietzsche contends, must start from these former and construct the latter out of them rather than vice versa. Hence, just as Nietzsche comes to conceive of "a thing" as "the sum of its effects" (*WP* 551), so, too, does he come to conceive of the subject as the sum of its actions and passions.

Nietzsche's initial premise is that the natural world in which we are situated and that we observe is, first and foremost, a world of becoming, that is, a world of myriad actions, happenings, effects, and appearances. Yet we can and do individuate this becoming into particular sets or assemblages. The subject, Nietzsche argues, is just such an assemblage. Subjectivity in general is characterized by a specific set of activities and appearances; and each particular subject is individuated by a peculiar subset of those activities, by a disposition to act in a particular manner and direction: " 'the subject' " he writes, "is [. . .] a created entity [. . .] a capacity [. . .]—fundamentally, action collectively considered with respect to all anticipated actions (action and the probability of similar actions)" (*WP* 556; cf. *WP* 485).

Yet, for Nietzsche, the subject is only a *relative* unity. The unity of the subject is that of a *disposition,* merely a probability that groups together a range of more or less similar and more or less connected activities for the purpose of simplification and calculation.[37] Subjects, Nietzsche tells us, are irreducible multiplicities.[38] The disposition that

36. This conception is developed more fully by the twentieth-century French Nietzschean Gilles Deleuze, for whom the empirical individual is a "concentration, accumulation, coincidence of a certain number of converging preindividual singularities" (*The Fold: Leibniz and the Baroque,* trans. Tom Conley [Minneapolis: University of Minnesota Press, 1993], 63), also called "pure events" or "pure becomings" (*The Logic of Sense,* ed. Constantin V. Boundas, trans. Mark Lester and Charles Stivale [New York: Columbia University Press, 1990]).

37. See *WP* 561: "All unity is unity *only as organization and co-operation:* no differently than a human community is a unity—as opposed to an atomistic anarchy; it is a *pattern of domination* that *signifies* a unity but *is* not a unity." Cf. *WP* 490.

38. See *BGE* 12, 19; *WP* 488–92, 636, 660. This Nietzschean conception of subjectivity has been advocated more recently by Gilles Deleuze and Michel Foucault. See Foucault and Deleuze, "Intellectuals and Power," *Language, Counter-Memory, Practice: Selected Essays and Interviews by Michel Foucault,* ed. Donald F. Bouchard, trans. Donald F. Bouchard and Sherry Simon (Ithaca: Cornell University Press, 1977), 206, and Foucault, "The Confession of the Flesh," trans. Colin Gordon, in *Power/Knowledge: Selected Interviews and Other Writings, 1972–1977,* ed. Colin Gordon (New York: Pantheon, 1980), 208.

composes them is itself made up of microdispositions—what Nietz-sche variously calls "drives" (*Triebe*), "desires" (*Begierden*), "instincts" (*Instinkte*), "powers" (*Mächte*), "forces" (*Kräfte*), "impulses" (*Reize, Impulse*), "passions" (*Leidenschaften*), "feelings" (*Gefühlen*), "affects" (*Affekte*), pathos (*Pathos*), and so on. Starting from the premise that there are, first and foremost, actions, becomings, and appearances, Nietz-sche posits "affects"[39] as the interior states that help to explain and pre-dict these actions, becomings, and appearances.[40]

These affects are as close as one comes to a "bottom floor" in Nietz-sche's multileveled theory of subjectivity. With this hypothesis, he would seem to be arguing that the subject is not an atomic, pre-given unity simply because it itself can be broken down further into component parts. That is, he would seem to be replacing one sort of "subject atom-ism" with another, taking considerable force away from his critique of "ego-substance."[41] Indeed, in the *Nachlaß*, Nietzsche seems to say that the "subjects" of interpretations and perspectives are affects:

> [M]oral evaluation is an *interpretation,* a way of interpreting. The interpre-tation itself is a *symptom* of certain physiological conditions, likewise of a certain spiritual level of ruling judgments: *Who interprets?*— Our affects. (*WP* 254; cf. *D* 119; *BGE* 187, 556)

> It is our needs *that interpret the world:* our drives and their For and Against. Every drive is a kind of lust to rule; each one has its perspective that it would like to compel all the other drives to accept as a norm. (*WP* 481; cf. *BGE* 6; *GM* III: 8; *Z*:1 "On Enjoying and Suffering the Passions"; *WP* 567)

Here, Nietzsche seems to argue that every affect is or has a particular "For and Against" (cf. *BGE* 284) that makes it a kind of instinctive in-terpretation, a particular manner of construing and responding to its

---

39. I use "affect" as a general term to encompass the host of other associated terms, because "affect" seems to combine the active senses of "drive" and "desire" with the more passive senses of "passion" and "feeling." (Heidegger attempts to distinguish these terms from one another, though he grants that Nietzsche himself often equates them and gives no real clues to help us sort out their different senses. See his *Nietzsche,* vol. 1, *The Will to Power as Art,* trans. David F. Krell [San Francisco: Harper, 1979], 44–53.) More-over, the term in its various forms (*affectus*/*affectio, der Affekt, l'affect*/*l'affection*) has a long and rich history in philosophy (from the Scholastics to Spinoza, Kant to Deleuze), rhetoric, and the aesthetics of music.

40. See *BGE* 36; *WP* 619, 635. Note that, in *WP* 619, the translation should read "an inner world [not 'will'] must be ascribed to it."

41. This charge is made by Davey, "Nietzsche and Hume on Self and Identity," 23, 26. Deleuze (*Nietzsche and Philosophy,* trans. Hugh Tomlinson [New York: Columbia University Press, 1983], chap. 2), too, seems to read Nietzsche this way, as positing two basic and irreducible forces: active and reactive.

environing conditions. On the basis of these texts, one could argue that there is a simple answer to the question "who or what is the subject of interpretations and perspectives?" and that this answer is simply: "our affects."[42]

Yet while affects are in some sense primitive, for Nietzsche, he refuses to conceive of them as entities, much less the atomic, singular, and unified entities that could be the proper bearers of perspectives and interpretations. First of all, on a micro-level, Nietzsche thinks of affects as an organic form of the basic "force-points" posited by Boscovich to replace the materialist atom.[43] Boscovich maintains that these basic items are "not [. . .] particles of matter in which powers somehow inhere"[44] but dynamic, differential "centers" or nodes within a force-field.[45] They are, as it were, temporary dams or accumulations of force rather than subsisting entities. Second, on a more macro-level, affects are tendencies and processes ("becomings") rather than definite entities ("beings").[46] "Fear," "love," "exuberance," "ressentiment," and "envy," for example, are not adequately described as "things"; rather, they are what Nietzsche calls "dynamic quanta of force or drive" that have their specific expression and direction. Third, affects are, by definition, relational: they relate one state of affairs to another. As the terms "drive" and "impulse" suggest, affects are a pulling or pushing of the organism in one direction or another. They are, as it were, the state between two states—what Nietzsche describes as "the state '*towards which*' [*der Zustand, von dem* weg]" or "the state '*away from which*' [*der Zustand, zu dem* hin]" (*BGE* 19). Finally, Nietzsche argues that it makes no sense to speak of an affect in isolation from other affects. We

---

42. Sarah Kofman (*Nietzsche and Metaphor,* trans. Duncan Large [Stanford: Stanford University Press, 1993], 93ff., 135ff.) takes this to be Nietzsche's position.

43. See *BGE* 12, 36. On Boscovich and Nietzsche's relationship to Boscovich, see chap. 2, n. 30.

44. Charles C. Gillispie, *The Edge of Objectivity: An Essay in the History of Scientific Ideas* (Princeton: Princeton University Press, 1960), 455, quoted in Kaufmann's note to *BGE* 12. Gillispie paraphrases the account provided by Michael Faraday (*Experimental Researches in Electricity,* vol. 2 [New York: Dover, 1965], 290), who brought Boscovich's notion into the mainstream of modern scientific theory.

45. Cf. Deleuze (*Nietzsche and Philosophy,* 6): "Every force is thus essentially related to another force. The being of force is plural, it would be absolutely absurd to think of force in the singular." This notion of being as an irreducible plurality is at the heart of Deleuze's reading of Nietzsche.

46. See *WP* 556: "One may not ask: '*who* then interprets?' for the interpretation itself, as a form of will to power, has existence (but not as a 'being,' but rather as a *process,* a *becoming*) as an affect."

have seen that he considers affects to be, in a rudimentary sense, interpretive. Like the interpretations described in *GM* III:12, each affect is
or has a "For and Against" [*Für und Wider*] "that it would like to compel all the other drives to accept as a norm" (*WP* 481). Yet just as interpretations are always essentially engaged in a struggle with other interpretations, just as each interpretation always begins from and tends
toward other interpretations that it reinterprets or by which it is reinterpreted, so, too, each affect is always engaged in a struggle with other
affects, each of which "would like to compel the other[s] to accept [it]
as a norm." Affects, Nietzsche tells us, are "dynamic quanta in a relation of tension to all other dynamic quanta: *their essence lies in their relation to all other quanta,* in their 'effect' upon the same" (*WP* 635, my
emphasis).[47] Indeed, the world is a "becoming," for Nietzsche, precisely
because it is composed entirely of these volatile relations. "My idea,"
Nietzsche writes (speaking here of "bodies," though the same holds for
affects and interpretations),

> is that every specific body strives to become master over all space and to ex-
> tend its force (—its will to power:) and to thrust back all that resists its ex-
> tension. But it continually encounters similar efforts on the part of other
> bodies and ends by coming to an arrangement ("union") with those of them
> that are sufficiently related to it: *thus they conspire together for power.* And
> the process goes on—. (*WP* 636; see chapter 5, below)[48]

Instead of individual affects, each with its own interpretation or perspective, then, what we encounter are always "unions" of affects. This
description comes closer to capturing Nietzsche's idea of "perspective"
or "interpretation." While each affect is or has an interpretation in a
rudimentary sense, Nietzsche tends to think of interpretations and perspectives as hierarchical aggregates of affects in which some dominate
and others are subordinate.[49] Instead of being the proper subjects of in-

---

47. Once again, the language of "dynamic quanta" is the language of "affect" extended to encompass "all efficient force" (*BGE* 36). What holds for the more general language of "dynamic quanta," therefore, also holds for the subcategory of "affect."

48. Cf. *GS* 333, where Nietzsche describes knowledge and understanding as a contract that temporarily settles accounts between struggling drives and relates them to one
another in a nonantagonistic way. Cf. also *WP* 567.

49. This view of interpretation has recently been suggested by Schrift, *Nietzsche and
the Question of Interpretation,* chap. 6, and Fowler, "Nietzschean Perspectivism" and
"Having a Perspective as Having a 'Will.'" Fowler ("Having a Perspective as Having a
'Will,'" 115–16) writes: "As I see it, a Nietzschean perspective can be correctly characterized as being a certain configuration of affects—or perhaps better, a certain 'common-

terpretations and perspectives, then, affects turn out to be "subjects" only in a political sense: namely, members of the hierarchical structure of an interpretation.[50]

This description recalls our earlier characterization of interpretations as systems of evaluation directed by particular needs. But what is it that unifies a particular system and what makes a particular set of needs dominant? Nietzsche tells us that every interpretation and perspective is oriented toward the preservation and enhancement of a specific level of organization in life, from the individual to the group, the species, and life as a whole.[51] Are the "subjects" of perspectivism, then, perhaps just these particular levels of life? In a sense, the answer is yes; for a particular perspective does represent the "point of view" of a particular type, group, culture, people, and so forth. Yet, once again, these perspectives are never encountered in isolation. That is, we never come across these perspectives independent of the individual human beings to whom they are attributed. And each individual cuts across all the various levels of life: human beings are individuals as well as members of communities, cultures, subcultures, races, classes, genders, nationalities, religions, political parties, and other groups. Thus, on the one hand, we always encounter perspectives within individual subjects, while, on the other hand, individual subjects are aggregates of these perspectives and their forms of life.[52]

For Nietzsche, the individual subject is an aggregate on at least two levels—what are usually called "the physical" and "the spiritual," "body" and "soul." According to Nietzsche, however, these do not form the two sides of an opposition between different kinds of entity but only mark differences of degree along a continuum from the more

wealth of affects.' [. . .] which are related in such a way that some of these affects are dominant and so responsible for imposing order on what would otherwise be a chaos of motives and emotions. [. . .] A perspective is just a structure of affects governed by a basic dominant affect (or small cluster of them)."

50. For a similar interpretation, in terms of the will to power, see Wolfgang Müller-Lauter, "Nietzsche's Teaching of Will to Power," trans. Drew Griffin, *Journal of Nietzsche Studies* 4–5 (1992–93): §3.

51. "Insight: all estimation of value involves a certain perspective: that of the *maintenance* of the individual, a community, a race, a state, a church, a faith, a culture" (*WP* 259). Elsewhere, Nietzsche puts the stress on "enhancement" and "flourishing" rather than "maintenance" and "preservation." See the discussion in §§5.2.3–5.2.4, below.

52. "[T]he concept 'individual' is an error because every being constitutes the *entire process* in its entire course (not merely as 'inherited,' but the process itself . . .)" (*WP* 785).

or less immutable to the more or less mutable.[53] First, a subject has a *quantitative* identity insofar as it is born with a basic physical unity: an integral body. Yet even this basic unity and identity are only relative, because, according to Nietzsche, the body itself is "a political structure," "an aristocracy" (*WP* 660, 490; *BGE* 259) or "oligarchy" (*GM* II:1): that is, a hierarchy of organs, tissues, and cells, each of which has a particular role and function. In a healthy body, these various parts fulfill their functions in service of the whole; while in a sick or dying body, this relation of parts to whole (and thus the integrity of the body) is threatened or dissolving.[54] Furthermore, the relatively pre-given unity of the body is not an eternal verity but the product or result of "interpretation" (in Nietzsche's extended sense of the word), that is, of millennia of evolutionary struggle.

Second, and more important for the present discussion, a subject has a *qualitative* identity insofar as it is or has a more or less stable "character" or "self." But this unity, too, is an aggregate, and, moreover, one that is intimately related to the physical, bodily aggregate.[55] Indeed, Nietzsche argues that the organizational unity of the body provides the proper model for theorizing about the "soul," "self," or "subject":

> The body and physiology as the starting point: why?—We gain the correct idea of the nature of our subject-unity, namely as regents at the head of a communality (not as "souls" or "life forces"), also of the dependence of these regents upon the ruled and of an order of rank and division of labor as the conditions that make possible the whole and its parts. In the same way, how living unities continually arise and die and how the "subject" is not eternal; in the same way, that the struggle expresses itself in obeying and commanding, and that a fluctuating assessment of the limits of power is part of life. The relative ignorance in which the regent is kept concerning individual activities and even disturbances within the communality is among the

---

53. I note that my discussion here owes much to Nehamas, *Nietzsche: Life as Literature*, chap. 6, to Davey, "Nietzsche and Hume on Self and Identity" and "Nietzsche, the Self and Hermeneutic Theory," and to Deleuze's work in general. On the notion of the body in Nietzsche and Deleuze, see Paul Patton, "Nietzsche and the Body of the Philosopher," in *Cartographies: Poststructuralism and the Mapping of Bodies and Spaces*, ed. Rosalyn Diprose and Robyn Ferrell (Sydney: Allen and Unwin, 1991), 43–54.

54. On this process of growth and decay, see *WP* 647, 678. Also see *GM* II:12 and *WP* 643, on "physiological organs" as interpretive constructions.

55. See *Z:1* "On the Despisers of the Body": "'Body am I, and soul'—thus speaks the child. [. . .] But the awakened and knowing say: body am I entirely, and nothing else; and soul is only a word for something about the body"; and *Z:2* "On Poets": "Since I have come to know the body better [. . .] the spirit is to me only quasi-spirit; and all that is permanent is also a mere parable." See also *GS* P:2 and *WP* 659.

conditions under which rule can be exercised. [. . .] The most important thing, however, is: that we understand that the ruler and his subjects are of the *same kind,* all feeling, willing, and thinking. (*WP* 492)

This last remark is important; for it suggests not only that the body presents the appropriate framework for a conception of the self but also that the latter is actually rooted in the former—in the affects, which are at once "physical" and "spiritual," that is, interpretive.[56] The affects, then, are the point of contact between "body" and "soul." In mirroring formulas, Nietzsche tells us that "the soul" is a "social structure of the drives and affects" (*BGE* 12), while the "body is but a social structure composed of many souls" (*BGE* 19). We could summarize this by saying that the self (the physical-spiritual "subject-unity") is a composition of many "souls," each of which has its own perspective, its own arrangement of drives and affects, Fors and Againsts. The self is thus an aggregate of many different perspectives and interpretations, each of which is affective, rooted in the various drives, impulses, desires, capacities, and passions of the body (see *GS* P:2). The unity of the self is the result of the ordering, organizing, and subordinating power of the dominant affective interpretation(s).

This idea runs throughout Nietzsche's discussions of subjectivity, selfhood, and character. For example, in two related notes from 1884, he writes:

[A]ll sorts of contradictory estimations and *therefore contradictory drives* swarm within *one* man. This is the *expression of the diseased condition in mankind,* in contrast to the animals, in which all existing instincts satisfy very specific tasks—this contradictory creature has however in its nature a great method of *knowledge:* he feels many Fors and Againsts—he raises himself *to justice*—to a comprehension *beyond the estimation of good and evil.* The wisest man would be *the richest in contradictions,* who has feelers for all kinds of men: and, in the midst, his great moments of *grandiose harmony*— a rare *occurrence* even in us!—a sort of planetary movement—. (*WP* 259)[57]

In contrast to the animals, man has cultivated an abundance of *contrary* drives and impulses within himself: thanks to this synthesis he is master of the earth.—Moralities are the expression of locally limited *orders of rank* in this multifarious world of drives: so that man should not perish through their *contradictions.* Thus a drive as master, its opposite weakened, refined,

56. See *BGE* 19: "we are at the same time the commanding *and* the obeying parties."
57. Cf. *GS* 297 and *KSA* 11:26[149]: "Justice, as the function of a broad panoramic power that looks beyond the narrow perspectives of good and evil and thus has a broader horizon of *advantage*—the intention to preserve something that is more than this or that person" (cited in Heidegger, *Nietzsche,* 3:147 [Krell's translation modified]).

as the *impulse* that provides the stimulus for the activity of the chief drive. The highest man would have the greatest multiplicity of drives, in the relatively greatest strength that can be endured. Indeed, where the plant "man" shows itself strongest, one finds driving instincts that powerfully *conflict* with one another [. . .], but are controlled. (*WP* 966; cf. *Z:* Prologue 3; *BGE* 284; *TI* "Skirmishes" 49; *WP* 881, 933)

Here, as elsewhere, Nietzsche argues that the human subject is a multiplicity. In contrast with animals, who are composed of only a few, very specific, instinctive "perspectives," human beings are far more complex—collections of a vast array of competing instincts, desires, drives, beliefs, and capacities and thus of a vast array of perspectives and interpretations.[58] Hence, human beings are at once the most "richly endowed" and "the most imperiled" creatures (*GM* III:13).[59]

Nietzsche contends that, for the most part, human beings have been unable to master or control the conflict of interpretations and perspectives that rages within them. Pushed and pulled in multiple directions, the majority of human beings have shown themselves to be incontinent, unable *not* to respond to the myriad stimuli to which they are continually subjected (see *BT* SC: 1; *BGE* 212, 258; *TI* "Socrates" 4, "Morality" 2, "Germans" 5; *A* 30; *WP* 778). As a defense against this wanton and painful condition, human beings have resorted to a drastic means of achieving order, control, and power: they have declared the entire range of affects evil and resolved to extirpate them (see *GM* III:13–14; *TI* "Morality"; *WP* 228, 383–88). Though it would appear to be a rather rare and extreme manifestation, Nietzsche argues that it is "one of the most widespread and enduring of all phenomena" (*GM* III:11; cf. *A* 8–9). He discerns this kind of evaluation not only in the practices of the religious ascetic but also in those of the rationalist philosopher (who draws an opposition between mind and body and subordinates the latter to the former) and the scholar-scientist

58. On the struggle for supremacy of the affects, see *D* 109, 119; *Z:*1 "On Enjoying and Suffering the Passions."

59. Cf. *A* 14 and *WP* 684: "The richest and most complex forms—for the expression 'higher type' means no more than this—perish more easily: only the lowest preserve an apparent indestructibility. [. . .] Among men, too, the higher types, the lucky strokes of evolution, perish most easily as fortunes change. They are exposed to every kind of decadence: they are extreme, and that almost means decadents. [. . .] This is not due to any special fatality or malevolence of nature, but simply to the concept 'higher type': the higher type represents an incomparably greater complexity—a greater sum of co-ordinated elements: so its disintegration is also incomparably more likely. The 'genius' is the sublimest machine there is—consequently the most fragile." Also see *GS* 301–2; *Z:*1 "On Enjoying and Suffering the Passions"; *GM* I:16.

(who strives for objectivity conceived as "contemplation without inter-
est") (see *GM* III:12, 23–28). Indeed, "[a]part from the ascetic ideal,"
Nietzsche maintains, "man, the human *animal,* had no meaning so far"
(*GM* III:28).[60]

The ascetic solution is not only extreme but self-defeating. For, in the
guise of extirpating the affects and denying the multiplicity of perspectives, it simply endorses one affective perspective and sets it against all
the others. It, too, manifests a will to power and thus a privileged interpretation and dominant set of affects. Disgusted with sensuous existence, it plots revenge through the separation of mind and body and the
elevation of the "spiritual" and "antinatural" over the bodily and natural. This condition is certainly paradoxical—for it pits a particular
will of life against life itself (see *GM* III:10–13; *TI* "Morality"), an affect against all affects (see *BGE* 117), "nature against something that is
also nature" (*WP* 228)—but it is nonetheless prevalent.

This strange phenomenon, Nietzsche argues, is "the *expression of
the diseased condition in man,*" a sign of nihilism, decadence, and the
degeneration of life.[61] In this condition, human beings are primarily
reactive and negative. They declare their contradictory nature evil and
surmise that there must be a better condition—a good, noncontradic-
tory, extranatural condition and world (see *WP* 579). Thus, they come
to exemplify that unnuanced, binary morality of *ressentiment,* which
declares an other (in this case, the natural and physical) "evil" and consequently infers that it (in this case the spiritual) must itself represent
"the good" (see *BGE* 260 and *GM* I:10).

However, the contradictory swarm of drives in human beings also
presents another possibility. Nietzsche contends that there are rare human beings in whom the many contrary drives, affects, perspectives,
and interpretations are managed and organized into a rich and powerful unity (see *GM* III:14). In such beings, all the affective perspectives
and interpretations are allowed to express themselves, but in the service
of the whole (see *BGE* 200; *TI* "Skirmishes" 49). Such human beings
"give style" to their characters. Nietzsche explains:

> To "give style" to one's character—a great and rare art! It is practiced by
> those who survey all the strengths and weaknesses of their nature and then

60. Cf. *Thus Spoke Zarathustra,* where Nietzsche contends that this asceticism is
such a pervasive feature that it can be said to characterize humanity as a whole; hence,
Zarathustra's condemnation of "man" and call for the "overman."
61. This theme runs throughout *GM* III, *TI,* and the notes on "nihilism" in the later
Nachlaß (see *WP* Book One)

fit them into an artistic plan until every one of them appears as art and reason and even weaknesses delight the eye. Here a large part of second nature has been added; there a piece of original nature has been removed—both times through long practice and daily work at it. Here the ugly that could not be removed is concealed; there it has been reinterpreted and made sublime [*Erhabene umgedeutet*]. Much that is vague and resisted shaping has been saved and exploited for distant views; it is meant to beckon toward the far and immeasurable. In the end, when the work is finished, it becomes evident how the constraint of a single taste governed and formed everything large and small. [. . .] It will be the strong and domineering natures that enjoy their finest gaiety in such constraint and perfection under a law of their own. [. . .] Conversely, it is the weak characters without power over themselves that *hate* the constraint of style. (GS 290)[62]

Against the sensualist and relativist who submits indiscriminately to all drives and perspectives, and against the ascetic who attempts to annihilate the passions altogether, Nietzsche opposes the "highest human," who affirms that life is essentially affective and that it essentially involves the will to power (the forming, shaping, organizing, expansive drive of all life). This "highest human" is one capable of incorporating the multiplicity of affective perspectives and employing them in the service of the whole. Thus, Nietzsche says, such a person raises him or herself to "knowledge," "justice," and "an estimation beyond good and evil."

Yet this necessitates a redescription of "knowledge" and "justice." "Knowledge" can no longer mean "objectivity [. . .] understood as 'contemplation without interest,'" for this is "a nonsensical absurdity" (GM III:12) that denies the affective character of life and the affective perspectives and interpretations that are the very conditions for any knowledge whatsoever. Similarly, "justice" can no longer mean the equalization of power, the prevention of struggle, and the insurance of

---

62. One finds this same idea throughout Nietzsche's notes of the late 1880s. See, e.g., WP 46, 384, 778, 881, 928, 933, 962ff., 1014. Yet this notion also appears in a much earlier text, where Nietzsche writes: "since we are the outcome of earlier generations, we are also the outcome of their aberrations, passions, and errors, and indeed of their crimes; it is not possible wholly to free oneself from this chain. If we condemn these aberrations and regard ourselves as free of them, this does not alter the fact that we originate in them. The best we can do is confront our inherited and hereditary nature with our knowledge of it, and through new, stern, discipline combat our inborn heritage and inplant in ourselves a new habit, a new instinct, a second nature, so that our first nature withers away. It is an attempt to give oneself, as it were *a posteriori*, a past in which one would like to originate in opposition to that in which one did originate:—always a dangerous attempt. [. . .] But here and there a victory is nonetheless achieved, and for the combatants [. . .] there is even a noteworthy consolation: that of knowing that this first nature was once a second nature and that every victorious second nature will become a first" (HL 3, pp. 76–77).

peace, for this represents "a principle *hostile to life*" (*GM* II:11), because it denies "the relations of supremacy under which the phenomenon of 'life' comes to be" (*BGE* 19).[63] Rather, for these "higher types," "knowledge" and "justice" signify the affirmation of affective life and of the organizing force that controls it in the service of the subject as a whole.

There is no better formulation of these aims than the passage on perspectivity cited at the outset. For the "higher types," "knowledge" and "justice" are precisely "the ability to have one's For and Against *under control* and to engage and disengage them, so that one knows how to employ a *variety* of perspectives and affective interpretations in the service of knowledge" (cf. *BGE* 212, 284). Such a nuanced, multifaceted estimation is indeed something other than the binary, slavish morality of "good and evil." It points toward a different ethics: a model of practice firmly rooted in the *ethos,* which affirms difference and variety and extols self-control and fine discrimination in the estimation of the particular passions and actions appropriate for any given situation. Indeed, in this sense, perspectivism might be seen as encapsulating Nietzsche's conception of practical wisdom: it advocates the cultivation of a variety of affective centers within an overall organization (the subject) that is finely attuned to its capacities and environment, aware of the affective perspectives that are appropriate to a given circumstance, and able skillfully to deploy these perspectives as required.[64]

63. Jean Granier ("Perspectivism and Interpretation," trans. David B. Allison, in *The New Nietzsche: Contemporary Styles of Interpretation,* ed. David B. Allison [Cambridge, Mass.: MIT Press, 1977], 199) construes "knowledge" and "justice" in just this way, that is, as attempts to see things as they are, to "be true" to a putative ontological ground: "the text of Being."

64. See *TI* "Skirmishes" 49, where Nietzsche praises Goethe for conceiving "a human being who would be strong, highly educated, skillful in all bodily matters, self-controlled, reverent toward himself, and who might dare to afford the whole range and wealth of being natural, being strong enough for such freedom." This passage and the conception of ethics presented above invite comparison with Aristotle's ethics of *areté, phronesis,* and *megalopsychia.* Robert C. Solomon ("A More Severe Morality: Nietzsche's Affirmative Ethics," in *From Hegel to Existentialism* [Oxford: Oxford University Press, 1987]) draws just such a comparison, arguing that Nietzsche's "affirmative ethics" is much closer to Aristotle's than to any other ethicist in the Western philosophical tradition. A similar comparison is made, with reservations, by Nehamas, *Nietzsche: Life as Literature,* 193. Walter Kaufmann discusses Nietzsche's debt to Aristotle's ethics in general and, particularly, to his conception of *megalopsychia* (*Nietzsche: Philosopher, Psychologist, Anti-Christ,* 4th ed. [Princeton: Princeton University Press, 1974], 382–84 and his note to *BGE* 212), while Bernd Magnus finds little of Aristotle's notion in Nietzsche ("Aristotle and Nietzsche: *Megalopsychia* and *Übermensch,*" in *The Greeks and the Good Life,* ed. David J. Depew [Indianapolis: Hackett, 1980]). Jean-François Lyotard draws on both Nietzsche's perspectivism and Aristotle's *phronesis* to develop more fully this "postmodern" conception of

3.3.4 THE SUBJECT *AS* INTERPRETATION

We can now make explicit the result of this discussion for the issue at hand, the issue of the "subject" of perspectivism. We have seen that the subjects of perspectivism are not simply biological species; for, according to Nietzsche, there is no such thing as, for example, "the human perspective," because the human subject is itself composed of a multiplicity of perspectives formed at the micro-level of affects. We have also seen that the subject of perspectivism cannot be the individual human knower presupposed as *atomic* and *given;* for Nietzsche maintains that the human subject is a *multiplicity* that is constantly being *achieved, accomplished, produced, constructed.* Moreover, the subject does not *have* these various perspectives and interpretations; rather, they are what the subject *is.* According to Nietzsche, the subject is nothing over and above the various physical/spiritual affective perspectives and interpretations—the complexes of belief, desire, action, perception, and thought—that compose it and the relationships between these perspectives and interpretations.

This is not mysterious provided that we take seriously Nietzsche's conception of the subject as a political organization. Every such organization is a more or less temporary union of various individuals and groups that often have different experiences, views, and desires but agree (or are made to agree) about some central ideas, practices, and goals that supervene and serve to unify the membership. The force of the organization resides in the collective power of its members, in their ability to struggle in a particular direction and yet be flexible and responsive to changing circumstances by drawing upon the capacities of individual members or subgroups. There is no organization without these members and no membership without the existence of the organization as a whole.

Nietzsche argues that the subject is just like this.[65] It is nothing over

---

ethics and justice. See Lyotard and Jean-Loup Thébaud, *Just Gaming,* trans. Wlad Godzich (Minneapolis: University of Minnesota Press, 1985), and Lyotard, *The Differend: Phrases in Dispute,* trans. Georges Van Den Abbeele (Minneapolis: University of Minnesota Press, 1988).

65. Along the lines of Quine's "web of belief," Rorty ("Inquiry as Recontextualization," 93) has described the subject in a similar fashion: as a self-reweaving web of beliefs and desires separate from which there is no subject or "self." Though a Nietzschean orientation is only implicit in their work, Ernesto Laclau and Chantal Mouffe have developed in detail this political model of subjectivity in *Hegemony and Socialist Strategy: Towards a Radical Democratic Politics* (London: Verso, 1985).

and above the sum and arrangement of the affective perspectives and interpretations that compose it. These are not, and need not be, homogeneous. Indeed, Nietzsche argues that the more heterogeneous they are—provided that they maintain some coherence—the richer and more flexible the whole will be. (This is a basic theme of Nietzsche's later work. See *GS* 295–97, 344, 373, 375; *BGE* 212; *GM* III: 12; *TI* "Morality" 3, 6; *WP* 259, 410, 600, 655, 881, 933, 1051.) This union, however, is "mortal"; it is a changeable entity. Different circumstances often force the acquisition of new perspectives and/or the loss of old ones, thus altering the overall structure. And if these changes are significant enough, or if particular factions cease to remain subordinate to the whole, that whole is threatened or falls apart. Nietzsche writes:

> No subject "atoms." The sphere of the subject constantly growing or decreasing, the center of the system constantly shifting; in cases where it cannot organize the appropriate mass, it breaks into two parts. On the other hand, it can transform a weaker subject into its functionary without destroying it, and to a certain degree form a new unity with it. No "substance," rather something that in itself strives after greater strength, and that wants to "preserve" itself only indirectly (it wants to *surpass* itself—). (*WP* 488; cf. *GS* 290 and *WP* 715)

We thus discover not only that the human subject is a fabricated entity but that its fabrication takes the same form as that of an interpretation. Recall that, in his highly generalized account of interpretation (*GM* II: 11), Nietzsche writes:

> whatever exists, having somehow come into being, is again and again reinterpreted to new ends, taken over, transformed, and redirected by some power superior to it;[66] all events in the organic world are a subduing, a becoming master, and all subduing and becoming master involves a fresh interpretation, an adjustment through which any previous "meaning" and "purpose" are necessarily obscured or obliterated.

If "all events in the organic world" are submitted to this process, it is not surprising that this description also applies to the formation of subjectivity. Indeed, we find that Nietzsche not only views the subject as a

---

66. I take it that "some power superior to it" does not refer to a subject outside the field of interpretation that controls that field from without. Rather, it refers to an affect, perspective, or interpretation—*within* the general field of interpretative struggle—that is able to dominate and subordinate the previous interpretation by assimilating the old terms into its new system (see, e.g., *WP* 492). For more on this conception of interpretation, see §5.3.1, below.

multiplicity of micro-interpretations and -perspectives; he also views the subject itself as a macro-interpretation. The point is simply that, for Nietzsche, interpretation goes all the way down and all the way up. Rather than positing the subject as something outside the realm of interpretation, something that stands behind and fabricates interpretations, Nietzsche maintains that the subject itself is fabricated by and as an interpretation. Thus, the famous passage that claims that there are no facts but only interpretations, concludes:

> "Everything is subjective," you say; but even this is interpretation [*Auslegung*]. The "subject" is nothing given [*nichts Gegebenes*], but something added, fabricated, and stuck behind [*etwas Hinzu-Erdichtetes, Dahinter-Gestecktes*].—Finally, is it necessary to posit an interpreter [*Interpreten*] behind the interpretation [*Interpretationen*]? Even this is fiction, hypothesis. (WP 481)[67]

3.4 THE "OBJECT" OF PERSPECTIVISM

Nietzsche thus reverses our grammatical and philosophical conceptions of the primacy of the subject. At the beginning of our analysis, we saw that, instead of first positing a given subject who then acts or is acted upon, Nietzsche argues that what is primary are those actions and passions and that the subject is constructed after the fact as a particular configuration of these. At the end of our analysis, we saw that this reversal extends to the notions of interpretation and perspective: instead of first positing a given subject who then acquires various perspectives and interpretations, Nietzsche maintains that interpretation is primary and that the subject is itself an effect of interpretation.

This conception inveighs against the view that the subjects of perspectivism are biological species that have, through evolution, acquired a fixed interpretation or perspective, because, for Nietzsche, the process of interpretation resists this fixity and, instead, involves the constant acquisition and/or forfeiture of perspectives and interpretations. It also inveighs against the view that the subjects of perspectivism are ordinary human knowers conceived of as pre-given entities that then acquire perspectives and interpretations, because, for Nietzsche, "the subject is

---

67. Cf. *BGE* 34: "Why couldn't the world *that concerns us*—be a fiction? And if somebody asked, 'but to a fiction there surely belongs an author?'—couldn't one answer simply: *why*? Doesn't this 'belongs' perhaps belong to the fiction, too? Is it not permitted to be a bit ironical about the subject no less than the predicate and object?" Also cf. WP 556.

nothing given, but something added, fabricated, and stuck behind"
(*WP* 481). In short, for Nietzsche, the subject is *a piece of* the incessantly transformative process of interpretation rather than something
other than, outside of, or prior to interpretation.

But Nietzsche's conception of interpretation no less alters our everyday and philosophical views about *objecthood*. On my reading, Nietzsche's theory of interpretation holds that objects are nothing given but
that they, too, are only ever constructions of one or another interpretation. While it is often granted that Nietzsche rejects *some* form of the
given, commentators have been reluctant to ascribe to Nietzsche the
radical and thoroughgoing holism that, I believe, is warranted.[68] Before
offering my own account of Nietzsche's perspectivist theory of objecthood, then, I want briefly to return to the accounts of perspectivism
considered above. Doing so will allow us to determine both where these
accounts are supported by Nietzsche's texts and where those texts render these readings problematic and call for an alternative view.

3.4.1 OBJECTHOOD, BECOMING, AND THE "CHAOS OF SENSATIONS"

In order for there to be perspectives or interpretations, there presumably must be some object upon which there are perspectives, or some
primary "text" that provides the impetus for the various interpretations. Prima facie, that is, the notions of perspective and interpretation
seem to rely upon some notion of "the given." Since Kant, philosophers
have come to identify two forms or levels of "the given": one can regard
"the given" ontologically as the objects or "world out there" that we
come to know (Kant's "thing in itself" or "noumenal world"); or one
can regard it epistemologically as the immediate contents of perceptual
awareness, the "sense data" that provide the raw material for conceptual understanding (Kant's "sensuous intuition"). While one may not
be able precisely to isolate these "given" elements in experience, it is
said that, nonetheless, they are necessary to avoid the untenable position Kant called "empirical idealism," according to which there exists

68. The exceptions, perhaps, are Schacht, *Nietzsche*, 140–56, and Nehamas, "Immanent and Transcendent Perspectivism in Nietzsche" and *Nietzsche: Life as Literature*. See
also Robert C. Solomon, *In the Spirit of Hegel* (New York: Oxford University Press,
1983), 328 n.

no ontologically distinct world to serve as the object, source, and goal of our knowledge.

According to the skeptical account of perspectivism, Nietzsche's view also relies upon these "given" elements in experience. The skeptical reading acknowledges that Nietzsche rejects Kant's notion of the thing in itself insofar as this notion falsely ascribes the intraphenomenal predicates of unity and individuation to an extraphenomenal world.[69] Yet it maintains that Nietzsche nonetheless posits the existence of a chaotic, undifferentiated "given" that provides the material for conceptual knowledge. This "given" is seen as taking one of the two forms mentioned above: what is "given" to knowledge is either the "world of becoming" or the "chaos of sense impressions."[70]

There is, of course, some evidence for this view. Nietzsche's later texts often claim that "logic," "grammar," and "the categories of reason" "falsify" or "simplify" something more basic, to which these descriptions do not properly apply.[71] Thus, he writes that "We operate only with things that do not exist: lines, planes, bodies, atoms, divis-

---

69. See, e.g., Danto, *Nietzsche as Philosopher,* 89, 96–97, and Grimm, *Nietzsche's Theory of Knowledge,* 2, 18, 30, 53, 67–68. For Nietzsche's rejection on these grounds of Kant's thing in itself, see *HH* 16 and *WP* 553–54.

70. Thus, on the one hand, skeptical accounts construe this "given" ontologically as: "the world of 'shifting,' 'evanescent' becoming" (Vaihinger, "Nietzsche and His Doctrine of Conscious Illusion," 84), "sheer, undifferentiated flux," "swirling complexity," "a blind, empty, structureless, thereness," "a primal undifferentiated *Ur-Eine*" (Danto, *Nietzsche as Philosopher,* 89, 96, 97), "the chaotic being of a groundless depth" (Granier, "Nietzsche's Conception of Chaos," trans. David B. Allison, in *The New Nietzsche,* ed. David B. Allison [Cambridge, Mass.: MIT Press, 1977], 139), "a chaotic becoming," "the everchanging stream of becoming which is the world" (Grimm, *Nietzsche's Theory of Knowledge,* 30, 32), the "unintelligible flux of becoming," "the radical flux of becoming" (Magnus, *Nietzsche's Existential Imperative,* 25, 169), "becoming in itself," "an evanescent stream of becoming" (Stack, "Nietzsche's Critique of Things-in-Themselves," 54, "Nietzsche and Boscovich's Natural Philosophy," *Pacific Philosophical Quarterly* 62 [1981]: 80), "a self-contradictory world of becoming and change" (Willard Mittelman, "Perspectivism, Becoming, and Truth in Nietzsche," *International Studies in Philosophy* 16 [1984]: 5), "an a-cosmic, unimaginable, unknowable chaos of power-centers" (Babich, "Nietzsche and the Philosophy of Scientific Power: Will to Power as Constructive Interpretation," *International Studies in Philosophy* 22 [1990]: 83). Or, on the other hand, these accounts construe this "given" epistemologically as "an archaic strata of sense" (Granier, "Nietzsche's Conception of Chaos," 137), "the 'flux' or 'continuum' of sensation," "the sensory manifold" (John T. Wilcox, *Truth and Value in Nietzsche: A Study of His Metaethics and Epistemology* [Ann Arbor: University of Michigan Press, 1974], 133, 149), "the formless, unformulable world of the chaos of sensations" (Babich, "Nietzsche and the Philosophy of Scientific Power," 83, citing *WP* 569), "a presumed, chaotic 'manifold' of sensory impressions" (Stack, "Kant, Lange, and Nietzsche: Critique of Knowledge," 35).

71. These themes can also be found in Nietzsche's early work, particularly in *TL*.

ible time spans, divisible spaces" (*GS* 112), with "erroneous articles of faith," which assert "that there are enduring things; that there are equal things; that there are things, substances, bodies," and so on (*GS* 110). Nietzsche also asserts that it is only "the prejudice of reason" that "forces us to posit unity, identity, permanence, substance, thinghood, being" (*TI* "Reason" 5) and thus "to impose upon becoming the character of being" (*WP* 617). "Being," however, "is an empty fiction" (*TI* "Reason" 2), and the philosopher's "world of being" is simply an imaginary world (*WP* 570; cf. *TI* "Reason" 6).

Such descriptions are "lies" (*TI* "Reason" 2), it seems, insofar as they cover over the "manifold one-after-another [*vielfaches Nacheinander*]," the "continuum," and "flux" that "in truth we are confronted by" (*GS* 112). "Continual transition forbids us to speak of 'individuals,'" Nietzsche writes, "the 'number' of beings is itself in flux" (*WP* 520). This "flux" is sometimes spoken of ontologically as "a world of becoming [*eine werdende Welt*]" (*WP* 517, 520), "becoming [*das Werden*]" (*WP* 617), or "chaos" (*GS* 109; *WP* 515, 711), while, at other times, it is spoken of epistemologically as the "chaos of sense-impressions," "the chaos of sensations" (*WP* 569), "a chaos of ideas" (*WP* 508), "the medley of sensations [*der Sensationen-Wirrwarr*]" (*WP* 552), "the multiplicity of sensations [*das Vielerei der Sensationen*]" (*WP* 517), or "the motley whirl of the senses [*der bunte Sinnen-Wirbel*]" (*BGE* 14).

Moreover, in these passages, Nietzsche often makes use of the Kantian distinctions between the knowable and the unknowable, form and matter, and the active and passive faculties. For Kant, knowledge is the result of an active imposition of the forms of sensibility and categories of the understanding upon the unknowable world in itself that is given to our sense receptivity. Similarly, Nietzsche often seems to claim that knowledge is the result of the active imposition of form upon the "chaos of sensations" or an unknowable "world of becoming."

> The material of the senses adapted by the understanding, reduced to rough outlines, made similar, subsumed under related matters. Thus the fuzziness and chaos of sense-impressions are, as it were, *logicized*. (*WP* 569; cf. *GS* 354)
>
> The character of the world of becoming as *unformulable*, as "false," as "self-contradictory." *Knowledge* and *becoming* exclude one another. (*WP* 517)
>
> A world of becoming could not, in the strict sense, be "comprehended" or "known"; only to the extent that the "comprehending" and "knowing" intellect encounters a coarse, already-created world, built out of nothing but appearances but become firm to the extent that this kind of appearance has

preserved life—only to this extent is there anything like "knowledge," a measuring of earlier and later errors by one another. (*WP* 520)

It thus seems that to know, for Nietzsche, is "to impose upon chaos as much regularity and form as our practical needs require" (*WP* 515), "to impose upon becoming the character of being" (617).[72]

These passages do lend credence to the view that Nietzsche conceives of the structure of knowledge in Kantian terms. Such a reading would certainly equivocate his own rejection of the appearance/reality distinction and put into doubt his expressed commitment to the primacy of the this-worldly (see, e.g., *GS* 54; *TI* "Reason" 2, 6, "World" 6; *WP* 552, 567), for it would commit him to the view that the world we know—the world of our experience—is built upon another, unknowable, primary, and pre-given world of becoming or chaos.

Yet there is another way to read these passages. This new reading would show that the above-cited passages are not only consistent with Nietzsche's naturalism but that they also repudiate the epistemological and metaphysical claims of Kantianism. On this reading, these passages simply continue the argument against the "prejudices" and "idiosyncrasies" of the metaphysicians, namely "their lack of historical sense; their hatred of the very idea of becoming, their Egypticism" (*TI* "Reason" 1–3); their habit of "confusing the last and the first" (*TI* "Reason" 4–6); their "faith in opposite values" (*BGE* 2; cf. *HH* 1); their belief in the "fictions" of "'pure reason,' 'absolute *Geistigkeit*,'[73] 'knowledge in itself,'" and "a 'pure, will-less, painless, timeless, knowing subject'" (*GM* III:12); and their "faith in immediate certainties" (*BGE* 16, 34; cf. *WP* 406–9).

One can read Nietzsche's comments concerning the primacy of becoming as empirical and phenomenological claims.[74] As such, Nietzsche simply wants to direct our attention to the fact that the world in

---

72. It should be said that, in *WP* 515, Nietzsche actually claims that such schematization and imposition of form is *not* "knowledge." The passage runs: "Not 'to know' but to schematize—to impose upon chaos as much regularity and form as our practical needs require . . . the need, not to 'know,' but to subsume, to schematize, for the purpose of intelligibility and calculation.—" Yet Nietzsche is not arguing that there is no such thing as knowledge. He is only arguing that there is no such thing as knowledge "in the strict sense" (*WP* 520), that is, knowledge conceived as a passive mirroring of the world. Against such a view, this passage and those that surround it are concerned to argue that there is knowledge only as the active imposition of form (see *WP* 517, 520).

73. I take this to be a reference to Hegel's notions of "Absolute Spirit" and "Absolute Knowing."

74. This idea is discussed further below, in §4.5.

which we live—and of which we ourselves are inescapably a part—
is continually undergoing change and transformation. Physical objects
that the naked eye perceives to be stable and durable are, when viewed
microscopically, shown to be a swarm of molecules and, when viewed
over large time spans, are shown to be undergoing various processes
of expansion, contraction, reorganization, disintegration, decay, and so
forth.[75] Moreover, though we always retrospectively construct ourselves
as unified and self-same entities, we are, in fact, always enmeshed in
physical processes of growth, procreation, degeneration, and death and
find ourselves to be an intellectual, psychological, and spiritual battle-
ground of competing beliefs, desires, impulses, and needs.

Our perception, thought, and memory are carried along in this stream
of lived experience. We have this perception or thought, then that. We
attempt to unify and systematize these perceptions, thoughts, and mem-
ories, yet some of them slip away, either through passive forgetting or
active repression. We constantly measure the new against the old, and
vice versa, each time coming to a temporary equilibrium before this stability is again disrupted by a new experience, a memory, or both. Never
do we achieve absolute knowing, the ideal point of totalization or stasis
when "all reports are in" and all of them are in perfect order. Nor does
the world ever stop its incessant movement and alteration to allow us to
summarize, calculate, and totalize it. Measured according to the ideal
of an absolute knowledge that comprehends a fixed and stable world of
being, our knowledge of the world and the world we know are "false."
Thus, Nietzsche writes: "The world *that concerns us* is false, i.e., is
no fact, but rather a fable and approximation on the basis of a mea-
ger sum of observations; it is 'in flux,' as something becoming [*etwas
Werdendes*], as an ever-shifting falsehood that never nears the truth:
for—there is no 'truth'" (*WP* 616; cf. *WP* 542–43).

This is not a lament. It expresses neither the nostalgia for a lost truth
nor the hope for a truth to come. On the contrary, it is an affirmative
renunciation of "truth" conceived as the final comprehension of a
world of being. Along with this renunciation comes a revaluation of the
world we know and of our knowledge itself, an affirmation of the ever-

75. For an empirical construal of Nietzsche's language of "becoming," see Morgan,
What Nietzsche Means, 244, 268, 271, 281. In "Kant, Lange, and Nietzsche: Critique of
Knowledge," 42 and *passim,* and "Nietzsche's Evolutionary Epistemology," 94 and *passim,* Stack also makes this point but then goes on to draw the unwarranted conclusion
that this entails a sort of skepticism.

changing and transforming world in which we exist as entities whose knowledge, too, is always relative to particular horizons that are forever shifting.

Of course, Nietzsche realizes that we do not experience the world as a radical flux. But he argues that this is because we have biologically and socially inherited and constructed elaborate conceptual and linguistic edifices that serve, at least partially, to simplify and stabilize ("logicize," "falsify") the actual fluidity of our experience. Once again, we should not read this as some nostalgia for a lost world of becoming. On the contrary, Nietzsche greatly admires this tendency of humanity and these edifices themselves, arguing that they represent the "genius of the species" (GS 354) and show humanity to be "a mighty genius of construction, [that] succeeds in piling up an infinitely complicated dome of concepts upon an unstable foundation, and, as it were, on running water" (TL p. 85). "In this man is greatly to be admired," he writes, "but not on account of his drive for truth or for pure knowledge of things" (TL p. 85).

Nietzsche's contention that such structures are "false" is not a claim that something else—for instance, the world of becoming—is true. Here, as elsewhere, he makes polemical use of the terms "true" and "false," reversing the assignments given to them within the old schema that he is attempting to dismantle. Contrary to the metaphysicians, he argues, such edifices do not grant us "the truth" conceived of as the total comprehension of a stable world of being. In this sense, then, they are "false." But that is because such "truth" is not forthcoming, and such "falsity"—such provisional and pragmatic horizons—is all we ever have, "for—there is no 'truth.'" Nietzsche's aim here is to show that, contrary to the metaphysical view, our conceptual and linguistic edifices ought not to be set over and against becoming and do not provide us with a glimpse of another "true world." Rather, they themselves are *a part of* becoming: that is, they are themselves instances of the construction and inhabitation of provisional, conditional, and contingent horizons that satisfy important needs and desires.

With this in mind, we can provide alternative renderings of the passages that seemed to give credence to the skeptical view. *Will to Power* §517, then, might be reread in the following manner:

> The character of the world of becoming as *unformulable*, as "false," as "self-contradictory." [We can never stabilize and totalize from without a world that is in constant transition and of which we ourselves are a part.]

Knowledge and *becoming* exclude one another. [Conceived as the totalizing comprehension of a world of being, knowledge will be confounded by the world of becoming in which we live.] *Consequently,* "knowledge" must be something else: there must first of all be a will to make knowable, a kind of becoming must itself create the *deception of beings.* [If we want to maintain some notion of knowledge, we must conceive it differently. Instead of setting it over and against "becoming," we should see it as itself "a kind of becoming," as a process *within* becoming—as an active interpretation rather than a passive mirroring, as the will of living beings to select from, simplify, and stabilize their world so as to insure their self-preservation and/or -enhancement. Such a simplification and stabilization constitutes a "deception" insofar as it is not uniquely correct, for there are other purposes toward the satisfaction of which one might construe the world differently; and there is no construal that conjoins all possible purposes.]

Similarly, we might translate *Will to Power* §520 as follows:

A world of becoming could not, in the strict sense, be "comprehended" or "known" [again, Nietzsche declares that knowledge, conceived as the full comprehension of things-in-themselves, is a bankrupt ideal]; only to the extent that the "comprehending" and "knowing" intellect encounters a coarse, already-created world, built out of nothing but appearances but become firm to the extent that this kind of appearance has preserved life—only to this extent is there anything like "knowledge"; a measuring of earlier and later errors by one another. [What is given to knowledge is never "things as they are in themselves" but only previous appearances, previous interpretations, previous formulations of the world that are oriented toward some purpose or another (cf. *GS* 57–58). Knowing, then, becomes the weighing against one another of these interpretations, which, since they are not "truths," can polemically be called "errors."]

Finally, we might reread *Will to Power* §569 as follows:

The antithesis of the phenomenal world is *not* "the true world," but the formless unformulable world of the chaos of sensations—*another kind* of phenomenal world, a kind "unknowable" for us. [. . .] The question is whether there could not be many other ways of creating such an *apparent* world. [What is excluded from the apparent world of our knowledge is not some "real, true, world in itself," but simply *another* apparent world, another arrangement of appearances. As Nietzsche writes in a note from the same period: "The 'real world,' however one has hitherto conceived it—it has always been the apparent world *once again*"(*WP* 566; cf. *TI* "Reason" 6). To put this another way, we might say that the world outside of our rational interpretation is not a fact or a given, but simply the world as fabricated by *another* interpretation. The latter might be "unknowable for us" in the sense that it does not conform to the rational structure of our ordinary experience (e.g., the indeterminate world of quantum mechanics or the world of the artist's manipulation),[76] but this does not rule out its actuality. In fact, Nietzsche wants to encourage such alternative constructions, especially aesthetic ones, and to insist that the more perspectives and interpretations we can construct, the richer our knowledge will be.][77]

Thus, Nietzsche's apparent oppositions between becoming and being, the world as it is known and the world as it is really is, turn out to be no oppositions at all. The world of becoming is nothing other than the world in which we live and of which we have experience; and being and knowledge are not opposed to but are indeed modes of this becoming. If Nietzsche occasionally reverses the standard metaphysical oppositions, this is to be seen as a polemical strategy directed against metaphysicians who are quick to sever being from becoming, reality from appearance, and to elevate the former to the status of Reality, Being, and Truth. Nietzsche's polemics on the part of becoming, appearance, and error, then, are to be seen not as skeptical hypotheses but as sobering reminders of our contingency and conditionality and affirmations of our creative power.

3.4.2 ORDINARY OBJECTS AND HUMAN FINITUDE

The realist account of perspectivism also acknowledges that "perspectivism" seems to require that there be something given to our perspectives; yet it maintains that this relationship between subject and object ought not to be construed skeptically. For this account holds that Nietz-

---

76. Think, for instance, of the way in which the dreamlike spatial and temporal manipulations made possible by cinema are "understandable," though such effects are "irrational" in comparison with our ordinary experience. This is precisely Nietzsche's point in "On Truth and Lies," where, against "the rational man of science," he sets "the intuitive man of art" for whom "anything is possible at each moment," "every tree can suddenly speak as a nymph, [. . .] a god in the shape of a bull can drag away maidens," "and all of nature swarms around man as if it were nothing but a masquerade of the gods," "as colorful, irregular, lacking in results and coherence, charming, and eternally new as the world of dreams" (p. 89).

77. See GM III:12; GS 373; WP 259, 410, 600. More recently, in *Ways of Worldmaking*, Nelson Goodman has argued that the world is capable of an immense variety of interpretations ("versions"); or rather, that there are as many "worlds" as there are "right versions" ("rightness," here, conceived as the result of a host of selective criteria: initial credibility, entrenchment, coherence, usefulness, edification, novelty, etc.). Goodman argues that there is no uniquely correct world-version, that new versions proceed from and reinterpret previous versions, that most versions are irreducible to, and not conjoinable with, most others, and that the goal of "understanding" ought to be to generate and accumulate as many of these versions as possible.

sche rejects skepticism with the same stroke as he rejects the thing in itself. The object of perspectivism, then, cannot be some unknowable "becoming" or preconceptual "chaos of sensations" but must be something readily available to our knowledge.

However, according to the realist account, Nietzsche also rejects idealism. As such, the object of perspectivism cannot itself be a representation but must be something independent of our knowledge and its representations. This account thus comes to hold that the objects of perspectivism are simply the "ordinary," "commonsense" things of our everyday experience.[78] And this makes perspectivism "an obvious and nonproblematic doctrine."[79] Thus, Maudemarie Clark writes:

> The perspectivist metaphor does invite us to think of a thing that is independent of the perspectives on it. If the same thing can be seen from different perspectives, its existence is not reducible to the existence of representations. It must be an extramentally existing thing, a thing with its own foothold in reality. Such a thing has *existence in itself,* as opposed to having only the kind of existence Berkeley or Schopenhauer would grant it: existence as a representation or appearance, *existence in relation to a mind.* However, this does not make it a thing-in-itself. The possession of extramental existence (*existence in itself*) is neither necessary nor sufficient for being a thing-in-itself. What is required is rather an *essence in itself,* an essence or nature that is independent of what it can appear to be. The affirmation of an independently existing thing (common sense realism) will seem to affirm a thing-in-itself (metaphysical realism) only if one conflates the thing/appearance and the reality/appearance distinctions. Given that conflation, it follows that a thing with extramental existence, that is, a thing that is independent of its appearances, must possess a reality that is independent of how it appears. [. . .] Without this conflation, we have no basis for assuming that an extramentally existing thing has a reality that is independent of how it can appear (i.e., that it is a thing-in-itself). Nietzsche's use of the metaphor of perspective helps us to see the conflation for what it is. It sets an independently existing thing over against the perspectives on it, but it does not thereby commit him to the existence of a thing-in-itself, for it equates the latter with something completely contradictory (what something looks like from nowhere).[80]

78. See Clark, *Nietzsche on Truth and Philosophy,* 107, 121.

79. Ibid., 135. Cf. Leiter ("Perspectivism in Nietzsche's *Genealogy of Morals,*" 351–52): "perspectivism turns out to be much less radical than is usually supposed: we get, as one writer recently put it, 'a Nietzsche who is merely rehashing familiar Kantian themes, minus the rigor of Kant's exposition.' [. . .] Yet this is not a problem, particularly since Nietzsche's primary concerns lie elsewhere," namely, "with philosophical theories of agency and value." Leiter's reference is to Ken Gemes, "Nietzsche's Critique of Truth," *Philosophy and Phenomenological Research* 52 (1992): 49.

80. Clark, *Nietzsche on Truth and Philosophy,* 136–37.

In a similar vein, Brian Leiter writes that Nietzsche's perspectivism urges us to

> give up [. . .] the metaphysical construal of the epistemic notions in our practice: e.g., the idea that truth might be glossed in a metaphysically realist sense, as that which is available from no perspective at all (i.e., independent of *all* human interests); or conversely, the vulgar idealist gloss that it is nothing other than what particular human interests take it to be. A metaphysical realism of this sort is rendered unintelligible because human interests are *conditions* of anything being true or knowable (whereas the metaphysical realist would have truth transcend *all* human interests). And a crude idealism is avoided because: interests are *only conditions* of our knowledge of objects; hence particular interests are not *constitutive* of objects. So just as it is a condition of seeing a thing that we see it from some perspective, so too it is a condition of knowing that we do so from the perspective of some interest (need, affect). Similarly, this epistemic interest—like the analogous visual perspective—determines what piece of the object of knowledge we pick out. But the object of knowledge is never constituted by that or *any other particular* interest. In that sense, it remains an independent object. Yet it is not—and this is the key point—a transcendent object, i.e. a thing-in-itself. For the thing-in-itself is the thing that would transcend *all* possible perspectives on it; but the thing—the object of knowledge—as conceived by Nietzsche would not be left over after all possible perspectives were taken. It would just be a *thing itself* (*not* in-itself).[81]

In short, the objects of perspectivism, according to the realist account, are simply the ordinary things with which we are acquainted in our everyday experience. Every such thing "*is* independent of its appearances," since it is not constituted by our perspectives; though it has no "*essence* or *nature* independent of what it can appear to be," since essence or nature is, presumably, attributed to it by our perspectives and interests. In other words, while it is a condition of our knowledge that we know the thing "from somewhere," this knowledge is not constitutive of the object, which has an existence of its own.

If we always know the object "from somewhere," there are an infinite number of such "somewheres," an infinite number of perspectives on the object. Hence, the force of the "metaphor of perspective," according to the realist account, is that human knowledge is necessarily finite. Clark writes:

> Our capacity for truth is limited [. . . T]here are always more truths than any human being can know. We are, after all, finite creatures with a limited

---

81. Leiter, "Perspectivism in Nietzsche's *Genealogy of Morals*," 350.

amount of time to discover truths, whereas there are surely an infinite number of truths to discover. We should therefore expect people with different interests to discover different truths (as well as many common ones). Our interests will determine where we look, and therefore what we see.[82]

Similarly, Leiter argues that one of the central features of Nietzsche's perspectivism is the "Infinity Claim," which stipulates that: "We will never exhaust all possible perspectives on the object of knowledge (there are an infinity of interpretive interests that can be brought to bear)."[83] He concludes that, for Nietzsche, "we do indeed have knowledge of the world, though it is never disinterested, never complete, and can always benefit from additional non-distorting perspectives."[84]

We see that the realist account duly attempts to respect Nietzsche's critique of ontological and epistemological dualism. Yet this account is problematic for two reasons. First, it harbors a fatal contradiction. Both Clark and Leiter argue that, while the object of perspectivism does have its own independent existence, it does not have an "essence," "nature," or "reality" of its own. Yet both commentators are concerned to counter the claim "that reality holds no epistemic constraint on our interpretations of the world."[85] They maintain that the goal of knowledge is "to correspond to [the independently existing world], that is, get it 'the way it is,'" or "know about its actual nature."[86] But one cannot have it both ways. If the independently existing thing or world has no "essence," "nature," or "reality" of its own, then it cannot constrain our various attributions to it of "essence" or "nature." If, however, it does so constrain our perspectival attributions, then it must have some "essence" or "nature" of its own—that is, it must be, in Clark's and Leiter's terms, a "thing-in-itself," making it objectionable on all accounts.

Second, and more important for this discussion, the realist account is not supported by Nietzsche's texts. Once again, this account assumes the ordinary distinctions between knower and known, subject and object, perspective and thing—distinctions that Nietzsche relentlessly

82. Clark, *Nietzsche on Truth and Philosophy*, 135.
83. Leiter, "Perspectivism in Nietzsche's *Genealogy of Morals*," 345–46.
84. Ibid., 346, cf. pp. 350–51.
85. Ibid., 347. Cf. Clark, *Nietzsche on Truth and Philosophy*, 39.
86. Clark, *Nietzsche on Truth and Philosophy*, 39; Leiter, "Perspectivism in Nietzsche's *Genealogy of Morals*," 345.

challenges. The view that the objects of perspectivism are simply ordinary, independently existing things is nowhere found in Nietzsche.
On the contrary, he vigorously argues against this view. In *The Gay
Science,* we find that only "erroneous articles of faith" cause us to hold
"that there are enduring things; that there are identical things; that
there are things" (110). And in *Twilight of the Idols,* he exposes "the lie
of thinghood" ("Reason" 2), arguing that it is only "the metaphysics of
language" and "the prejudice of reason"—a projection of the "faith
in the ego-substance"—that "forces us to posit [. . .] thinghood"
("Reason" 5; cf. *TI* "Errors" 3). Moreover, he rejects the distinction between independent existence and attributed essence, maintaining that
"[i]f I remove all the relationships, all the 'properties,' all the 'activities'
of a thing, the thing does *not* remain over; because thingness has only
been fabricated by us [. . .] to bind together the multiplicity of relationships, properties, activities" (*WP* 558).[87]

Clark acknowledges that such passages might seem to put the realist interpretation in question. Yet she contends that they reject only
"the metaphysical concept of a substance, the concept of an unchanging substrate that underlies all change" and not "the ordinary concept of a thing," "the common sense idea of an enduring thing or substance."[88] The above-cited passages from Nietzsche clearly do reject
the former, "metaphysical" conception of a thing. But Nietzsche does
not make Clark's distinction between this "metaphysical" conception
and an "ordinary" or "common sense" conception of thinghood. One
might see this lack of distinction as simply intellectual carelessness on
Nietzsche's part. Yet I think it is something else and that this points to a
deep difference between Nietzsche's ontology and the commonsense realist account of it.

This difference becomes apparent once we consider Nietzsche's comments on the "lie of thinghood" within the larger framework of his theory of "interpretation," which we have seen to be so central and pervasive in his later work. In this light, we see that Nietzsche's perspectivism
accepts neither the world of commonsense realism nor the thesis that
this world is infinite and our knowledge of it finite. On the contrary, we

---

87. Though both Clark and Leiter take only the published work as worthy of consideration, this passage from the *Nachlaß* seems to me simply an extension of the passages
from the published work quoted in conjunction with it.
88. Clark, *Nietzsche on Truth and Philosophy,* 107, 121.

come to see that, for Nietzsche, there is no sense in speaking of "the world" outside of every interpretation and that the plurality of such interpretations follows not from "the world" being too much but from it being too little.

3.4.3 OBJECTHOOD AS INTERPRETIVE CONSTRUCT: NIETZSCHE VERSUS IDEALISM AND REALISM

Nietzsche conceives of the thing in itself in a twofold sense, both of which he rejects. On the one hand, he construes it in the Kantian sense: as a general posit naming that which gives content to our knowledge but which exists outside the structure of this knowledge. In this sense, the thing in itself is distinguished from the thing as it appears to our knowledge (see, e.g., GS 54; WP 553–54). Yet Nietzsche also thinks of the thing in itself more literally, as akin to the Cartesian conception of substance, namely, the pre-individuated, self-identical, unconditional, independently existing thing.[89] In this sense, the thing in itself is distinguished from the conditional or relational thing (see, e.g., WP 555–60).

This latter construal is not simply a misreading of Kant.[90] Nietzsche wants to extend his critique of the distinction between the thing in itself and appearance to a critique of the distinctions between substance and attribute, the absolute and the relational, the unconditional and the conditional. All the former terms, he argues, name entities and notions that are perniciously super-natural and metaphysical. Never in our experience of the natural world do we come across absolute and unconditional entities or things as they are in themselves. Everything we know to exist owes its genesis and continued existence to its dependence upon, and relations with, other things, forces, and events, past and present. Indeed, it is logically impossible for us to encounter such absolute

---

89. Thus, Descartes (*Principles of Philosophy*, in *Descartes: Philosophical Writings*, ed. and trans. Elizabeth Anscombe and Peter Thomas Geach [Indianapolis: Bobbs-Merrill, 1971], 192), writes: "We can mean by *substance* nothing other than a thing existing in such a manner that it has need of no other thing in order to exist." Cf. the reply to Arnauld ("Reply to the Fourth Set of Objections," in *The Philosophical Works of Descartes*, vol. 2, ed. and trans. Elizabeth S. Haldane and G. R. T. Ross [Cambridge: Cambridge University Press, 1967], 101): "Really the notion of *substance* is just this—that which can exist by itself, without the aid of any other substance."

90. A charge leveled by Wilcox, *Truth and Value in Nietzsche*, 120, and Houlgate, "Kant, Nietzsche, and the 'Thing in Itself,'" 128.

and unconditional things, because such an encounter would place them in a conditional relationship to us.[91] If things in themselves and absolute, unconditional things do not and cannot exist in our contingent, conditional, and relational world, they must exist in another world. But because this posit of the otherworldly arises within us, and because we are thoroughly contingent and conditional creatures with no extranatural source of knowledge or insight, Nietzsche concludes that this posit expresses nothing but a perverse desire for self- and world-negation.

Nietzsche thus rejects these notions and attempts to formulate an ontological theory that does without them. Following his usual strategy, he begins with the naturalistic premise that all the evidence we have for our ontology is sensory. But sensory evidence, Nietzsche acknowledges, reveals only so many appearances and effects, not the substantial "things" or "causes" that are said to underlie these appearances and effects.[92] He thus proposes that "things" and "causes" simply designate particular assemblages of appearances, dispositions to particular manifestations.[93] It is this line of thought that leads Nietzsche to claim that a " 'thing' is the sum of its effects, synthetically united by a concept, an

91. See WP 555: "One would like to know how *things in themselves* are obtained; but behold, there are no things in themselves! But even supposing there were an in-itself, an unconditioned thing, it would for that reason be *unknowable!* Something unconditioned cannot be known; otherwise it would *not* be unconditioned! Knowing is always but 'placing-oneself-in-a-conditional-relation-to-something'—one who seeks to know the unconditioned desires that it should not concern him. [. . .] This involves a contradiction. [. . .]"

92. See, e.g., WP 551: "We have absolutely no experience of a cause. [. . .] There is no such thing as a cause. [. . .] In fact, we invent causes after the schema of the effect: the latter is known to us." And see, e.g., GS 54: "What is 'appearance' for me now? Certainly not the opposite of some essence: what could I say about any essence except to name the attributes of its appearance! Certainly not a dead mask that one could place on an unknown x or remove from it!"

93. Nietzsche's view is, then, a particular kind of phenomenalism, as he himself grants in GS 354 and WP 475, 477–79. Yet, unlike traditional phenomenalism, Nietzsche's theory of knowledge does not rest upon the "givenness" of "sense data," nor does it take the knowing subject as something "given" to which appearances appear. While he thus grants that all we have are appearances, and that these appearances depend upon the stimulation of our sense organs, Nietzsche also holds that appearances only ever present themselves within the context of an interpretation. His position is thus closer to that of W. V. Quine and Nelson Goodman, for whom physical objects are not "given" but are simply the "posits" (or, as Quine occasionally calls them, "myths") of physicalistic systems, which are superior to other systems only in relation to a particular set of objectives. See Quine, "On What There Is," in *From a Logical Point of View* (Cambridge: Harvard University Press, 1961), 17ff., and "Two Dogmas of Empiricism," in *From a Logical Point of View*, 44–46, and Goodman, "The Way the World Is," in *Problems and Projects* (Indianapolis: Bobbs-Merrill, 1972), *Languages of Art*, 3–10, and *Ways of Worldmaking*, 8, 117, and *passim*.

image" (*WP* 551), that "objects" are only "complexes of events apparently durable in comparison with other complexes" (*WP* 552), and that
"the 'thing' in which we believe was only *invented and added* as a foundation for the various attributes" (*WP* 561).[94]

The notion that objects are particular complexes of "appearances"
and "effects" calls for a specification of that *to which* they appear and
that *which* they effect; for "appearances" and "effects" do not exist "in
themselves" but only relative to a particular standpoint. Nietzsche thus
comes to hold that objects are what they are only under a particular description, for a particular perspective or interpretation. He writes:

> That things possess a *constitution in themselves* entirely apart from interpre-
> tation and subjectivity, is *a totally idle hypothesis:* it presupposes that *inter-*
> *pretation and subjectivity* are *not* essential, that a thing freed from all rela-
> tionships would still be a thing. (*WP* 560)

> The "what is that?" is an *establishment of meaning* from some other view-
> point. The *"essence,"* the *"being"* [«Wesenheit»] is something perspectival
> that already presupposes a plurality [i.e., a relationship between the thing
> and that for-which the thing is a thing]. At bottom, there always lies "what
> is that for *me?"* (for us, for all that lives, etc.) [. . .] In short: the being
> [*Wesen*] of a thing is only an *opinion* about the "thing." Or rather: *"it is con-*
> *sidered"* [*es gilt*] is the actual *"it is,"* the only "this is." (*WP* 556)[95]

We should be careful to distinguish this position from any simple-
minded relativism, subjectivism, or solipsism. Nietzsche is not making

94. Charles Guignon (*Heidegger and the Problem of Knowledge,* 47–48) notes that
"this holistic conception of substance has a long and dignified history" and that it "holds
a distinguished place in German philosophy, running through Spinoza, Hegel, Schopenhauer, and Schelling, to Dilthey, Heidegger, and more recently Gadamer." Guignon neglects to mention Nietzsche; yet his description of this holistic ontology nicely captures
Nietzsche's view. "On the holistic view of substance," he writes, "the being of an entity is
determined by the totality of its relations to other entities within a whole field or system.
Hence, there is no way meaningfully to pick out or identify an entity without at least implicitly referring to the entire context in which it finds its place. [. . .] One consequence
of this emphasis on the context of the whole is that relations are raised to prominence
while the relata are dissolved into the network of relations in which they stand. The priority of relations over individuals leads to a 'philosophy of internal relations' in which
each concept serves to pick out a nexus in a field rather than an object. If all relations are
internal, then changes in any term in the network will have repercussions across the
whole. [. . . I]t seems that claiming that a relation is internal to an entity is always relativized to a particular description of that entity. [. . .] If an entity's being is fully circum-
scribed by its place in a totality, then it is not clear that another entity could take its place
without changing the meaning of the whole. As a result, the essence of an entity is inextricably bound up with its actual locus in the totality. It cannot be picked out or identified
independently of its position in that context." Cf. *WP* 553–70.
95. Cf. *GS* 58 and *WP* 625. Note that, in all these passages, Nietzsche does not make
Clark's distinction between essence-in-itself and existence-in-itself. For Nietzsche, a thing
removed from its network of relationships has neither essence nor existence.

the claim that everything is subjective such that no one person can ever know how the world appears to another. We have seen that the term "perspective," for Nietzsche, does not characterize the private point of view of an individual but, instead, designates the particular interpretive horizon of a form of life, defined as an evaluative center situated anywhere from the micro-level of affects to the macro-level of cultural, social, and political organizations. And we have seen that the individual is a configuration of these micro- and macro-perspectives, not an atomic entity with a unique perspective of its own.[96] We have also seen that Nietzsche conceives of these perspectives not as radically disjoint from one another but as always engaged in a struggle that incessantly leads to the blurring of old boundaries between interpretations and to the construction of new hybrids. Finally, we have seen that, for Nietzsche, the "active and interpreting forces" that constitute a particular perspective are that "through which alone seeing becomes a seeing-*something*" (*GM* III: 12, my emphasis)—that is, that interpretations determine what is to count as an object or thing.

In Nietzsche's usage, then, a perspective is not a private point of view but a public system of evaluation that assembles, selects, organizes, and hierarchizes appearances deemed relevant to its particular purposes and projects. In this light, we can see that Nietzsche's perspectival ontology has little in common with facile subjective relativism. It does, however, have much in common with the systematic and public "ontological relativity" more recently defended by American philosophers such as W. V. Quine, Nelson Goodman, Catherine Elgin, Hilary Putnam, and Richard Rorty.[97] In a general sense, this doctrine of "ontological

96. Recall *WP* 481: "'Everything is subjective,' you say; but even this is interpretation. The 'subject' is nothing given, but something added, fabricated, and stuck behind."
97. See Quine, "Ontological Relativity"; Goodman, "The Way the World Is" and *Ways of Worldmaking;* Goodman and Elgin, *Reconceptions in Philosophy;* Elgin, "The Relativity of Fact and the Objectivity of Value," in *Relativism: Interpretation and Confrontation,* ed. Michael Krausz (Notre Dame: University of Notre Dame Press, 1989); and Putnam, "Reflections on Goodman's *Ways of Worldmaking*" and "Irrealism and Deconstruction," in *Starmaking: Realism, Anti-Realism, and Irrealism,* ed. Peter J. McCormick (Cambridge, Mass.: MIT Press, 1996). Rorty sides with this view throughout his work. Of course, there are significant differences among the various formulations of this theory. Yet I am concerned only with general features shared by most of these formulations, e.g., the relativity of ontology to theory, the absence of a uniquely correct theory, and, thus, the absence of a unique ontology. For discussion of the differences between various formulations of the theory, see Putnam, "The Way the World Is," in *Realism with a Human Face* (Cambridge, Mass.: Harvard University Press, 1990), and "Irrealism and Deconstruction." While these philosophers are generally more concerned with differences between *scientific* systems (e.g., phenomenalistic vs. physicalistic systems, macro-physical vs. micro-physical systems), Goodman and Elgin make it clear that the theory is also ap-

relativity" holds: (1) that it makes no sense to give an absolute description of "what there is"; (2) that it only makes sense to say "what there is" relative to a background theory, which will have its own purposes, principles, and criteria of individuation; (3) that there exist a host of such theories, many of which are equally warranted yet incompatible with one another; and thus (4) that there is no uniquely correct "way the world is" but rather as many "ways the world is" as there are warranted theories.

This view proceeds from the naturalistic premise that we never encounter "the world as it is in itself" but always "the world as it appears under a particular description." Because there is no comparing a "description of the world" with "the world as it is under no description at all," this latter notion turns out, at best, to be superfluous. All we ever can do is compare descriptions with other descriptions. And because there is no One True World, there is no description that could show itself to be the One True Description by "corresponding to" that World. Thus there will always be many descriptions and no single, independent world that they all describe. Each *description,* then, is actually a *prescription* that constructs a world, leaving us with no World but many worlds.[98]

Moreover, this multiplicity is a permanent condition rather than the

plicable to those systems that are closest to Nietzsche's concerns, e.g., the evaluative systems of art and morality. See Goodman, *Languages of Art,* and Goodman and Elgin, *Reconceptions in Philosophy.*

98. The notion that every valid description constructs a "world" or "world-version" is proposed by Goodman in *Ways of Worldmaking.* It has generated considerable controversy, even among those who are otherwise sympathetic to Goodman's project. Critics argue that the notion that we simultaneously inhabit many worlds is metaphysical at worst and misleading at best. See, for example, Quine, "Goodman's *Ways of Worldmaking,*" in *Theories and Things* (Cambridge, Mass.: Harvard University Press, 1981); the articles by C. G. Hempel, Israel Scheffler, and Hilary Putnam in McCormick, ed., *Starmaking;* and Rorty, "Introduction: Pragmatism and Philosophy," in *Consequences of Pragmatism* (Minneapolis: University of Minnesota Press, 1982), xlvii. Despite these criticisms, Goodman makes clear his reasons for the formulation: because there is no World of which all descriptions are valid, and because descriptions delineate modes of composing, weighting, and ordering entities, qualities, and their relationships, we seem justified in saying that there are many "worlds" or "world-versions" provided that we conceive of these worlds as the specifiable, *actual* worlds of our practice and not the merely *possible* worlds of metaphysical speculation. In addition to *Ways of Worldmaking,* see Goodman, *Of Mind and Other Matters* (Cambridge, Mass.: Harvard University Press, 1984), chap. 2. I think that the term "world" has a distinct advantage over the term "perspective" and even "interpretation" insofar as it does not as easily invite us to think of the points of view of pre-given subjects on pre-given objects. On Nietzsche, the death of God, and the multiplicity of worlds, see also Gilles Deleuze, *Difference and Repetition,* trans. Paul Patton (New York: Columbia University Press, 1994), 55–56, 68–69, and *The Logic of Sense,* 171–74, 259–65.

temporary result of inadequate knowledge. The ontological relativist repudiates the idea that all these world-versions may eventually converge
to form a total picture of the World. If one follows such theorists as
Thomas Kuhn and Michel Foucault, such an ideal is not even to be
hoped for in the world of science, from whence it originates. The move
from one scientific paradigm to another is seen as not so much a progressive accumulation as a series of perceptual and conceptual gestalt shifts,
like those required when considering very different works of art.[99] Even
if the scientific world is conceived as progressive and cumulative, beside
it sits the many worlds of art, religion, politics, and so on, which do not
share these features and which can never be reduced to the scientific
without remainder. Thus, we inhabit many worlds at once, and "objectivity" comes to name a competence in the many ways of worldmaking
and the ability to shift skillfully and appropriately from one to another.

Nietzsche affirms each of these theses. For Nietzsche, there are only
descriptions, interpretations, or perspectives . . .

> There is *only* a perspective seeing, *only* a perspective "knowing." (*GM* III: 12)

. . . and no One True World of which they are all descriptions:

> The "apparent" world is the only one: the "true" world is merely *added by
> a lie.* (*TI* "Reason" 2)

> There is no "other," no "true," no essential being. [. . .] The antithesis of
> the apparent world and the true world is reduced to the antithesis "world"
> and "nothing." (*WP* 567)

Each perspective fabricates a world and its entities:

> The question "what is that?" is an *establishment of meaning* from some other
> viewpoint. The "*essence*," the "*being*" is something perspectival. (*WP* 556)

> The *perspective* therefore determines the character of the "appearance."
> (*WP* 567)

There are many different, coexisting perspectives:

> No limit to the ways in which the world can be interpreted. (*WP* 600)

> The world [. . .] has no meaning behind it, but countless meanings. (*WP*
> 481)[100]

---

99. See Thomas Kuhn, *The Structure of Scientific Revolutions*, 2d ed. (Chicago: University of Chicago Press, 1970), and Michel Foucault, *The Order of Things: An Archaeology of the Human Sciences*, trans. Alan Sheridan (London: Tavistock, 1970).

100. Cf. *KSA* 12:1[120]: "The same text permits countless interpretations: there is
no 'correct' interpretation." Also see *GS* 374 and *GM* II: 12–13.

Thus there are many different, coexisting worlds; and "the world" is nothing other than the sum total of these "apparent" worlds:

> Every center of force adopts a *perspective* toward the entire *remainder,* i.e., its own particular *valuation,* mode of action, and mode of resistance. The "apparent world," therefore, is reduced to a specific mode of action on the world, emanating from a center. Now there is no other mode of action whatever; and the "world" is only a word for the totality of these actions. (*WP* 567)

This collection is not a congruent synthesis but an assemblage of differences:

> The world, apart from our condition of living in it, [. . .] does *not* exist as a world "in-itself"; it is essentially a world of relations; it has [. . .] a *differing aspect* from every point; its being is essentially different from every point; it presses upon every point, every point resists it—and the sum of these is in every case quite *incongruent.* (*WP* 568)

Nor is this assemblage cumulative, since each step of the way

> involves a fresh interpretation, an adaptation through which any previous "meaning" and "purpose" are necessarily obscured or even obliterated. (*GM* II:12)

Finally, for Nietzsche, "objectivity" no longer means the attempt to see the world under no description at all, or the achievement of an absolute knowing that could synthesize all these perspectives and aspects, but rather the cultivation of a variety of perspectives and the ability skillfully to shift among them:

> "Objectivity" [ought to be understood] as the ability to have one's For and Against *under control* and to engage and disengage them, so that one knows how to employ a *variety* of perspectives and affective interpretations in the service of knowledge. (*GM* III:12)

> The wisest man would be the one richest in contradictions. (*WP* 259)[101]

---

101. Cf. *BGE* 12: "a philosopher—if today there could be philosophers—would be compelled to find the greatness of man, the concept of 'greatness,' precisely in his range and multiplicity, in his wholeness in manifoldness. He would even determine value and rank in accordance with how much and how many things one could bear and take upon himself, how *far* one could extend his responsibility."

Not only does Nietzsche's perspectivism have nothing to do with solipsism or subjectivist relativism, it also has nothing to do with idealism, contrary to the suggestions of some of his commentators.[102] In the first place, Nietzsche short-circuits idealism by rejecting the notion that subjects or minds are primary or given (see *WP* 481).[103] As we have seen, both "subjects" and "objects," for Nietzsche, are what they are only by virtue of their relationships, that is, by virtue of their actions, reactions, and the ways in which these relate to the actions and reactions of the entities with which they coexist. Rejecting the notions of the noumenal self and the self-as-substance, Nietzsche argues that we know ourselves only empirically[104] and that this self-apprehension and self-knowledge is a complex and ongoing process of balancing the ways in which we appear to ourselves and the ways in which we are described and situated by others.[105] In short, then, for Nietzsche, "the subject," too, is a collection of appearances organized by an interpretation—the latter encompassing, rather than proceeding from, a conscious subject and extending far beyond the realm of consciousness and subjectivity to include the instinctive and, perhaps, even the inorganic.

Nor does Nietzsche deny the reality of the external world or claim that we can make interpretations, worlds, subjects, and objects any way we please. He understands that there are always constraints upon our worldmaking. He only refuses to grant that there is some pre-given world that can or should ultimately serve as that constraint. Rather,

102. See Danto, *Nietzsche as Philosopher*, 231–32; Wilcox, *Truth and Value in Nietzsche*, 121–22; Davey, "Nietzsche and Hume on Self and Identity," 21–21; and Julian Young, *Nietzsche's Philosophy of Art* (Cambridge: Cambridge University Press, 1992), 95. For the suggestion that Goodman's view is an idealism, see Putnam, "Irrealism and Deconstruction," 180, 189. Against this view, see Goodman, "Comments," in McCormick, ed., *Starmaking*; and Rorty, "Introduction" to *Consequences of Pragmatism*, xxxix–xl; and Goodman, *Ways of Worldmaking*, x, 119.

103. See §3.3, above, and Strong, *Friedrich Nietzsche and the Politics of Transfiguration*, 298.

104. See *GS* 354: "It was only as a social animal that man acquired self-consciousness"; and cf. *WP* 524: "It is essential that one should not make a mistake over the role of 'consciousness': it is our *relation with the 'outer world' that evolved it*. [. . . I]t is only a *means of communication*: it evolved through social intercourse and with a view to the interests of social intercourse . . . '[i]ntercourse' here understood to include the influences of the outer world and the reactions they compel on our side; also our effect *upon* the outer world." For more on "the phenomenality of the inner world," see *WP* 475, 477–79, 504.

105. For instance, Nietzsche's descriptions of both the man of *ressentiment* and the man of nobility characterize self-consciousness as essentially bound up with social relations: in the former case, those between oneself and a foreign other, in the latter case, those between oneself and one's peers.

what reality there is and what constraints there are, Nietzsche argues, are provided solely by *the dominant, existing interpretations*.[106] We are born into and live among the worlds that have been fabricated by our forebears.[107] These worlds need not be accepted in full, but neither can they be rejected altogether or even in large part. For, if we have relinquished the notion that there exists a pre-given world, nothing can serve as a foil for an interpretation except *another interpretation;* and, to perform a compelling transformation, we must use old interpretations as a lever.[108] Transformation is effected only by slow and patient work, which proceeds by appealing to at least some of the accepted criteria in the service of novel construction.[109] "We can destroy only as creators!" Nietz-

---

106. See *GS* 58. Cf. Goodman (*Ways of Worldmaking*, 6): "The many stuffs—matter, energy, waves, phenomena—that worlds are made of are made along with the worlds. But made from what? Not from nothing, after all, but from other worlds. Worldmaking as we know it always starts from worlds already on hand; the making is a remaking."

107. That is, we cannot help but be "burdened with those estimates of things that have their origin in the passions and loves of former centuries" (*GS* 57).

108. See *GM* III:10. This is a theme common to many recent versions of antifoundationalism and holism. It is, for instance, a central feature of Donald Davidson's view in "On the Very Idea of a Conceptual Scheme" and of much of the early work of Jacques Derrida (*Of Grammatology*, trans. Gayatri C. Spivak [Baltimore: Johns Hopkins University Press, 1974], 138–39), who writes: "The already-there-ness of instruments and concepts cannot be undone or reinvented. In that sense the passage from desire to discourse loses itself in *bricolage*, it builds its castles with debris. [. . . T]he most radical discourse, the most inventive and systematic engineer are surprised and circumvented by a history, a language, etc., a world (for 'world' means nothing else) from which they must borrow their tools, if only to destroy the former machine. [. . .] The idea of the engineer breaking with all *bricolage* is dependent on a creationist theology." Cf. Derrida, "Structure, Sign, and Play in the Discourse of the Human Sciences," in *Writing and Difference*, trans. Alan Bass (Chicago: University of Chicago Press, 1978), 280–81.

109. It is not surprising, then, that Nietzsche's preferred manner of critique and construction is genealogical. Contrary to "history," which, according to Nietzsche, is imbued with the false notion that development or evolution is a continuous progress from origin to goal, "genealogy" sees the past as "a continuous sign-chain of ever new interpretations and adaptations whose causes do not even have to be related to one another but, on the contrary, in some cases succeed and alternate with one another in a purely chance fashion," as "a succession of more or less profound, more or less mutually independent processes of subduing, plus the resistances they encounter" (*GM* II:12). Genealogical inquiry, then, investigates the past to reveal the contingency of the dominant interpretations and to discover resources with which to counter those interpretations. This methodology, and the antifoundationalism and antiessentialism that necessitate it, has profoundly influenced Nietzsche's heirs. It is evident in Heidegger's conception of the *destruktion* of the history of ontology and Derrida's conception of the "deconstruction" of metaphysics, both of which reject radical novelty and take their task to involve a de-construction and re-construction, that is, a desedimentation of past interpretations so as to open up possibilities that had thus far been foreclosed by the interpretive tradition. See Heidegger, *Being and Time*, §6, and Derrida, *Of Grammatology*, 10ff. On the distinction between "genealogy" and "history" in Nietzsche, see Foucault, "Nietzsche, Genealogy, History," in *Language, Counter-Memory, Practice*.

sche writes. "But let us not forget this either: it is enough to create new names and estimations and probabilities in order to create in the long run new 'things'" (GS 58).[110]

If Nietzsche's ontological theory is, thus, not an idealism, neither is it a realism, whether "metaphysical" or "common sense." For Nietzsche holds: (1) that we never encounter a pre-given world (whether of "becoming" or of "ordinary objects"); (2) that the world we encounter is the world as constructed by one or another interpretation; and (3) that all interpretation is reinterpretation. In short, for Nietzsche, there is no escaping the world of interpretation; and, indeed, without interpretation, there is no "world."

Several important passages underscore these points. Nietzsche begins Book Two of *The Gay Science* with a section that foregrounds this "antirealism." Addressing his remarks to "the realists," he writes:

> You sober people who feel well armed against passion and fantasy and would like to turn your emptiness into a matter of pride and an ornament: you call yourselves realists and hint that the world really is the way it appears to you. As if reality stood unveiled before you alone. [. . .] But in your unveiled state are not even you still very passionate and dark creatures [. . .] and still far too similar to an artist in love?[. . .] You are still burdened with those estimates of things that have their origin in the passions and loves of former centuries. Your sobriety still contains a secret and inextinguishable drunkenness. Your love of "reality," for example—oh that is a primeval "love." In every sensation and every sense impression there is a piece of this old love; and some fantasy, some prejudice, some unreason, some ignorance, some fear, and ever so much else has woven it and worked on it. That mountain there! That cloud there! What is "real" in that? Subtract the phantasm and every human *ingredient* from it, you sober ones! If you *can!* If you can forget your descent, your past, your training—all of your humanity and animality. There is no "reality" for us—not for you either, you sober ones[.] (GS 57; cf. GS 54)

Here we find a series of reversals: the "realist" is a kind of "artist," her "reality" the product of a "fantasy," her "sobriety" a form of "drunkenness," her "objectivity," "reason," and "knowledge" forms of "passion," "prejudice," "unreason," and "ignorance." This is more than simply a gratuitous attack on "realism," "science," and "objectivity." As with so much in Nietzsche, the rhetoric of this passage is motivated by an important insight that issues from his thoroughgoing naturalism.

110. Cf. *HL* 3, quoted p. 135n. 62, above.

"Realism" is attacked only for deluding itself with sham ideals and for denying its actual cognitive and instinctual operations. It is attacked only for wanting "to see the world as it really is," stripped of every interpretation (see *GM* III:24) and the background of "descent," "past," and "training" that is the condition of seeing anything *as* anything at all (see *GM* III:12). Put in the affirmative, Nietzsche's point is simply that all "finding" is "creating," that all "science" is "art," insofar as science, too, necessarily involves "interpretation," a notion generally consigned to the realm of the aesthetic (which itself has been traditionally subordinated to the scientific due to its preoccupation with "appearances" and "styles," its conscious "fabrication," and its lack of concern with "truth").[111]

Even the *notion* of "reality" and the *desire* to "lay it bare," Nietzsche argues, are the products of interpretation—of an antinaturalistic interpretation based on the central belief that there must be another, better, real, true world that contains indubitable facts, certainties, and foundations. Thus, later in *The Gay Science,* Nietzsche writes: "The truthful man, in the audacious and ultimate sense presupposed by faith in science, *thereby affirms another world* than the world of life, nature, and history; and insofar as he affirms this 'other world,' does this not

---

111. It is this primacy of interpretation that leads Nietzsche to argue for the primacy of art over science. This idea is found throughout Nietzsche's work, from *The Birth of Tragedy* and "On Truth and Lies" (especially §2 of that essay) to the *Genealogy of Morals.* In the *Genealogy,* Nietzsche writes: "*Art*—to say it in advance, for I shall one day return to this subject at greater length—art, in which precisely the *lie* is sanctified and the *will to deception* has a good conscience, is much more fundamentally opposed to the ascetic ideal than is science: this was instinctively sensed by Plato, the greatest enemy of art Europe has yet produced. Plato versus Homer: that is the complete, the genuine antagonism—there the sincerest advocate of the 'beyond,' the great slanderer of life; here the instinctive deifier, the *golden* nature" (*GM* III:25). In a passage that resonates in more than a few ways with Nietzsche's point that, for the naturalist, science involves art and artifice, Quine ("Two Dogmas of Empiricism," 44) writes: "Physical objects are conceptually imported into [the prediction of future experience] as convenient intermediaries—not by definition in terms of experience, but simply as irreducible posits comparable, epistemologically, to the gods of Homer. For my part I do, qua lay physicist, believe in physical objects and not in Homer's gods; and I consider it a scientific error to do otherwise. But in point of epistemological footing the physical objects and the gods differ only in degree and not in kind. Both sorts of entities enter our conception only as cultural posits. The myth of physical objects is epistemologically superior to most in that it has proved more efficacious than other myths as a device for working a manageable structure into the flux of experience." This is precisely the way that, in "On Truth and Lies," Nietzsche describes the "man of science," who differs from "the man of art" only insofar as his world-interpretation is primarily directed toward utility for survival. See *TL* pp. 88–91. For a more recent statement of the position that science is art by other means, see Goodman, *Languages of Art,* 242–64, and *Ways of Worldmaking,* 102, 106–7, 139–40. This idea is more fully discussed above in §1.7, above.

mean that he has to deny its antithesis, this world, *our* world?" (*GS* 344). This view is restated in that important passage from the *Genealogy of Morals* (III:24) in which Nietzsche argues that modern science is still ascetic and metaphysical insofar as it preserves an unconditional faith in truth, wishing to uncover "the *factum brutum*" and renounce all interpretation.

The point of these passages, I take it, is that there are "things" and "facts" only within the framework of an interpretation; and that, without interpretation—that is, without some system that makes ontological commitments and accords its entities meaning and value—there are no "facts" or "things" at all. Paraphrasing Nietzsche, we might say that the antithesis of the world of interpretation and world in itself is the antithesis "world" and "nothing" (see *WP* 567).

3.5 THE FINITUDE AND INFINITUDE OF INTERPRETATION: NIETZSCHE'S ANTIESSENTIALISM

Nietzsche's ontological theory, then, presumes neither a pre-given world of unknowable becoming nor a pre-given world of ordinary objects. Against all realisms, Nietzsche maintains that every ontology is the construction of an interpretation and that no world would remain over after the subtraction of every interpretation. Against idealism, he argues that interpretations are not the productions of isolated subjects or minds but complexes of evaluation and power that traverse the entire spectrum of organic life and are discernible even in the inorganic world. Indeed, Nietzsche short-circuits the distinction between idealism and realism by dissolving the poles of subject and object into the unified field of interpretation or will to power.

In the remaining chapters, I examine Nietzsche's ontological theory in detail. Yet before turning to this, I want to draw attention to one final consequence of the account of perspectivism presented above. I began by arguing that the term "perspectivism" is misleading, because it suggests that a visual analogy provides the key to Nietzsche's theory of knowledge. I argued that this is not the case and, instead, recommended that we refigure Nietzsche's conception of knowledge within a general theory of interpretation. We can now bring into relief an important contrast between the visual and interpretive conceptions of perspectivism.

The visual account maintains that the force of Nietzsche's doctrine lies in its assertion of the finitude of human knowledge and the infinitude of the world's being. Our field of vision is always only partial, largely ignorant of features and occurrences outside of it. The visual account of perspectivism takes Nietzsche to be making a similar point about human knowledge. Thus, for example, Jean Granier writes: "The idea of the fundamental perspectivism of knowledge has as its precise function the uprooting of the metaphysical conviction that subjectivity is capable of dominating the totality of Being. [. . .] The epistemological subject is necessarily situated, his field of knowledge is finite; thus no one perspective can exhaust the richness of reality."[112] Arguing that truth is dependent upon our cognitive interests but independent of our cognitive capacities, Clark writes: "There are always more truths than any human being can know. We are, after all, finite creatures with a limited amount of time to discover truths, whereas there are surely an infinite number of truths to discover."[113] Finally, Leiter writes that, according to Nietzsche's perspectival view of knowledge: "We will never exhaust all possible perspectives on the object of knowledge. [. . . W]e do indeed have knowledge of the world, though it is never disinterested, never complete, and can always benefit from additional non-distorting perspectives."[114]

Relying on the optical analogy, these accounts presume a passive conception of knowledge, an essentialist conception of ontology, and a correspondence theory of truth. That is, they conceive of knowledge as prompted by, and directed toward, the accurate representation of the richness of an antecedent reality. Knowing is modeled on the accumulation of successive visual representations of a static object. Though total comprehension will always be impossible for finite creatures like ourselves, it nonetheless remains a cognitive ideal. Thus, conceiving the world as a text, Granier writes:

> The rules of philology require that we sacrifice interest and utility for the demands of a textual understanding, one that would restore, to the extent to which it is possible, the original meaning of the text. The text is not a plaything of human subjectivity. [. . .] Here we must set out to discover this primordial ground, upon which every interpretation grows. For the noblest and most courageous spirits, one voice speaks louder than that of their own vital interests, commanding us to do justice to nature, to reveal things as they are in their own being.[115]

112. Granier, "Perspectivism and Interpretation," 190.
113. Clark, *Nietzsche on Truth and Philosophy*, 135.
114. Leiter, "Perspectivism in Nietzsche's *Genealogy of Morals*," 345–46.
115. Granier, "Perspectivism and Interpretation," 199. Evidence for this view appears in *A* 52, where, against theological hermeneutics, Nietzsche celebrates the virtues of

Clark, too, conceives of perspectival knowledge in this manner. On her view, perspectivism satisfies "the minimal correspondence theory of truth," according to which "our beliefs are about an independently existing world" and "they can be true only if they correspond to it, that is, get it 'the way it is.'"[116] Following Clark's lead, Leiter holds that perspectival knowledge seeks correspondence with the external world. On his account, "the Perspectivist Thesis (Proper)" states that:

> Knowledge of objects in any particular case is always conditioned by particular interpretive interests that direct the knower to corresponding features of the object of knowledge. [. . .] If they are not to distort the real (but non-transcendent) nature of objects, however, these particular interests must be adequate to relevant respects of [. . .] reality.[117]

This version of Nietzsche's perspectivism is rendered problematic by the account of the doctrine I have presented above. I have argued that perspectivism is poorly conceived as developing an optical analogy and best read as functioning within a generalized conception of interpretation. Thus, Nietzsche regards all entities as interpretive complexes situated within a network of other such complexes, each of which constantly attempts to extend its range and power by interpolating, adjusting, and reworking the interpretations (or parts of interpretations) with which it is presented. On this model, then, interpretations strive not for the adequate representation of an ontologically distinct world but for power and influence over (via the incorporation and assimilation of) other interpretations.[118] Thus, it makes no sense to say that the world

---

"philology," construed as "the art of reading well—of reading facts *without* falsifying them through interpretation" (cf. *BGE* 38 and *WP* 479). This passage does pose a problem for the interpretation I have proposed. Yet the view it presents is so unusual in Nietzsche's corpus, and is so greatly outweighed by passages that express the opposite view (that there are no uninterpreted facts: *GM* III:24 marks a particularly striking contrast), that it is hard to take it at face value. I think we ought to read the passage as expressing Nietzsche's outrage at the mendaciousness and intellectual laziness of Christian interpretations and his frustration at their persistence in everyday life, despite the event of "God's death." For Nietzsche, such Christian interpretations must still submit to the challenge of scientific reason; only then can they submit to his own post-positivistic discourse. In short, I think this passage ought to be taken as part of Nietzsche's campaign for "intellectual conscience," which, as we saw in chapter 1, ultimately supports, rather than denies, the irreducibility of interpretation.

116. Clark, *Nietzsche on Truth and Philosophy*, 39.

117. Leiter, "Perspectivism in Nietzsche's *Genealogy of Morals*," 351.

118. See *GM* II:11–12 and *WP* 636–44. The drive for power will, no doubt, often involve fidelity to existing standards of representation but only as a means toward greater power. A similar point, I think, is made by Nelson Goodman (*Ways of Worldmaking*, 18): "The scientist who supposes that he is single-mindedly dedicated to the search for truth deceives himself. He is unconcerned with the trivial truths he could grind out endlessly;

outside of perspective and interpretation is "infinitely rich," because, for Nietzsche, there is no such world. "In itself" the world has neither existence nor essence: both are interpretive constructions.[119]

However, even on this antidualist rendering of Nietzsche's perspectivism, there is still some sense in which interpretations are finite and the world infinite. But the reasons for this are precisely the opposite of those appealed to by the visual conception of perspectivism. Alluding to Nietzsche, Jacques Derrida provides an appropriate formulation of the different conceptions of finitude under consideration here. He writes:

> There are two ways of conceiving the limit of totalization. [. . .] Totalization can be judged in the classical style: one then refers to the empirical endeavor of either a subject or a finite discourse in a vain and breathless quest of an infinite richness which it can never master. There is too much, more than one can say. But nontotalization can also be determined in another way: no longer from the standpoint of a concept of finitude as relegation to the empirical, but from the standpoint of the concept of *play.* If totalization no longer has any meaning, it is not because the infiniteness of the field cannot be covered by a finite glance or a finite discourse, but because the nature of the field [. . .] excludes totalization. This field is in effect that of *play,* that is to say, a field of infinite substitutions only because it is finite, that is to say, because instead of being an inexhaustible field, as in the classical hypothesis, instead of being too large, there is something missing from it: a center which arrests and grounds the play of substitutions.[120]

The first of these "two ways of conceiving the limit of totalization" summarizes the notion of finitude assumed by the visual account of per-

---

and he looks to the multifaceted and irregular results of observations for little more than suggestions of overall structures and significant generalizations. He seeks system, simplicity, and scope; and when he is satisfied on these scores, he tailors truth to fit. He as much decrees as discovers the laws he sets forth, as much designs as discerns the patterns he delineates." And, one might add, he decrees and designs in the interest of greater control over the environing world.

119. See, e.g., *WP* 556 ("'essence,' the 'essential nature' is something perspectival") and *GM* II:12, which argues that form, meaning, existence, and essence are the constructions of an interpretive will to power. Cf. also *WP* 643.

120. Derrida, "Structure, Sign, and Play," 289. Note that the Bass translation inadvertently omits the words "discourse in a vain and breathless quest of an infinite." The distinction between these two conceptions of "nontotalization" is also discussed by Nelson Goodman, who attempts to sort out the difference between the claims of "the mystic" and those of "the ontological relativist" or "pluralist." While both parties seem to agree that no description can ever be faithful to the world as it is, the former maintains that this is because the essence of the world is too great and ineffable for us to grasp, while the latter maintains that this is because the world is nothing in itself, because the world is something only insofar as it is construed by one of the many incompatible, true descriptions of it. See Goodman, "The Way the World Is."

spectivism. On this view, perspectivism describes "the empirical endeavor of either a subject or a finite discourse in a vain and breathless quest of an infinite richness which it can never master." Such a view presupposes the existence of a pre-given world that always remains outside of our perspectival grasp and dreams of an omniscient being who could encompass this infinite richness. But this is not Nietzsche's view. Nietzsche's perspectivism is captured in the second formulation, according to which the world is infinite and nontotalizable "not because the richness of the field cannot be covered by a finite glance or a finite discourse, but [. . .] because, instead of being too large, there is something missing from it: a center which arrests and grounds the play of substitutions." Translating this into Nietzsche's idiom, "the world has become 'infinite'" (GS 374) precisely insofar as it is seen as *lacking* an essence, since essence is perspectival and perspectives are always contested, engaged in a perpetual struggle that forces the incessant substitution of one interpretation for another. For Nietzsche, there are "infinite interpretations" (GS 374)—and therefore world-versions— precisely because there is no World and no super-natural judge that could settle the struggle once and for all.

Recalling Nietzsche's description of this struggle in the *Genealogy of Morals* (II 12), Michel Foucault puts the point nicely:

> If interpretation can never be brought to an end, it is simply because there is nothing to interpret. There is nothing absolutely primary to interpret, because at bottom everything is already interpretation. [. . .] There is never, if you will, an *interpretandum* which is not already an *interpretans*, so that there is established in interpretation a relation of violence as much as of elucidation. In fact, interpretation does not illuminate an interpretive topic that would offer itself passively to it; it can only violently seize an interpretation already there, which it must reverse, return, shatter with blows of a hammer.[121]

Along with Derrida's, this formulation allows us to see that the world of ubiquitous interpretation is one of becoming and will to power and that these doctrines do not name some primary essence or *interpretandum* but are simply different ways of describing the struggle of interpretation itself. Thus, the doctrine of "becoming" holds that there is being only according to an interpretation and that one interpretation always passes

121. Michel Foucault, "Nietzsche, Freud, Marx," trans. Alan D. Schrift, in *Transforming the Hermeneutic Context: From Nietzsche to Nancy,* ed. Gayle L. Ormiston and Alan D. Schrift (Albany: State University of New York Press, 1990), 64.

over into another, forming a "continuous sign-chain of ever new interpretations and adaptations." Thus, "will to power," too, names this incessant process of substitution—victorious new interpretations "becoming master" over previous and existing interpretations (*GM* II:12)
and maintaining their hegemony only by subduing rebellious forces from
within and encroachments from without. We must now turn to these
doctrines to fill out these suggestions and the antidualist reading of
Nietzsche's epistemology and ontology I have proposed.

CHAPTER FOUR

Becoming and Chaos,
or *Différance* and *Chaosmos*

[Heraclitus] denied the duality of totally diverse worlds. [. . .]
He no longer distinguished a physical world from a metaphysical one.[. . .] And after this first step, nothing could
hold him back from a second, far bolder negation: he -
altogether denied being.[. . .] Heraclitus proclaimed:
"I see nothing other than becoming."

    Nietzsche, Philosophy in the Tragic Age of the Greeks §5

Heraclitus will remain eternally right with his assertion that
being is an empty fiction. The "apparent" world is the only
one: the "true" world is only added by a lie.

    Nietzsche, Twilight of the Idols *"Reason"* 2

4.1 NIETZSCHE AND THE "BATTLE OF GIANTS CONCERNING BEING"

From his early study of the Presocratics through the writings of his last
productive year, Nietzsche relentlessly criticizes the philosophical obsession with being and asserts the priority of its conceptual opposite:
becoming. Viewing the history of philosophy as a protracted celebration
of Parmenides' victory over Heraclitus in what Plato called the "battle
of giants concerning being," Nietzsche aims to revive this ancient *agon*
and reverse its outcome.[1]

    Nietzsche's ontological sympathies and fondness for Heraclitus are
well known. But this alone tells us little, for Nietzsche's great nineteenth-
century rival, Hegel, also fancied himself a disciple of Heraclitus.[2] The

---

    1. "*Gigantomachia peri tēs ousias*" (Plato, *Sophist,* 246a).
    2. Thus, Hegel writes, "there is no proposition of Heraclitus which I have not adopted
in my Logic" (*Lectures on the History of Philosophy,* vol. 1, *Greek Philosophy to Plato,*
trans. E. S. Haldane [Lincoln: University of Nebraska Press, 1995], 279).

crucial questions remain: "What is Nietzsche's 'becoming'?" and "Who is Nietzsche's Heraclitus?" These questions are commonly answered by reading Nietzsche as a Kantian skeptic and metaphysician for whom "becoming" names a sort of unknowable noumenon. After presenting and criticizing this view, I suggest another. I maintain that, as with Nietzsche's other doctrines, "becoming," too, must be seen through the twin lenses of naturalism and interpretation: that is, on the one side, Nietzsche's "becoming" is a naturalistic doctrine intended to counter the metaphysical preoccupation with being, stasis, and eternity by fore-grounding the empirically evident ubiquity of change in the natural world; on the other, "becoming" describes the incessant shift of per-spectives and interpretations in a world that lacks a grounding essence.

4.2 BECOMING AS NOUMENON: NIETZSCHE AMONG THE NEO-KANTIANS

The story is often told: Nietzsche was drawn from philology to philoso-phy by his discovery of Schopenhauer in the mid-1860s. Attracted by Schopenhauer's tragic pessimism—so much at odds with the optimism of Hegel and the positivists—Nietzsche also absorbed Schopenhauer's Kantian dualism, which distinguishes the phenomenal from the noume-nal world, the realm of appearance from that of things in themselves. Nietzsche's first published book, *The Birth of Tragedy,* explicitly pays homage to Kant and Schopenhauer and centers on what appears to be a dualistic schema: the Dionysian swarm of becoming, chaos, and indefi-niteness that is represented by us as an Apollinian gallery of being, or-der, and definition. Yet whereas Schopenhauer was repulsed by the surg-ing chaos he saw at the heart of things, Nietzsche and his tragedians were allured by it. Increasingly struck by this difference in attitude, Nietzsche became dismayed with Schopenhauer's crypto-Christian rejec-tion of the physical world and retreat into the metaphysical solitude of timeless forms. By the late 1870s, this dismay had developed into out-right repudiation.

Here the story becomes more controversial. Nietzsche is often read as implicitly maintaining a Kantian–Schopenhauerian framework even in his later writings. He is said to have supplemented Kant and Schopen-hauer with Heraclitus, Boscovich, Darwin, and Lange to arrive at a conception of the world in itself as a "becoming," "chaos," or "will to power"—a fluid, impermanent, and undifferentiated *Urwelt* to which the categories of knowledge (identity, substance, causality, etc.) do not apply. This reading of Nietzsche was advocated early in Nietzsche studies by the prominent neo-Kantian Hans Vaihinger and has continued to find supporters, among them Arthur Danto, and, more recently, Julian Young and Stephen Houlgate.[3]

This interpretation of becoming proceeds from a skeptical epistemology, which it traces throughout Nietzsche's corpus.[4] Thus, from the

3. "Neo-Kantian" here refers to the skeptical version presented in the previous chapter, not to its realist variant, which has little to say about becoming. For versions of this interpretation of Nietzsche's epistemology and ontology, see Hans Vaihinger, "Nietzsche and His Doctrine of Conscious Illusion," in *Nietzsche: A Collection of Critical Essays*, ed. Robert C. Solomon (Notre Dame: University of Notre Dame Press, 1973); Karl Jaspers, *Nietzsche: An Introduction to the Understanding of His Philosophical Activity*, trans. Charles F. Walraff and Frederick J. Schmitz (South Bend, Ind.: Regnery Gateway, 1979); Martin Heidegger, *Nietzsche*, vol. 3, *The Will to Power as Knowledge and as Metaphysics*, trans. Joan Stambaugh et al. (San Francisco: Harper, 1987); Arthur Danto, *Nietzsche as Philosopher* (New York: Columbia University Press, 1965), 80, 95–97; Jean Granier, "Perspectivism and Interpretation" and "Nietzsche's Conception of Chaos," trans. David B. Allison, in *The New Nietzsche*, ed. David B. Allison (Cambridge, Mass.: MIT Press, 1977); John T. Wilcox, *Truth and Value in Nietzsche: A Study of His Metaethics and Epistemology* (Ann Arbor: University of Michigan Press, 1974), 132–34; Rüdiger Grimm, *Nietzsche's Theory of Knowledge* (Berlin: Walter de Gruyter, 1977), 30, 53, and *passim;* George J. Stack, "Nietzsche's Critique of Things-In-Themselves," *Dialogos* 36 (1980): 50ff., *Lange and Nietzsche* (Berlin: Walter de Gruyter, 1983), and "Kant, Lange, and Nietzsche: Critique of Knowledge," in *Nietzsche and Modern German Thought,* ed. Keith Ansell-Pearson (London: Routledge, 1991); Willard Mittelman, "Perspectivism, Becoming, and Truth in Nietzsche," *International Studies in Philosophy* 16 (1984): 3–22; Eric Blondel, *Nietzsche: The Body and Culture,* trans. Seán Hand (Stanford: Stanford University Press, 1991), 98; Julian Young, *Nietzsche's Philosophy of Art* (Cambridge: Cambridge University Press, 1992), 3, 41, 96–97, 160–61; and Stephen Houlgate, "Kant, Nietzsche, and the 'Thing in Itself,'" *Nietzsche-Studien* 22 (1993): 133, 135.

4. For instance, Arthur Danto (*Nietzsche as Philosopher,* 38) writes: "In a precocious essay, written in 1873 [. . .] Nietzsche asks the old, cynical question, What is truth? It was to be a question that occupied him throughout his entire philosophical life, and the answer he gave it here [. . .] was one he never saw fit to modify in any essential respect." Daniel Breazeale concurs: "it is not only true that, as Arthur Danto has contended, Nietzsche never modified 'in any essential respect' the theory of truth which he advanced in his unpublished writings of the early 1870's, but it is also true that these same writings contain by far his most explicit, detailed, and sustained treatments of basic epistemological issues. Not only are most of his later published remarks on this subject compatible with these early discussions, they actually seem in some cases to presuppose them" ("Introduction," *Philosophy and Truth: Selections from Nietzsche's Notebooks of the Early 1870's,* ed. and trans. Daniel Breazeale [Atlantic Highlands, N.J.: Humanities Press, 1979], xlvi). While disagreeing with Danto that Nietzsche's epistemological position remained unchanged over the course of his career, Wilcox (*Truth and Value in Nietzsche,* 127) writes: "[Nietzsche] denies that anything is 'true' or that we 'know' anything in any sense which presupposes insight into the thing in itself, the transcendental reality which Kant thought had to be distinguished from appearance or phenomena. Doubt about *that kind* of truth or knowledge was not uncommon in the nineteenth century, largely because of the efforts of Kant. [. . .] That kind of intellectual pessimism, despair about that kind of truth, was

early essay "On Truth and Lies in a Nonmoral Sense" (which maintains that "truths are illusions that we have forgotten are illusions" [p. 84]) through the notes on epistemology in the later *Nachlaß* (one of which claims that "truth is the kind of error without which a certain species of life could not live" [*WP* 493]), Nietzsche is seen as consistently holding the Kantian position that our knowledge is limited to the phenomenal world of our own construction and can say little if anything about things as they are in themselves. Thus, we can hope for no correspondence between our language or thought and the world as it really is.[5]

For Kant, this restriction of knowledge to phenomena is no cause for despair. On the contrary, it serves two of his aims. Insofar as it rejects as useless speculation any claim to knowledge concerning metaphysics and morality, this limitation can be said to place philosophy on a more firm, scientific foundation. Moreover, Kant's view can claim to "make way for faith" concerning those metaphysical and moral concerns that are now judged to lie beyond the scope of knowledge but within reach of Reason. Yet, for Nietzsche, who held no such faith in God, reason, or morality, this skeptical insight is said to have led to a more deeply felt sense of our fundamental ignorance about the world.[6] Thus, in an early text, he claims that

> despair of truth [. . .] attends every thinker who sets out from the Kantian philosophy, provided he is a vigorous and whole man in suffering and desire and not a mere clattering thought- and calculating-machine. [. . .] If Kant ever should begin to exercise any wide influence we shall be aware of it in the form of a gnawing and disintegrating skepticism and relativism; and only in the most active and noble spirits who have never been able to exist in a state of doubt would there appear instead that undermining and despair of all truth. [. . .] (*SE* 3, p. 140)

---

one of Nietzsche's concerns from early to late." In a similar vein, George Stack ("Nietzsche's Critique of Things-In-Themselves," 50) writes that Nietzsche "never really retreats from [the] theme" that "knowledge, especially of the Kantian variety, entails 'falsification.'" Note that my presentation of this skeptical interpretation is a composite that brings together the many different textual and historical strands of this interpretation as it is found among a host of commentators on Nietzsche.

5. On this point, see Danto, *Nietzsche as Philosopher,* 72ff.; Grimm, *Nietzsche's Theory of Knowledge,* 44–65 and *passim;* George Stack, "Nietzsche's Evolutionary Epistemology," *Dialogos* 59 (1992): 83; and Young, *Nietzsche's Philosophy of Art,* 41.

6. See Wilcox, *Truth and Value in Nietzsche,* 125–27; Stack, "Nietzsche's Evolutionary Epistemology," 83. In *Nietzsche as Philosopher,* Danto deems Nietzsche's view an epistemological and ontological "nihilism."

Similarly, toward the end of his career, Nietzsche describes the Copernican revolution in astronomy and epistemology[7] as "the self-belittlement of man":

> Alas, the faith in the dignity and uniqueness of man, in his irreplaceability in the great chain of being, is a thing of the past—he has become an *animal*, literally and without reservation or qualification, he who was, according to his old faith, almost God. [. . .] Since Copernicus, man seems to have got himself on an inclined plane—now he is slipping faster and faster away from the center into—what? into nothingness? into a "*penetrating* sense of his nothingness"? (*GM* III:25)

According to the neo-Kantian view, Nietzsche places himself among those "most active and noble spirits" who are overcome by Kantian "skepticism." Beyond the island of our knowledge, we see only "a blind, empty, structureless thereness" "tossing blackly like the sea, chaotic relative to our distinctions and perhaps to all distinctions, but there nonetheless."[8]

This reading is aided by historical investigations into the sources of Nietzsche's putative skepticism. George Stack has done the most to promote the view that the later Nietzsche's perspectivist epistemology is an outgrowth of his early acceptance of the skeptical position held by many nineteenth-century neo-Kantian philosophers of science, particularly F. A. Lange.[9] According to Stack, Lange followed Kant in claiming that we have only a mediated knowledge of the world and that what performs this mediation is a conceptual apparatus that arranges the world for us in terms of substance, cause and effect, unity, identity, continuous and irreversible time, and so forth. Kant took this intuitional and categorial framework to be given in our cognitive constitution. His transcendental arguments sought to show the necessary and universal

7. Nietzsche clearly intends his description of the Copernican revolution to cover not only Copernicus's "defeat of theological astronomy" but also "Kant's *victory* over the dogmatic concepts of theology." Indeed, his discussion of astronomy moves directly into a discussion of Kant's critique.

8. Danto, *Nietzsche as Philosopher*, 96. This view has been endorsed more recently by Young, *Nietzsche's Philosophy of Art*, 96–97. The island analogy is presented by Kant in the *Critique of Pure Reason*, trans. Norman Kemp Smith (New York: St. Martin's Press, 1929), 257.

9. This argument is made in many of Stack's books and essays on Nietzsche. See, e.g., Stack, *Lange and Nietzsche*, and "Kant, Lange, and Nietzsche." For more on the importance of Lange to Nietzsche, see Vaihinger, "Nietzsche and His Doctrine of Conscious Illusion," 83–84, 104, and Robert Nola, "Nietzsche's Theory of Truth and Belief," *Philosophy and Phenomenological Research* 47 (1987): 528–33 and *passim*.

operation of the forms of sensuous intuition and categories of the understanding in human thought and experience. Lange, however, rejected Kant's transcendental account in favor of an evolutionary account of the existence and scope of the categorial system. What Kant took to be logically and conceptually a priori Lange viewed as having only a temporal and evolutionary priority. That is, what Kant maintained to be necessary and universal for rational thought and experience Lange saw as only the contingent product of a particular "physico-psychological organization," [10] itself a result of the natural selection of traits that have proven their practical value for the survival of the species.[11]

Lange's neo-Kantian evolutionism, the story continues, was taken up by Nietzsche, who argued in similar fashion that "the world of which we can become conscious is only a surface and sign-world" (GS 354), a world determined by "those primeval basic errors" "which were continually inherited, until they became almost part of the basic endowment of the species" (GS 110).[12] Such "errors," for both Lange and Nietzsche, define the parameters of our "perspective," construed as a species-concept and not as an individual point of view.[13] Due to their different "physico-psychological" constitutions and organizations, different species are supposed to have different "perspectives."[14] According to the skeptical interpretation, this is what leads Nietzsche to claim that

> the human intellect cannot avoid seeing itself in its own perspectives, and *only* in these. We cannot look around our own corner: it is hopeless curiosity that wants to know what other kinds of intellects there *might* be. [. . .] But I should think that today we are at least far from the ridiculous immodesty that

10. See Stack, "Nietzsche's Critique of Things-In-Themselves," 33–37, and "Kant, Lange, and Nietzsche," 39. Other commentators, such as Mary Warnock, "Nietzsche's Conception of Truth," in *Nietzsche's Imagery and Thought: A Collection of Essays,* ed. Malcolm Pasley (Berkeley: University of California Press, 1978), 41ff., have argued that what determines the parameters of our "perspective," for Nietzsche, is our language and grammar.

11. Stack, "Nietzsche's Critique of Things-In-Themselves," 33–35.

12. Cf. *HH* 16: "That which we now call this world is the outcome of a host of errors and fantasies that have gradually arisen and grown entwined with one another in the course of the overall evolution of the organic being, and are now inherited by us as the accumulated treasure of the entire past—as treasure: for our humanity now depends upon it." Cf. also *GS* 57. Houlgate, "Kant, Nietzsche, and the 'Thing in itself,'" 145–46 and *passim,* offers an interpretation similar to Stack's, though on exclusively textual, rather than historical, grounds.

13. Stack, "Kant, Lange, and Nietzsche," 39–40.

14. Ibid., 44–45. Cf. Danto, *Nietzsche as Philosopher,* 40–41. For a critique of this conception of perspective, see §3.3.1, above.

would be involved in decreeing from our corner that perspectives are permitted only from this corner. (*GS* 374)[15]

This skeptical account of Kant's, Lange's, and Nietzsche's epistemologies is also an account of their ontologies. If the phenomenal world—the world as it exists for a particular perspective—is a "mediated" world, a world of "representations" or "appearances," by inference there must be some "real," "unmediated," "original" world that these perspectives distort, filter, or represent. For Kant, this is the noumenal world, the realm of things in themselves that is apprehended by the sensuous intuition and worked up by the categories of the understanding before it can be considered knowable. For Lange, this "original" world is the "evanescent stream" of "'unknowable' becoming," a "presumed chaotic 'manifold' of sensory impressions."[16] Finally, according to this view, Nietzsche is said to maintain that the world in itself is a "becoming," "chaos," or "will to power," a world devoid of definition and organization.[17] The categories of knowledge, which define the pa-

15. An earlier statement of this view appears in "On Truth and Lies" (p. 79), where Nietzsche writes: "how miserable, how shadowy and transient, how aimless and arbitrary the human intellect looks within nature. [. . . T]his intellect has no additional mission which would lead it beyond human life. Rather, it is human, and only its possessor and begetter takes it so solemnly—as though the world's axis turned within it. But if we could communicate with the gnat, we would learn that he likewise flies through the air with the same solemnity, that he feels the flying center of the universe within himself." Pages later (p. 86), he continues: "If but for an instant [man] could escape from the prison walls of this faith, his 'self-consciousness' would be immediately destroyed. It is even a difficult thing for him to admit to himself that the insect or the bird perceives an entirely different world from the one that man does, and that the question of which one of these perceptions of the world is the more correct one is quite meaningless, for this would have to have been decided previously in accordance with the criterion of the *correct perception,* which means, in accordance with a criterion which is *not available.*" Cf. WP 616.

16. Stack, "Nietzsche and Boscovich's Natural Philosophy," *Pacific Philosophical Quarterly* 62 (1981): 80. Stack, "Kant, Lange, and Nietzsche," 35.

17. This formulation appears explicitly or implicitly in: Vaihinger, "Nietzsche and His Doctrine of Conscious Illusion," 84 and *passim;* Jaspers, *Nietzsche,* 212–13, 321, 351–52; Heidegger, *Nietzsche,* vol. 1, *The Will to Power as Art,* trans. David F. Krell (San Francisco: Harper, 1979), 3–6, and *Nietzsche,* 3:3–9, 64ff.; George A. Morgan, *What Nietzsche Means* (New York: Harper and Row, 1941), 267ff.; Danto, *Nietzsche as Philosopher,* 80, 96–97; Granier, "Perspectivism and Interpretation" and "Nietzsche's Conception of Chaos"; Sarah Kofman, "Appendix: Genealogy, Interpretation, Text," in *Nietzsche and Metaphor,* trans. Duncan Large (Stanford: Stanford University Press, 1993), 138–39; Peter Heller in the "Discussion" following Paul De Man, "Nietzsche's Theory of Rhetoric," *Symposium* (Spring 1974): 46; Wilcox, *Truth and Value in Nietzsche,* 132–33; Grimm, *Nietzsche's Theory of Knowledge,* 30 and *passim;* Bernd Magnus, *Nietzsche's Existential Imperative* (Bloomington: Indiana University Press, 1978), 25–32; Stack, "Nietzsche's Critique of Things-In-Themselves," 5off., and "Kant, Lange, and Nietzsche"; Mit-

rameters of our "perspective," impose order on this becoming and thus
help us to cope with it and increase our chances for survival. Yet, for
Nietzsche, "the categories are 'truths' only insofar as they are conditions of life for us" (*WP* 515). And "[i]t is improbable that our 'knowledge' should extend further than is strictly necessary for the preservation of life" (*WP* 494). As Karl Jaspers succinctly puts it: "Life quite
properly believes in being, and were it to believe in becoming instead, it
would perish. . . . [B]ecoming [is] a doctrine that [Nietzsche] considers
'true, but deadly.' " [18]

4.3 A CRITIQUE OF THE NEO-KANTIAN VIEW

Without a doubt, then, there exists some textual, historical, and critical
support for the neo-Kantian interpretation of Nietzsche's ontology. Yet
this interpretation is problematic, for it is deeply inconsistent with positions central to Nietzsche's work, particularly his resolute antidualism.
The claim that Nietzsche endorses a skeptical epistemology and a metaphysical ontology does not fit well with his explicit rejection of Kant's
notion of the "thing in itself" and the very distinction between a "real"
and an "apparent" world. This distinction is rejected in the very passage in which the notion of perspectivism is introduced. Having claimed
that "the world of which we become conscious is only a surface- and
sign-world," Nietzsche writes:

> You will guess that it is not the opposition of subject and object that con-
> cerns me here: this distinction I leave to the epistemologists [*Erkenntniss-
> theoretikern*] who have become entangled in the snares of grammar (the
> metaphysics of the people). It is even less the opposition of "thing in it-
> self" [»*Ding an sich*«] and appearance [*Erscheinung*]; for we do not "know"

telman, "Perspectivism, Becoming, and Truth in Nietzsche"; Charles Taylor, "Foucault
on Freedom and Truth," in *Foucault: A Critical Reader,* ed. David Couzens Hoy (Oxford:
Basil Blackwell, 1986), 93; Houlgate, *Hegel, Nietzsche, and the Criticism of Metaphysics*
(Cambridge: Cambridge University Press, 1986), 56–95, and "Kant, Nietzsche, and the
'Thing in itself,' " 133, 135; Nola, "Nietzsche's Theory of Truth and Belief"; Barry Allen,
"Government in Foucault," *Canadian Journal of Philosophy* 21 (1991): 423, and "Nietzsche's Question: 'What Good Is Truth?' " *History of Philosophy Quarterly* 9 (1992): 238;
and Babette E. Babich, *Nietzsche's Philosophy of Science: Reflecting Science on the
Ground of Art and Life* (Albany: State University of New York Press, 1994), 87 and *passim.* A more novel interpretation is presented by Blondel (*Nietzsche: The Body and Culture,* 98), who argues that "Nietzsche gives a *reality,* as a thing 'in itself,' to the *body.*"
    18. Jaspers, *Nietzsche,* 351.

[»*erkennen*«] nearly enough even to be allowed to *distinguish* in this way. (*GS* 354)

This may sound like a skeptical argument. Yet it actually amounts to a rejection of skepticism. Nietzsche's point is that, without access to a God's-eye view capable of confirming the existence of a thing in itself and distinguishing it from its appearances, we have no basis for making such a distinction at all and thus no basis for skepticism. Earlier in *The Gay Science*, Nietzsche makes a similar point: "What is 'appearance' [»*Schein*«] for me now? Certainly not the opposite of some essence [*eines Wesens*]: what could I say about any essence except to name the attributes of its appearance! Certainly not a dead mask that one could place over an unknown *x* or remove from it!" (*GS* 54).

This critique of the distinction between appearance and its putative opposites (and of the subordination of the former to these latter) is taken up again in later texts. For example, in *Twilight of the Idols*, Nietzsche writes:

> The reasons for which "this" world has been characterized as "apparent" [*scheinbar*] are the very reasons which indicate its reality [*Realität*]; any *other* kind of reality is absolutely indemonstrable. . . . The criteria which have been bestowed on the "true being" [»*wahren Sein*«] of things are the criteria of not-being, of *naught*; the "true world" [»*wahre Welt*«] has been constructed out of contradiction to the actual world [*wirklichen Welt*]. (*TI* "Reason" 6; cf. *WP* 584)

> The true world [*wahre Welt*]—we have abolished. What world has remained? The apparent [*scheinbare*] one perhaps? But no! *With the true world we have also abolished the apparent one.* (*TI* "World" 6; cf. "Reason," 2)[19]

These points are underscored in *Nachlaß* notes from the same period:

> The antithesis of the apparent [*scheinbaren*] world and the true [*wahren*] world is reduced to the antithesis "world" and "nothing." (*WP* 567)

> The antithesis "thing in itself" [»*Ding an sich*«] and "appearance" [»*Erscheinung*«] is untenable; with that, however, the concept of "*appearance*" also disappears. (*WP* 552)

---

19. Reading this passage against the background of a dualistic, Kantian interpretation of Nietzsche's epistemology and ontology, Daniel W. Conway ("Beyond Realism: Nietzsche's New Infinite," *International Studies in Philosophy* 22 [1990]: 103) construes it as a "warning" rather than a celebration. Yet Conway's reading is implausible, especially since the passage goes on to characterize this event of abolition in a highly affirmative tone: "Noon; moment of briefest shadow; end of the longest error; high point of humanity; INCIPIT ZARATHUSTRA" (*TI* "World" 6).

Of course, these passages do not employ a consistent terminology: at times, Nietzsche explicitly refers to Kant's distinction between *Ding an sich* and *Erscheinung* while, at others, he refers to the Platonic or Christian distinction between *die wahre Welt* and *die scheinbare Welt*. Yet I think this vacillation is not mere terminological carelessness. Rather, Nietzsche wishes to equate the Kantian distinction between the thing in itself and appearance with the Platonic–Christian distinction between the true world and the apparent world:

> Any distinction between a "true" [»*wahre*«] and an "apparent" [»*scheinbare*«] world—whether in the Christian manner or in the manner of Kant (in the end, an *underhanded* Christian)—is only a suggestion of decadence, a symptom of the *decline* of life. (TI "Reason" 6)[20]

Taken together, these passages present the following naturalistic argument. Kant's distinction between the thing in itself and appearance is merely a version of the Platonic–Christian distinction between the true world and the apparent world (the un-earthly world of pure, unlimited knowledge, goodness, beauty, and peace versus the earthly, sensual world of ignorance and suffering). According to Nietzsche, this latter distinction is unjustified, because the only world with which we are acquainted [*erkennen*] is the "apparent world." How, then, does the notion of "the true world" (and thus the "thing in itself") arise? Nietzsche sees it as "constructed out of contradiction to the actual world," that is, as originating out of a hatred of this world on the part of a this-worldly creature, a hatred that has led to the fictitious fabrication and elevation of "another world," which, as the antithesis to this "merely apparent" world, is deemed a "true world," a world "in itself."

This argument is pervasive in Nietzsche's later writings. How, then, can such passages and arguments be squared with the neo-Kantian interpretation according to which Nietzsche is a skeptic who maintains that there is a world in itself of becoming? One might argue that Nietzsche does not object to Kant's notion of a noumenal world but only to the characterization of that world as a world of "*things* in themselves" or a "*true* world." Nietzsche might be said to parallel Kant in claiming that the world of becoming, like the world of things in themselves, is unknowable. Thus, following Kant's claim that "knowledge has to do

<hr>

20. Recall that Nietzsche also calls Christianity "Platonism for 'the people'" (*BGE* P), thus completing the equation between Platonism, Christianity, and Kantianism. On Kant's "underhanded Christianity," see also *GS* 335 and *GM* III:25.

only with appearances and must leave the thing in itself as indeed real per se, but as not known by us,"[21] Nietzsche writes:

> *Knowledge* and *becoming* exclude one another. (*WP* 517)
>
> Knowledge in itself in a world of becoming is impossible. (*WP* 617)
>
> A world of becoming could not, in the strict sense, be "comprehended" or "known"; only to the extent that the "comprehending" and "knowing" intellect encounters a coarse already-created world, built out of nothing but appearances [*Scheinbarkeiten*] but become firm to the extent that this kind of appearance [*Schein*] has preserved life—only to this extent is there anything like "knowledge." (*WP* 520)[22]

In these passages, it would seem that Nietzsche is making the Kantian argument that what is available to our knowledge is only a world of appearance—the noumenal world filtered through the forms of intuition and categories of the understanding (Kant) or our "physico-psychological" apparatus (Lange).[23] Were this the case, Nietzsche's only objection would be that Kant conceives of this noumenal world as a world of "things" that exist "in themselves." Perhaps Nietzsche disapproves of this conception only insofar as it falsely attributes the intraphenomenal notions of unity, individuation, and duration to a world that is really "a sheer, undifferentiated flux"[24] or "an ever-flowing, ever-changing, chaotic 'reality.'"[25] For the same reason, one might argue that it is wrong to characterize the world of becoming as a "true" world, because truth and knowledge require states of affairs that remain distinct and durable over time.[26] Thus, Nietzsche might be said to argue that there is an ultimate, noumenal reality (the world of becoming); but, contrary to the Kantian and Platonic–Christian views,[27] it is not a

---

21. Kant, *Critique of Pure Reason*, 24.

22. Mittelman, "Perspectivism, Becoming, and Truth in Nietzsche," 5, and Stack, "Nietzsche's Critique of Things-In-Themselves," 52–53, draw upon these passages in support of their skeptical interpretation.

23. See §3.4.1, above, for a different reading of these passages.

24. Danto, *Nietzsche as Philosopher*, 89, see also 96–97.

25. Grimm, *Nietzsche's Theory of Knowledge*, 18, see also 2, 30, 53, 67–68. Magnus (*Nietzsche's Existential Imperative*, 25, 196, xiv) writes of "the [. . .] unintelligible flux of becoming," "the radical flux of becoming," "an [. . .] incoherent stratum" upon which we "impose form."

26. See Danto, *Nietzsche as Philosopher*, 75; Grimm, *Nietzsche's Theory of Knowledge*, 46–47 and *passim*; Mittelman, "Perspectivism, Becoming, and Truth in Nietzsche," 4–5.

27. Of course, Kant never calls the world of things in themselves (or of noumena) a "true" world. Nevertheless, the noumenal world is, for Kant, the realm of those supreme Ideas—God, freedom, and immortality—which it is the purpose of the first *Critique* to

"true" but a "false" world, insofar as it is a "self-contradictory world of becoming and change." [28]

Yet this version of the skeptical interpretation no more adequately solves the problem. Once again, it has Nietzsche both asserting the unknowability of becoming *and* positively characterizing it. But even if we leave aside this difficulty, other problems remain. In the above-cited passages from *The Gay Science, Twilight,* and the *Nachlaß,* it is clear that Nietzsche is not merely opposed to characterizing the noumenal world as a "true" world of "things"; rather, he is opposed to the very notion of a noumenal world and to *every* dualistic view that contrasts "appearance" with something other than "appearance." "The 'apparent' world," he maintains, "is the only world"; "any other kind of reality is absolutely indemonstrable" (*TI* "Reason" 2, 6). We must recall that, with his rejection of Kantian, Platonic–Christian, and all other dualisms, Nietzsche proposes to abolish the very notion of "appearance" (*TI* "Reason" 6, "World" 6; *WP* 567, 552), for this notion has only ever functioned in opposition and subordination to "that which appears," namely, the world as it is in itself. [29]

Indeed, Kant had to posit the "thing in itself" for just this reason. In the preface to the second edition of the first *Critique,* he writes:

> [A]ll possible speculative knowledge of reason is limited to mere objects of *experience.* But our further contention must also be duly borne in mind, namely that though we cannot *know* these objects as things in themselves, we must yet be in position to at least *think* them as things in themselves; otherwise we should be landed in the absurd conclusion that there can be appearance without anything that appears. [30]

Thus is Kant led into the notorious "problem of affection." [31] He maintains that, for thought to have any content, our faculty of sensibility

---

"make way for" (*Critique of Pure Reason,* 29). In this sense, then, Nietzsche has some justification for calling Kant an "underhanded Christian" (*TI* "Reason" 6) and for claiming that Kant's Copernican revolution is "the straightest route to—the *old* ideal" (*GM* III:25; cf. *GS* 335).

28. Mittelman, "Perspectivism, Becoming, and Truth in Nietzsche," 5.

29. This point is also made by Alan D. Schrift, *Nietzsche and the Question of Interpretation: Between Hermeneutics and Deconstruction* (New York: Routledge, 1990), 190–91.

30. Kant, *Critique of Pure Reason,* 27. Other relevant passages are collected and discussed in Henry Allison, *Kant's Transcendental Idealism: An Interpretation and Defense* (New Haven: Yale University Press, 1983), 238ff. and 363 n 15.

31. See Allison, *Kant's Transcendental Idealism,* 247ff., for a nice discussion of this problem.

must be affected from without. That is, the world of phenomena or appearance, with which our knowledge is concerned, must have something outside it as its "cause" or "ground." [32] This "something" cannot be an appearance, since Kant rejects the idealist thesis that a representation—that is, something in us—is the cause of our representations; but neither can this "something" be a thing in itself, for that would mean extending to things in themselves the category of causality, which, Kant himself claims, has only intraphenomenal validity.

We need not discuss in detail either this problem as it arises in Kant or the various solutions to it offered by Kant's commentators. I raise the issue only because Nietzsche joins the host of Kant's critics on this point, and because this criticism helps us to see that Nietzsche holds no skeptical or dualist position with regard to epistemology and ontology. In the *Nachlaß* Nietzsche criticizes Kant on precisely this issue:

> The sore spot of Kant's critical philosophy has gradually become visible even to dull eyes: Kant no longer has a right to his distinction "appearance" and "thing in itself"—he had deprived himself of the right to go on distinguishing in this old familiar way, in so far as he rejected as impermissible making inferences from phenomena to the cause of phenomena—in accordance with his conception of causality and its purely intra-phenomenal validity. (*WP* 553)[33]

Nietzsche's point here is clearly that, if Kant's only justification for positing a thing in itself is that it is a necessary causal corollary to the notion of appearance, then he is unjustified in making this posit according to his own view that causality cannot apply to things in themselves.

Yet, as Nietzsche is well aware, Kant provides another justification

---

32. See Kant, *Critique of Pure Reason,* 441ff.

33. Nietzsche mounts this critique of Kant even in *Human, All Too Human.* In a section entitled "Appearance and Thing in Itself [Erscheinung und Ding an sich]," he writes: "Philosophers are accustomed to station themselves before life and experience—before that which they call the world of appearance—as before a painting that has been unrolled once and for all and unchangeably depicts the same scene: this scene, they believe, has to be correctly interpreted, so as to draw a conclusion as to the nature of the being that produced the picture: that is to say, as to the nature of the thing in itself, which it is customary to regard as the sufficient reason [*zureichende Grund*] for the world of appearance. Against this, more rigorous logicians, having clearly identified the concept of the metaphysical as that of the unconditioned, consequently also unconditioning, have disputed any connection between the unconditioned (the metaphysical world) and the world we know: so what appears in appearance is precisely *not* the thing in itself, and no conclusion can be drawn from the former as to the nature of the latter" (16). Nietzsche clearly agrees with this logical critique of the thing in itself, though he goes on to mount another, evolutionary, critique of the notion.

for positing a realm of things in themselves or noumena. The passage from the first *Critique* quoted above continues as follows:

> Now let us suppose that the distinction, which our Critique has shown to be necessary, between things as objects of experience and those same things as they are in themselves, had not been made. In that case all things in general, as far as they are efficient causes, would be determined by the principle of causality, and consequently by the mechanism of nature. I could not, therefore, without palpable contradiction, say of one and the same being, for instance the human soul, that its will is free and yet is subject to natural necessity, that is, is not free. For I have taken the soul in both propositions *in one and the same sense,* namely as a thing in general, that is, as a thing in itself [*Sache selbst*]; and save by means of a preceding critique, could not have done otherwise. But if our Critique is not in error in teaching that the object is to be taken *in a twofold sense,* namely as appearance and as thing in itself [. . .] then there is no contradiction in supposing that one and the same will is, in the appearance, that is, in its visible acts, necessarily subject to the law of nature, and so far *not free,* while yet, as belonging to a thing in itself, it is not subject to that law, and is therefore *free.*[34]

We see here the more fundamental reason that Kant posits a world of things in themselves or noumena: to save the metaphysical Ideas of God, freedom, and the soul from their elimination by a thoroughgoing empiricism and naturalism.[35] Nietzsche recognizes this and criticizes Kant on this account as well. From early on (see *BT* 18–19), he admires Kant for having dismissed metaphysical talk as unintelligible, for having restricted knowledge to "appearance," and for having granted that the objects of our knowledge are constructions. Yet, in his later work, Nietzsche is more critical of what he takes to be the real motivation behind Kant's critique—the restoration of those metaphysical, anti-natural specters: God, free will, and the soul. Nietzsche writes, in *The Gay Science:*

> And now don't cite the categorical imperative, my friend! This term tickles my ear and makes me laugh despite your serious presence. It makes me think of the old Kant who had obtained "the thing in itself"—another very ridiculous thing!—*by stealth* and was punished for this when the "categorical imperative" crept stealthily into his heart and led him *astray—back* to "God," "soul," "freedom," and "immortality," like a fox who loses his way and goes

34. Kant, *Critique of Pure Reason,* 27–28.
35. See Kant, *Prolegomena to Any Future Metaphysics,* trans. James W. Ellington (Indianapolis: Hackett, 1977), 103.

astray back into his cage. Yet it had been *his* strength and cleverness that had *broken open* the cage! (335)[36]

This critique is reiterated in the 1886 preface to *Daybreak*:

> [T]o create room for *his* "moral realm" [Kant] saw himself obliged to posit an indemonstrable world, a logical "Beyond"—it was for precisely that that he had need of his critique of pure reason! In other words: *he would not have had need of it* if one thing had not been more vital to him than anything else: to render the "moral realm" unassailable, even better incomprehensible to reason. (3)

Thus, while Nietzsche praises Kant's critique of the possibility of metaphysical "knowledge," he criticizes the antinaturalistic motivation that lurks behind this critique: Kant's attempt to reinvigorate "faith" and metaphysics via the opposition between appearances and things in themselves.

Nietzsche's criticism of Kant, then, is not merely a critique of the notion of "*things* in themselves." It is a criticism of the very dualism between appearance and something other than appearance. Neither in his criticism of Kant's notion of "affection" nor in his criticism of Kant's metaphysical designs does Nietzsche object to the characterization of noumena as individual items: "*things* in themselves." Rather, he objects to the very distinction between noumena and phenomena. Indeed, Nietzsche's objection to the notion that phenomena are "affected" by things in themselves would apply equally well to the notion that "becoming" is the ontological ground of perspectival knowledge. For, were Nietzsche to claim that an unknowable becoming is the cause or ground of appearance, he would be subject to the same criticism he levels against Kant: namely, that nothing in our experience of the world, not even the notion of causality, can lead us to an extra-phenomenal world. "For we do not 'know' nearly enough even to be allowed to *distinguish* in this way" (GS 354).

For Nietzsche, as for Kant, we are led to this distinction only through the desire to justify such theological and metaphysical notions as God,

---

36. Cf. A 55. Also cf. GM III:25, where Nietzsche argues that the Copernican revolution, though superficially antitheological, is really theological and ascetic through and through. Also cf. WP 578: "*Moral values even in theory of knowledge:* [. . .] the transcendent world invented, in order that a place remains for 'moral freedom' (in Kant)."

free will, soul, and immortality. Yet, unlike Kant, Nietzsche has no faith
or belief in such ideas. Indeed, his naturalism aims to get rid of them altogether. He argues that, just as the notion of God is a manifestation of
certain human beings' desire to be other than they are, so "things in
themselves" and "essences" are manifestations of a desire that there be
a world beyond that of "mere appearance." Nietzsche staunchly maintains, however, that there is no such world. For Nietzsche, the origin of
the "true or real world" is not to be found outside appearance but
within it. In naturalistic fashion, he argues that the noumenal world has
only ever been a guise of the phenomenal world: the human fantasy that
there is "another, better world." This is the meaning of Nietzsche's
aphorism: "The 'real world,' however one has hitherto conceived it—it
has always been the apparent world *once again* " (*WP* 566).[37] For Nietzsche, the question is not "what 'things in themselves' may be like, apart
from our sense receptivity and the activity of our understanding. [. . .]
The question is *whether there could not be many other ways of creating
such an* apparent *world*" (*WP* 569, my emphasis). That is, the question
is not what "other world" is indicated by our metaphysical ideas but
rather what "*this*-worldly" features could have given rise to such ideas.

4.4 NIETZSCHE, BECOMING, HERACLITUS

Whatever "becoming" is, for Nietzsche, it does not characterize some
ineffable noumenal realm. Rather, it must describe something about the
world we inhabit and know: the natural, physical world, the world of
"appearance" (if this term can still function free of its discredited conceptual opposite).

To begin to answer our question, "What is Nietzsche's 'becoming'?"
we must turn to our other question, "Who is Nietzsche's Heraclitus?";
for it is from Heraclitus that Nietzsche inherits the notion of becoming and to whom he often turns when discussing it. Moreover, while
Nietzsche's infatuation with Schopenhauer and Kant was brief, his allegiance to Heraclitus is as evident in his first writings as in his last. Thus,

37. Cf. *TI* "Reason" 6: "Any distinction between a 'true' and an 'apparent' world
[. . .] is only a suggestion of decadence, a sign of *decline* of life. That the artist esteems
appearance higher than reality is no objection to this proposition. For 'appearance' in this
case means reality *once again,* only by way of selection, reinforcement, and correction.
The tragic artist is no pessimist. [. . .]"

in one of his final statements—*Ecce Homo*'s discussion of *The Birth of Tragedy*—he writes:

> I [. . .] understand myself as the first *tragic philosopher*, that is, the most extreme opposite and antipode of a pessimistic philosopher. Before me [. . .] *tragic wisdom* was lacking; I have looked in vain for signs of it even among the *great* Greeks in philosophy, those of the two centuries *before* Socrates. I retained some doubt in the case of *Heraclitus*, in whose proximity I feel warmer and better than anywhere else. The affirmation of passing away *and destroying*, which is the decisive feature of a Dionysian philosophy; saying yes to opposition and war; *becoming*, along with the repudiation of the very concept of *being*—all this is clearly more closely related to me than anything else thought to date. ("Books" BT:3)

And in another text from the same year, having criticized "the philosophers' [. . .] hatred of the very idea of becoming," "the senses," and "appearance" in favor of "being" and "what does not become," Nietzsche writes:

> With the highest respect, I except the name of *Heraclitus*. When the rest of the philosophic folk rejected the testimony of the senses because they showed multiplicity and change, he rejected their testimony because they showed things as if they had permanence and unity. Heraclitus too did the senses an injustic. [. . .][38] But Heraclitus will remain eternally right with his assertion that being is an empty fiction. (*TI* "Reason" 2)

These passages recapitulate the conclusions of Nietzsche's early work on Greek philosophy, where the justification for them is presented in much greater detail. For a characterization of Nietzsche's Heraclitus, we must turn to *Philosophy in the Tragic Age of the Greeks,* a study of the Presocratics Nietzsche left unpublished but to which he returned throughout the 1870s.[39] This text is significant for a number of reasons.

---

38. On this passage, see p. 194n. 56 below.

39. The text seems to have been left unpublished primarily because it was to be included in the "historical" half of a larger "historical-theoretical" study, *Das Philosophenbuch* (*The Philosopher's Book*), the second half of which was never completed but which was to include "On Truth and Lies in a Nonmoral Sense." (See *Grossoktavausgabe,* 2d ed., vol. 10, *Nachgelassene Werke* [Leipzig: Naumann, 1903], which collects together all the texts, fragments, and plans for the proposed *Philosopher's Book.*) *Philosophy in the Tragic Age of the Greeks* was written in 1873 and based on a series of lectures first delivered in 1872 and repeated, with revisions, in 1873 and 1876. A fair copy of the text was made the next year, and minor corrections and additions were incorporated in 1879. For a discussion of this and related texts, see Breazeale's "Introduction" to *Philosophy and Truth.* Breazeale writes that Nietzsche "devoted great care to the preparation of this course of lectures" (liii), which were "clearly his personal favorite" (xviii). Breazeale goes on to de-

It provides Nietzsche's most sustained treatment of Heraclitus, clearly the text's protagonist. Not surprisingly, then, it is also a text in which the notion of becoming figures centrally.[40] Moreover, far from displaying the reverence toward Schopenhauer and Kant one is supposed to find in Nietzsche's early work, the text is highly critical of these philosophers, with Heraclitus playing Nietzsche against Anaximander and Parmenides, whose interpretations of becoming and being are glossed with quotations from Schopenhauer and Kant. Indeed, instead of revealing a juvenile Nietzsche, this text shows him advancing positions and views that are central to his later work: naturalism and antidualism; a repudiation of "being" in favor of an "innocent becoming"; the characterization of becoming as a perpetual "artist's *agon*" or dice game; the promotion of an aesthetic versus a moral interpretation of the world; praise of an aphoristic and esoteric philosophical style; an empiricist and nominalist critique of the notions of substance and essence, and so on.

The text begins with a discussion of Thales. But this is only a prologue to the main drama, which stages a contest among the interpretations of becoming and being proposed by Anaximander, Heraclitus, and Parmenides. The problem of becoming first appears in the discussion of Anaximander, "the first philosophical author of the ancients" (4, p. 45), for whom "all becoming [is] an illegitimate emancipation from eternal being, a wrong for which destruction is the only penance" (4, p. 46).[41] "Enigmatic proclamation of a true pessimist," Nietzsche

scribe *Philosophy in the Tragic Age of the Greeks* as a "polished text" (liii n 4), "a relatively finished historical survey of the development of ancient philosophy" (xxii). In his "Nachwort" to the first volume of the *Kritische Studienausgabe,* Giorgio Colli calls the text Nietzsche's "central work" of the period immediately following *The Birth of Tragedy* (p. 916).

40. In his introductory lecture for the course, Nietzsche claims: "This is the true distinguishing mark of the philosophical drive: wonder concerning what is lying in front of everyone's nose. The most ordinary phenomenon is becoming, and with it Ionian philosophy begins. The problem reappears in an infinitely intensified form in the Eleatics. [. . .] All subsequent philosophies struggle against Eleaticism" (cited in Breazeale's "Introduction" to *Philosophy and Truth,* xliii–xliv).

41. Nietzsche's interpretation is based on the only extant fragment of Anaximander, which Kirk and Raven translate into English as follows: "And the source of coming-to-be for existing things is that into which destruction, too, happens, 'according to necessity; for they pay penalty and retribution to each other for their injustice according to the assessment of Time'" (*The Presocratic Philosophers: A Critical History with a Selection of Texts,* ed. G. S. Kirk and J. E. Raven [Cambridge: Cambridge University Press, 1957], 117). Though they tell us much about the interpreter himself, Nietzsche's interpretations of the Presocratics are surely a matter for debate. Even so, his reading, particularly of Heraclitus, accords with such canonical accounts as that of W. K. C. Guthrie, *A History of Greek Philosophy,* vol. 1, *The Earlier Presocratics and Pythagoreans* (Cambridge: Cambridge University Press, 1962). It bears mentioning that Nietzsche's heir, Heidegger, also

declares and immediately likens Anaximander's doctrine to that of "[t]he only serious moralist of our century" (4, p. 46), Schopenhauer, whose *Parerga* Nietzsche quotes in support. On the next page, Anaximander's distinctions between being and becoming, the indefinite and the definite, are presented as parallels to Kant's distinction between the thing in itself and appearance: "This ultimate unity of the 'indefinite,' the womb of all things, can, it is true, be designated by human speech only as a negative, as something to which the existent world of becoming can give no predicate. We may look upon it as the equal of the Kantian *Ding an sich*" (4, p. 47).[42]

Those who view Kant as a sober epistemologist will have trouble making sense of this strange affiliation of Kant with Anaximander. Yet recall that Nietzsche does not read Kant this way. Rather—and not implausibly—he sees Kant as one for whom epistemology and metaphysics are means to an end. Nietzsche perceives that, at bottom, what motivates Kant, Schopenhauer, and Anaximander is a *metaphysical-moral interpretation of the world*. Thus, with the names "Schopenhauer" and "Kant" still resonating, Nietzsche remarks that:

> Anaximander was no longer dealing with the question of the origins of this world in a purely physical way. Rather [. . .] he grasped with bold fingers the tangle of the profoundest problem in ethics. [. . .] From this world of injustice [. . .] Anaximander flees into a metaphysical fortress from which he leans out, letting his gaze sweep the horizon. (4, p. 48)

Thus far, one might still read this text in the way that *The Birth of Tragedy* is often read: as supporting a Kantian dualism and a Schopenhauerian pessimism. Yet the entrance of Heraclitus quickly disconfirms this reading. For Heraclitus appears bearing a new world-interpretation with which Nietzsche is clearly in sympathy:

> [Heraclitus] denied the duality of totally diverse worlds—a position which Anaximander had been compelled to assume. He no longer distinguished a physical world from a metaphysical one, a realm of definite qualities from an undefinable "indefinite." And after this first step, nothing could hold him back from a second, far bolder negation: he altogether denied being. For this one world which he retained [. . .] nowhere shows a tarrying, an indestruc-

---

revisits the Presocratics in an attempt to reassess the foundations of European philosophy. Unlike Nietzsche's, however, Heidegger's analysis has less clearly defined protagonists and antagonists. See Heidegger's collection, *Early Greek Thinking*, trans. David Farrell Krell and Frank A. Capuzzi (San Francisco: Harper and Row, 1984).

42. Note that, in this passage, becoming is contrasted with, rather than assimilated to, "the Kantian *Ding an sich*."

tibility, a bulwark in the stream. Louder than Anaximander, Heraclitus pro-claimed: "I see nothing other than becoming. Be not deceived. It is the fault of your short-sightedness, not of the essence of things, if you believe you see land somewhere in the ocean of becoming and passing-away. You use names for things as though they rigidly, persistently endured; yet even the stream into which you step a second time is not the one you stepped into before." (5, pp. 51–52)

This passage tells us much about Nietzsche's Heraclitus and the view of becoming these two philosophers share. Unlike Anaximander (and Kant and Schopenhauer), Nietzsche's Heraclitus is an antidualist and anti-metaphysician for whom there is only "one world," a world of "becoming" that is entirely physical and evident to those who are not swayed by the conceptual and linguistic reifications that convince the "short-sighted" of being and persistence.

This antidualism and critique of the concept of being also leads Heraclitus to deny the distinctions between substance and accident, essence and appearance. Just as Nietzsche himself later proclaims that "a 'thing' is the sum of its effects [*Wirkungen*]" (*WP* 551), Nietzsche's Heraclitus declares that "the whole nature of reality [*Wirklichkeit*] lies simply in its acts [*Wirken*] and [. . .] for it there exists no other sort of being" (5, p. 53); "[t]he many perceivable qualities are neither eternal substances [*ewige Wesenheiten*] nor phantasms of our senses [. . .] neither rigid autonomous being nor fleeting semblance flitting through human minds" (6, p. 58). Rejecting these oppositions, Nietzsche asserts that there is only the empirically evident world of becoming, a vast and shifting assemblage of effects, forms, appearances, and perspectives.

Heraclitus' world of becoming and appearance is characterized by Nietzsche in a network of images and figures that recur throughout the Nietzschean corpus: the images of the *agon* and the game, the figures of the artist and the child.[43]

Ordinary people think they see something rigid, complete and permanent; in truth, however, light and dark, bitter and sweet are attached to each other and interlocked at any given moment like wrestlers of whom sometimes one, sometimes the other is on top. [. . .] The strife of opposites gives birth to all

43. Preference for these figures and images, and for figurative, imagistic, or "intu-itive" language in general, is not the only stylistic trait Nietzsche inherits from Heraclitus. He also shares a penchant for the terse, dense, and provocative aphorism that offends common sense but strikes "those with ears to hear." For Nietzsche's own praise of Hera-clitus's style, see *PTA* 7, pp. 64–65. For an analysis of Heraclitus's style and mode of thought that bears an uncanny resemblance to Nietzsche's discussion of these issues, see Guthrie, *History of Greek Philosophy*, 1:437–39. Cf. *PTA* 5, pp. 52–53.

that becomes; the definite qualities which look permanent to us express the momentary ascendancy of one partner. But this by no means signifies the end of the war; the contest endures to all eternity. (5, pp. 54–55)

In this world only the play of artists and children exhibits becoming and passing away, building and destroying, without any moral additive, in forever equal innocence. And as artists and children play, so plays the ever-living fire, building up and destroying, in innocence. Such is the game that the aeon plays with itself. [. . . I]t builds towers of sand like a child at the seashore, piling them up and trampling them down. From time to time it starts the game anew. A moment of satiety, and again it is seized by its need, as the artist is seized by the need to create. Not hybris but the ever-newly-awakened impulse to play calls new worlds into being. (7, p. 62)[44]

Here, Nietzsche pauses to acknowledge that Schopenhauer, too, presents an image of becoming as an everlasting struggle. Yet, after quoting a representative passage from *Die Welt als Wille und Vorstellung*, he notes that "the basic tone of [Schopenhauer's] description is quite different from that which Heraclitus offers," because, for Schopenhauer, becoming is "a self-consuming, menacing and gloomy drive, a thoroughly frightful and by no means blessed phenomenon" (5, p. 56).[45] Here we find the crucial difference between the Anaximandrian–Kantian–Schopenhauerian and the Heraclitean–Nietzschean interpretations of becoming: the former is a *moral* interpretation that paints a "thoroughly gloomy" picture of guilt and penance, while the latter is an *aesthetic* interpretation that sees becoming as "blessed" and "innocent."[46]

---

44. This passage seems to allude to Heraclitus' fr. 52: "Time is a child playing a game of draughts; the kingship is in the hands of a child" (*Ancilla to the Pre-Socratic Philosophers*, trans. Kathleen Freeman [Cambridge, Mass.: Harvard University Press, 1948], 28). Yet it more closely approximates an epic simile in Homer that unites the figures of *agon* and game: "[The Trojans] streamed over / in massed formation, with Apollo in front of them holding / the tremendous aegis, and wrecked the bastions of the Achaians / easily, as when a little boy piles sand by the sea-shore / when in his innocent play he makes sand towers to amuse him / and then, still playing, with hands and feet ruins them and wrecks them" (*The Iliad of Homer*, trans. Richmond Lattimore [Chicago: University of Chicago Press, 1951], 319). In "On the Pathos of Truth," an 1872 "preface to an unwritten book," Nietzsche calls upon Diogenes Laertius's description of Heraclitus "watching the games of noisy children [. . .] pondering something never before pondered by a mortal on such an occasion, viz., the play of the great world-child, Zeus, and the eternal game of destruction and origination" (in Breazeale, ed. and trans., *Philosophy and Truth*, 64). Cf. *BGE* 94 and *WP* 797.

45. Recall the 1886 preface to *The Birth of Tragedy*, in which Nietzsche maintains that this book "tried laboriously to express by means of Schopenhauerian and Kantian formulas strange and new valuations which were basically at odds with Kant's and Schopenhauer's spirit and taste!" (*BT* SC: 6).

46. Cf. *TI* "Errors" 7: "there is in our eyes no more radical opposition than that of the theologians, who continue with the concept of a 'moral world-order' to infect the innocence of becoming by means of 'punishment' and 'guilt'."

" 'It is a game,' " Nietzsche's Heraclitus says. " 'Don't take it so patheti-cally, and—above all—don't make morality of it!' " (7, p. 64): "Be-coming is not a moral but an aesthetic phenomenon" (19, p. 113).[47]

With the entrance of Parmenides, the Heraclitean interpretation of becoming is provided an even starker contrast. In these sections, Nietz-sche casts aside the mode of explication and adopts a stridently critical tone. Moreover, the language and content of this critique are nearly identical to those found in a text written fifteen years later—the section of Twilight of the Idols entitled " 'Reason' in Philosophy," in which Nietzsche criticizes the basic traits that have hitherto dominated the philosophical disposition. Indeed, in Nietzsche's Parmenides, we find the archetype of the philosopher, a condensation of Plato, Descartes, and Kant. Here we discover the true origin of that philosophical "hatred of the very idea of becoming" (TI "Reason" 1); for Parmenides is the first to proclaim "the doctrine of Being," a position that Nietzsche deems "un-Greek as no other in the two centuries of the Tragic Age" (PTA 9, p. 69). With "purest absolutely bloodless abstraction, unclouded by any reality" (9, p. 69), Parmenides declares:

> That which truly is must be eternally present; one cannot say of it that "it was," or "it will be." What has being cannot have become. [. . .] It is the same with passing-away. Passing-away is just as impossible as becoming, as is all change, all decrease, all increase. In fact the only valid proposition that can be stated is "Everything of which you can say 'it has been' or 'it will be' is not; of what has being you can never say 'it is not.' " (10, p. 78)[48]

Along with this denial of becoming, Nietzsche's Parmenides rejects the testimony of the senses—which deceive us into believing in becom-ing—and draws a fateful distinction between the mind and the body:

> "Whatever you do, do not be guided by your dull eyes," is [Parmenides'] im-perative, "nor by your resounding ears, nor by your tongue, but test all things

47. Nietzsche attributes this view to Anaxagoras, who, however, is seen as following Heraclitus. See PTA 19, 112–13.
48. Cf. TI "Reason" 1: "You ask me which of the philosophers' traits are really idio-syncrasies? For example, their lack of historical sense, their hatred of the very idea of be-coming, their Egypticism. They think that they show their respect for a subject when they de-historicize it, sub specie aeterni—when they turn it into a mummy. All that philoso-phers have handled for thousands of years have been concept-mummies; nothing real es-caped their grasp alive. When these honorable concept-idolators worship something, they kill it and stuff it; they threaten the life of everything they worship. Death, change, old age, as well as procreation and growth, are to their minds objections—even refutations. Whatever is does not become; whatever becomes is not."

with the power of your thinking alone."[49] Thus he accomplished the immensely significant first critique of man's apparatus for knowledge, a critique as yet inadequate but disastrous in its consequences. By wrenching apart the senses and the capacity for abstraction, in other words by splitting up reason as though it were composed of two quite separate capacities, he demolished the intellect itself, encouraging that wholly erroneous distinction between "mind" and "body" which, especially since Plato, lies upon philosophy like a curse. All sense perceptions, says Parmenides, yield but deceptions.[. . .] All the multiplicity and colorfulness of the world known to experience, the transformations of its qualities, the orderliness of its ups and downs, are mercilessly cast aside as mere semblance and delusion. (10, p. 79)[50]

If Anaximander was criticized for "flee[ing] into a metaphysical fortress" (4, p. 48), Parmenides retreats even further and solicits from Nietzsche an even stronger reproach:

When one makes as total a judgment as does Parmenides about the whole of the world, one ceases to be a natural scientist [ein Naturforscher], an investigator into any of the world's parts. One's sympathy toward phenomena atrophies; one even develops a hatred for phenomena including oneself, a hatred for being unable to get rid of the eternal deceitfulness of the senses. Henceforth truth shall live only in the palest, most abstracted generalities, in the empty husks of the most indefinite terms, as though in a house of cobwebs. And beside such "truth" now sits the philosopher, as bloodless as his abstractions, in the spun-out fabric of his formulas. A spider at least wants blood from his victims. The Parmenidean philosopher hates most of all the blood of his victims, the blood of empirical reality which was sacrificed and shed by him. (10, pp. 79–80)[51]

Thus do we also find in Parmenides the origin of "the other idiosyncrasy of the philosophers," which "consists in confusing the last and the first": "They place that which comes at the end—unfortunately! for it ought not to come at all!—namely, the 'highest concepts,' which means

49. See Parmenides, frr. 7–8.
50. Cf. TI "Reason" 1: "Now [the philosophers] all believe, desperately even, in what has being. But since they never grasp it, they seek for reasons why it is kept from them. 'There must be mere appearance, there must be some deception which prevents us from perceiving what has being: where is the deceiver?'—'We have found him,' they cry ecstatically; 'it is the senses! [. . .] Moral: let us free ourselves from the deception of the senses, from becoming, from history, from lies. [. . .] And above all, away with the *body*, this wretched *idée fixe* of the senses, disfigured by all the fallacies of logic, refuted, even impossible, although it is impudent enough to behave as if it were real!'"
51. Cf. TI "Reason" 2: "Today we possess science precisely to the extent that we have decided to *accept* the testimony of the senses [. . .] The rest is miscarriage and not-yet-science. [. . .]"; also see n. 50, above.

the most general, the emptiest concepts, the last smoke of evaporating reality, in the beginning, *as* the beginning" (*TI* "Reason" 4). Nietzsche's Parmenides

> flee[s] from an over-abundant reality [. . .] into the rigor mortis of the coldest, emptiest concept of all, the concept of being. [. . .] Instead of being corrected and tested against reality (considering that they are in fact derived from it) the concepts, on the contrary, are supposed to measure and direct reality and, in case reality contradicts logic, to condemn the former. (*PTA* 11, pp. 80–81; 12, p. 87)[52]

To the two presented in *Twilight,* we might add a third "idiosyncrasy" that Nietzsche exposes elsewhere: "the demand for certainty." [53] According to Nietzsche, it, too, has its source in Parmenides:

> What astonishes us is the degree of schematism and abstraction (in a Greek!), above all, the terrible energetic striving for *certainty* [*Strebens nach* Gewiß-heit] in an epoch which otherwise thought mythically and whose imagination was highly mobile and fluid. "Grant me, you gods, but one certainty," runs Parmenides' prayer, "even if it be but a log's breadth on which to lie, on which to ride upon the sea of uncertainty. Take away everything that becomes, everything lush, colorful, blossoming, deceptive, everything that charms and is alive. Take all these for yourselves and grant me but the one and only, poor empty certainty." [. . .] Experience nowhere offered him being as he imagined it, but he concluded its existence from the fact that he was able to think it. (11, pp. 81–82)

It is Descartes, not Schopenhauer, who is the fruit of this Parmenidean seed.[54] And Nietzsche takes pains to distinguish this form of ascetic world-denial from the mystical, ecstatic form found among "the Hindu

---

52. Nietzsche's struggle against the philosophical tendency "to confuse the last and the first" helps to explain some of the puzzling language of *PTA* 11 and *TL,* both written in the same year. In these texts, Nietzsche appears to lapse into the skeptical, metaphysical-realist view that words and concepts can never "touch upon absolute truth," "that knowing and being are the most opposite of all spheres" (*PTA* 11, 83). This language is surely misleading. Yet I think that what motivates these claims is simply the point that words and concepts are only pragmatic simplifications and reifications of the rich, sensual, world of becoming and that—contra the rationalist—the former are derived from the latter rather than the reverse. Thus, too, we find Nietzsche, both early and late, supporting the claims of "intuition" over those of "reason," his somewhat idiosyncratic terms for "sensuality" and "conceptuality," respectively. Cf., e.g., *WP* 488: "All our *categories of reason* are of sensual origin: derived from the empirical world"; and *TI* "Reason" 2: "[The senses] do not lie at all. What we *make* of their testimony, that alone introduces lies. [. . .] 'Reason' is the cause of our falsification of the testimony of the senses."

53. See *GS* 2, 347; *BGE* 10; and the discussion of these passages above, in §1.6.2.

54. Cf. W. K. C. Guthrie, *A History of Greek Philosophy,* vol. 2, *The Presocratic Tradition from Parmenides to Democritus* (Cambridge: Cambridge University Press, 1965), 20.

philosophers" (11, p. 81) of whom Schopenhauer was a disciple. Yet, despite important differences among the Hindu, Buddhist, Platonic, Christian, Cartesian, Kantian, and Schopenhauerian world-interpretations, Nietzsche sees in them a basic similarity: they are all forms of what he would later call "the ascetic ideal," that "hatred of the human, and even more of the animal, and more still of the material, this horror of the senses, of reason itself, this fear of happiness and beauty, this longing to get away from all appearance, change, becoming, death, wishing, from longing itself" (*GM* III:28). This "ascetic ideal," this "moral interpretation of the world" in its various guises, Nietzsche asserts, "has hitherto *dominated*" not only "all philosophy" (III:24) but all of "[humanity's] existence on earth" (III:28). "Apart from [it], man, the human *animal*, had no meaning so far" (III:28). Consequently, "the death of God," which signals the eclipse of this world-interpretation, leads to the profound crisis of "nihilism." As diagnostician and physician of this condition, Nietzsche heralds a new interpretation. All but alone, he draws strength and inspiration from that world-interpretation foreclosed by the Parmenidean-ascetic: the Heraclitean view that "becoming is not a moral but an aesthetic phenomenon" (*PTA* 19, p. 113).

4.5 BECOMING AND NIETZSCHE'S NATURALISM

We now have an answer to the question, "Who is Nietzsche's Heraclitus?" With this, we have also begun to answer the main question, "What is Nietzsche's 'becoming'?" We can further pursue this question by focusing on the traits of becoming outlined above. It is evident that neither Heraclitus nor Nietzsche takes the world of "becoming" to be a metaphysical, noumenal world. On the contrary, their notions of "becoming" are consistent with a thoroughgoing naturalism. Nietzsche's Heraclitus "denie[s] the duality of totally diverse worlds" and "no longer distinguishe[s] a physical world from a metaphysical one" (*PTA* 5, p. 51). The world of becoming that both philosophers take to be the only reality is simply the physical, natural world that we inhabit and with which we are familiar. As Nietzsche remarks in his lecture course on the Presocratics, "becoming" is "the most ordinary phenomenon"; it "[lies] in front of everyone's nose." [55] Rather than discovering

---

55. This passage is found in the introduction to Nietzsche's lectures on the Presocratics (*KGW* II/4, pp. 215–16), quoted in Breazeale's "Introduction" to *Philosophy and Truth,* xliv.

reality in the abstract realm of concepts, names, and mathematical or logical forms, Heraclitus and Nietzsche find it in "the present many-colored and changing world that presses upon us in all our experiences" (*PTA* 5, p. 52), in "[a]ll the multiplicity and colorfulness of the world known to experience, [with] all the changes of its qualities" (10, p. 79). That is, the world of becoming is the sensuous world, the world available to the senses, a world of myriad and ever-changing appearances.[56] "Insofar as the senses show becoming, passing away, and change," Nietzsche writes, "they do not lie at all" (*TI* "Reason" 2).

Not the product of a speculative metaphysics, then, the notion of becoming is drawn from an empirical examination of the world around us. It simply marks the fact that, within the physical world, nothing is exempt from alteration; and those entities that appear stable differ only in their slower tempo of change or the degree to which it is apparent to the unaided senses (see *WP* 521, 552, 568, 580, and *GS* 112). What common sense takes to be a solid object, the physicist considers a more or less stable swarm of molecules. And while common sense has a pragmatic justification for treating this swarm as a single enduring entity, Nietzsche and Heraclitus remind us that this is a simplification. As an illustration, Heraclitus offers the image of the bow or lyre,[57] to which W. K. C. Guthrie provides this helpful gloss:

> Look at a strung bow lying on the ground or leaning against a wall. No movement is visible. To the eyes it appears a static object, completely at rest. But in fact a continuous tug-of-war is going on within it, as will become evident if the string is not strong enough or is allowed to perish. The bow will immediately take advantage, snap it and leap to straighten itself, thus showing that each had been putting forth effort all the time.[58]

Such is the case with every natural entity—the only ones to which Nietzsche and Heraclitus grant existence. Every "thing" is but a tension of forces and materials that soon enough alter, becoming other. Tables,

---

56. If Nietzsche later chides Heraclitus for doing an "injustice" to the senses ("he rejected their testimony because they showed things as if they had permanence and unity," *TI* "Reason" 2), it is only to remind him, and us, that it is not the senses themselves that are to blame but the falsification of their testimony by a reifying conceptual apparatus. Nietzsche and Heraclitus are not far apart, here. See the discussion of Nietzsche's empiricism above, in §§2.2.4–2.3.1, and Heraclitus's empiricism below, in §4.5, and in Guthrie, *History of Greek Philosophy*, 1:429ff.

57. See fr. 51: "They [ordinary people] do not grasp how by being at variance it [the Logos, cosmos, or natural order] agrees with itself, a backward-turning adjustment like that of the bow or lyre" (trans. Guthrie, *A History of Greek Philosophy*, 1:439).

58. Guthrie, *History of Greek Philosophy*, 1:440.

hands, cups, water, doorknobs, trees, stones, and all other natural things expand, contract, grow, decay, fuse, divide, solidify, melt, evaporate, and so on.[59] And none of this is mysteriously unavailable to the scrupulous and patient inquirer.[60]

Indeed this notion of becoming is the conclusion of a thoroughgoing empiricism that accepts the evident ubiquity of change in the universe without viewing it as issuing from, or tending toward, some being. We have already seen that both philosophers reject the notion that becoming's appearances and accidents are rooted in some underlying substratum. So, too, do they reject the supposition that being is the *archē* or *telos* of the process of becoming. Against the Milesians, Heraclitus rejects cosmogony in favor of a perpetual becoming ("[t]his world-order [. . .] none of the gods nor of men has made, but it was always and is and shall be");[61] while, against Hegel and Kelvin, Nietzsche maintains that "[t]he world [. . .] becomes, it passes away, but it has never begun to become and never ceased from passing away" (*WP* 1066).[62] For both Heraclitus and Nietzsche, the world is a perpetual *agon* that witnesses periodic victories but "endures in all eternity" (*PTA* 5, pp. 54–55).

This empiricism and naturalism of Nietzsche and his Heraclitus is directed against an idealist tradition that stretches from Parmenides and Plato through Christianity to Kant and Schopenhauer. If the idealist tradition travels Parmenides' "way of Truth," which leads it toward spirit, mind, thought, and being,[63] Nietzsche and his Heraclitus tread

59. See Heraclitus, fr. 126: "Cold things grow hot, hot things cold, moist dry, dry wet" (trans. Guthrie, *History of Greek Philosophy*, 1:445).
60. See *WP* 688: "It is simply a matter of experience that change *never ceases.*"
61. Fr. 30, trans. Guthrie, *History of Greek Philosophy*, 1:454. For a discussion of this rejection of cosmogony, see Guthrie, *The Greek Philosophers: From Thales to Aristotle* (New York: Harper and Row, 1950), 45, and *History of Greek Philosophy*, 1:441. Like Nietzsche, Guthrie rejects interpretations that read Heraclitus as hypothesizing "alternate states of harmony and discord, unity and plurality," maintaining that, for Heraclitus, "tension is never resolved. Peace and war do not succeed each other in turn: always in the world there is both peace and war. Cessation of struggle would mean the disintegration of the cosmos" (p. 437). See also Guthrie's rejection of the attribution to Heraclitus of a notion of *ecpyrosis* (the periodic destruction of the world by fire) in *History of Greek Philosophy*, 1:454ff.
62. See the rest of this note, as well as *WP* 708, 1062, 1064, and 1067. That Nietzsche maintained this idea throughout his career can be seen by comparing these passages to *PTA* 13, written more than a decade earlier, and the notes from 1873 presented by Walter Kaufmann in *The Portable Nietzsche* (New York: Viking Press, 1968), 39ff.
63. See Parmenides, frr. 2–8, and *Presocratic Philosophers,* ed. Kirk and Raven, 269–78. Though Kant carves out a limited domain for experience and natural science, his real concern, too, lies outside this domain: in the sphere of morality, the universal and necessary presuppositions of which are the products of pure reason "scrupulously cleansed of

---

the opposite path, "the way of seeming,"[64] which leads them back toward nature, body, sensation, and becoming. Contrary to Plato's claim that "[t]hat which is conceived by opinion with the help of sensation and without reason is always in the process of becoming and perishing and never really is,"[65] Nietzsche and his Heraclitus maintain that *there is only* the world of nature, life, history, becoming, and appearance and that "any other kind of reality is absolutely indemonstrable" (*TI* "Reason" 6). If Parmenides and Plato discover "absolute reality" in mental entities that "remain always constant and invariable never admitting any alteration in any respect or in any sense,"[66] Nietzsche and his Heraclitus, as we have seen, maintain that these mental entities are secondary to—"are in fact derived from"—the world of nature, experience, and becoming (*PTA* 12, p. 87).

4.6 BECOMING, APPEARANCE, AND INTERPRETATION

4.6.1. BEYOND GOD AND BEING: THE AFFILIATION OF BECOMING AND APPEARANCE

This conception of becoming as perpetual alteration and movement is certainly the best-known and most obvious characterization of the notion as it appears in Heraclitus and Nietzsche. But there is also another facet to their conception of becoming. If we examine this aspect, we find that Nietzsche's becoming does not name the primal ontological ground that no epistemological perspective can grasp but rather is a feature of his "perspectivism" itself.

We have seen that the world according to Heraclitus and Nietzsche is a "becoming" in the sense that no part of it is exempt from change. A commitment to naturalism and empiricism leads both philosophers to this view. Yet we have also seen that Nietzsche is no traditional empiricist. He rejects the positivistic notion that there are "brute facts" and

everything empirical" (*Groundwork of the Metaphysic of Morals*, trans. H. J. Paton [New York: Harper and Row, 1948], 56).

64. See Parmenides, frr. 8–19, and *Presocratic Philosophers*, ed. Kirk and Raven, 278–83. On "the way of seeming," see chapter 1, above.

65. Plato, *Timaeus* 27d–28a, in *The Collected Dialogues of Plato*, ed. Edith Hamilton and Huntington Cairns (Princeton: Princeton University Press, 1961), 1161. Robert Bolton ("Plato's Distinction between Being and Becoming," *Review of Metaphysics* 29 [1975]: 67) writes that this passage is, "[b]y general agreement, the definitive statement of the distinction [between being and becoming in Plato's work]."

66. Plato, *Phaedo* 78c–78d, in *Collected Dialogues of Plato*, 61.

instead espouses a holistic or hermeneutic view, according to which sense evidence is always relative to one or another background interpretation (see §2.3.1, above). Neither is Heraclitus a traditional empiricist. While acknowledging a preference for "[t]he things of which there is seeing and hearing and perception,"[67] Heraclitus also warns that "eyes and ears" are "evil witnesses [. . .] for men if they have souls that do not understand their language."[68] That is, for Heraclitus, as for Nietzsche, there is no *simple* perception; perception is always already interpretation.[69]

This insight is tremendously important to Heraclitus, for one who neglects it might succumb to the illusion that simple sense perception directly reveals the way the world really is. In a number of the fragments, Heraclitus rejects this realist view: "The sea is the purest and most polluted water, drinkable and salutary for fishes, undrinkable and deadly to men" (fr. 61); "Pigs like mud [but men do not]" (fr. 13); "Donkeys prefer rubbish to gold, [men gold to rubbish]" (fr. 9); "cutting and burning [which are normally bad] call for a fee when done by a surgeon" (fr. 58).[70] These observations about ordinary life aim to remind us that every description is relative to an interpretation and that every interpretation is rooted in a set of interests, desires, needs, capacities, and standpoints. Given the absurdity of declaring some one set of these to be absolutely true and right, we are to conclude that there is not one "true" description of the world but many.

67. Fr. 55, *Presocratic Philosophers*, ed. Kirk and Raven, 189. Cf. Sextus Empiricus's presentation of Heraclitus's view: "in sleep, when the channels of perception are shut, our mind is sundered from its kinship with the surrounding. [. . .] But in the waking state it again peeps out through the channels of perception as through a kind of window, and meeting with the surrounding it puts on its power of reason" (quoted and discussed in Kirk and Raven, *Presocratic Philosophers*, 207–8). On this passage, also see Guthrie, *History of Greek Philosophy*, 1:430.

68. Fr. 107, trans. Kirk and Raven, *Presocratic Philosophers*, 189.

69. Cf. Heidegger: "What we 'first' hear is never noises or complexes of sounds, but the creaking wagon, the motor-cycle. We hear the column on the march, the north wind, the woodpecker tapping, the fire crackling" (*Being and Time*, trans. John Macquarrie and Edward Robinson [New York: Harper and Row, 1962], 207).

70. Fr. 61, trans. Guthrie, *History of Greek Philosophy*, 1:445; frr. 13, 9, and 58, trans. Kirk and Raven, *Presocratic Philosophers*, 190. Cf. Nelson Goodman's remark: "If I were asked what is the food for men, I should have to answer 'none.' For there are many foods. And if I am asked what is the way the world is, I must likewise answer, 'none,' " ("The Way the World Is," in *Problems and Projects* [Indianapolis: Bobbs-Merrill, 1972], 31). Indeed, Goodman writes: "The pre-Socratics, I have long felt, made almost all the advances and mistakes in the history of philosophy" (*Ways of Worldmaking* [Indianapolis: Hackett, 1978], 97). Later in the same text, he refers to Heraclitus in support of the notion that "worlds seem to depend on conflict for their existence"(119).

We have already seen this to be the upshot of Nietzsche's perspectivism (see chapter 3). But the Heraclitean source is important for our
discussion of becoming. Terence Irwin has shown that, according to
both Plato and Aristotle, Heraclitean becoming must be seen as more
than simply the view that "everything undergoes constant local movement and qualitative alteration."[71] In addition to this notion of becoming, which Irwin calls "self-change," Heraclitean becoming must also
be taken to involve what Irwin calls "aspect-change," "things with
compresent opposite properties," "especially the compresence resulting from dependence on different situations," for example, "the road
up and down, the straight and crooked writing, the food which is good
(for some people) and bad (for others)."[72] Irwin's analysis follows that
of Guthrie, who remarks that the two central Heraclitean doctrines,
"everything is in continuous motion and change" and "harmony is of
opposites,"[73] are "only different ways of explaining the same truth."[74]

But how is this the case? How are these seemingly different notions
related? Self-change involves transformation over time, aspect-change
need not. The former seems to describe the alteration of a particular object, the latter a change in the viewpoint from which it is considered.[75]
Despite these differences, what joins these two kinds of change is *the rejection of being,* in its many forms.[76]

If self-change concerns "becoming" in the usual sense, aspect-change
concerns what is usually termed "appearance," variation in the way an

71. Terence Irwin, "Plato's Heracleiteanism," *Philosophical Quarterly* 27 (1977): 4.
Like Irwin, Guthrie maintains that there is good reason to accept Plato's account of
Heraclitus. For Guthrie (*History of Greek Philosophy,* 1:436–37), Plato was "perhaps
the first to appreciate the full boldness of [Heracleitus's] thought" and Plato "warrants
confidence in anything that he has to say about this difficult thinker." This confidence is
in part due to the fact that Plato and his contemporaries "possess[ed] either Heraclitus'
book or at least a much more comprehensive collection of his sayings than we have"
(p. 452n). I thank John Richardson for pointing me toward Irwin's essay.
72. Irwin, "Plato's Heracleiteanism," 4, 5.
73. Guthrie (*History of Greek Philosophy,* 1:435ff.) notes that the term "harmony"
is "misleading" "because it carries psychological overtones which are biased in a Pythago-
rean direction." That is, we tend to take the term as naming a calm resolution of tension
and struggle, which, for Heraclitus, is impossible. The Heraclitean doctrine is perhaps better described by Gilles Deleuze's phrase "the affirmation of difference." See, e.g., Deleuze,
The Logic of Sense, ed. Constantin V. Boundas, trans. Mark Lester and Charles Stivale
(New York: Columbia University Press, 1990), 172–73.
74. Guthrie, *History of Greek Philosophy,* 1:435.
75. See Irwin, "Plato's Heracleiteanism," 4. We will quickly see that this opposition
of object and subject, known and knower is problematized by the conception of becoming under discussion here.
76. For Nietzsche's endorsement of Heraclitus' rejection of being, see *PTA* 5, 51–52,
TI "Reason" 2 and *EH* "Books" BT:3, all three of which are quoted in §4.4, above.

object can seem or appear. But "becoming" and "appearance" are intimately related to one another. From its inception, the philosophical tradition has associated "becoming" and "appearance" as forms of alterity, of that which does not remain the same but constantly becomes-other. Thus, Parmenides arrived at his concept of Being through a rejection of both becoming and appearing (or seeming). This association was later taken up and canonized by Platonism and Christianity, which took the natural, empirical world as a derivative realm of mere becoming and mere appearance in relation to the meta-physical world of true being.[77] It is not surprising, then, that Nietzsche's naturalism—that is, his rejection of ontological dualism and his revaluation of the natural world—comes to privilege becoming not only in the sense of self-change but also in the sense of aspect-change (i.e., his perspectivism).

Yet Nietzsche's rejection of being connects "becoming" and "appearance" in a deeper sense as well. In the metaphysical tradition, true being serves as origin, aim, essence, and substance for the rest of existence. Thus, the Platonic Form is both a template for empirical entities and that which renders intelligible these entities by distilling the essence from their various guises. The Form also provides an absolute standard by which to judge true and false claimants (who is the true statesman? the true lover? the true philosopher?) and thus establishes a hierarchy of the more or less real that measures each entity according to its distance from true being.[78] So, too, for the Western tradition, has God been synonymous with Being itself: at once creator, providential director, essence, substance, and end of all existence. The Christian tradition, too, produces a hierarchy of entities, at the top of which stands "man," created "in the image of God," and at the bottom of which stands inanimate nature. Moreover, for modern rationalism, God is that which guarantees all knowledge (Descartes), sorts out better from worse and actual from merely possible worlds (Leibniz), exists as the sole substance, of which all else is expression or attribute (Spinoza),[79] and serves as the ultimate unity and ground of all possible experience (Kant). In

77. For Nietzsche's critique of philosophy's obsession with true being and its rejection of becoming, appearance, and the senses, see *TI* "Reason" 1. Note that Nietzsche's critique of the philosophical tradition excepts only Heraclitus (*TI* "Reason" 2).

78. For an analysis of Plato along these lines, see Deleuze, "Plato and the Simulacrum," in *Logic of Sense*, 253–66, and *Difference and Repetition*, trans. Paul Patton (New York: Columbia University Press, 1994), 59–69.

79. Of course, Spinoza is a special case, since, for him, "God is Nature" rather than some meta-physical entity. Nietzsche praises Spinoza for this, as do Nietzscheans such as Deleuze. Nonetheless, Spinoza still follows the metaphysical-theological tradition in us-

short, true Being has always been that which guarantees the existence, unity, necessity, completeness, continuity, and hierarchy of all knowing and being.

Consequently, "the rejection of being" or "the death of God" (the two phrases are nearly synonymous)[80] means a fragmentation of this unity and continuity, a withdrawal of this origin, a subversion of this hierarchy, a deviation of this teleology. Of the two tasks that are to follow God's death (see *GS* 109 and chapter 2, above), "the naturalization of humanity" means a rejection of the hierarchy that places human beings closest to God and establishes "a false order of rank in relation to animals and nature" (*GS* 115).[81] "The de-deification of nature" means the rejection of any simple and absolute origin, the denial of providence and teleology, and a repudiation of the model–copy relationship and the associated distinctions between substance and accident, essence and appearance, identity and difference. For Nietzsche, following Heraclitus, "being is an empty fiction. The 'apparent' world is the only one" (cf. *TI* "World" 6). If being finds its ideal and sanction in God, "the death of God" inaugurates the reign of becoming and appearance. In place of the opposition of being (or essence or substance) and appearance, there remain only "degrees of apparentness and, as it were, lighter and darker shadows and shades of appearance" (*BGE* 34). In short, the rejection of being amounts to a rejection of every transcendent grounding principle, any form of—what, following Derrida, we could call—"being-presence": origin, aim, unity, essence, substance, and so on.[82] Cast adrift from these anchors, the world *becomes*.

Thus, just as the two central Heraclitean doctrines—"everything is in continuous motion and change" and "harmony is of opposites"—are "only different ways of explaining the same truth," so, too, are the two Nietzschean doctrines, "becoming" and "perspectivism." The terms

ing "God" to name this essence and source of all existence. This idea is discussed further in §4.7.1, below.

80. Compare *PTA* 11 with *TI* "Reason" 4. See also *TI* "Reason" 5, where Nietzsche writes that "every word we say and every sentence speak in [. . .] favor" of "the error concerning being" and concludes that "we are not rid of God because we still have faith in grammar."

81. Cf. *GM* III:25: "Alas, the faith in the dignity and uniqueness of man, in his irreplaceability in the great chain of being, is a thing of the past—he has become an *animal*, literally and without reservation or qualification, he who was, according to his old faith, almost God ('child of God,' 'God-man')."

82. For some representative passages, see *GS* 54, 109, 285, 357; *TI* "Errors" 7–8; *WP* 552, 556, 561, 567, 1062–67.

of this latter pair are not related to one another as object to subject, known to knower. Rather, they describe different facets of a world beyond being. Such a world "becomes" not only in the sense that, natural in its entirety, it is subject to incessant alteration over time. It "becomes" also insofar as "essence" has been dissolved into "appearance," the "world 'in itself'" into "a world of relations." "It has *a differing aspect* from every point," and thus "its being is essentially different from every point." [83] Hence, any characterization of the world as a whole or any entity within it will be perpetually displaced by another—"and the sum of these is in every case quite *incongruent*" (*WP* 568).

4.6.2 BECOMING AND THE CONTEST OF INTERPRETATIONS

Let us pursue this further. To account for the ubiquity and perpetuity of change in the world, both Heraclitus and Nietzsche call upon the metaphor of war and struggle: "war is the father of all" (fr. 53),[84] says the former; "[t]he world [. . .] is 'will to power' and nothing besides" (*BGE* 36), declares the latter, explaining that:

> every specific body strives to become master over all space and to extend its force (—its will to power:) and to thrust back all that resists its extension. But it continually encounters similar efforts on the parts of other bodies and ends by coming into an arrangement ("union") with those of them that are sufficiently related to it: *thus they conspire together for power.* And the process goes on. (*WP* 636)

"[T]he process goes on" because these unions are unstable, each part bent on power; and so "the contest endures in all eternity" (*PTA* 5, p. 55). This contest could not have had a simple beginning, because it requires at least two contestants and the difference and tension between them. And the projection of an end to this struggle Nietzsche views as merely the dream of those for whom this world of becoming ought to be other than it is (see *WP* 708).

---

83. Cf. *GS* 54, 335; *WP* 556ff.; and *WP* 625 ("there is no 'essence-in-itself,' it is only relations that constitute an essence").

84. Nietzsche quotes this fragment in *GS* 92 and celebrates war and warriors throughout his writing: see, e.g., *HC; GS* 283, 285, 377; *Z:*1 "On Reading and Writing," *Z:*3 "On Old and New Tablets"; *BGE* 76; *GM* I:5, I:7, II:9, II:24, III:epigram, III:10, III:25; *TI* "Morality" 3, "Skirmishes" 24; *EH* "Wise" 7; and *WP* 1040.

Moreover, for Nietzsche and Heraclitus, there is no place outside this struggle:

> While Heraclitus' imagination saw this restless motion of the universe, this "reality," with the eyes of a blissful spectator who is watching innumerable pairs of contestants wrestling in joyous combat and refereed by stern judges, he was overcome by an even greater idea: he could no longer see the contesting pairs and their referees as separate; the judges themselves seemed to be striving in the contest and the contestants seemed to be judging them. (*PTA* 6, p. 57)

That is, we who witness this becoming are ourselves a part of it; our interpretations are contestants in the game or *agon*. Rejecting the notion that the world simply reveals itself as it is, Nietzsche and Heraclitus maintain that the world always appears under the aegis of one or another interpretation. Yet, lacking both a fixed essence and a detached judge who could determine it, no one of these interpretations can ever be granted ultimate priority. While surely there are "momentary ascendanc[ies]" during which particular interpretations dominate, the contest continues without end. "A thing would be defined," Nietzsche writes, "once all creatures had asked 'what is that?' and had answered their question. Supposing one single creature, with its own relationships and perspectives for all things were missing, then the thing would not yet be 'defined'" (*WP* 556). Thus is any final characterization of a "thing"—and, indeed, of the world as a whole—forever contested and, hence, deferred.

4.6.3 BECOMING AS *DIFFÉRANCE*

We can summarize the discussion thus far by calling upon a notion the inspiration for which is both Heraclitean and Nietzschean: Jacques Derrida's conception of *différance*.[85] Derrida provides this gloss:

> The verb "to differ" [Fr. *différer;* L. *differre*] seems to differ from itself. On the one hand, it indicates difference as distinction, inequality, or discernibility; on the other, it expresses the interposition of delay, the interval of a *spacing* and *temporalizing* that puts off until "later" what is presently denied, the pos-

---

85. See Jacques Derrida, "Différance," in *Speech and Phenomena and Other Essays on Husserl's Theory of Signs,* trans. David B. Allison (Evanston: Northwestern University Press, 1973), 148ff. and 154, where Nietzsche and Heraclitus are cited as having foreshadowed the notion of *différance.* On the Nietzschean inspiration, see also Derrida, "Implications," in *Positions,* trans. Alan Bass (Chicago: University of Chicago Press, 1981), 9–10.

sible that is presently impossible. Sometimes the *different* and sometimes the *deferred* correspond [in French] to the verb "to differ." [. . .] In the one case "to differ" signifies nonidentity; in the other case it signifies the order of the *same.* Yet there must be a common, although entirely differant [*différante*], root within the sphere that relates the two movements of differing to one another. We provisionally give the name *différance* to this *sameness* which is not *identical:* by the silent writing of its *a,* it has the desired advantage of referring to differing, *both* as spacing/temporalizing and as the movement that structures every dissociation.[86]

Derrida's neologism (or neographism) is perhaps a better name for the complex notion of "becoming" we have been discussing. It captures both senses of "becoming" we have found at work in Heraclitus and Nietzsche: becoming as "self-change" and as "aspect-change." As "self-change," *différance* designates difference within "the order of the *same*": the one that, in time, becomes-other, postponing any definitive characterization. As "aspect-change," *différance* "signifies non-identity," "difference as distinction, inequality, or discernibility": the one that is simultaneously other—"the road up," which both is and is not "the road down." Furthermore, it serves to highlight several features not immediately evident in Nietzsche's and Heraclitus's notion but that we have seen are central to it. First, it discards the image of becoming as a fluid, primary, pre-formed plenum and instead figures it as an assemblage of differences, of forces in struggle, as "a 'productive,' conflictual movement which cannot be preceded by any identity, any unity, or any original simplicity."[87] It thus serves to remind us that, if Nietzsche and Heraclitus at times picture becoming as a "river," it is one in which "different and different waters flow."[88] Second, *différance* describes "an allergic or polemical otherness," "the 'active,' moving discord of different forces, and difference of forces," thus highlighting the agonistic quality we have seen to be so crucial in Heraclitus's and Nietzsche's notions of becoming.[89] Third, it emphasizes that becoming is not *something that happens to beings* but rather constitutes *the rejection of*

86. Derrida, "Différance," 129–30. Note that David B. Allison's translation of "Différance" includes a brief introduction (from which I quote above) that appeared in the original version of the essay, published in *Théorie d'ensemble* (Paris: Editions Seuil, 1968), but was omitted in the version reprinted in *Marges de la philosophie* (*Margins of Philosophy*).

87. Jacques Derrida, *Dissemination*, trans. Barbara Johnson (Chicago: University of Chicago Press, 1981), 6.

88. Heraclitus, fr. 12, trans. Kirk and Raven, *Presocratic Philosophers*, 217.

89. Jacques Derrida, "Différance," in *Margins of Philosophy*, trans. Alan Bass (Chicago: University of Chicago Press, 1982), 8, 18.

being, "the operation of differing which at one and the same time both fissures and retards [being-] presence, submitting it simultaneously to primordial division and delay."[90] Finally, if Heraclitus's "becoming" has lost some of its force through its long service in the metaphysical vocabulary, Derrida's neographism restores this force and draws attention to what both Nietzsche and Derrida see as the decisive feature of our modernity (or postmodernity): the differing and deferring of being and presence that follows the "death of God."[91]

4.7 CHAOS AND NECESSITY

4.7.1 FROM CHAOS TO *CHAOSMOS*

Nietzsche alternately describes this world of becoming or *différance* as a "chaos" [*Chaos*]. No less than "becoming," this notion has been subject to a misunderstanding of its ontological status. Like "becoming," Nietzschean "chaos" has been taken to name a primordial ground, a world in itself that surges beneath the regular and ordered world of our experience and knowledge. Nietzschean "chaos" is thus construed in the traditional manner, as describing a lack of order, form, discernibility, stasis, intelligibility; and Nietzsche is read in the manner of Kant, as maintaining that, though the world in itself comes to us as a chaos (Kant speaks of a "manifold" or "mass" of sensations), we impose form upon it and thus make it intelligible.[92] In our discussion of "becoming," we saw that Nietzsche severely criticizes this sort of Kantian dualism. This gives us prima facie evidence against a Kantian reading of Nietz-

90. Derrida, *Speech and Phenomena,* 88.
91. Derrida ("Différance," trans. Allison, 135–36, 130) writes that *différance* is "the theme most proper to think out [. . .] what is most characteristic about our 'epoch',", that, in *différance,* we "see the juncture [. . .] of what has been most decisively inscribed in the thought of what is conveniently called our 'epoch.' " Indeed, we can see this conception of *différance* at work in contemporary art and science as well. For suggestions along these lines, see Umberto Eco, "The Poetics of the Open Work," in *The Role of the Reader: Explorations in the Semiotics of Texts* (Bloomington: Indiana University Press, 1979), 57ff.; Ilya Prigogine and Isabelle Stengers, *Order out of Chaos: Man's New Dialogue with Nature* (New York: Bantam Books, 1984), 111, 136; and Alistair Moles, "Nietzsche's Eternal Recurrence as Riemannian Cosmology," *International Studies in Philosophy* 21 (1989): 21–40.
92. Heidegger reminds us of this in *Nietzsche,* 3:77. For this reading of Nietzsche on chaos, see Danto, *Nietzsche as Philosopher,* 96–98; Granier, "Perspectivism and Interpretation" and "Nietzsche's Conception of Chaos"; Taylor, "Foucault on Freedom and Truth," 93; Young, *Nietzsche's Philosophy of Art,* 96–97, 160–61; and Babich, *Nietzsche's Philosophy of Science,* 107, 149, 152ff.

sche's notion of "chaos." And, indeed, a close reading of the passages in which this notion appears reveals that Nietzsche construes the notion otherwise.

Nietzsche defines his terms in use, and so, to understand his conception of "chaos," we need to examine how the term functions within the textual networks in which it, and associated terms, appear. In the published work, Nietzsche speaks of "chaos" most frequently and poignantly in *The Gay Science*. The most famous passage is the by now familiar one in which the project of "naturalizing humanity" and "de-deifying nature" is introduced. Having criticized a number of world-interpretations, and before proceeding to criticize others, Nietzsche writes, "[t]he total character of the world [. . .] is in all eternity chaos—in the sense not of a lack of necessity but a lack of order, arrangement, form, beauty, wisdom, and whatever other names there are for our aesthetic anthropomorphisms" (*GS* 109).[93] At first glance, one might well take this passage as an assertion of the Kantian thesis that none of our conceptions adequately comprehend the world as it really is, for this world is an ungraspable "chaos." Yet the appearance of the term elsewhere shows that this sort of paradoxical noumenon is not at all what Nietzsche has in mind.

Gay Science §277 asks that we "face [. . .] up to the beautiful chaos of existence and den[y] it all providential reason and goodness." As in §109, the notion of "chaos" is here contrasted with a conception of the world as divinely created and unfolding according to a grand plan. Instead, Nietzsche contends that "becoming" is "innocent," that it is not the product of divine intention and its movement does not have any particular direction or destination.[94] The term "chaos" also appears in §322, where Nietzsche writes: "Those thinkers in whom all stars move in cyclic orbits are not the most profound. Whoever looks at himself as into vast space and carries galaxies within himself, also knows how irregular galaxies are; they lead into the chaos and labyrinth of existence."[95] Here, Nietzsche all but repeats a few lines from §109: "Let us beware of positing generally and everywhere anything as elegant as the

93. The passage is quoted in full in section §2.3.2, above.
94. Cf. *GS* 357, quoted in §1.2. This passage is also quoted in *GM* III:27. See also *TI* "Errors" 8; *WP* 340 and 1062.
95. This notion of human beings as containing a "chaos" appears frequently in Nietzsche's writings of the 1880s. See, e.g., *Z*:Prologue 5; *BGE* 224–35; *KSA* 10:5[1]; *WP* 842 and, especially, *WP* 83: "'*Without the Christian faith*,' Pascal thought, 'you, no less than nature and history, will become for yourselves *un monstre et un chaos*.' This prophecy we

cyclical movements of our neighboring stars; even a glance into the galaxy raises doubts whether there are not far coarser and more contradictory movements there, as well as stars with eternally linear paths, etc." The later passage (§322) describes human beings as microcosms whose perspectival movements are analogous to the macrocosmic orbits of stars presented in the earlier passage (§109). The later passage also sheds considerable light on the notion of "chaos" presented in the earlier. Read together, these passages suggest that Nietzsche's "chaos" is not characterized by an absolute lack of order but by a set of "irregular," "contradictory" movements. That is, the "chaotic" universe is one that moves not teleologically but errantly; it follows no simple linear or cyclical path but a "labyrinthine" one. So, too, is the "chaotic" person a wanderer and experimenter. As Nietzsche puts it in the final section of *Human, All Too Human:*

> He who has attained to only some degree of freedom of mind cannot feel other than a wanderer on the earth—though not as a traveler *to* a final destination: for this destination does not exist. But he will watch and observe and keep his eyes open to see what is really going on in the world; for this reason he may not let his heart adhere too firmly to any individual thing; within him too there must be something wandering that takes pleasure in change and transience. (638)

Here we begin to see that "chaos" involves not only an errant or labyrinthine world-trajectory but also a perspectival or interpretive multiplicity. We find further evidence of this in another set of passages from *The Gay Science* that clearly resonate with those that make more explicit mention of "chaos." In §2, Nietzsche celebrates what he calls "this *rerum concordia discors*" (discordant concord of things),[96] "this whole marvelous uncertainty and interpretive multiplicity of existence [*Vieldeutigkeit der Daseins*]" and reproaches those who do not, or cannot bear to, see it as such. This is echoed in §373, where Nietzsche chides those who "wish to divest existence of its *multiply interpretable* character [*seines* vieldeutigen *Charakters*]" in favor of a single mathe-

---

have *fulfilled.* [. . .]" On perspectivism and "the chaos we are," see §3.3.3, above. On the human being as analogous to a solar system, see *WP* 676.

96. A particularly Heraclitean formulation. Derrida ("Différance," trans. Allison, 154) is more explicit, referring his notion of *différance* to "the Heraclitean play of the *hen diapheron heautoi,* of the one differing from itself, of what is in difference with itself." Derrida alludes to Heraclitus's fr. 51 (trans. Freeman, *Ancilla to the Pre-Socratic Philosophers,* 28): "They do not understand how that which differs with itself is in agreement: harmony consists of opposing tension, like that of the bow and the lyre."

matical or mechanistic interpretation. The "chaos and labyrinth of existence" would thus seem to describe the errant and divergent movements of both world and world-interpretation.

This becomes clearer once we see that, like "becoming," this conception of "chaos" follows from the "death of God." If God guaranteed a single world-trajectory and world-interpretation, the "death of God" unleashes a series of "irregular," "contradictory" movements and opens the way for an "interpretive multiplicity." Gilles Deleuze summarizes this situation well and offers perhaps the most Nietzschean characterization of this "chaos." For Deleuze, Nietzsche is a posttheological Leibniz. If Leibniz's God creates an infinity of divergent, incompossible worlds but chooses to actualize only one—"the best"—on which all monadic perspectives converge,[97] Nietzsche's atheological "perspectivism" and "becoming" deny the existence of any privileged world and worldview and instead affirm the coexistence of divergent, irreducible worlds and worldviews. For Deleuze, Nietzsche's "chaos" describes the *complication* of these divergent worlds and worldviews, their coexistence within "the same world."[98] It does not describe some pre-cosmic jumble but a world of difference, the coexistence of irreducibly different and divergent worlds and worldviews. And, because this "chaos" is no longer opposed to a "cosmos" (to the cosmic ordering of the demiurge), because it simply describes the posttheological world, this "chaos," Deleuze suggests, is better termed a *chaosmos*.[99]

97. On God, the infinity of worlds, and the choice of the best, see Leibniz, *The Monadology* §53, and *Theodicy* §§225, 414–17. On the multiple monadic perspectives on the same world, see *The Monadology* §57; *Discourse on Metaphysics* §9; and *Theodicy* §357.

98. In this setting, "the same world" is to be taken not as the point of convergence for all worldviews (Leibniz) but rather as the incongruous assemblage of all world-interpretations and their worlds (Nietzsche). If, for Nietzsche, "a 'thing' is the sum of its effects," the "world" is the sum of its interpretations, and this sum is not convergent but divergent, "*incongruent*" (WP 568). Cf. Goodman, *Ways of Worldmaking* and *Of Mind and Other Matters* (Cambridge, Mass.: Harvard University Press, 1984), chap. 2; Richard Rorty, "Introduction: Pragmatism and Philosophy," in *Consequences of Pragmatism* (Minneapolis: University of Minnesota Press, 1982), xlvii; and §3.4.3, above.

99. These suggestions are scattered throughout Deleuze's writings of the late 1960s. See, e.g., Deleuze, *Logic of Sense*, 172–76, 264, 260–66 and *Difference and Repetition*, 40–41, 46–50, 55–58, 66–69, 123–24, 280, 299. They reappear in his book on Leibniz, *The Fold: Leibniz and the Baroque*, trans. Tom Conley (Minneapolis: University of Minnesota Press, 1993), 59–82. The term *chaosmos* is taken from James Joyce's *Finnegans Wake*, which Deleuze sees as an artistic manifestation of our posttheological condition. A similar assessment is offered by Eco ("Poetics of the Open Work," 54, 58), who writes that Joyce "deliberately seeks to offer an image of the ontological and existential situation of the contemporary world," with all its "openness," "multiplicity," "indeterminacy," and "discontinuity." I thank Daniel W. Smith for helpful discussion of these issues.

On Deleuze's view, Nietzsche is also a posttheological Spinoza.[100] For Spinoza, all entities originate, and converge, in a single substance: God. All of nature expresses God's being; and, in turn, God's being contains all of nature. Thus, Spinoza can say: "Deus sive Natura [God or Nature]."[101] Like Spinoza, Nietzsche is a naturalist and antidualist. He grants that there is nothing other than nature and that all entities and attributes are natural. Yet, for Nietzsche, nature can no longer be identified with God. After the "death of God," nature is no longer a point of convergence but a zone of divergence, no longer one, but multiple. Thus, Nietzsche reformulates Spinoza's equation: "Chaos sive Natura [Chaos or Nature]" (*KSA* 9:11[197]). Nature de-deified is "chaos."

This passage returns us to the one with which we began, *Gay Science* §109, which calls for a "de-deification of nature" and names this nature "chaos." Contrary to the neo-Kantian reading, we have seen that this notion of "chaos" does not describe an ungraspable metaphysical world. Rather, it describes the natural, physical world, the world we know — or rather, the world Nietzsche believes will be disclosed to us once we discard our ontotheological[102] prejudices: a world of becoming or *différance,* a world without origin or end, the "true" character, essence, or being of which is incessantly differed and perpetually deferred.[103]

4.7.2 NECESSITY AND CHANCE

A THROW OF THE DICE ... WILL NEVER
... ABOLISH ... CHANCE

Stéphane Mallarmé (1897)

We can further clarify this conception of "chaos" by examining the notion of "necessity" [*Nothwendigkeit*] Nietzsche associates with it. The

100. See Deleuze, *Difference and Repetition,* 40ff. Also see Richard Schacht, "The Nietzsche-Spinoza Problem: Spinoza as Precursor?" in *Making Sense of Nietzsche* (Urbana: University of Illinois Press, 1995).

101. *Ethics,* in *Works of Spinoza,* vol. 2, trans. R. H. M. Elwes (New York: Dover), 188; cf. *WP* 1062.

102. The term is borrowed from Heidegger (*Identity and Difference,* trans. Joan Stambaugh (New York: Harper and Row, 1969), 54: "Western metaphysics [. . .] has eminently been both ontology and theology. [. . . T]his means: metaphysics is ontotheology." On the identity of God and Being in Nietzsche, see §4.6.1, above. For more on this Heideggerian term, see my introduction, §0.3.

103. Cf. *WP* 584 on "the properties that constitute [the world's] reality: change, becoming, multiplicity, opposition, contradiction, war." Also see *WP* 616: "The world *with which we are concerned* is false [. . .] it is 'in flux,' as something becoming, as a falsehood always changing but never getting near the truth: for—there is no 'truth.'"

latter term appears frequently in Nietzsche's presentations of his own cosmological view. To quote it once again, *Gay Science* §109 maintains that: "The total character of the world [. . .] is in all eternity chaos— in the sense not of a lack of *necessity* but of a lack of order, arrangement, [etc.] Let us beware of saying there are laws in nature. There are only *necessities:* there is nobody who commands, nobody who obeys, nobody who trespasses [my emphasis]." This language is echoed in two later passages. In *Beyond Good and Evil* §22, Nietzsche rejects the world-interpretation according to which "nature conforms to law" and proceeds to sketch his own picture of the world as "will to power." Such a world, he writes, "has a 'necessary' and 'calculable' course, *not* because laws obtain in it, but because they are absolutely lacking, and every power draws its ultimate consequences at every moment." Similarly, the section of *Twilight of the Idols* called "The Four Great Errors" culminates with this statement of Nietzsche's own worldview:

> One is necessary, one is a piece of fatefulness, one belongs to the whole, one *is* in the whole; there is nothing which could judge, measure, compare, or sentence our being, for that would mean judging, comparing, or sentencing the whole. *But there is nothing besides the whole!* That nobody is held responsible any longer, that the mode of being may not be traced back to a *causa prima,* that the world does not form a unity either as a sensorium or as "spirit"—*that alone is the great liberation;* with this alone is the *innocence* of becoming restored. The concept of "God" was until now the greatest *objection* to existence. We deny God, we deny the responsibility in God: only *thereby* do we redeem the world. ("Errors" 8; cf. *WP* 552)

Finally, in two related notes from the *Nachlaß*, Nietzsche states:

> [I]f becoming *could* resolve itself into being or nothingness [. . .] then [given infinite time] this state must have been reached. But it has not been reached: from which it follows [that it cannot and will not be reached]. (*WP* 1066)

> I seek a conception of the world that takes this fact into account. Becoming must be explained without recourse to final intentions; becoming must appear justified at every moment (or incapable of being evaluated; which amounts to the same thing). [. . .] "Necessity" not in the shape of an overreaching, dominating total force, or that of a prime mover; even less as a necessary condition for something valuable. To this end, it is necessary to deny a total consciousness of becoming, a "God."[. . .] Fortunately such a summarizing power is missing (—a suffering and all-seeing God, a "total sensorium" and "cosmic spirit" would be the greatest objection to being). More strictly one must admit nothing that has being—because then becoming would lose its value and actually appear meaningless and superfluous. [. . .] Becoming is of equivalent value every moment; the sum of its val-

ues always remains the same; in other words, it has no value at all, for anything against which to measure it and in relation to which the word "value"
could have any meaning, is lacking. *The total value of the world cannot be
evaluated.* (*WP* 708)

Taken together, these passages present a number of overlapping ideas:
becoming is innocent and without beginning, end, intention, or direction; it is lawless yet necessary and fateful; it is incapable of being
judged or measured as a whole but is of equal value at every moment.
What are we to make of this set of ideas and how do they cast light on
the notions of "chaos" and "necessity"?

As with "becoming" and "chaos," Nietzsche's affirmation of "necessity" proceeds from the rejection of God and being. "Necessity"
is set against divine "purpose" and human "free will," both of which
require the posit of an extra-natural world of uncaused causes (see
§3.3.2, above). For Nietzsche, becoming is "necessary" in the sense that
it neither originates from nor is directed by the "purposes" and "intentions" of any transcendent being. Rather, its errant movements are
solely the result of immanent conditions and forces. But this does not
mean that the "necessity" attributed to becoming and chaos sanctions
a determinism. Nietzsche sees the deterministic picture of the world as
itself theological: a closed system, timeless, static, in equilibrium, governed by universal laws—"the great captious web of causality" behind
which lies "God as some alleged spider of purpose" (*GM* III:9).[104]
Indeed, the deterministic world subordinates becoming to being, time
to eternity: past and future are given in every moment, bound together
in an eternal Present.[105] Finally, behind determinism, there lurks that
"demand for certainty" condemned by Nietzsche for its willed ignorance of the "whole marvelous uncertainty and interpretive multiplicity
of existence" (*GS* 2).[106]

104. Cf. *Z*:3 "Before Sunrise" on the "eternal spider" and "spider web of reason."
Cf. Gaston Bachelard (*The New Scientific Spirit,* trans. Patrick A. Heelan [Boston: Beacon Press, 1984], 100): "Terrestrial phenomena are too obviously fluid and diverse to permit, without prior psychological preparation, the elaboration of an objective, deterministic physics. Determinism descended from heaven to earth."
105. See Prigogine and Stengers, *Order out of Chaos,* 11, 60, and Stephen H. Kellert,
In the Wake of Chaos: Unpredictable Order in Dynamical Systems (Chicago: University
of Chicago Press, 1993), 53–54. See also Deleuze, *Logic of Sense,* 162–68. Ilya Prigogine
(*From Being to Becoming: Time and Complexity in the Physical Sciences* [New York:
W. H. Freeman and Co., 1980]) describes the deterministic world of classical dynamics
precisely as "a world of being," which, since the discovery of thermodynamics in the nineteenth century, has given way to a "world of becoming."
106. See Kellert, *In the Wake of Chaos,* 51–55.

In place of both the theological notion of becoming as divinely constructed and purposive and the scientific picture of it as thoroughly calculable and predictable, Nietzsche maintains that becoming is a dice game.[107] In the language of *Zarathustra*, the gods are dice players and the earth is their table.[108] The natural world and everything in it, ourselves included, are combinations that have turned up in this game of chance. But this chance is not opposed to necessity. While the throw of the dice is an act of freedom, it is powerless to determine the resulting combination. Once the dice leave the hand, the rest is left to necessity. And, while, one can retrospectively determine the conditions and forces that led to a particular result, no prospective inference will enable one to determine the results of future throws, each of which will, once again, affirm both chance and necessity.[109] "Those iron hands of necessity which shake the dice-box of chance play their game for an infinite length of time," Nietzsche writes; and "we ourselves shake the dice-box with iron hands, [. . .] we ourselves in our most intentional actions do no more than play the game of necessity" (*D* 130). Such a game denies transcendent purpose and control and instead affirms "divine accidents" (*Z:*3 "Before Sunrise").[110] It is this sort of nonrational, nonpurposive "necessity" that Nietzsche wants to ascribe to becom-

107. See *PTA* 14, 91; *D* 130; *Z:*3 "Before Sunrise," 16; *WP* 1066. See also Gilles Deleuze, *Nietzsche and Philosophy,* trans. Hugh Tomlinson (New York: Columbia University Press, 1983), 25ff.

108. See *Z:*3 "Before Sunrise" and "The Seven Seals." Cf. *D* 130.

109. Chaos theory discovers a similar feature in physical systems. On the model presented by Prigogine and Stengers (*Order out of Chaos,* 177), Nietzsche's "throw of the dice" corresponds to a "bifurcation point," where "deterministic description breaks down." At such points, "fluctuations or random elements would play an important role, while between bifurcations the deterministic aspects would become dominant" (176; cf. 73 and Prigogine, *From Being to Becoming,* 106). "Both the deterministic character of the kinetic equations whereby the set of possible states and their respective stability can be calculated, and the random fluctuations 'choosing' between or among the states around bifurcation points are inextricably connected. This mixture of necessity and chance constitutes the history of the system" (Prigogine and Stengers, *Order out of Chaos,* 170). On dice throws and bifurcations, see Prigogine, *From Being to Becoming,* 203, and Prigogine and Stengers, *Order out of Chaos,* 162. Prigogine and Stengers (*Order Out of Chaos,* 111, 136) cite Nietzsche as a philosophical precursor to the move in physics from being to becoming, substance to relation, equivalence to difference, determinism to chance. Neither these authors nor I want to claim that Nietzsche is a chaos theorist *avant la lettre*. Rather, Nietzsche's attempt to provide a rigorously atheological conception of nature leads him to *philosophically* anticipate features of the world that resemble those later *experimentally* discovered by chaos physics.

110. Nietzsche shares with Hume the notion that the world (human beings included) operates neither according to "chance" nor "necessity," in their strict senses. It does not operate according to pure "chance," because there appears to be some order and regularity in our experience; nor does it operate according to "necessity," whether transcendent or

ing.[111] Becoming is seen as a series of dice throws, each of which is complete in itself ("justified at every moment") and has no further end beyond sparking an interest in new throws and different combinations.

This game of chance and necessity, this nonpurposive becoming, is what Nietzsche elsewhere calls "chaos." Thus, at one point, Zarathustra speaks of "that heavenly need that constrains even accidents to star dances" (Z:3 "The Seven Seals"); while, at another point, echoing *Gay Science* §322, he says that "one must still have chaos in oneself to give birth to a dancing star" (Z:Prologue 5). That is, Nietzschean "chaos" is not some arbitrary jumble from which we, like the demiurge, create order. Rather, it is a redescription of the world we know and in which we exist, an image of what our world would look like were we to eliminate all the "shadows of God." Whether dubbed an "innocent becoming" or a "chaos," such a world is without origin, purpose, aim, unity, or total character. And it is precisely this that makes it a world of *play*, for there is nothing to halt this becoming and differing, no transcendent principle to direct or constrain it, no calculation that could totalize it once and for all.[112]

---

immanent, because divine providence is indemonstrable or superfluous and induction can, at best, provide only probabilities.

111. See *PTA* 19, 116: "But absolute free will can only be imagined as purposeless, roughly like a child's game or an artist's creative play impulse." See also *HH* 107: "Everything is necessity—thus says the new knowledge; and this knowledge itself is necessity. Everything is innocence: and knowledge is the path to insight into this innocence."

112. Cf. Derrida ("Différance," trans. Allison, 135): "on the eve and aftermath of philosophy, [the concept of play] designates the unity of chance and necessity in an endless calculus."

CHAPTER FIVE

Will to Power

The De-Deification of Nature

> The world viewed from inside, the world defined and deter-
> mined according to its "intelligible character"—it would be
> "will to power" and nothing besides.
>
> Nietzsche, Beyond Good and Evil §36

> Supposing that this also is only interpretation—and you will
> be eager enough to make this objection?—well, so much the
> better.
>
> Nietzsche, Beyond Good and Evil §22

5.1 THE PROBLEM OF WILL TO POWER

The doctrine of "will to power" is surely the most controversial in Nietzsche's philosophy. While, for the most part, it has been rescued from its
association with unsavory political and ethical programs, the doctrine
still poses a host of philosophical problems. Its centrality to Nietzsche's
later thought is undeniable.[1] But its import is far from clear. At times, it
appears to be an ontological view (*"the world is will to power—and
nothing besides"* [WP 1067; cf. BGE 36]); while, at other times, it appears in a more epistemological guise ("[t]ruth [. . .] is a word for the
'will to power'" [WP 552; cf. BGE 211]; "interpretation itself [. . . is]
a form of the will to power" [WP 556; cf. GM II:12]). The scope of the
doctrine is also indeterminate: is it meant to characterize human psychology? animal life? organic activity? or nature as a whole? This raises

---

1. For example, among the many dozen appearances of the phrase in the published
work alone, one finds the following: "[w]here I found the living, there I found will to
power" (Z:2 "On Self-Overcoming"); "life itself is *will to power*" (BGE 13); "[t]he world
viewed from inside [. . .] would be 'will to power' and nothing besides" (BGE 36); "the will
to power [. . .] is the will of life" (GS 349); "in all events a *will to power* is operating"
(GM II:12); "[l]ife itself is to my mind the instinct for growth, for durability, for an accumulation of forces, for *power:* where the will to power is lacking there is decline" (A 6).

a final question: is will to power a metaphysical doctrine (an a priori theory about ultimate reality) or an empirical one? If the former, it would seem to violate Nietzsche's rejection of metaphysics. If the latter, it would seem highly dubious and hence dispensable.[2]

These questions have been posed repeatedly in the literature on Nietzsche; and nearly every permutation of answers has been given. For my part, I think that these questions are answered and these problems solved once we see will to power as a product of Nietzsche's naturalism and interpretive holism. Viewed in this light, will to power is indeed an empirical theory that follows from Nietzsche's thesis that "God is dead." On my account, will to power is Nietzsche's attempt to challenge the dominant scientific theories of the late nineteenth century (particularly mechanistic physics and evolutionary biology) and to formulate a new conception of nature from which all theological posits have been withdrawn. Among these residues of theology, Nietzsche maintains, are the firm distinctions between "subject" and "object," "knower" and "known," "epistemology" and "ontology." In place of these dualisms, will to power conceives all of nature as engaged in an active "interpretation" (in Nietzsche's extended sense) that produces a becoming no longer subordinate to God or being.

5.2 WILL TO POWER AND NIETZSCHE'S NATURALISM

Will to power is not a metaphysical theory, if by "metaphysics" is meant some "transcendent" account of the world, a view "from outside." Nietzsche's criticism of such conceptions is most vehement in exactly those texts in which will to power plays a central role. Indeed, the doctrine is introduced precisely as an effort to view the world "from inside" (BGE 36). It is intended as an "interpretation" (BGE 22) of nature that competes with other such interpretations. That is, it is an empirical theory—a broad, hypothetical attempt to provide a unifying explanation for the observable features of the natural world.[3] In this

---

2. Maudemarie Clark (*Nietzsche on Truth and Philosophy* [Cambridge: Cambridge University Press, 1990], chap. 7) poses this dilemma and reviews some of the critical literature on this issue. For an earlier analysis of various ways of interpreting will to power, see Walter Kaufmann, *Nietzsche: Philosopher, Psychologist, Anti-Christ*, 4th ed. (Princeton: Princeton University Press, 1974), 204–7.

3. Scientific theories are general, systematic schemes that attempt to account for empirical observations but are not reducible to them. They regularly have recourse to unobservable explanatory posits (e.g., forces, classes, quarks). To call on W. V. Quine's famous analogy, a theory is "like a field of force whose boundary conditions are experience. [...]

sense, it is akin to scientific theories such as mechanism, thermodynamics, and evolutionary theory; and Nietzsche affirms it as such. Yet will to power is meant to challenge just these theories, which, according to Nietzsche, still manifest what he calls "shadows of God." Thus Nietzsche proposes will to power as the naturalistic theory par excellence, a rigorously antimetaphysical attempt to account for the multiplicity and perpetual becoming of the natural world without recourse to ontotheological posits.

We have seen that, for Nietzsche, nature encompasses all there is. The spiritual, the mental, and the divine no longer occupy a world apart but are natural or explicable in naturalistic terms. Moreover, on Nietzsche's view, nature is univocal, without ontological hierarchy.[4] Thus he rejects any strict opposition between mind (or spirit) and body (see *PTA* 10, p. 79; *Z*:1 "On the Despisers of the Body"; *BGE* 36; *A* 14), human and animal (see *HC*; *GS* 115; *A* 14), organic and inorganic matter (see *GS* 109; *BGE* 36; *WP* 655, 676; *KSA* 9:11[70]). The rejection

---

But the total field is [. . .] underdetermined by its boundary conditions. [. . .] No particular experiences are linked with any particular statements in the interior of the field, except indirectly, through considerations of equilibrium affecting the field as a whole" ("Two Dogmas of Empiricism," in *From a Logical Point of View* [Cambridge: Harvard University Press, 1961], 44–45). Or see Norwood Russell Hanson (*Patterns of Discovery: An Inquiry into the Conceptual Foundations of Science* [Cambridge: Cambridge University Press, 1958], 109): "Philosophers sometimes regard physics as a kind of mathematical photography and its laws as formal pictures of regularities. But the physicist often seeks not a general description of what he observes, but a general pattern of phenomena within which what he observes will appear intelligible. [. . .] The great unifications of Galileo, Kepler, Newton, Maxwell, Einstein, Bohr, Schrödinger and Heisenberg were pre-eminently discoveries of terse formulae from which explanations of diverse phenomena could be generated as a matter of course; they were not discoveries of undetected regularities."

4. In *BGE* 36, Nietzsche asserts "the right to determine *all* efficient force univocally [*eindeutig*] as—*will to power.*" (Cf. *A* 14: "every living being stands beside [man] on the same level of perfection.") Gilles Deleuze (*Difference and Repetition*, trans. Paul Patton [New York: Columbia University Press, 1994], 304) has more fully developed this conception of "univocity," the notion that "[being] is said in a single same sense throughout all its forms" even if "[t]hat of which it is said [i.e., beings . . .] differs." Deleuze sees Nietzsche as the last of three great thinkers of the univocity of being. In medieval philosophy, Duns Scotus asserted the heretical view that the ontological relationship of God to the rest of being is not analogical (Aquinas) or negative (Meister Eckhart) but univocal: distributed equally and neutrally, without hierarchy. In modern philosophy, this thesis is proclaimed by Spinoza, for whom God is immanent in all of nature, which, in turn, expresses or explicates God: "Deus sive Natura." Finally, Nietzsche accepts the univocal distribution of being asserted by Duns Scotus and Spinoza but eliminates God as the alleged source and point of convergence. Thus Nietzsche reformulates Spinoza's dictum: "Chaos sive Natura." See Deleuze, *Difference and Repetition*, 35–42, and *The Logic of Sense*, ed. Constantin V. Boundas, trans. Mark Lester and Charles Stivale (New York: Columbia University Press, 1990), 177–80, and §§4.6–4.7, above. Of course, this is not to say that, for Nietzsche, there is no such thing as hierarchy. It is only to say that Nietzschean hierarchy is one of *power* and *relative value*, not one of *reality* or *being*.

of these oppositions opens the way for a unified account of all natural phenomena. This is precisely the direction taken by modern science. Hence, mechanistic physics sees all material entities, regardless of kind, as governed by a limited number of forces and explains all physical movements and processes in terms of these. Modern chemistry follows suit. Rejecting vitalism, it maintains that all matter is explicable by the same set of physical and chemical principles and that living organisms differ not by the incorporation of some extra-natural substance but only by their different organization of natural material.[5] Lastly, post-Darwinian biology dismisses creationism and essentialism, maintaining instead the continuity of "higher" with "lower" forms of life.[6]

These scientific revolutions constitute major victories for naturalism in its struggle against metaphysics and theology; and Nietzsche allies himself with them on this count.

> When I think of my philosophical genealogy, I feel myself connected with [. . .] the mechanistic movement (reduction of all moral and aesthetic questions to physiological ones, of all physiological ones to chemical ones, of all chemical ones to mechanical ones). (*KSA* 11:26[432])

> We no longer derive man from "the spirit" or "the deity"; we have placed him back among the animals. [. . .] As regards the animals, Descartes was the first to have dared, with admirable boldness, to understand the animal as machine: the whole of our physiology endeavors to prove this claim. And we are consistent enough not to except man, as Descartes still did: our knowledge of man today goes just as far as we understand him mechanistically. (*A* 14; cf. *BGE* 230)

Yet Nietzsche is also a sharp critic of both mechanistic physics and evolutionary biology (see *GS* 109, 373; *BGE* 22; *GM* I:1, II:12; *WP* 618–58). What explains this equivocal attitude? It is that, for Nietzsche, these theories are preferable to metaphysical and theological positions, but they are still *not naturalistic enough*. While they appear to advocate a thoroughly materialist conception of the world and an immanent con-

---

5. See Ernst Mayr, *Toward a New Philosophy of Biology: Observations of an Evolutionist* (Cambridge, Mass.: Harvard University Press, 1988), 12.

6. In a margin note, Darwin admonishes a progressivist author: "Never say higher or lower" (quoted in Ernst Mayr, *One Long Argument: Charles Darwin and the Genesis of Modern Evolutionary Thought* [Cambridge, Mass.: Harvard University Press, 1991], 62, and Stephen Jay Gould, *Full House: The Spread of Excellence from Plato to Darwin* [New York: Harmony, 1996], 137). Taking his cue from the naturalist advances of modern science, Nietzsche extends this rejection of essential oppositions ("[t]he fundamental faith of the metaphysicians" [*BGE* 22]) into the moral domain and attempts to construct a moral theory that is "beyond good and evil." See, e.g., *GS* 1, 4; *BGE* 2, 24; *WP* 124.

ception of natural change, Nietzsche argues that they maintain a number of ontotheological posits that must be eliminated for nature to be fully "de-deified" and for becoming to appear in all its "innocence."

5.2.1 MECHANISM AND THE "SHADOWS OF GOD"

We can begin with mechanism. Nietzsche's objections to mechanistic physics proceed from his "rejection of being" (see §4.6.1, above). If mechanism sees the world as "matter in motion," Nietzsche argues that it has a false conception of "matter" and an inadequate conception of "motion." Mechanism views matter as composed of irreducible material atoms. Against this view, Nietzsche maintains that, like every atomism, "materialistic atomism" is the result of an ontological, psychological, and linguistic prejudice. It is founded on the privilege of being, the insistence that, somewhere, the earth "stands fast," "the belief in 'substance,' in 'matter,' in the earth-residuum" (*BGE* 12); and this privilege and insistence are inscribed in the very structure of our language:

> Everywhere [language] sees a doer and a doing; it believes in will as *the* cause; it believes in the "ego" [*das »Ich«*: the "I"], in the ego as being, in the ego as substance, and it *projects* this faith in the ego-substance upon all things— only thereby does it first *create* the concept of "thing." Everywhere "being" is projected by thought, *pushed underneath*, as the cause; the concept of "being" follows, and is derivative of, the concept of "ego." In the beginning there is that great calamity of error that the will is something which is *effective*, that will is a *capacity*. Today we know that it is only a word. [. . .] I am afraid we are not rid of God because we still have faith in grammar. (*TI* "Reason" 5; cf. *TI* "Errors" 3; *WP* 488)

This dense passage—which moves swiftly from the grammatical "I" to "substance," "thinghood," "being," "free will" and "God"—contains, in aphoristic form, an argument widespread throughout Nietzsche's later work (see WS 11; *BGE* 12, 17; *GM* I:13; *TI* "Reason" 5; *WP* 624–25, 634–35). Nietzsche's view is that the grammatical subject, the idea of substance, and the posit of thinghood all rest on a conception of being as primary, prior to all becoming and activity. This conception is concomitant with the idea of free will, the alleged capacity of the subject to initiate proximal becomings while remaining outside the chain of becoming. And this idea of free will is but an incarnation of that ultimate, transcendent source of all becoming: God, Being itself.

Thus, the very posit of thinghood—and the separation of being from becoming, doer from deed, entity from activity—is, on Nietzsche's view, the product of ontotheology. Insofar as its atomism is a form of thing-ontology, mechanism is darkened by a "shadow of God." Of course, the mechanistic worldview explicitly claims to do without such notions as "free will," advocating instead a purely deterministic system of cause and effect, action and reaction. Yet for it to become as naturalistic as it takes itself to be, Nietzsche believes that mechanism must forgo its thing-ontology in favor of an event- or force-ontology. Hence, against classical mechanics, he sides with Boscovich, who, rejecting the dualism of matter and force, asserts that force is primary and that material entities are but nodes in a field of force.[7]

> [T]he older atomism sought, besides the operating "power," that lump of matter in which it resides and out of which it operates. More rigorous minds [e.g., Boscovich],[8] however, learned at last to get along without this "earth residuum." (*BGE* 17)[9]
>
> [T]here is no such substratum: there is no "being" behind doing, effecting, becoming; "the doer" is merely a fiction added to the deed—the deed is everything. (*GM* I 13)
>
> If we eliminate these additions, no things remain over but only dynamic quanta, in a relation of tension to all other dynamic quanta: their essence lies in their relation to all other quanta, in their "effect" upon the same. (*WP* 635)

But there are still other problems with the mechanistic worldview, as Nietzsche sees it. While it rejects the motive force of "free will," mech-

---

7. Boscovich's conception of matter and force, proposed in 1769 but neglected for nearly a century, has become a central feature of contemporary physical theory (see Jonathan Powers, "Atomism," in *The Concise Encyclopedia of Western Philosophy and Philosophers,* ed. J. O. Urmson and Jonathan Rée [London: Unwin Hyman, 1989], 32, and J. D. Bernal, *Science in History,* vol. 2, *The Scientific and Industrial Revolutions* [Cambridge, Mass.: MIT Press, 1954], 676). Boscovich was rescued from obscurity when, in 1844, his view was advocated by the great theorist of electromagnetism, Michael Faraday (*Experimental Researches in Electricity,* vol. 2 [New York: Dover, 1965], 290): "[T]he atoms of Boscovich appear to me to have a great advantage over the usual notion," Faraday wrote. "His atoms, if I understand him aright, are mere centres of forces or powers, not particles of matter, in which the powers themselves reside. If, in the ordinary view of atoms, we call the particle of matter away from the powers *a,* and the system of forces in and around it *m,* then in Boscovich's theory *a* disappears, or is a mere mathematical point, whilst in the usual notion it is a little unchangeable, impenetrable piece of matter, and *m* is an atmosphere of force grouped around it." Cf. the passages from Nietzsche cited in the text, below.
8. Cf. *BGE* 12: "Boscovich has taught us to abjure belief in the last part of the earth that 'stood fast'—belief in 'substance,' in 'matter,' in the earth-residuum and particle-atom."
9. Cf. *BGE* 36: "'Will,' of course, can affect only 'will'—and not 'matter'."

anism does not replace this with any more immanent or naturalistic principle that would explain "motion" or "becoming." It does not tell us what motivates one entity to affect another—except that this motion is itself the effect of a prior "cause" and so on, producing a regress that terminates with the only genuinely active force: God the Watchmaker who sets the world-mechanism in motion.[10] Thus, according to Nietzsche, mechanism is superficial, reactive, passive, and theological: "superficial" because it only "describes" immanent motions without "explaining" them, without *getting inside* them (see *BGE* 14; *WP* 618; 628–32, 660, 688); "reactive" and "passive" because every immanent "action" is truly only a "reaction" (see *GM* I: 1, II: 12); and "theological" because the true principle of motion lies outside the system in a transcendent cause (see *WP* 1062, 1066).

The mechanistic view is ontotheological in another sense as well. It sees the world as essentially static—a system closed, reversible, and in equilibrium. It posits a universe in which, from any given state, all other states, past and future, could, theoretically, be calculated. For classical dynamics, as one writer recently put it, "[a]ll is given in one moment— the changing 'now' is just our subjective window for experiencing the eternally present one instant at a time."[11] It is this theoretical vantage point, this God's-eye view of an eternal present, to which the mechanistic physicist aspires.[12] From this vantage-point, time, becoming, and

10. Cf. Ilya Prigogine and Isabelle Stengers: "Why was natural motion conceived of in the image of a rationalized machine? [. . .] Why did the clock almost immediately become the very symbol of world order? In this last question lies perhaps some elements of an answer. A watch is a *contrivance* governed by a rationality that lies outside itself, by a plan that is blindly executed by its inner workings. The clock world is a metaphor suggestive of God the Watchmaker, the rational master of a robotlike nature. At the origin of modern science, a 'resonance' appears to have been set up between theological discourse and theoretical and experimental activity" (*Order out of Chaos: Man's New Dialogue with Nature* [New York: Bantam Books, 1984], 46, see also 47–50). Elsewhere (*Order out of Chaos*, 6–7), they write: "Western thought has always oscillated between the world as an automaton and a theology in which God governs the universe. [. . .] In fact these visions are connected. An automaton needs an external god."
11. Stephen H. Kellert, *In the Wake of Chaos: Unpredictable Order in Dynamical Systems* (Chicago: University of Chicago Press, 1993), 54.
12. This idea was made famous by Pierre Laplace, who hypothesized that a being like us, but with far greater powers of calculation, could, beginning from any given state, determine any event in the universe, whether past and future. See Laplace, *A Philosophical Essay on Probabilities*, trans. F. W. Truscott and F.L. Emory (New York: John Wiley and Sons, 1917), 4. Nietzsche remarks that this Laplacean aspiration and the mechanistic language of the "laws" of nature "savors of morality" (*WP* 630). They interpret the fact that something "always act[s . . .] thus and thus as a result of obedience to a law or lawgiver, while it would be free to act otherwise were it not for the 'law'" (*WP* 632). That is, "laws

difference are reduced to the eternal present, being, and the equivalent, to "a sort of shifting and place-changing on the part of a 'being,' of something constant" (*WP* 631). And even if the thermodynamic revolution of the nineteenth century alters this picture by introducing time, irreversibility, and openness, it does so only to reintroduce stasis, indifference, and being as the *telos* of the system: entropic equilibrium.[13]

5.2.2 BEYOND MECHANISM: WILL TO POWER

Nietzsche aims to correct these defects and eliminate these residues of theology. Denying both free will and mechanistic determinism, he attempts to formulate a theory of motion, change, and becoming the principle of which is immanent, active, and explanatory. He begins, as we have seen, by rejecting the dualisms of doer and deed, matter and force, and proposes instead an ontology according to which "the deed is everything" (*GM* I 13) and there exist "only dynamic quanta, in a relation of tension to all other dynamic quanta" (*WP* 635). In opposition to the passive and reactive character of mechanism, this ontology is fundamentally active; and the principle of its activity, motion, and becoming is not transcendent (as with the divine watchmaker or free will) but immanent:

> In our science, where the concept of cause and effect is reduced to the relationship of equivalence, with the object of proving that the same quantum of force is present on both sides, the *driving force* is *lacking:* we observe only results, and we consider them equivalent in content and force. (*WP* 688)

> The victorious concept of "force," by means of which our physicists have created God and the world, still needs to be completed: an inner world must be ascribed to it, which I designate as "will to power." (*WP* 619)[14]

---

of nature" language explains the regularity of nature as the result of nature's submission to, and governance by, an external authority, i.e., God—hence Newton's eighteenth-century reputation as the "new Moses" (see Prigogine and Stengers, *Order out of Chaos,* 27ff.). Ernst Mayr (*Toward a New Philosophy of Biology,* 18–21) remarks that the biological revolution of the past two centuries has led to the need to replace the language of scientific "laws" with that of scientific "theories."

13. It is for this reason that Nietzsche rejects the conclusions of thermodynamics: "If, e.g., the mechanistic theory cannot avoid the consequence, drawn for it by William Thompson, of leading to a final state, then the mechanistic theory stands refuted" (*WP* 1066; cf. *WP* 639).

14. Note that the Kaufmann/Hollingdale translation mistakenly renders Nietzsche's "an inner world [*eine innere Welt*]" as "an inner will."

This "will to power" must not be thought of as a capacity that inheres in individual entities. For Nietzsche repeatedly criticizes both this conception of "things" and this conception of "the will":

> Is "will to power" a kind of "will" or identical with the concept "will"? Is it the same thing as desiring? or commanding? Is it that "will" of which Schopenhauer said it was the "in itself of things"? My proposition is: that the *will* of psychology hitherto is an unjustified generalization, that this will *does not exist at all* [. . .] one has *eliminated* the character of the will by *subtracting* from it its content, its "whither?" (*WP* 692)

> *There is no will*: there are only treaty drafts of will [*Willens-Punktationen*] that are constantly increasing or losing their power. (*WP* 715; see also *GS* 127; *BGE* 16, 19; *TI* "World" 5, "Errors" 3; *A* 14; *WP* 46, 488, 668, 671, 765)

That is, in place of an ontology of atomic unities each of which contains "will" as an effective capacity, Nietzsche substitutes a holistic ontology of relatively stable power-complexes essentially bound to one another by lines of force (resistance, domination, submission, alliance, etc.). Hence, each of these complexes exists in an intricate web of tension with neighboring power-complexes; and "will"—"will to power"—is just a name for this state of tension, this straining "towards which" and "*away from which*" (*BGE* 19; cf. *WP* 636). Moreover, this struggle is just as much internal as external. Each power-complex strives to maintain its integrity, its dominance or control over its component powers, which constantly threaten to revolt or secede (see *WP* 492 and §3.3.3, above).

Change, then, is no longer a matter of "cause" and "effect," conceived on the classic billiard-ball model as a rigid, one-directional system of colliding atoms; rather, it is a matter of myriad macro- and microscopic struggles and the new configurations of power which result:

> Two successive states, the one "cause," the other "effect": this is false. [. . .] It is a question of a struggle between two elements of unequal power: a new arrangement of forces is achieved according to the measure of power of each of them. The second condition is something fundamentally different from the first (*not* its effect): the essential thing is that the factions in struggle emerge with different quanta of power. (*WP* 633; cf. *BGE* 19; *WP* 631, 688–89)

Indeed, this change or becoming does not leave the original parties intact. Rejecting the conception of substance maintained by the mechanistic-atomistic worldview, Nietzsche asserts that change is not merely the qualitative alteration of essentially enduring entities but the constant production of new entities:

> There are no durable ultimate units, no atoms, no monads: here, too, "beings" are only *introduced* [hineingelegt] by us. [. . .] "Forms of domination"; the sphere of that which is dominated continually growing or periodically increasing and decreasing according to the favorability or unfavorability of circumstances. [. . .] "Value" is essentially the standpoint for the increase or decrease of these dominating centers ("multiplicities" in any case; but "units" are nowhere present in the nature of becoming)—a quantum of power, a becoming, in so far as none of it has the character of "being." (*WP* 715; cf. *WP* 488)

"Becoming," then, is the result of this pressure and tension of forces and powers. Just as the work of a system is a function of the differences in temperature, level, pressure, and potential of its component parts, the dynamic force of will to power is a function of the difference of powers and the tension between them.[15] A generalized equivalence or equilibrium of forces, then, would signal an end to this power-struggle and, hence, an end to becoming. But Nietzsche denies this possibility ("the adiaphoristic state is missing," he writes, "though it is thinkable" [*WP* 634]) and views the very supposition as ontotheological, merely another attempt to subordinate becoming to being.[16] His rejection of God and being requires the elimination of both an absolute origin and an absolute end to becoming (see §4.6.1, above). Dismissing the hypothesis of "a creative God" (*WP* 1062) and "a created world" (*WP* 1066), Nietzsche maintains "the temporal infinity of the world in the past." Given this premise,

> [i]f the world could in any way become rigid, dry, dead, *nothing,* or if it could reach a state of equilibrium, or if it had any kind of goal that involved

15. Cf. Prigogine and Stengers (*Order out of Chaos,* 111): "Nietzsche was one of those who detected the echo of creations and destructions that go far beyond mere conservation or conversion. Indeed, only difference, such as difference of temperature or potential energy, can produce results that are also differences. Energy conversion is merely the destruction of a difference, together with the creation of another difference. The power of nature is thus concealed by the use of equivalences."

16. For the same reason, he sees equalizing measures on the social level (socialism, democracy, peace) to be disastrous and antinatural: "from the highest biological standpoint, legal conditions can never be other than *exceptional conditions,* since they constitute a partial restriction of the will of life, which is bent upon power, and are subordinate to its total goal as a single means: namely, as a means of creating *greater* units of power. A legal order thought of as sovereign and universal, not as a means in the struggle between power-complexes but as a means of *preventing* all struggle in general [. . .] would be a principle *hostile to life,* an agent of the dissolution and destruction of man, an attempt to assassinate the future of man, a sign of weariness, a secret path to nothingness" (*GM* II:11).

duration, immutability, the once-and-for-all (in short, speaking metaphysically: if becoming *could* resolve itself into being or into nothingness), then this state must have been reached. But it has not been reached: from which it follows. (*WP* 1066; cf. *HL* 9; *WP* 639, 688, 1064)

With this, Nietzsche challenges both the mechanistic hypothesis of God the watchmaker and the thermodynamic hypothesis of thermal equilibrium or "heat death." If the nineteenth century saw the introduction of time, history, and becoming into a previously static scientific and philosophical worldview, Nietzsche, at the end of that century, seeks to eliminate teleology, the last bulwark of God, eternity, and being.[17]

5.2.3 EVOLUTIONARY THEORY AND THE "SHADOWS OF GOD"

No modern scientific theory did more to challenge the static, closed, deterministic, deistic view of the world than Darwin's evolutionary biology.[18] The Darwinian revolution opposed the physical worldview of Descartes and Newton and biological worldview of Lyell and Agassiz. Against these, it asserted the primacy of time, becoming, chance, and struggle in nature and liberated this becoming from being, essence, and God. Rejecting the belief in a constant world, Darwin revealed a nature in incessant alteration and transformation.[19] In place of the doctrines of creation and design prevalent among natural theologians and biologists alike, Darwin proposed the mechanisms of random variation and natural selection and candidly described a nature that is, by moral standards, "capricious, cruel, arbitrary, wasteful, [and] careless."[20] Op-

17. In doing so, he philosophically anticipates the experimental discoveries of the "Brussels School," which has reinterpreted the second law of thermodynamics to include spontaneous transformations from disorder to order, from simplicity and equivalence to complexity and difference. See, e.g., Prigogine and Stengers, *Order out of Chaos, passim.* Also see p. 211n. 109.

18. See Mayr, *One Long Argument,* 35–67.

19. This summary presentation draws heavily on Stephen Jay Gould's and Ernst Mayr's superb accounts of the essential features of Darwin's revolution. See Gould, "In Praise of Charles Darwin," in *Darwin's Legacy,* ed. Charles L. Hamrum (San Francisco: Harper and Row, 1983), and Mayr, *One Long Argument,* chaps. 4–5. While I find them particularly compelling, these reconstructions of Darwinism are not uncontroversial. For criticisms, see, e.g., Robert J. Richards, *The Meaning of Evolution: The Morphological Construction and Ideological Reconstruction of Darwin's Theory* (Chicago: University of Chicago Press, 1992), 169–79, and Daniel Dennett, *Darwin's Dangerous Idea: Evolution and the Meanings of Life* (New York: Simon and Schuster, 1995), 229–312.

20. D. L. Hull, quoted in Mayr, *One Long Argument,* 14. Nietzsche uses remarkably similar language in *BGE* 9 and 22 to combat the design theories of the Stoics and mechanists. On Darwin's arguments against creation and design, see Gould, "In Praise of Charles

posing philosophical and biological essentialisms, Darwin discovered
that there are no essential disjunctions between species and showed
that every species is itself only a statistical abstraction over a popula-
tion of irreducibly unique individuals, a variation without which evolution would be impossible.[21] Moreover, Darwin refused to grant any divine exception to human beings, viewing them as material through and
through and continuous with the rest of nature.[22] Biological evolution
also seemed to contradict the trajectory of thermodynamics. If the latter
hypothesized a solar system becoming steadily more uniform and disor-
dered, the former revealed a world in which difference and complexity
increase, rather than decrease, over time.[23]

The Darwinian revolution thus effected a profound de-deification of
nature and naturalization of humanity—a fact occasionally acknowledged by Nietzsche (see *HL* 9; *GS* 357; *GM* III:25; *A* 14). Yet Nietzsche seems to have known Darwin primarily through what Stephen Jay
Gould has recently called "Darwin's spin doctors," who, under the
guise of disseminating Darwinism, continued to insinuate ontotheological posits into the theory of natural selection.[24] In his quest to eliminate

---

Darwin," 5–6, and Richard Dawkins, *The Blind Watchmaker* (New York: W. W. Norton,
1986).
    21. See Mayr, *One Long Argument,* 39–42, and Stephen Jay Gould, *The Flamingo's
Smile: Reflections in Natural History* (New York: W. W. Norton, 1985), 160–66. We
have seen, in §2.2.4, that Nietzsche, too, argues against essentialism along these nominalist lines. Indeed, Mayr (*One Long Argument,* 41) presents an argument concerning the
linguistic basis of essentialism that reads like a paraphrase of passages in *TL* and *TI*: "Essentialism's influence was great in part because its principle is anchored in our language,
in our use of a single noun in the singular to designate highly variable phenomena of our
environment, such as mountain, home, water, horse, or honesty. Even though there is a
great variety in kinds of mountain and kinds of home, and even though the kinds do not
stand in direct relation to one another (as do the members of a species), the simple noun
defines the class of objects."
    22. See Stephen Jay Gould, *Ever Since Darwin: Reflections in Natural History* (New
York: W. W. Norton, 1977), 21–27, and "In Praise of Charles Darwin," 6.
    23. See Jacques Monod, *Chance and Necessity: An Essay on the Natural Philosophy
of Modern Biology,* trans. Austryn Wainhouse (New York: Vintage, 1972), 18, and Prigogine and Stengers, *Order out of Chaos,* 127–28.
    24. Gould, *Full House,* 19. Gould argues that, in both the popular and the scholarly
literature, the evolutionary story continues to be "spun" in this manner and that we still
need to "complete Darwin's revolution" (see *Full House,* chap. 2). Nietzsche's critique thus
remains as relevant today as it was more than a century ago. In his recent book on philosophy and evolutionary theory, Daniel Dennett (*Darwin's Dangerous Idea,* 181–83, 461–
67) explicitly acknowledges the significance of Nietzsche's Darwinian critique of "Darwinism." Yet his presentation of Nietzsche's position is both superficial and patronizing.
Moreover, Dennett dedicates a substantial portion of this book to a critique of Gould (*Darwin's Dangerous Idea,* 229–312), who is seen as fortifying Darwin's theory with superfluous metaphysical posits. I do not find this in Gould. Indeed, I read Gould as sharing

the "shadows of God," Nietzsche subjects such "Darwinism" to a naturalizing critique.[25]

This critique appears throughout Nietzsche's corpus—from the 1873 essay, "On Truth and Lies," to the sections and notes of 1888 entitled "Anti-Darwin" (*TI* "Skirmishes" 14; *WP* 647, 684–85). Recurrent in these texts is an argument against a notion of evolutionary progress that takes human beings to be the goal and pinnacle of nature. In "On Truth and Lies," Nietzsche remarks that the pride of humanity—the human intellect—is an evolutionary variation no better, and in many ways worse, than the "sharp teeth of beasts of prey" and that human existence will surely turn out to be but a "shadowy and transient," "aimless and arbitrary" moment in geological time (*TL*, pp. 79–80).[26] Evolutionary progressivism and anthropocentrism, Nietzsche suggests elsewhere, are merely secular translations of biblical creationism—attempts to shift the ontotheological weight from the origin to the end of history:

> Formerly, one sought the feeling of the grandeur of man by pointing to his divine *origin*: this has now become a forbidden way, for at its portal stands the ape, together with other gruesome beasts, grinning knowingly as if to say: no further in this direction! One therefore now tries the opposite direction: the way mankind is *going* shall serve as proof of his grandeur and kinship with God. Alas this, too, is in vain! [. . .] However high mankind may have evolved—and perhaps at the end it will stand even lower than at the beginning!—it cannot pass over into a higher order, as little as the ant and the earwig can at the end of its "earthly course" rise up to kinship with God and eternal life. (*D* 49)

> We have become more modest in every way. We no longer derive man from "the spirit" or "the deity"; we have placed him back among the animals. We consider him the strongest animal because he is the most cunning: his intellectuality [*Geistigkeit*] is a consequence of this. On the other hand, we oppose the vanity that would raise its head again here too—as if man had been the great hidden purpose of the evolution of the animals. Man is by no means

---

Nietzsche's commitment to the thorough elimination, from evolutionary theory, of all the "shadows of God."

25. "Darwinism," here refers to the view of the "spin doctors," not to Darwin's view itself, with which Nietzsche, albeit unbeknownst to Nietzsche himself, is in very substantial agreement.

26. Cf. Gould, *Full House*, 18: "If we are but a tiny twig on the floridly arborescent bush of life, and if our twig branched off just a geological moment ago, then perhaps we are not a predictable result of an inherently progressive process (the vaunted trend to progress in life's history); perhaps we are, whatever our glories or accomplishments, a momentary cosmic accident that would never rise again if the tree of life could be replanted from seed and regrown under similar conditions."

the crown of creation: every living being stands beside him on the same level
of perfection . . . And even this is saying too much: relatively speaking, man
is the most bungled of all the animals, the sickliest, the one who has strayed
the most dangerously from its instincts. (*A* 14)[27]

Despite Darwin's antiprogressivism, evolutionary theorists continued to see the phenomenon of evolutionary "adaptation" as progressive.
According to a view promoted by Herbert Spencer, one of Nietzsche's
prime targets (see *GM* II:12), natural selection gradually promotes an
increasingly better fit between organisms and their environment. But
such "adaptationism" projects into the evolutionary process a false teleology, amounting to a revival of the "argument from design" that Darwin's theory explicitly opposed.[28] Thus, Gould writes:

> Evolutionary biologists have too often slipped into a seductively appealing
> mode of argument about the phenomenon of adaptation. We tend to view
> every structure as designed for a definite purpose, thus building (in our imag-
> ination) a world of perfect design not much different from that concocted by
> eighteenth-century natural theologians who "proved" God's existence by the
> perfect architecture of organisms. [. . .] But [the] current utility [of traits]
> does not imply that they were built directly by natural selection for the pur-
> pose they now serve. [. . .] We do not inhabit a perfected world where nat-
> ural selection ruthlessly scrutinizes all organic structures and then molds
> them for optimal utility. [. . .] The primary flexibility of evolution may arise
> from nonadaptive by-products that occasionally permit organisms to strike
> out in new and unpredictable directions. What "play" would evolution have
> if each structure were built for a restricted purpose and could be used for
> nothing else? How could humans learn to write if our brain had evolved for
> hunting, social cohesion, or whatever and could not transcend the adaptive
> boundaries of its original purpose? [. . .] Selection works for the moment. It
> cannot sense what may be of use ten million years hence in a distant descen-
> dant. [. . .] Future utility is an important consideration in evolution, but it
> cannot be the explanation for current preservation. Future utilities can only
> be the *fortuitous effects* of other direct reasons for immediate favor. (The
> confusion of current utility with reasons for past historical origin is a logical
> trap that has plagued evolutionary thinking from the start.)[29]

27. Cf. *HL* 9; *GM* III:25; *WP* 90, 401, 684–85. Also see Gould, *Full House,* for an extended argument against the notion of evolutionary progressivism and anthropocentrism.
28. Thus Darwin wrote in his *Autobiography:* "The old argument from design in nature, as given by Paley . . . fails, now that the law of natural selection has been discovered.
We can no longer argue that, for instance, the beautiful hinge of the bivalve shell must have
been made by an intelligent being, like the hinge of a door by man. There seems to be no
more design in the variability of organic beings and in the action of natural selection, than
in the course which the wind blows" (quoted in Mayr, *One Long Argument,* 57).
29. Gould, *Hen's Teeth and Horse's Toes* (New York: W. W. Norton, 1983), 155–56,
170. This argument runs throughout Gould's work. The most sustained version is pre-

Nietzsche makes a strikingly similar point in §12 of the *Genealogy*'s second essay, which bears citing again in this context:

> [T]he cause of the origin of a thing and its eventual utility, its actual employ-ment and place in a system of purposes, lie worlds apart; whatever exists, having somehow come into being, is again and again reinterpreted to new ends, taken over, transformed, and redirected by some power superior to it; all events in the organic world are a *subduing, becoming master,* and all sub-duing and becoming master involves a fresh interpretation, an adjustment through which any previous "meaning" and "purpose" are necessarily ob-scured or even obliterated. However well one has understood the utility of a physiological organ [. . .], this means nothing regarding its origin: how-ever uncomfortable and disagreeable this may sound to older ears—for one had always believed that to understand the demonstrable purpose, the utility of a thing, a form, or an institution, was also to understand the rea-son why it originated—the eye being made for seeing, the hand made for grasping. [. . . P]urposes and utilities are only *signs* that a will to power has become master of something less powerful and imposed upon it the charac-ter of a function; and the entire history of a "thing," an organ, a custom can in this way be a continuous sign-chain of ever new interpretations and adap-tations whose causes do not even have to be related to one another but, on the contrary, in some cases succeed and alternate with one another in purely chance fashion. The "evolution" of a thing, a custom, an organ is thus by no means its *progressus* toward a goal, even less a logical *progressus* by the shortest route and with the smallest expenditure of force—but the succes-sion of more or less profound, more or less mutually independent processes of subduing, plus the resistances they encounter, the attempts at transforma-tion for the purpose of defense and reaction, and the results of successful counteractions.[30]

In place of the steady upward climb imagined by the progressivists and adaptationists, Gould and Nietzsche view the trajectory of evolution as an unpredictable, ateleological movement. "Adaptation" and "success" are local and contingent; and subsequent forms can claim only tempo-rary victory in a perpetual and shifting *agon* rather than global advance on "the ladder of progress."

Neither the longevity of an organism nor its complexity or later ap-pearance are any evidence of progress or superiority. Gould points out that, however simple, "bacteria, by any reasonable criterion, were in

---

sented in Gould and Richard Lewontin, "The Spandrels of San Marco and the Pangloss-ian Paradigm: A Critique of the Adaptationist Programme," *Proceedings of the Royal Society of London* B205 (1979): 581–98.

30. For an earlier critique of progressivism and adaptationism as manifested in the Hegelian dialectic, see *HL* 8–9.

the beginning, are now, and ever shall be the most successful organisms on earth" [31] and that the relatively late and rare appearance of complex organisms such as *Homo sapiens* is no sign of an inherent tendency to complexity but only a consequence of life's diversification in the only direction available to it.[32] As Nietzsche puts it:

> [M]an as a species does not represent any progress compared to any other animal. The whole animal and vegetable kingdom does not evolve from the lower to the higher—but all at the same time, in utter disorder, over and against one another. The richest and most complex forms—for the expression "higher type" means no more than this—perish more easily: only the lowest preserve an apparent indestructibility. The former are achieved fairly rarely and maintain their superiority with difficulty. (*WP* 684)

In short, criteria of progress or excellence are criteria of *value;* and such criteria are not *found* or *given* in the nature of things but must be *made* and *defended*. Once we give up the notion that a teleology is inherent in the evolutionary process, criteria other than preservation, survival, and adaptation become available for assessing excellence.[33] Thus Nietzsche remarks: "Greatness ought not to depend on success"; "the goal of humanity cannot lie in [. . . the] end [of history], but only in its highest exemplars" (*HL* 9, p. 111).[34] Given the central role Darwin's theory assigns to chance,[35] we can liken evolution to a dice game. On this model, Nietzsche suggests, excellence need not be assigned to statistical averages or probabilities but to those rare "lucky throws" [*Glückswürfen*].[36] "The brief spell of beauty, of genius," he writes, "is *sui generis*: such things are not inherited" (*WP* 684; cf. 685).

> Mankind does *not* represent a development toward something better or stronger or higher in the sense accepted today. "Progress" is merely a modern idea, that is, a false idea. The European of today is vastly inferior to the European of the Renaissance: further development is altogether *not* accord-

31. Gould, *Full House*, 38, see also 175–216.
32. Ibid., 167–75.
33. See Nietzsche's 1873 notes on history (in *The Portable Nietzsche*, 39ff.), and *HL* 9; *D* 106, 108; *GM* I:17, II:12; *TI* "Skirmishes" 44; *A* 14; *WP* 647–48, 684–85.
34. See *GM* I:9, where Nietzsche's irony hints that the "success" of "slave," "mob," "herd," or "democratic" ideals is no indication of their superiority. Also see Nietzsche's various remarks to the effect that "one always has to defend the strong against the weak" (*WP* 685; cf. *WP* 864, *GM*:III:14).
35. See Mayr, *One Long Argument*, 48–49; Gould, "In Praise of Charles Darwin," 5; and Monod, *Chance and Necessity*.
36. See *GM* II:16: "From now on, man is *included* among the most unexpected and exciting lucky throws in the dice game of Heraclitus' 'great child,' be he called Zeus or chance." See also *GM* III:14; *A* 3–4; *WP* 684–85, 864.

ing to any necessity in the direction of elevation, enhancement, or strength. In another sense, success in individual cases is constantly encountered in the most widely different places and cultures: here we really do find a *higher type*, which is, in relation to mankind as a whole, a kind of overman. Such lucky strokes [*Glücksfälle*] of great success have always been possible and will perhaps always be possible. (*A* 4; cf. *WP* 881)

5.2.4 BEYOND THE "STRUGGLE FOR EXISTENCE": WILL TO POWER

This argument forms part of a wider polemic against views that assert the primacy of preservation and adaptation in the natural world. Nietzsche contends that organisms do not, first and foremost, struggle to *live,* to *survive,* to *preserve* themselves. Such a conception is both too reactive and too teleological: it locates the impetus for natural becoming in a reactive attempt to adapt to environing conditions and takes the aim of this adaptation to be the preservation of existence for as long as possible (see *BGE* 13; *GM* II:12; *WP* 70, 647, 681, 684). Nietzsche writes:

> Physiologists should think before putting down the instinct of self-preservation as the cardinal instinct of an organic being. A living thing seeks above all to *discharge* its strength—life itself is will to power; self-preservation is only one of the indirect and most frequent *results.* In short, here as everywhere else, let us beware of *superfluous* teleological principles!—one of which is the instinct of self-preservation. (*BGE* 13; cf. *Z:*2 "On Self-Overcoming"; *WP* 650, 688)

This view is repeated and elaborated in the fifth book of the *Gay Science:*

> The wish to preserve oneself is the symptom of a condition of distress, of a limitation of the really fundamental instinct of life which aims at *the expansion of power* and, wishing for that, frequently risks and even sacrifices self-preservation. [. . . O]ur modern natural sciences have become so thoroughly entangled in this [. . .] dogma [concerning the instinct of self-preservation] (most recently and worst of all Darwinism with its incomprehensibly one-sided doctrine of the "struggle for existence").[37] [. . . But] in nature it is not conditions of distress that are *dominant* but overflow and squandering, even to the point of absurdity. The struggle for existence is only an *exception,* a temporary restriction of the life-will. The great and small struggle always revolves around superiority, around growth and expansion, around power—in

---

37. The famous title and subject of *On the Origin of Species,* chap. 3.

accordance with the will to power which is the will of life. (*GS* 349; cf. *TL* §2;
Z:2 "On Self-Overcoming"; *BGE* 262; *GM* II:11; *TI* "Skirmishes" 14, 44)

There is an apparent equivocation, in these passages, about the nature
of "will to power." On the face of it, will to power would seem to be the
drive to *acquire* power; yet both passages assert that it essentially concerns the *expenditure* ("discharge," "sacrifice," "overflow and squandering") of power, "even to the point of absurdity." Furthermore, having criticized one "superfluous teleological principle," the instinct of
self-preservation, Nietzsche seems to substitute another, the desire for
power. Lastly, this desire (*for* power) would seem to signify a fundamental lack (*of* power), that is, a fundamental indigence and distress,
which, however, here and elsewhere, Nietzsche repeatedly denies is the
basic condition of nature.[38]

These difficulties rest on a teleological interpretation of will to power
and disappear as soon as we begin to understand Nietzsche's doctrine
otherwise. If the fundamental condition of life is one of superabundance
and exuberance rather than indigence and distress, power is not primarily something an organism *wants* or *needs* but something an organism *is* or *has* and *must exercise*. Will to power, then, is not a teleological principle but a dynamic force, like a stretched spring or a dammed
river.[39] The "willing" of will to power, Nietzsche writes, "is *not* 'desir-
ing,' striving, demanding"; rather, it is "[t]hat *state of tension* by virtue
of which a force seeks to discharge itself" (*WP* 668).[40]

If Nietzsche's language is puzzling, his basic hypothesis is fairly
straightforward. It is one later taken up and developed by the French

---

38. This rejection of indigence and utility, and the assertion of superabundance and
exuberance as the *primum mobile* of life, are basic themes in Nietzsche's work from beginning to end. See, e.g., *BT passim* and *BT* SC:1, SC:4, SC:5; *TL*, pp. 90–91 (on the in-
digent scientific vs. the free artistic intellect); *Z*:Prologue 1, 4, *Z*:2 "On Self-Overcoming";
GS 370; *BGE* 260, 262; *GM* I (on master vs. slave morality); *TI* "Skirmishes" 8–9, "Ancients" 4–5; *EH* "Books" BT:2; *WP* 797, 802, 843, 864, 1050.

39. For various metaphors of power as superabundance, see *GS* 285, 370; *Z* Prologue
1, *Z*:1 "On the Gift-Giving Virtue," *Z*:2 "On Self-Overcoming"; *BGE* 260, 262; *TI*
"Skirmishes" 8–9, 44, "Ancients" 3; *A* 1; *EH* "Books" BT:2; *WP* 576, 802, 846, 852,
1022.

40. Thus, in *GM* II:17–18, Nietzsche calls will to power "the *instinct for freedom*"
that must "discharge and vent itself." *TI* "Ancients" 3 describes it as an "inner explosive
[...]," a "tremendous inner tension." In *Z*:2 "On Self-Overcoming," will to power is "the
unexhausted procreative will of life," and life is "*that which must always overcome itself.*"
Resonating with these passages is *BT* SC:5, which glorifies the "amoral artist-god [...]"
who, creating worlds, frees himself from the *distress* of fullness and *overfullness*."

Nietzschean Georges Bataille: namely, that the dynamic force of nature (that which propels growth, sexuality, procreation, struggle, and death) and of culture[41] (production, form-giving, creativity, and play) is the superabundance of energy in the biosphere and the compulsion to expend it.[42] As Bataille puts it, *"it is not necessity but its contrary, 'luxury,' that presents living matter and mankind with their fundamental problems."*[43] For both Bataille and Nietzsche, the source and archetype of this expenditure is the sun and its prodigality:

> Solar energy is the source of life's exuberant development. The origin and essence of our wealth are given in the radiation of the sun, which dispenses energy—wealth—without any return. The sun gives without receiving. [. . .] Solar radiation results in a superabundance of energy on the surface of the globe. But, first, living matter receives this energy and accumulates it within the limits given by the space that is available to it. It then radiates or squanders it, but before devoting an appreciable share to this radiation it makes maximum use of it for growth. Only the impossibility of continuing growth makes way for squander.[44]

In the natural world, growth constitutes a temporary accumulation of energy; but this accumulation eventually ceases, often giving way to procreation, a luxurious expenditure through which life is given to an-

---

41. This distinction between "nature" and "culture" does not mark an opposition between two fundamentally different domains but only a conventional division of the same domain: Nature writ large. Nietzsche's point is, precisely, that will to power operates throughout both "nature" and "culture."

42. See Georges Bataille, "The Notion of Expenditure," in *Visions of Excess: Selected Writings, 1927–1939,* ed. Allan Stoekl (Minneapolis: University of Minnesota Press, 1985), and *The Accursed Share: An Essay on General Economy,* vol. 1, *Consumption,* trans. Robert Hurley (New York: Zone, 1988). Nietzsche, too, attempts to view "[t]he organic functions translated back to the basic will, the will to power" (WP 658); cf. Z:2 "On Self-Overcoming"; BGE 36; WP 651–57, 680, 688.

43. Bataille, *Accursed Share,* 12.

44. Ibid., 28–29. Cf. *Zarathustra,* which opens with praise of the sun, that "overrich star," that "cup that wants to overflow, that the water may flow from it golden and carry everywhere the reflection of [its] delight" (Z:Prologue 1). Later in the Prologue, Zarathustra echoes this passage, proclaiming: "I love him whose soul squanders itself, who wants no thanks and returns none: for he always gives away and does not want to preserve himself" (4). See also the section on "The Gift-Giving Virtue"—"the highest virtue," which, like gold, "is uncommon and useless and gleaming and gentle in its splendor; it always gives of itself" (Z:1 "On the Gift-Giving Virtue"). For further discussion of the gift-giving theme in Nietzsche's work and suggestions concerning its relationship to Bataille's conception of "general economy," see Gary Shapiro, *Alcyone: Nietzsche on Gifts, Noise, and Women* (Albany: State University of New York Press, 1991), 13–51, and Alan D. Schrift, *Nietzsche's French Legacy: A Genealogy of Poststructuralism* (New York: Routledge, 1995), 82–101.

other.[45] So, too, is it within the domain of "culture." Nietzsche notes that peoples are acquisitive and conservative until they reach such a point of power and abundance that they burst the bounds of their moralities and ranks, producing a flood of individualities and new systems of value (*BGE* 262).[46] If law and justice temporarily stem this tide, Nietzsche insists that,

> from the highest biological standpoint, legal conditions can never be other than *exceptional conditions,* since they constitute a partial restriction of the will of life, which is bent upon power, and are subordinate to its total goal as a single means: namely, as a means of creating *greater* units of power. A legal order thought of as sovereign and universal, not as a means in the struggle between power-complexes but as a means of *preventing* all struggle in general [. . . ,] would be a principle *hostile to life,* an agent of the dissolution and destruction of man, an attempt to assassinate the future of man, a sign of weariness, a secret path to nothingness. (*GM* II:11; cf. *BGE* 259; *GM* II:12; and *WP* 728)

In short, while provisional limits and restrictions can be imposed upon the impulse to expenditure, this accumulation can only ever be in the service of a more magnificent squandering. Ultimately, the movement of expenditure can only be channeled, not thwarted.[47] Denied outward discharge, the will to power turns inward (*GM* II:16). And even the ascetic who attempts to negate life and will to power implicitly affirms them, for asceticism, Nietzsche famously argues, is merely a perverse will of life against life itself, "*a will to nothingness*" that, nevertheless, "remains a *will!*" (*GM* III:28; cf. *GM* III:10–13; *TI* "Morality").

The affirmation of life, then, requires an affirmation of will to power as the will to expenditure, the drive to discharge strength and exude energy. According to both Nietzsche and Bataille, human history and anthropology reveal the extent and variety of forums developed for the satisfaction of this drive. Festivals, spectacles, games, athletic and aesthetic contests, orgies, feasts, sacrifices, wars, monumental construction, gambling, nonreproductive sex, and sumptuous gifts all attest to this impulse to dissipate energy and discharge strength at the cost of preser-

45. See Bataille, *Accursed Share,* 33–35; and Nietzsche, *Z*:2 "On Self-Overcoming"; *TI* "Ancients" 4; *WP* 655–58, 680.
46. Cf. *WP* 933: "A culture of the exception, the experiment, the danger, the nuance as a consequence of a great *abundance of powers: this* is the tendency of *every* aristocratic culture. Only when a culture has an excess of powers at its disposal can it also constitute a hothouse of luxury cultivation" (modified on the basis of the original, *KSA* 12:9[139]).
47. See Bataille, *Accursed Share,* 21, 25.

vation and the utility of resources.[48] Yet, as we have seen, will to power is not only concerned with the expenditure and dissipation of strength. It is also taken up with "growth and expansion," the acquisition of strength and power in the service of an even more grandiose expenditure. Hence, it favors neither total dissipation of power nor complete destruction of the object on which power is exercised. Such results will only negate, rather than affirm, the will of life. In contrast, Nietzsche sees will to power as exemplified by the Greek *agon*. These contests are not "fights of annihilation" (*HC*, p. 35), which manifest what, following Hesiod, Nietzsche calls "the evil Eris": struggles motivated only by *ressentiment* and the desire to destroy.[49] Rather, they affirm Hesiod's "good Eris," fostering an ongoing forum for the release of strength, the testing of claims to power, and the drive for competitive distinction.[50] Because "will to power can manifest itself only against resistances," every contestant "seeks that which resists it" (*WP* 656). Competing forces will be worthy opponents only if their respective strengths and directions are more or less similar. The exemplary contestant derives no satisfaction from competing against an inferior power, nor does he or she wish to dominate the field absolutely. Such situations undermine the contest; and the proper response to these situations, Nietzsche suggests, is "ostracism," the banishment of these over-bearing contestants (see *HC*, p. 36). For the good contestant "resist[s] any ultimate peace," and, instead, "will[s] the eternal recurrence of war and peace" (*GS* 285).

The *agon* may well result in the acquisition of strength and the feeling of power that accompanies it. Yet, again, this condition is not its aim: will to power is ateleological.[51] It desires not a final state but the perpetuation of the contest. Paradoxically, power can be acquired only through expenditure (think, for instance, of athletic training); and its acquisition leads once again to this desire to expend. Bataille illustrates this well with his privileged manifestation of the will to expenditure, the

---

48. See Bataille, "Notion of Expenditure," 118–23, *Accursed Share, passim*; and Nietzsche, *HC; HL* 9; *GM* II:6–7; *TI* "Ancients" 3–5.

49. The notion of *ressentiment* appears nowhere in "Homer's Contest." But I think Nietzsche's characterization of "the evil Eris" in this text has much in common with his description of the *ressentiment* that characterizes the slave's will to power in the *Genealogy of Morals*, Essay I.

50. See *HC*, p. 35, and Hesiod, *Works and Days*, lines 1–50.

51. One is reminded of a claim repeated throughout Nietzsche's corpus: "every power draws its ultimate consequences at every moment" (*BGE* 22). Cf. *HL* 1, p. 66; *BT* SC: 5; *WP* 55, 634, 708. Also cf. Bataille ("Notion of Expenditure," 118): activities of expenditure "have no end beyond themselves."

ritual of potlatch practiced by a number of Native American tribes of the Northwest Coast.[52] "Potlatch," Bataille explains,

> is, like commerce, a means of circulating wealth, but it excludes bargaining. More often than not it is the solemn giving of considerable riches, offered by a chief to his rival for the purpose of humiliating, challenging and obligating him. The recipient has to erase the humiliation and take up the challenge; he must satisfy the *obligation* that was contracted by accepting. He can only reply, a short time later, by means of a new potlatch, more generous than the first: He must pay back with interest.[53]

Bataille remarks that "[t]here would be no potlatch if, in a general sense, the ultimate problem concerned the acquisition and not the dissipation of useful wealth." [54] Yet, it gives rise to a paradox:

> We need to give away, lose or destroy. But the gift would be senseless (and so we would never decide to give) if it did not take on the meaning of an acquisition. Hence *giving* must become *acquiring a power.* Gift-giving has the virtue of a surpassing of the subject who gives, but in exchange for the object given, the subject appropriates the surpassing: He regards his virtue, that which he has had the capacity for, as an asset, as a *power* that he now possesses. He enriches himself with a contempt for riches, and what he proves to be miserly of is in fact his generosity.[55]

> [I]t turns out that the giver has only apparently lost. Not only does he have the power over the recipient that the gift has bestowed on him, but the recipient is obligated to nullify that power by repaying the gift. The rivalry even entails the return of a greater gift: In order to *get even* the giver must not only redeem himself, but he must also impose the "power of the gift" on his rival in turn. In a sense the presents are repaid *with interest.* Thus the gift is the opposite of what it seemed to be: To give is obviously to lose, but the loss apparently brings a profit to the one who sustains it.[56]

Bataille maintains, however, that this acquisitive interpretation of potlatch is misleading. Acquisition is only a moment in the endless cycle of

---

52. Though the term "potlatch" properly describes the practice of a particular group of peoples, Bataille (*Accursed Share,* 67) notes that "[e]thnographers now employ this term to designate institutions functioning on a similar principle; they find traces of it in all societies." Indeed, he writes, "a good many of our behaviors are reducible to the laws of potlatch; they have the same significance as it does" (69). For his anthropological data, Bataille draws heavily on Marcel Mauss's extremely influential "Essay on the Gift" (1923–24), itself based on the work of Davy, Boas, Swanton, and Malinowski. See Claude Lévi-Strauss, *Introduction to the Work of Marcel Mauss,* trans. Felicity Baker (London: Routledge and Kegan Paul, 1987), 37.

53. Bataille, *Accursed Share,* 67–68; cf. "Notion of Expenditure," 121.

54. Bataille, *Accursed Share,* 68.

55. Ibid., 69.

56. Ibid., 70.

potlatch: every gift prompts, in response, an even greater gift, a more glorious expenditure. One does not give in order to acquire; acquisition is merely an effect of one's giving.[57] "[I]f it is ultimately a source of profit," Bataille writes, "the principle of [potlatch] is nevertheless determined by a resolute squandering of resources that in theory could have been acquired."[58] Moreover, in this endless cycle of gift-giving, what is genuinely acquired is not *things* but *rank*, esteem, value, glory. And this rank is determined, principally, not by what one *has*, but by what one is able to *risk, expend, put in play*: "the players can never retire from the game, their fortunes made; they remain at the mercy of provocation."[59] As soon as one retires from the game, one's prestige becomes a thing of the past.

The example of "potlatch," of agonistic giving, may appear to be an anthropological curiosity. Yet Bataille sees in it something characteristic not only of human activity but of natural life as a whole: the burden of excess energy and the need to expend it. So, too, does Nietzsche see in his privileged metaphor of the *agon* not a rarefied cultural practice but something characteristic of natural processes generally. Bataille's "potlatch" and Nietzsche's *agon* are exemplary instances of will to power, intended to help us see that "power" is not primarily about acquisition, not primarily something a being wants or can have for its own, but something that circulates through living beings and that propels the myriad movements of organic life.

5.2.5 BEYOND MECHANISM AND VITALISM: NIETZSCHE'S MATERIALISM

Recall, however, that Nietzsche rejects any fundamental distinction between organic and inorganic nature. As we have seen, he believes that the hypothesis of will to power helps to explain even the most basic inorganic, physical processes. The solar power that animates the biosphere,

---

57. Cf. *BGE* 13 and *GS* 349, cited above. See *WP* 935: "True graciousness, nobility, greatness of soul proceed from abundance; do not give in order to receive—do not try to *exalt* themselves by being gracious;—*prodigality* as the type of true graciousness, abundance of *personality* as its presupposition." Cf. *WP* 943, 864.

58. Bataille, *Accursed Share*, 70.

59. Bataille, "Notion of Expenditure," 122–23. Thus Bataille: "power is characterized as power to lose" (122; cf. *Accursed Share*, 71), and Nietzsche: "how much injury [one] can endure without suffering from it becomes the actual *measure* of [one's] wealth" (*GM* II:10). Cf. also *WP* 949.

then, must be only one of many forms of energy that drive natural becoming. Let me, then, conclude this discussion by working backward from the domain of culture, life, and biology to the realm of the inorganic from which we began.

Darwin's revolution promoted the conception of a naturalized humanity thoroughly enmeshed in a de-deified nature. Rejecting creationism, essentialism, progressivism, adaptationism, and teleology, it saw species as mere statistical generalizations, viewed all living beings as derived from a common ancestor, and refused to see human beings as apart from, or as the pinnacle of, this natural distribution. Indeed, Darwin espoused a thoroughgoing materialism that denied the immateriality of the soul (or mind) and the existence of any extra-natural vital force in the organic world.[60]

Nonetheless, scientists and laypeople alike continued to view human beings as fundamentally different in kind from animals and to make an analogous separation between living and nonliving matter.[61] It is in this context that Nietzsche intervenes to complete Darwin's revolution.[62] The rigorous naturalist cannot accept such essential divisions in nature. If Nietzsche and Bataille often restrict their hypothesis of will to power and expenditure to the realm of life, Nietzsche, at least, often realizes the inadmissibility of this restriction and seeks to extend it to the whole of nature. Thus, Nietzsche counts among "man's four errors" that "he endowed himself with fictitious attributes [. . .] and placed himself in a false order of rank in relation to animals and nature" (GS 115). Against vitalist evolutionary theorists, and despite his critique of mechanism, Nietzsche retains the materialism promoted by classical physical theory, which asserts the continuity of the organic with the inorganic world (see KSA 11:26[432] and A 14, quoted in §5.2, above). Organic matter is the result of a set of peculiar chemical reactions that took place in "the primeval soup" and set off the evolutionary chain. Hence, though

60. See Howard E. Gruber, Darwin on Man: A Psychological Study of Scientific Creativity, together with Darwin's Early and Unpublished Notebooks, ed. Paul H. Barrett (New York: E. P. Dutton, 1974); Gould, Ever Since Darwin, 21–27, and "In Praise of Charles Darwin," 5–6.

61. See Stephen Jay Gould, "Eternal Metaphors of Palaeontology," in Patterns of Evolution as Illustrated by the Fossil Record, ed. A. Hallam (Amsterdam: Elsevier, 1977), 14 and passim.

62. Again, like many nineteenth- and twentieth-century scientists and laypeople, Nietzsche seems not to have fully appreciated the radical nature of Darwin's de-deification and naturalization. Despite this ignorance, Nietzsche undertakes a philosophical campaign that, in many respects, continues and furthers Darwin's revolution.

remarkable in many ways, living beings are not so by virtue of any extra-natural origin or endowment. "The entire distinction" between "the inorganic and the organic world," Nietzsche writes, "is a prejudice" (*WP* 655). "The living is merely a type of what is dead, and a very rare type" (*GS* 109).

Recall that Nietzsche criticizes mechanism for promoting a passive, reactive principle of natural movement that could only have been made possible by an original divine push. Similarly, he criticizes biology for taking a reactive principle, "adaptation," to be the driving force of evolutionary change.[63] In place of these, Nietzsche seeks an active principle that can explain natural movement and change without recourse to ontotheological posits. Moreover, Nietzsche's naturalism requires that this principle apply equally to mechanical, chemical, biological, and cultural change. It is this that leads him to propose will to power as a unifying theory. Thus, after noting that all human functions (including thought and reason) and, indeed, all organic functions (nutrition, excretion, procreation, etc.) can be explained in terms of the interrelation of "desires," "passions," and "drives," he suggests that this might "be *sufficient* for also understanding [. . .] the so called mechanistic (or 'material') world" (*BGE* 36). "In short," Nietzsche continues, "conscience of *method* demands" that we "risk the hypothesis whether will does not affect will wherever 'effects' are recognized—and whether all mechanical occurrences are not, insofar as force is active in them, will-force, will-effects." If one grants this hypothesis, "one would have gained the right to determine *all* efficient force univocally as—*will to power*. The world viewed from inside, the world defined and determined according to its 'intelligible character'—it would be 'will to power' and nothing besides."[64]

63. See *GM* II:12, and *WP* 70, 647, 681, 684. Cf. Gould ("Eternal Metaphors of Palaeontology," 21–22): "physical scientists are forever trying to extend their 'billiard ball' models to major events in the history of life. (By 'billiard ball model,' I refer to a habit of explanation that treats organisms as inert substances, buffeted by an external environment and reacting immediately to physical stress without any counteracting, intrinsic control or even temporary resistance.) [. . .] I have labeled as 'physicalist' these purely environmental explanations, based upon billiard ball models: i.e., stimulus leads to immediate and passive response. [. . .] For all my general support of environmental control, I applaud the attempt of several palaeontologists to counteract these physicalist explanations by asserting the independence and internal dynamic of biological processes in complex systems, particularly of ecological interaction and the genetic and morphological prerequisites of complexity."

64. Cf. *WP* 619: "one is obliged to understand all motion, all 'appearances,' all 'laws,' only as symptoms of an inner event and to employ man as an analogy to this end.

One could take this hypothesis as an attempt to resolve the quarrel between mechanism and vitalism by asserting a sort of hypervitalism that would extend the vital force over the entire domain of matter. But this is not Nietzsche's move. Time and again he asserts that human beings and life itself must be "translated back into nature," not the reverse: "life is merely a *special case* of the will to power" (*WP* 692), he writes. On the issue of mechanism and vitalism, Nietzsche advocates the position held by most twentieth-century scientists: that the very distinction ought to be rejected.[65] For Nietzsche, the trouble is that both positions retain theological posits: vitalism proceeds from the spiritual conviction that life must be more than, higher than, different from the rest of the material world; and mechanism maintains a passive and deterministic conception of matter that is incapable of explaining becoming and the production of difference without recourse to an extra-natural motive force. Instead, Nietzsche looks at matter and everywhere sees motion and change, from the simplest chemical reactions and the most basic material forces to the nutritive and reproductive activity of animals and plants and the formative activity of artists and athletes. Everywhere this motion and change is driven by struggle and *pathos*: by attraction, repulsion, tension, resistance, integration, disintegration, assimilation, incorporation, alliance, and so on. Having rejected any transcendent source, Nietzsche comes to hold that the principle of this becoming and struggle must lie in material things themselves, things considered as "dynamic quanta, in a relation of tension to all other dynamic quanta" (*WP* 635). In the words of Nobel laureate Ilya Prigogine: "since there is no one to build nature, we must give to its very 'bricks'—that is, to its microscopic activity—a description that accounts for that building process. [. . . M]atter is no longer the passive substance described in the mechanistic world view but is associated with spontaneous activity."[66]

In the case of an animal, it is possible to trace all its drives to the will to power; likewise all the functions of organic life to this one source."

65. See, e.g., Gould, *Flamingo's Smile*, 377–91, and Mayr, *Toward a New Philosophy of Biology*, 8–21.

66. Prigogine and Stengers, *Order Out of Chaos*, 7, 9. Nietzsche's view might also be compared with that of another materialist, atheist, antidualist critic of mechanism, Denis Diderot, who asserts "a simple hypothesis that explains everything—sensitivity as a property common to all matter or as a result of the organization of matter" (*Rameau's Nephew* and *D'Alembert's Dream*, ed. and trans. Leonard Tancock [Harmondsworth: Penguin, 1966], 159).

5.3 WILL TO POWER AND INTERPRETATION

5.3.1 WILL TO POWER AS INTERPRETATION

Opposing Schopenhauer's "will to live" and Darwin's "struggle for existence," Nietzsche calls this fundamental activity of things "will to power." Yet it goes by another name, as well: "interpretation." Throughout his later work, Nietzsche closely links these two notions. "The will to power *interprets*," he writes in a note from 1885–86, "interpretation is itself a means of becoming master of something" (*WP* 643). This view is elaborated in the *Genealogy of Morals*, where Nietzsche remarks that interpretation "*essentially*" involves "forcing, adjusting, abbreviating, omitting, padding, inventing, [and] falsifying" (III:24).[67] In the *Genealogy*'s "Second Essay," the connection between "interpretation" and "will to power" is drawn more explicitly and the two terms become nearly synonymous: "[W]hatever exists," he writes, is essentially involved in processes of "*subduing,* [. . .] *becoming master,* and all subduing and becoming master involves a fresh interpretation." There is "interpretation" whenever something is "taken over, transformed and redirected by some power superior to it" and "will to power" whenever something has "become master of something less powerful and imposed on it the character of a function." The section concludes that "the essence of life, *will to power*" is revealed in those "spontaneous, aggressive, expansive, form-giving forces that give new interpretations and directions" (*BGE* 12).

Earlier, we saw that Nietzsche's notion of "interpretation" extends well beyond its ordinary domain (see §3.2). Indeed, its scope is precisely as broad as that of will to power. Thus, just as "all organic functions could be traced back to this will to power and one could also find in it the solution to the problem of procreation and nourishment" (*BGE* 36), so, too, "all events in the organic world" are said to involve "interpretation" (*GM* II:12). "The organic process constantly presupposes *interpreting*," Nietzsche writes elsewhere; thus, for example, "it is a question of interpretation when an organ is constructed" (*WP* 643;

67. This language resonates with that of another passage, which asserts that, as will to power, "life operates *essentially,* that is in its basic functions, through injury, assault, exploitation, destruction, and simply cannot be thought of at all without this character" (*GM* II:11). See also *BGE* 259: "'Exploitation' does not belong to a corrupt or imperfect and primitive society: it belongs to the *essence* of what lives, as a basic organic function; it is a consequence of the will to power, which is after all the will of life." See also *Z:2* "On Self-Overcoming."

cf. *GM* II:12). And because, consistent with his thoroughgoing naturalism, Nietzsche sees fit to extend will to power over inanimate nature,[68] we could view even inorganic events and entities (e.g., chemical reactions and bonds) as "interpretations" in Nietzsche's extended sense.

This will strike many as a bizarre and idiosyncratic move. Yet I take it to be a polemical strategy intended to make a serious naturalistic point. Just as Nietzsche asserts that the "soul is only a word for something about the body" (*Z*:1 "On the Despisers of the Body")[69] and that "thinking is merely a relation of [. . .] drives to each other" (*BGE* 36), he asks us to see "interpretation"—one of the "highest" intellectual operations—as simply one manifestation of a process found throughout the natural world. Thus, if the interpretation of texts involves the selection, incorporation, assimilation, weighting, ordering, and elaboration (or, in Nietzsche's more polemical formulation: "forcing, adjusting, abbreviating, omitting, padding, inventing, [and] falsifying" [*GM* III:24]) of textual material in the interest of intellectual mastery and the production of meaning, so, too, do breathing and eating, for example, consist in the exploitation, incorporation, and assimilation of a select portion of the natural world in the service of preservation, growth, enhancement, and power. Indeed, Nietzsche suggests that "'the spirit' is relatively most similar to a stomach" (*BGE* 230).[70] He elaborates:

> That commanding something which the people call "spirit" wants to be master in and around its own house and wants to feel that it is master; it has the will from multiplicity to simplicity, a will that ties up, tames, and is domineering and truly masterful. Its needs and capacities are so far the same as those which physiologists posit for everything that lives, grows, and multiplies. The spirit's power to appropriate the foreign stands revealed in its inclination to assimilate the new to the old, to simplify the manifold, and to overlook or repulse whatever is totally contradictory—just as it involuntarily emphasizes certain features and lines in what is foreign, in every piece of the "external world," retouching and falsifying the whole to suit itself. Its intent in all this is to incorporate new "experiences," to file new things in old files— growth, in a word—or, more precisely, the *feeling* of growth, the feeling of increased power.

68. Thus, to take the two passages cited above, *BGE* 36 concludes that "*all* efficient force" ought to be determined as "*will to power*," and *GM* II:12 concludes that "in all events a *will to power* is operating."
69. In *BGE* 12, Nietzsche deems "the soul" a "social structure of the drives and affects." On this issue, see §3.3.3, above.
70. Cf. *Z*:3 "On Old and New Tablets" (§16): "For verily, my brothers, the spirit *is* a stomach."

This will to "appropriate," "assimilate," "simplify," "overlook," "emphasize," "retouch," "falsify," and "incorporate" Nietzsche here calls "will to power."[71] Elsewhere he calls it "interpretation." Indeed, this allows us to make sense of the initially puzzling idea that "the general renunciation of all interpretation (of forcing, adjusting, abbreviating, omitting, padding, inventing, falsifying, and whatever else is of the *essence* of interpreting) [. . .] expresses, broadly speaking, as much ascetic virtue as any denial of sensuality" (*GM* III:24). If the essence of life and nature is will to power, and if will to power essentially involves interpretation (in the broad sense), then "the general renunciation of all interpretation" would signify an ascetic rejection of life and nature. Conversely, if will to power is the naturalistic theory par excellence, and if will to power essentially involves interpretation, the naturalist is led to assert the primacy and irreducibility of interpretation.

5.3.2 BEYOND EPISTEMOLOGY AND ONTOLOGY

This identification of will to power with interpretation and our exposition of Nietzsche's broad conception of interpretation allow us to answer the last of our initial questions: is will to power an epistemological or an ontological doctrine? The answer is that it is both, or neither: both, because it offers an account of knowing *and* being; neither, because it collapses the rigorous distinctions between subject and object, knower and known, upon which epistemology and ontology are traditionally founded.

To make sense of this we need to return to the gastronomic metaphor presented above. For Nietzsche, "knowing" is "interpreting" (that is, "taking possession of things," "equalization and ordering," "simplification," "adjustment," "schematizing," "forming, shaping, and reshaping" "for the purpose of intelligibility and calculation").[72] And this cognitive apprehension or interpretation is simply a kind of in-gestion or in-corporation, which forms "the basic will" not only of the body but also of the "spirit"—for " 'the spirit' is relatively most similar to a stomach" (*BGE* 229–30).[73] On this model, then, the "knowing subject" is

---

71. He does so even more explicitly in passages that employ nearly identical language, e.g., *BGE* 259; *GM* II:11; and *WP* 511.

72. A list of predicates for "knowledge" drawn from *WP* 503, 500, 515, and 656, the earliest written in 1884, the latest in 1888.

73. Elsewhere, Nietzsche remarks that the cognitive process "is the same as the process of incorporation of appropriated material in the amoeba" (*WP* 501), that "[t]his whole

no more detached from the "objects" it apprehends than the body is detached from the solids, liquids, and gases it ingests. That which ingests (the knower, the interpreter, the consumer) is not different in kind from that which is ingested (other natural material), for the latter is also a consumer and interpreter (in the extended sense) in its own right. Thus, the designations subject and object, knower and known, interpreter and interpreted, eater and eaten are relative and perspectival, since, from one point of view all matter is the former, while from another it is the latter. "[A]ll existence" *is* "essentially an *interpreting* existence" (*GS* 374), Nietzsche writes; and all *knowing* is a form of "interpreting." That is, what things *are* is determined by interpretation (both by cognitive and noncognitive forms of appropriation and assimilation); and what things *do* is interpret (including that rarefied form we call "knowing" or "cognition").

In short, for Nietzsche, the natural world is fundamentally interpretive. There is no world other than the natural and nothing outside the interpretive web that constitutes this natural world. If "epistemology" names the attempt to conceive of the knowing subject as prior to interpretation, the attempt to found a prior science, to view the world "from the outside," then will to power (which resolutely views the world "from inside") is anti-epistemological. In Richard Rorty's formulation, it is "hermeneutical," because it substitutes for the epistemological dualism of subject and object the web of "interpretation," which encompasses and articulates both subjects and objects.[74] There is only this web of interpretation; which is to say, there is only will to power: "*This world is will to power—and nothing besides!* And you yourselves are also this will to power—and nothing besides!" (*WP* 1067).

5.3.3 WILL TO POWER AS AN INTERPRETATION

This assertion of the primacy and irreducibility of interpretation can only mean that "will to power" is itself an interpretation. And Nietz-

---

process corresponds exactly to that external, mechanical process (which is its symbol) by which the *protoplasm* makes what it appropriates equal to itself and fits it into its own forms and files" (*WP* 510).

74. See Richard Rorty, *Philosophy and the Mirror of Nature* (Princeton: Princeton University Press, 1979), part 3, and "Inquiry as Recontextualization: An Anti-Dualist Account of Interpretation," in *Objectivity, Relativism, and Truth: Philosophical Papers,* vol. 1 (Cambridge: Cambridge University Press, 1991). On the notion of subject and object as interpretive constructs, see chapter 3 and *WP* 481; *BGE* 34; and *WP* 556, which are quoted at the end of §3.3.4 above.

sche affirms it as such: "Supposing that this ['will to power'] also is only interpretation—" he writes, "and you will be eager enough to make this objection?—well, so much the better" (*BGE* 22). Nietzsche is not a dogmatic metaphysician for whom will to power could be a transcendent Truth; nor is he a positivist for whom will to power could be founded on indubitable "facts." Indeed, in the closing sections of the *Genealogy,* he argues that dogmatic metaphysics and positivism are secret allies, because both are motivated by the same "unconditional will to truth" that demands "the renunciation of all interpretation" (*GM* III: 24). For Nietzsche, however, such renunciation is impossible and the very attempt at it antinatural.

How, then, can Nietzsche avoid vicious circularity and legitimate his claim that will to power is the best available world-interpretation? This problem of circularity confronts every philosophy that abjures foundationalism.[75] But the circle will appear vicious only to the foundationalist who assumes that there must be some way of exiting it. For the holist, there is no such exit. But this does not mean that the holist lacks a platform for critique, for the proposal of positive views, and for the determination of value. What it does mean is that critique can only take place *from within,* that it must draw its resources from that which it criticizes.[76] That is why Nietzsche's critique of metaphysics and theology takes the form not of a definitive refutation but of elaborate fallibilistic *genealogies,*[77] which provide deflationary psychological, philological, and historical redescriptions that draw attention to the ascetic ideal's *pudenda origo* (*D* 42; *WP* 254), its shameful origins and ends. Nietzsche's positive conceptions are justified in the same manner: by ap-

75. See, e.g., the problem of the hermeneutic circle in Martin Heidegger, *Being and Time,* trans. John Macquarrie and Edward Robinson (New York: Harper and Row, 1962), §§2, 32, 63; in Jacques Derrida, "Structure, Sign, and Play in the Discourse of the Human Sciences," in *Writing and Difference,* trans. Alan Bass (Chicago: University of Chicago Press, 1978), 280ff, and *Of Grammatology,* trans. Gayatri C. Spivak (Baltimore: Johns Hopkins University Press, 1974), 162; in Nelson Goodman, *Fact, Fiction, and Forecast* (Indianapolis: Bobbs-Merrill, 1965), 63–64; and in W. V. Quine, "Epistemology Naturalized," in *Ontological Relativity and Other Essays* (New York: Columbia University Press, 1969), 75–76.

76. To call on Quine's analogy ("Natural Kinds," in *Ontological Relativity,* 127), drawn from Neurath, we are at sail in "a boat which [. . .] we can rebuild only at sea while staying afloat in it" (cf. *Word and Object* [Cambridge, Mass.: MIT Press, 1960], 3). Or, to use Derrida's analogy (*Of Grammatology,* 139), drawn from Lévi-Strauss, we are "bricoleurs" who can only "build [. . . new] castles with debris."

77. Thus, in the preface to the *Genealogy of Morals,* Nietzsche writes, "[W]hat have I to do with refutations!—but, as becomes a positive spirit, to replace the improbable with the more probable, possibly one error with another" (4).

peal to something within the tradition that allows it to be deconstructed and then reconstructed otherwise. In chapter 1, we saw that Nietzsche's endorsement of art (or the aesthetic) as the naturalistic discourse par excellence is premised upon a genealogy of European thought, specifically upon a radical extension of the naturalistic tendency implicit in its latest, scientific, moment. And, in the present chapter, we have seen that will to power is proposed as an effort finally to rid contemporary scientific accounts of "the shadows of God." Will to power, then, is justified not transcendently but immanently—by recourse to a tradition, an interpretation, a story that it takes over and recasts.

As such, Nietzsche's project bears some resemblance to that of the other great nineteenth-century German holist, Hegel. Both Nietzsche and Hegel reject foundationalism and traditional epistemology in favor of a holistic, historicist account of the succession of interpretations that constitute the European intellectual tradition, a tradition which, for both philosophers, can only be altered via an immanent critique.[78] Yet, for Nietzsche, the Hegelian project remains ontotheological in its teleological trajectory toward "absolute knowledge," the dream of an end to becoming, multiplicity, struggle, and contingency, the desire for a final interpretation. The "death of God" proclaimed in Hegel's *Glauben und Wissen* is only a religious death, because it is followed by a philosophical resurrection.[79] For Nietzsche, "the death of God" means a rejection

78. Hence, Jacques Derrida ("Positions," in *Positions*, trans. Alan Bass [Chicago: University of Chicago Press, 1981], 44) writes that his Nietzschean conception of *différance* operates "at a point of almost absolute proximity to Hegel." See also "The Original Discussion of 'Différance,'" in *Derrida and Differance*, ed. David Wood and Robert Bernasconi (Evanston: Northwestern University Press, 1982), 95. For Derrida, as for Deleuze (*Nietzsche and Philosophy*, trans. Hugh Tomlinson [New York: Columbia University Press, 1983], 8ff., 147ff.), the contemporary debate is not between antifoundationalism and foundationalism but between the Hegelian and Nietzschean forms of antifoundationalism.

79. See Hegel, *Faith and Knowledge*, trans. Walter Cerf and H. S. Harris (Albany: State University of New York Press, 1977), 190–91, and *Phenomenology of Spirit*, trans. A. V. Miller (Oxford: Oxford University Press, 1977), §808. In this sense, even if, with Robert C. Solomon ("The Secret of Hegel [Kierkegaard's Complaint]: A Study in Hegel's Philosophy of Religion," in *From Hegel to Existentialism* [Oxford: Oxford University Press, 1987]), we grant Hegel's "atheistic humanism," Hegel remains a closet theologian insofar as his "humanism" maintains "the shadows of God." For Gilles Deleuze and Michel Foucault, this is the significance of Nietzsche's doctrine of the *Übermensch*: that humanism remains theological and that not only God, but man, too, must be overcome. "No we do not love humanity," Nietzsche writes (*GS* 377); "[m]an is something that shall be overcome" (Z:Prologue 3). See Deleuze, *Nietzsche and Philosophy*, 147–94, *Foucault*, trans. Seán Hand (Minneapolis: University of Minnesota Press, 1988), 124–32; and Michel Foucault, *The Order of Things: An Archaeology of the Human Sciences*, trans. Alan Sheridan (London: Tavistock, 1970), 303–87.

not only of God but also of his epistemological and ontological "shadows," that is, of all transcendent interpretations and posits. It means not an elevation toward spirit but the reassertion of nature and embodiment, not "dusk" but "midnight," "daybreak," or "noon," not peace and rest but struggle and becoming, not "the end of history" but "the end of an error," not "experience" but a return to the "innocence" of Heraclitus's child.

With the doctrine of "will to power," Nietzsche reasserts Heraclitus's claim that "war is the father of all." He affirms the irreducible multiplicity and conflict of "interpretations" and thus the perpetual becoming (or *différance*) of the interpretive field. Before and after theology, will to power places us in the space of "the pagan," to adopt Jean-François Lyotard's term for our postmodern condition: a condition defined by the perpetual *agon* of multiple and irreducible discourses in the absence of a God or metadiscourse that could resolve disputes once and for all.[80] And Nietzsche places the doctrine of will to power in this very space, a space it does not govern but in which it, too, can only be a move in the game. Will to power, too, "is no matter of fact, no 'text,' but [. . . an] interpretation [. . .]; and somebody might come along who, with opposite intentions and modes of interpretation, could read out of the same 'nature,' and with regard to the same phenomena," something altogether different (*BGE* 22). Nietzsche acknowledges this and responds "so much the better," because this supposition ensures the continuation of the *agon*. For the moment and in our current situation, Nietzsche is satisfied that his interpretations are victorious. But this satisfaction is that of victory, not of peace; and it is hoped that the peace be short rather than long (*Z*:1 "On War and Warriors"; cf. *HC*, p. 38, and *GS* 285). Since the *agon* that is nature, life, and history "abominates the rule of one" (*HC*, p. 37), Nietzsche "looks for" (*EH* "Wise" 7), indeed "craves" (*BT* SC:1), new enemies, new struggles, and new contests.

80. See Jean-François Lyotard, "Lessons in Paganism," in *The Lyotard Reader,* ed. Andrew Benjamin (Oxford: Blackwell, 1989), and Lyotard and Jean-Loup Thébaud, *Just Gaming,* trans. Wlad Godzich (Minneapolis: University of Minnesota Press, 1985).

Bibliography

I. NIETZSCHE'S WORKS IN ENGLISH

PUBLISHED WORKS*

The Antichrist (written 1888). In *The Portable Nietzsche,* ed. and trans. Walter
    Kaufmann. New York: Viking Press, 1968.
Assorted Opinions and Maxims (1879). Volume II, Part 1 of *Human, All Too
    Human.* Trans. R. J. Hollingdale. Cambridge: Cambridge University Press,
    1986.
Beyond Good and Evil (1886). In *Basic Writings of Nietzsche,* ed. and trans.
    Walter Kaufmann. New York: Modern Library, 1966.
The Birth of Tragedy (1872). In *Basic Writings of Nietzsche,* ed. and trans.
    Walter Kaufmann. New York: Modern Library, 1966.
The Case of Wagner (1888). In *Basic Writings of Nietzsche,* ed. and trans. Walter
    Kaufmann. New York: Modern Library, 1966.
Daybreak (1881). Trans. R. J. Hollingdale. Cambridge: Cambridge University
    Press, 1982.
Ecce Homo (written 1888). In *Basic Writings of Nietzsche,* ed. and trans. Walter
    Kaufmann. New York: Modern Library, 1966.
The Gay Science (Books I–IV: 1882; Book V: 1887). Trans. Walter Kaufmann.
    New York: Vintage Books, 1974.
Human, All Too Human, Vol. I (1878). Trans. R. J. Hollingdale. Cambridge:
    Cambridge University Press, 1986.

* Note that, though completed and prepared for publication in 1888, *Ecce Homo* and
The Antichrist were not actually published until after Nietzsche's collapse, the former in
1895, the latter in 1908. Nevertheless, both texts are conventionally classed among the
"published works."

On the Genealogy of Morals (1887). In *Basic Writings of Nietzsche,* ed. and
   trans. Walter Kaufmann. New York: Modern Library, 1966. Roman numerals indicate essay number.
"On the Use and Disadvantage of History for Life" (1874). In *Untimely Meditations,* trans. R. J. Hollingdale. Cambridge: Cambridge University Press,
   1983. References to this text provide both section and page numbers from
   this edition.
"Schopenhauer as Educator" (1874). In *Untimely Meditations,* trans. R. J. Hollingdale. Cambridge: Cambridge University Press, 1983. References to this
   text provide both section and page numbers from this edition.
Thus Spoke Zarathustra (Parts I–II: 1883; Part III: 1884; Part IV: 1885). In *The
   Portable Nietzsche,* ed. and trans. Walter Kaufmann. New York: The Viking
   Press, 1968. Arabic numerals indicate the Part number, followed by the chap-
   ter title.
Twilight of the Idols (written 1888). In *The Portable Nietzsche,* ed. and trans.
   Walter Kaufmann. New York: The Viking Press, 1968. The eleven major di-
   visions of this text are indicated by abbreviations of their titles: "Maxims,"
   "Socrates," "Reason," "World," "Morality," "Errors," "Improvers," "Ger-
   mans," "Skirmishes," "Ancients," and "Hammer."
The Wanderer and His Shadow (1880). Vol. II, Part 2, of *Human, All Too
   Human.* Trans. R. J. Hollingdale. Cambridge: Cambridge University Press,
   1986.

UNPUBLISHED WORKS AND NOTES

"Homer's Contest" (written 1872). In *The Portable Nietzsche,* ed. and trans.
   Walter Kaufmann. New York: Viking Press, 1968. Page numbers refer to
   this edition.
"On Truth and Lies in a Nonmoral Sense" (written 1873). In *Philosophy and
   Truth: Selections from Nietzsche's Notebooks of the Early 1870's,* ed. and
   trans. Daniel Breazeale. Atlantic Highlands: Humanities Press International,
   1979. Page numbers refer to this edition.
Philosophy in the Tragic Age of the Greeks (written 1873), trans. Marianne
   Cowan. Washington, DC: Regnery Gateway, 1962. References to this text
   provide both section and page numbers from this edition.
The Will to Power (selected notes from 1883–88). Ed. Walter Kaufmann. Trans.
   Walter Kaufmann and R. J. Hollingdale. New York: Vintage Books, 1967.

II. NIETZSCHE'S WORKS IN GERMAN

English translations have been checked against the now-standard Colli-Montinari edition of Nietzsche's *Werke.* Among other benefits, this edition finally
standardizes the emphases in the *Nachlaß;* and I have accordingly altered the
emphases in the English translations. References to the Colli-Montinari *Studienausgabe* are indicated by the acronym *KSA* followed by the volume number,
a colon, and the fragment number(s) (e.g., *KSA* 12:5[71]):

Friedrich Nietzsche, *Kritische Studienausgabe.* Ed. Giorgio Colli and Mazzino Montinari. Berlin/New York, Walter de Gruyter, 1967–88.

For material not contained in the *KSA,* I refer to the more comprehensive *Kritische Gesamtausgabe,* references to which are indicated by the acronym *KGW,* followed by the volume numbers, a colon, and the fragment number(s) (e.g., *KGW* II/4:4[73]):

Friedrich Nietzsche, *Kritische Gesamtausgabe.* Ed. Giorgio Colli and Mazzino Montinari. Berlin, Walter de Gruyter, 1967–.

III. SECONDARY WORKS

Allen, Barry. "Government in Foucault." *Canadian Journal of Philosophy* 21 (1991): 421–40.
———. "Nietzsche's Question: 'What Good Is Truth?'" *History of Philosophy Quarterly* 9 (1992): 225–40.
Allison, Henry E. *Kant's Transcendental Idealism: An Interpretation and Defense.* New Haven: Yale University Press, 1983.
Babich, Babette E. "Nietzsche and the Philosophy of Scientific Power: Will to Power as Constructive Interpretation." *International Studies in Philosophy* 22 (1990): 79–92.
———. *Nietzsche's Philosophy of Science: Reflecting Science on the Ground of Art and Life.* Albany: State University of New York Press, 1994.
Bachelard, Gaston. *The New Scientific Spirit.* Trans. Patrick A. Heelan. Boston: Beacon Press, 1984.
Bataille, Georges. *The Accursed Share: An Essay on General Economy,* vol. 1, *Consumption.* Trans. Robert Hurley. New York: Zone, 1988.
———. "The Notion of Expenditure." In *Visions of Excess: Selected Writings, 1927–1939,* ed. Allan Stoekl. Minneapolis: University of Minnesota Press, 1985.
Bernal, J. D. *Science in History,* vol. 2, *The Scientific and Industrial Revolutions.* Cambridge, Mass.: MIT Press, 1954.
Bernstein, Richard J. *Beyond Objectivism and Relativism: Science, Hermeneutics, and Praxis.* Philadelphia: University of Pennsylvania Press, 1983.
Bittner, Rüdiger. "Nietzsche's Begriff der Wahrheit." *Nietzsche-Studien* 16 (1987): 70–90.
Blanchot, Maurice. *The Infinite Conversation.* Trans. Susan Hanson. Minneapolis: University of Minnesota Press, 1993.
Blondel, Eric. *Nietzsche: The Body and Culture.* Trans. Seán Hand. Stanford: Stanford University Press, 1991.
Bolton, Robert. "Plato's Distinction between Being and Becoming." *Review of Metaphysics* 29 (1975): 66–96.
Breazeale, Daniel. 1971. "Introduction." *Philosophy and Truth: Selections from Nietzsche's Notebooks of the Early 1870's.* Ed. and trans. Daniel Breazeale. Atlantic Highlands, N.J.: Humanities Press, 1979.

Cartwright, Nancy. *How the Laws of Physics Lie*. Oxford: Oxford University Press, 1983.

Clark, Maudemarie. *Nietzsche on Truth and Philosophy*. Cambridge: Cambridge University Press, 1990.

Conway, Daniel W. "Beyond Realism: Nietzsche's New Infinite." *International Studies in Philosophy* 22 (1990): 93–109.

———. "The Eyes Have It: Perspectives and Affective Investment." *International Studies in Philosophy* 23 (1991): 103–13.

Crawford, Claudia. *The Beginnings of Nietzsche's Theory of Language*. Berlin: Walter de Gruyter, 1988.

Crowell, Steven G. "Nietzsche's View of Truth." *International Studies in Philosophy* 19 (1987): 3–18.

Danto, Arthur. *Nietzsche as Philosopher*. New York: Columbia University Press, 1965.

Davey, Nicholas. "Nietzsche and Hume on Self and Identity." *Journal of the British Society for Phenomenology* 18 (1987): 14–29.

———. "Nietzsche, the Self, and Hermeneutic Theory." *Journal of the British Society for Phenomenology* 18 (1987): 272–84.

Davidson, Donald. "Afterthoughts, 1987." In *Reading Rorty*, ed. Alan R. Malachowski. Oxford: Blackwell, 1990.

———. "On the Very Idea of a Conceptual Scheme." In *Inquiries into Truth and Interpretation*. Oxford: Clarendon Press, 1984.

———. "Radical Interpretation." In *Inquiries into Truth and Interpretation*. Oxford: Clarendon Press, 1984.

Dawkins, Richard. *The Blind Watchmaker*. New York: W. W. Norton, 1986.

Deleuze, Gilles. *Difference and Repetition*. Trans. Paul Patton. New York: Columbia University Press, 1994.

———. *The Fold: Leibniz and the Baroque*. Trans. Tom Conley. Minneapolis: University of Minnesota Press, 1993.

———. *Foucault*. Trans. Seán Hand. Minneapolis: University of Minnesota Press, 1988.

———. *The Logic of Sense*. Ed. Constantin V. Boundas, trans. Mark Lester and Charles Stivale. New York: Columbia University Press, 1990.

———. *Nietzsche and Philosophy*. Trans. Hugh Tomlinson. New York: Columbia University Press, 1983.

Deleuze, Gilles, and Félix Guattari. *A Thousand Plateaus: Capitalism and Schizophrenia*. Trans. Brian Massumi. Minneapolis: University of Minnesota Press, 1987.

De Man, Paul. "Nietzsche's Theory of Rhetoric." *Symposium* (Spring 1974): 33–51.

Dennett, Daniel. *Darwin's Dangerous Idea: Evolution and the Meanings of Life*. New York: Simon and Schuster, 1995.

Derrida, Jacques. "Différance." In *Speech and Phenomena and Other Essays on Husserl's Theory of Signs*, trans. David B. Allison. Evanston: Northwestern University Press, 1973.

———. "Différance." In *Margins of Philosophy*, trans. Alan Bass. Chicago: University of Chicago Press, 1982.

———. *Dissemination*. Trans. Barbara Johnson. Chicago: University of Chicago Press, 1981.

———. "Implications." In *Positions*, trans. Alan Bass. Chicago: University of Chicago Press, 1981.

———. *Of Grammatology*. Trans. Gayatri C. Spivak. Baltimore: Johns Hopkins University Press, 1974.

———. "The Original Discussion of 'Différance.'" In *Derrida and Différance*, ed. David Wood and Robert Bernasconi. Evanston: Northwestern University Press, 1982.

———. "Positions." In *Positions*, trans. Alan Bass Chicago: University of Chicago Press, 1981.

———. *Speech and Phenomena and Other Essays on Husserl's Theory of Signs*. Trans. David B. Allison. Evanston: Northwestern University Press, 1973.

———. *Spurs: Nietzsche's Styles*. Trans. Barbara Harlow. Chicago: University of Chicago Press, 1978.

———. "Structure, Sign, and Play in the Discourse of the Human Sciences." In *Writing and Difference*, trans. Alan Bass. Chicago: University of Chicago Press, 1978.

Descartes, René. *Principles of Philosophy*. In *Descartes: Philosophical Writings*, ed. and trans. Elizabeth Anscombe and Peter Thomas Geach. Indianapolis: Bobbs-Merrill, 1971.

———. "Reply to the Fourth Set of Objections." In *The Philosophical Works of Descartes*, vol. 2, ed. and trans. Elizabeth S. Haldane and G. R. T. Ross. Cambridge: Cambridge University Press, 1967.

Diderot, Denis. *Rameau's Nephew* and *D'Alembert's Dream*. Ed. and trans. Leonard Tancock. Harmondsworth: Penguin, 1966.

Dreyfus, Hubert L. *Being-in-the-World: A Commentary on* Being and Time, *Division I*. Cambridge, Mass.: MIT Press, 1990.

Eco, Umberto. "The Poetics of the Open Work." In *The Role of the Reader: Explorations in the Semiotics of Texts*. Bloomington: Indiana University Press, 1979.

Elgin, Catherine Z. "The Relativity of Fact and the Objectivity of Value." In *Relativism: Interpretation and Confrontation*, ed. Michael Krausz. Notre Dame: University of Notre Dame Press, 1989.

Faraday, Michael. *Experimental Researches in Electricity*, vol. 2. New York: Dover, 1965.

Feyerabend, Paul. *Against Method*. London: Verso, 1978.

Fink, Eugen. "Nietzsche's New Experience of the World," trans. Michael A. Gillespie. In *Nietzsche's New Seas: Explorations in Philosophy, Aesthetics, and Politics*, ed. Michael A. Gillespie and Tracy B. Strong. Chicago: University of Chicago Press, 1988.

Foucault, Michel. "The Confession of the Flesh," trans. Colin Gordon. In *Power/Knowledge: Selected Interviews and Other Writings, 1972–1977*, ed. Colin Gordon. New York: Pantheon, 1980.

———. "Nietzsche, Freud, Marx," trans. Alan D. Schrift. In *Transforming the Hermeneutic Context: From Nietzsche to Nancy*, ed. Gayle L. Ormiston and Alan D. Schrift. Albany: State University of New York Press, 1990.

————. "Nietzsche, Genealogy, History." In *Language, Counter-Memory, Practice: Selected Essays and Interviews by Michel Foucault,* ed. Donald F. Bouchard, trans. Donald F. Bouchard and Sherry Simon. Ithaca: Cornell University Press, 1977.

————. *The Order of Things: An Archaeology of the Human Sciences.* Trans. Alan Sheridan. London: Tavistock, 1970.

————. "Truth and Power," trans. Colin Gordon. In *Power/Knowledge: Selected Interviews and Other Writings, 1972–1977,* ed. Colin Gordon. New York: Pantheon, 1980.

Foucault, Michel, and Gilles Deleuze. "Intellectuals and Power." In *Language, Counter-Memory, Practice: Selected Essays and Interviews by Michel Foucault,* ed. Donald F. Bouchard, trans. Donald F. Bouchard and Sherry Simon. Ithaca: Cornell University Press, 1977.

Fowler, Mark. "Having a Perspective as Having a 'Will': Comment on Professor Conway's 'The Eyes Have It.'" *International Studies in Philosophy* 23 (1991): 115–18.

————. "Nietzschean Perspectivism: 'How Could Such a Philosophy Dominate?'" *Social Theory and Practice* 16 (1990): 119–62.

Freeman, Kathleen. *Ancilla to the Pre-Socratic Philosophers.* Cambridge, Mass.: Harvard University Press, 1948.

Gadamer, Hans-Georg. *Truth and Method,* 2d ed. Trans. John Cumming and Garrett Barden. New York: Continuum, 1989.

Gemes, Ken. "Nietzsche's Critique of Truth." *Philosophy and Phenomenological Research* 52 (1992): 47–65.

Gibson, Roger F, Jr. *Enlightened Empiricism: An Examination of W. V. Quine's Theory of Knowledge.* Tampa: University of South Florida Press, 1988.

Gillispie, Charles C. *The Edge of Objectivity: An Essay in the History of Scientific Ideas.* Princeton: Princeton University Press, 1960.

Goodman, Nelson. "Comments." In *Starmaking: Realism, Anti-Realism, and Irrealism,* ed. Peter J. McCormick. Cambridge, Mass.: MIT Press, 1996.

————. *Fact, Fiction, and Forecast.* Indianapolis: Bobbs-Merrill, 1965.

————. *Languages of Art,* 2d ed. Indianapolis: Hackett, 1976.

————. *Of Mind and Other Matters.* Cambridge, Mass.: Harvard University Press, 1984.

————. "The Way the World Is." In *Problems and Projects.* Indianapolis: Bobbs-Merrill, 1972.

————. *Ways of Worldmaking.* Indianapolis: Hackett, 1978.

Goodman, Nelson, and Catherine Z. Elgin. *Reconceptions in Philosophy and Other Arts and Sciences.* Indianapolis: Hackett, 1988.

Gould, Stephen Jay. "Eternal Metaphors of Palaeontology." In *Patterns of Evolution as Illustrated by the Fossil Record,* ed. A. Hallam. Amsterdam: Elsevier, 1977.

————. *Ever Since Darwin: Reflections in Natural History.* New York: W. W. Norton, 1977.

————. *The Flamingo's Smile: Reflections in Natural History.* New York: W. W. Norton, 1985.

———. *Full House: The Spread of Excellence from Plato to Darwin*. New York: Harmony, 1996.

———. *Hen's Teeth and Horse's Toes*. New York: W. W. Norton, 1983.

———. "In Praise of Charles Darwin." In *Darwin's Legacy*, ed. Charles L. Hamrum. San Francisco: Harper and Row, 1983.

Gould, Stephen J., and Richard Lewontin. "The Spandrels of San Marco and the Panglossian Paradigm: A Critique of the Adaptationist Programme." *Proceedings of the Royal Society of London* B205 (1979): 581–98.

Granier, Jean. "Nietzsche's Conception of Chaos," trans. David B. Allison. In *The New Nietzsche: Contemporary Styles of Interpretation*, ed. David B. Allison. Cambridge, Mass.: MIT Press, 1977.

———. "Perspectivism and Interpretation," trans. David B. Allison. In *The New Nietzsche: Contemporary Styles of Interpretation*, ed. David B. Allison. Cambridge, Mass.: MIT Press, 1977.

———. *Le problème de la vérité dans la philosophie de Nietzsche*. Paris: Éditions du Seuil, 1966.

Grimm, Rüediger. "Circularity and Self-Reference in Nietzsche." *Metaphilosophy* 10 (1979): 289–305.

———. *Nietzsche's Theory of Knowledge*. Berlin: Walter de Gruyter, 1977.

Gruber, Howard E. *Darwin on Man: A Psychological Study of Scientific Creativity*, together with *Darwin's Early and Unpublished Notebooks*, ed. Paul H. Barrett. New York: E. P. Dutton, 1974.

Guignon, Charles B. *Heidegger and the Problem of Knowledge*. Indianapolis: Hackett, 1983.

Guthrie, W. K. C. *The Greek Philosophers: From Thales to Aristotle*. New York: Harper and Row, 1950

———. *A History of Greek Philosophy*, vol. 1, *The Earlier Presocratics and Pythagoreans*. Cambridge: Cambridge University Press, 1962.

———. *A History of Greek Philosophy*, vol. 2, *The Presocratic Tradition from Parmenides to Democritus*. Cambridge: Cambridge University Press, 1965.

Haase, Marie-Louise, and Salaquarda, Jörg. "Konkordanz Der Wille Zur Macht: Nachlass in chronologischer Ordnung der kritischen Gesamtausgabe." *Nietzsche-Studien* 9 (1980): 446–90.

Hales, Steven D., and Robert C. Welshon. "Truth, Paradox, and Nietzschean Perspectivism." *History of Philosophy Quarterly* 11 (1994): 101–19.

Hanson, Norwood Russell. *Patterns of Discovery: An Inquiry into the Conceptual Foundations of Science*. Cambridge: Cambridge University Press, 1958.

Heath, Stephen. *Questions of Cinema*. Bloomington: Indiana University Press, 1981.

Hegel, G. W. F. *Faith and Knowledge*. Trans. Walter Cerf and H. S. Harris. Albany: State University of New York Press, 1977.

———. *Lectures on the History of Philosophy*, vol. 1, *Greek Philosophy to Plato*. Trans. E. S. Haldane. Lincoln: University of Nebraska Press, 1995.

———. *Phenomenology of Spirit*. Trans. A. V. Miller. Oxford: Oxford University Press, 1977.

Heidegger, Martin. *Being and Time*. Trans. John Macquarrie and Edward Robinson. New York: Harper and Row, 1962.

——. *Early Greek Thinking*. Trans. David Farrell Krell and Frank A. Capuzzi. San Francisco: Harper and Row, 1984.

——. *Identity and Difference*. Trans. Joan Stambaugh. New York: Harper and Row, 1969.

——. *Nietzsche*, vol. 1, *The Will to Power as Art*. Trans. David F. Krell. San Francisco: Harper, 1979.

——. *Nietzsche*, vol. 2, *The Eternal Recurrence of the Same*. Trans. David F. Krell. San Francisco: Harper, 1984.

——. *Nietzsche*, vol. 3, *The Will to Power as Knowledge and as Metaphysics*. Trans. Joan Stambaugh, David Farrell Krell, and Frank A. Capuzzi. San Francisco: Harper, 1987.

——. "The Word of Nietzsche: 'God Is Dead.'" In *The Question Concerning Technology and Other Essays*, trans. William Lovitt. New York: Harper and Row, 1977.

Heller, Erich. "Wittgenstein and Nietzsche." In *The Importance of Nietzsche: Ten Essays*. Chicago: University of Chicago Press, 1988.

Hiley, David R., James F. Bohman, and Richard M. Shusterman, eds. *The Interpretive Turn: Philosophy, Science, Culture*. Ithaca: Cornell University Press, 1991.

Hinman, Lawrence M. "Nietzsche, Metaphor, and Truth." *Philosophy and Phenomenological Research* 43 (1982): 179–99.

Hollingdale, R. J. *Nietzsche*. London: Routledge and Kegan Paul, 1973.

Homer. *The Iliad of Homer*. Trans. Richmond Lattimore. Chicago: University of Chicago Press, 1951.

Houlgate, Stephen. *Hegel, Nietzsche, and the Criticism of Metaphysics*. Cambridge: Cambridge University Press, 1986.

——. "Kant, Nietzsche, and the 'Thing in Itself.'" *Nietzsche-Studien* 22 (1993): 115–57.

Hoy, David C. *The Critical Circle: Literature, History, and Philosophical Hermeneutics*. Berkeley: University of California Press, 1978.

——. "Heidegger and the Hermeneutic Turn." In *The Cambridge Companion to Heidegger*, ed. Charles Guignon. Cambridge: Cambridge University Press, 1993.

——. "Nietzsche, Hume, and the Genealogical Method." In *Nietzsche as Affirmative Thinker*, ed. Yirmiyahu Yovel. Dordrecht: Martinus Nijhoff, 1986.

——. "Philosophy as Rigorous Philology? Nietzsche and Poststructuralism." *New York Literary Forum* 8–9 (1981): 171–85.

——. "Post-Cartesian Interpretation: Hans-Georg Gadamer and Donald Davidson." In *The Philosophy of Hans-Georg Gadamer*, ed. Lewis E. Hahn. La Salle, Ill.: Open Court, 1997.

——. "Two Conflicting Conceptions of How to Naturalize Philosophy: Foucault versus Habermas." In *Metaphysik nach Kant?* ed. Dieter Henrich and Rolf-Peter Horstmann. Stuttgarg: Klett-Cotta, 1988.

Irwin, Terence. "Plato's Heracleiteanism." *Philosophical Quarterly* 27 (1977): 1–13.

Jaspers, Karl. *Nietzsche: An Introduction to the Understanding of His Philosophical Activity.* Trans. Charles F. Walraff and Frederick J. Schmitz. South Bend, Ind.: Regnery Gateway, 1979.

Kant, Immanuel. *Critique of Pure Reason.* Trans. Norman Kemp Smith. New York: St. Martin's Press, 1929.

———. *Groundwork of the Metaphysic of Morals.* Trans. H. J. Paton. New York: Harper and Row, 1948.

———. *Prolegomena to Any Future Metaphysics.* Trans. James W. Ellington. Indianapolis: Hackett, 1977.

Kaufmann, Walter. "Editor's Introduction." In Friedrich Nietzsche, *The Will to Power,* ed. Walter Kaufmann, trans. Walter Kaufmann and R. J. Hollingdale. New York: Vintage Books, 1967.

———. *Nietzsche: Philosopher, Psychologist, Anti-Christ,* 4th ed. Princeton: Princeton University Press, 1974.

Kellert, Stephen H. *In the Wake of Chaos: Unpredictable Order in Dynamical Systems.* Chicago: University of Chicago Press, 1993.

Kirk, G. S. and J. E. Raven. *The Presocratic Philosophers: A Critical History with a Selection of Texts.* Cambridge: Cambridge University Press, 1957.

Klein, Wayne. *Nietzsche and the Promise of Philosophy.* Albany: State University of New York Press, 1997.

Kofman, Sarah. "Appendix: Genealogy, Interpretation, Text." In *Nietzsche and Metaphor,* trans. Duncan Large. Stanford: Stanford University Press, 1993.

———. *Nietzsche and Metaphor,* trans. Duncan Large. Stanford: Stanford University Press, 1993.

Kuhn, Thomas S., *The Structure of Scientific Revolutions,* 2d ed. Chicago: University of Chicago Press, 1970.

Laclau, Ernesto, and Chantal Mouffe. *Hegemony and Socialist Strategy: Towards a Radical Democratic Politics.* London: Verso, 1985.

Laplace, Pierre Simon, Marquis de. *A Philosophical Essay on Probabilities,* trans. F. W. Truscott and F. L. Emory. New York: John Wiley and Sons, 1917.

Leibniz, Gottfried Wilhelm. *Discourse on Metaphysics* and *The Monadology.* Trans. George Montgomery with revisions by Albert R. Chandler. In *The Rationalists.* Garden City, N.Y.: Doubleday.

———. *Theodicy: Essays on the Goodness of God, the Freedom of Man, and the Origin of Evil.* Ed. Austin Farrer. Trans. E. M. Huggard. La Salle, Ill.: Open Court, 1988.

Leiter, Brian. "Nietzsche and Aestheticism." *Journal of the History of Philosophy* 30 (1992): 275–88.

———. "Perspectivism in Nietzsche's *Genealogy of Morals.*" In *Nietzsche, Genealogy, Morality: Essays on Nietzsche's Genealogy of Morals,* ed. Richard Schacht. Berkeley: University of California Press, 1994.

Lévi-Strauss, Claude. *Introduction to the Work of Marcel Mauss.* Trans. Felicity Baker. London: Routledge and Kegan Paul, 1987.

Lyotard, Jean-François. *The Differend: Phrases in Dispute.* Trans. Georges Van Den Abbeele. Minneapolis: University of Minnesota Press, 1988.

————. "Lessons in Paganism," trans. David Macey. In *The Lyotard Reader,* ed. Andrew Benjamin. Oxford: Blackwell, 1989.

————. *The Postmodern Condition: A Report on Knowledge.* Trans. Geoff Bennington and Brian Massumi. Minneapolis: University of Minnesota Press, 1984.

Lyotard, Jean François, and Jean-Loup Thébaud. *Just Gaming.* Trans. Wlad Godzich. Minneapolis: University of Minnesota Press, 1985.

Magnus, Bernd. "Aristotle and Nietzsche: *Megalopsychia* and *Übermensch.*" In *The Greeks and the Good Life,* ed. David J. Depew. Indianapolis: Hackett, 1980.

————. "Nietzsche and the Project of Bringing Philosophy to an End." In *Nietzsche as Affirmative Thinker,* ed. Yirmiyahu Yovel. Dordrecht: Martinus Nijhoff, 1983.

————. *Nietzsche's Existential Imperative.* Bloomington: Indiana University Press, 1978.

————. "Nietzsche's Mitigated Skepticism." *Nietzsche-Studien* 9 (1980): 260–67.

————. "Nietzsche's Philosophy in 1888: *The Will to Power* and the *Übermensch.*" *Journal of the History of Philosophy* 24 (1986): 79–98.

Mallarmé, Stéphane. "A Throw of the Dice/Un Coup de Dés." In *Collected Poems,* trans. Henry Weinfield. Berkeley: University of California Press, 1994.

Malpas, J. E. *Donald Davidson and the Mirror of Meaning: Holism, Truth, Interpretation.* Cambridge: Cambridge University Press, 1992.

Marx, Karl. *Economic and Philosophical Manuscripts.* In *Marx: Selections,* ed. Allen W. Wood. New York: Macmillan, 1988.

Mauss, Marcel. *The Gift: Forms and Functions of Exchange in Archaic Societies.* Trans. Ian Cunnison. New York: W. W. Norton, 1967.

Mayr, Ernst. *One Long Argument: Charles Darwin and the Genesis of Modern Evolutionary Thought.* Cambridge, Mass.: Harvard University Press, 1991.

————. *Toward a New Philosophy of Biology: Observations of an Evolutionist.* Cambridge, Mass.: Harvard University Press, 1988.

McCormick, Peter J., ed. *Starmaking: Realism, Anti-Realism, and Irrealism.* Cambridge, Mass.: MIT Press, 1996.

Megill, Allan. *Prophets of Extremity: Nietzsche, Heidegger, Foucault, Derrida.* Berkeley: University of California Press, 1985.

Mittelman, Willard. "Perspectivism, Becoming, and Truth in Nietzsche." *International Studies in Philosophy* 16 (1984): 3–22.

Moles, Alistair. "Nietzsche's Eternal Recurrence as Riemannian Cosmology." *International Studies in Philosophy* 21 (1989): 21–40.

————. *Nietzsche's Philosophy of Nature and Cosmology.* Berlin: Peter Lang, 1990.

Monod, Jacques. *Chance and Necessity: An Essay on the Natural Philosophy of Modern Biology.* Trans. Austryn Wainhouse. New York: Vintage, 1972.

Montinari, Mazzino. "Nietzsche's Nachlaß 1885–1888 und der 'Wille zur Macht.'" In Friedrich Nietzsche, *Kritische Studienausgabe,* vol. 14. Ed. Giorgio Colli and Mazzino Montinari. Berlin: Walter de Gruyter, 1988.

Morgan, George A. *What Nietzsche Means.* New York: Harper and Row, 1941.

Müller-Lauter, Wolfgang. *Nietzsche: Seine Philosophie der Gegensätze und die Gegensätze seiner Philosophie.* Berlin: Walter de Gruyter, 1971.

———. "Nietzsche's Teaching of Will to Power," trans. Drew Griffin. *Journal of Nietzsche Studies* 4–5 (1992–93): 37–101.

———. "On Associating with Nietzsche," trans. R. J. Hollingdale. *Journal of Nietzsche Studies* 4–5 (1992–93): 5–35.

Nancy, Jean-Luc. "'Our Probity!' On Truth in the Moral Sense in Nietzsche." In *Looking After Nietzsche,* ed. Laurence A. Rickels. Albany: State University of New York Press, 1990.

Nehamas, Alexander. "Immanent and Transcendent Perspectivism in Nietzsche." *Nietzsche-Studien* 12 (1983): 473–94.

———. *Nietzsche: Life as Literature.* Cambridge, Mass.: Harvard University Press, 1985.

Nielsen, Kai. *Naturalism without Foundations.* Amherst, N.Y.: Prometheus Books, 1996.

Nola, Robert. "Nietzsche's Theory of Truth and Belief." *Philosophy and Phenomenological Research* 47 (1987): 525–62.

Papineau, David. *Philosophical Naturalism.* Oxford: Blackwell, 1993.

Patton, Paul. "Nietzsche and the Body of the Philosopher." In *Cartographies: Poststructuralism and the Mapping of Bodies and Spaces,* ed. Rosalyn Diprose and Robyn Ferrell. Sydney: Allen and Unwin, 1991.

Plato. *The Collected Dialogues of Plato.* Ed. Edith Hamilton and Huntington Cairns. Princeton: Princeton University Press, 1961.

Powers, Jonathan. "Atomism." In *The Concise Encyclopedia of Western Philosophy and Philosophers,* ed. J. O. Urmson and Jonathan Rée. London: Unwin Hyman, 1989.

Prigogine, Ilya. *From Being to Becoming: Time and Complexity in the Physical Sciences.* New York: W. H. Freeman and Co., 1980.

Prigogine, Ilya, and Isabelle Stengers. *Order out of Chaos: Man's New Dialogue with Nature.* New York: Bantam Books, 1984.

Prior, A. N. "Correspondence Theory of Truth." In *Encyclopedia of Philosophy.* Vol. 2, ed. Paul Edwards. New York: Macmillan, 1967.

Putnam, Hilary. "Irrealism and Deconstruction." In *Starmaking: Realism, Anti-Realism, and Irrealism,* ed. Peter J. McCormick. Cambridge, Mass.: MIT Press, 1996.

———. "Realism and Reason." *Proceedings and Addresses of the American Philosophical Association* 50 (1977): 483–98.

———. *Reason, Truth, and History.* London: Cambridge University Press, 1981.

———. "Reflections on Goodman's *Ways of Worldmaking.*" In *Starmaking: Realism, Anti- Realism, and Irrealism,* ed. Peter J. McCormick. Cambridge, Mass.: MIT Press, 1996.

———. "The Way the World Is." In *Realism with a Human Face.* Cambridge, Mass.: Harvard University Press, 1990.

Quine, W. V. "Epistemology Naturalized." In *Ontological Relativity and Other Essays.* New York: Columbia University Press, 1969.

————. "Goodman's *Ways of Worldmaking*." In *Theories and Things*. Cambridge, Mass.: Harvard University Press, 1981.

————. "Natural Kinds." In *Ontological Relativity and Other Essays*. New York: Columbia University Press, 1969.

————. "Ontological Relativity." In *Ontological Relativity and Other Essays*. New York: Columbia University Press, 1969.

————. "On What There Is." In *From a Logical Point of View*. Cambridge, Mass.: Harvard University Press, 1961.

————. "Structure and Nature." *Journal of Philosophy* 89 (1992): 5–9.

————. "Two Dogmas of Empiricism." In *From a Logical Point of View*. Cambridge, Mass.: Harvard University Press, 1961.

————. *Word and Object*. Cambridge, Mass.: MIT Press, 1960.

Rabinow, Paul, and William M. Sullivan. "The Interpretive Turn: Emergence of an Approach." In *Interpretive Social Science*, ed. Paul Rabinow and William M. Sullivan. Berkeley: University of California Press, 1979.

Ramberg, Bjørn. *Donald Davidson's Philosophy of Language: An Introduction*. Oxford: Basil Blackwell, 1989.

Richards, Robert J. *The Meaning of Evolution: The Morphological Construction and Ideological Reconstruction of Darwin's Theory*. Chicago: University of Chicago Press, 1992.

Richardson, John. "Reply to Professor Robin Small." *International Studies in Philosophy* 21 (1989): 135–37.

Rorty, Richard. "Inquiry as Recontextualization: An Anti-Dualist Account of Interpretation." In *Objectivity, Relativism, and Truth: Philosophical Papers*, vol. 1. Cambridge: Cambridge University Press, 1991.

————. "Introduction: Pragmatism and Philosophy." In *Consequences of Pragmatism*. Minneapolis: University of Minnesota Press, 1982.

————. "Is Natural Science a Natural Kind?" In *Objectivity, Relativism, and Truth: Philosophical Papers*, vol. 1. Cambridge: Cambridge University Press, 1991.

————. *Philosophy and the Mirror of Nature*. Princeton: Princeton University Press, 1979.

————. "Pragmatism without Method." In *Objectivity, Relativism, and Truth: Philosophical Papers*, vol. 1. Cambridge: Cambridge University Press, 1991.

————. "Solidarity or Objectivity?" In *Objectivity, Relativism, and Truth: Philosophical Papers*, vol. 1. Cambridge: Cambridge University Press, 1991.

Rouse, Joseph. *Knowledge and Power: Toward a Political Philosophy of Science*. Ithaca: Cornell University Press, 1987.

Schacht, Richard. "Beyond Scholasticism: On Dealing with Nietzsche and His *Nachlaß*." In *Making Sense of Nietzsche*. Urbana: University of Illinois Press, 1995.

————. *Nietzsche*. London: Routledge and Kegan Paul, 1983.

————. "Nietzsche's *Gay Science*, Or, How to Naturalize Cheerfully." In *Reading Nietzsche*, ed. Robert C. Solomon and Kathleen Higgins. New York: Oxford University Press, 1988.

————. "The Nietzsche-Spinoza Problem: Spinoza as Precursor?" In *Making Sense of Nietzsche*. Urbana: University of Illinois Press, 1995.

Schrift, Alan D. *Nietzsche and the Question of Interpretation: Between Hermeneutics and Deconstruction.* New York: Routledge, 1990.
———. *Nietzsche's French Legacy: A Genealogy of Poststructuralism.* New York: Routledge, 1995.
Shapiro, Gary. *Alcyone: Nietzsche on Gifts, Noise, and Women.* Albany: State University of New York Press, 1991.
Silverman, Kaja. *The Subject of Semiotics.* New York: Oxford University Press, 1983.
Solomon, Robert C. *In the Spirit of Hegel.* New York: Oxford University Press, 1983.
———. "A More Severe Morality: Nietzsche's Affirmative Ethics." In *From Hegel to Existentialism.* Oxford: Oxford University Press, 1987.
———. "The Secret of Hegel (Kierkegaard's Complaint): A Study in Hegel's Philosophy of Religion." In *From Hegel to Existentialism.* Oxford: Oxford University Press, 1987.
Spinoza, Benedict de. *The Ethics.* In *The Chief Works of Spinoza,* vol. 2. Trans. R. H. M. Elwes. New York: Dover Publications, 1951.
Stack, George J. "Kant, Lange, and Nietzsche: Critique of Knowledge." In *Nietzsche and Modern German Thought,* ed. Keith Ansell-Pearson. London: Routledge, 1991.
———. *Lange and Nietzsche.* Berlin: Walter de Gruyter, 1983.
———. "Nietzsche and Boscovich's Natural Philosophy." *Pacific Philosophical Quarterly* 62 (1981): 69–87.
———. "Nietzsche and the Correspondence Theory of Truth." *Dialogos* 38 (1981): 93–117.
———. "Nietzsche's Critique of Things-In-Themselves." *Dialogos* 36 (1980): 33–57.
———. "Nietzsche's Evolutionary Epistemology." *Dialogos* 59 (1992): 75–101.
Strong, Tracy B. *Friedrich Nietzsche and the Politics of Transfiguration.* Exp. ed. Berkeley: University of California Press, 1988.
Stroud, Barry. "The Charm of Naturalism." *Proceedings and Addresses of the American Philosophical Association* 70 (1996): 43–55.
Taylor, Charles. "Foucault on Freedom and Truth." In *Foucault: A Critical Reader,* ed. David Couzens Hoy. Oxford: Basil Blackwell, 1986.
Vaihinger, Hans. *Nietzsche als Philosoph.* Berlin: Reuther und Reichard, 1902.
———. "Nietzsche and His Doctrine of Conscious Illusion." In *Nietzsche: A Collection of Critical Essays,* ed. Robert C. Solomon. Notre Dame: University of Notre Dame Press, 1973.
Warnock, Mary. "Nietzsche's Conception of Truth." In *Nietzsche's Imagery and Thought: A Collection of Essays,* ed. Malcolm Pasley. Berkeley: University of California Press, 1978.
Warren, Mark. *Nietzsche and Political Thought.* Cambridge, Mass.: MIT Press, 1988.
West, Cornel. "Nietzsche's Prefiguration of Postmodern American Philosophy." In *Why Nietzsche Now?* ed. Daniel O'Hara. Bloomington: Indiana University Press, 1985.

Westphal, Kenneth R. "Nietzsche's Sting and the Possibility of Good Philology." *International Studies in Philosophy* 16 (1984): 71–89.

Wheeler, Samuel C. "True Figures: Metaphor, Social Relations, and the Sorites." In *The Interpretive Turn: Philosophy, Science, Culture,* ed. David R. Hiley, James F. Bohman, and Richard M. Shusterman. Ithaca: Cornell University Press, 1991.

Wilcox, John T. "Nietzsche Scholarship and 'the Correspondence Theory of Truth': The Danto Case." *Nietzsche-Studien* 15 (1986): 337–57.

———. "Nietzsche's Epistemology: Recent American Discussions." *International Studies in Philosophy* 15 (1983): 67–77.

———. "A Note on Correspondence and Pragmatism in Nietzsche." *International Studies in Philosophy* 12 (1980): 77–80.

———. *Truth and Value in Nietzsche: A Study of His Metaethics and Epistemology.* Ann Arbor: University of Michigan Press, 1974.

Wittgenstein, Ludwig. *The Blue and Brown Books.* New York: Harper and Row, 1958.

———. *Philosophical Investigations.* Trans. G. E. M. Anscombe. Oxford: Basil Blackwell, 1953.

Young, Julian. *Nietzsche's Philosophy of Art.* Cambridge: Cambridge University Press, 1992.

Concordance

NIETZSCHE'S NACHGELASSENE FRAGMENTE

The concordance below pairs passages in *The Will Power* (WP) referred to in my
text and footnotes with corresponding passages in the *Kritische Studienausgabe*
(*KSA*). A complete concordance between *The Will and Power* and the *Kritische
Gesamtausgabe* (*KGW*) is provided by Marie-Luise Haase and Jörg Salaquarda
in *Nietzsche-Studien* 9 (1980): 446–90. Haase and Salaquarda's concordance
can be converted into a complete concordance between *The Will to Power* and
the *Kritische Studienausgabe* by noting that *KGW* VII 1–24 = *KSA* 10, *KGW*
VII 25–45 = *KSA* 11, *KGW* VIII 1–10 = *KSA* 12, *KGW* VIII 11–25 = *KSA* 13.

WP	KSA	WP	KSA
Preface	13:11[411]	83	12:9[182]
1	12:2[127]	90	13:15[8]
2	12:9[35]	114	12:5[71]
3	12:10[192]	120	12:10[53]
4	12:5[71]	124	12:9[121]
5	12:5[71]	171	13:14[57]
12	13:11[99]	172	12:10[184]
22	12:9[35]	228	11:44[6]
23	12:9[35]	229	13:14[179]
37	12:9[107]	253	12:2[165]
46	13:14[219]	254	12:2[189]–[190]
47	13:14[219]	258	12:2[165]
55	12:5[71]	259	11:26[119]
70	12:2[175]	270	12:10[121]

WP	KSA	WP	KSA
279	12:7[6]	491	12:2[102]
293	13:14[31]	492	11:40[21]
298	12:10[194]	493	11:34[253]
339	13:11[226]	494	11:36[19]
340	12:10[170]	495	11:25[470]
370	12:9[108]	499	11:41[11]
383	13:14[163]	500	12:2[92]
384	12:1[122]	501	12:5[65]
385	12:10[206]	503	11:26[61]
386	12:10[164], [203]	504	12:7[9]
387	13:11[310]	505	12:2[95]
388	12:10[128]	508	10:24[5]
401	13:14[137], [138], [140]	509	12:7[41]
		510	12:7[9]
404	12:5[58]	511	12:2[90]
405	12:2[207]	512	11:40[13]
406	12:1[93]	513	12:6[11]
407	11:26[300]	514	13:14[105]
408	11:26[100]	515	13:14[152]
409	11:34[195]	516	12:9[97]
410	12:2[161]	517	12:9[89]
452	13:15[46]	518	12:2[91]
455	13:15[58]	519	12:7[55]
456	13:14[160]	520	11:36[23]
457	13:15[52]	521	12:9[144]
459	13:15[77]	522	12:5[22]
460	13:14[109]	523	13:14[144]–[145]
462	12:9[8], 10[28]	524	13:11[145]
466	13:15[51]	525	13:16[56]
470	12:2[155]	526	13:14[144]
474	13:11[120]	527	12:5[68]
475	12:2[204]	528	12:5[55]
477	13:11[113]	529	13:14[146]
478	13:14[152]	530	12:7[4]
479	13:15[90]	531	12:2[84]
481	12:7[60]	536	13:15[118]
482	12:5[3]	540	11:34[230]
483	11:38[3]	542	cf. 13:16[21]
484	12:10[158]	543	13:11[115]
485	12:10[19]	545	11:36[25]
486	12:2[87]	546	12:2[145]
487	12:7[63]	547	12:2[158]
488	12:9[98]	548	12:2[193]
489	12:5[56]	549	11:36[26]
490	11:40[42]	550	12:2[83]

WP	KSA		WP	KSA
551	13:14[98]		635	12:14[79]
552	12:9[91]		636	12:14[186]
553	12:5[4]		637	11:36[20]
554	12:2[139]		638	12:2[143]
555	12:2[154]		639	12:10[138]
556	12:2[149]–[152]		640	10:24[17]
557	12:2[85]		641	10:24[14]
558	12:10[202]		642	11:36[22]
559	13:11[134]		643	12:2[148]
560	12:9[40]		644	12:7[9]
561	12:2[87]		647	12:7[25]
562	10:24[13]		648	12:7[9]
563	12:5[36]		649	12:7[44]
564	12:2[157]		650	12:2[63]
565	12:6[14]		651	13:11[121]
566	13:11[50]		652	13:14[174]
567	13:14[184]		653	12:10[13]
568	13:14[93]		654	12:1[118]
569	12:9[106]		655	11:36[21]
570	13:11[5]		656	12:9[151]
576	13:18[16]		657	12:5[64]
578	12:9[160]		658	12:35[15]
579	12:8[2]		659	12:36[35]–[36]
580	12:9[62]		660	12:2[76]
584	13:14[153]–[154]		666	12:7[1]
590	12:2[77]		668	13:11[114]
591	12:3[5]		671	10:24[32], [34]
600	12:2[117]		676	10:24[16]
604	12:2[82], [86]		678	12:7[2]
605	12:9[48]		680	12:7[9]
606	12:2[174]		681	12:7[9]
616	12:2[108]		682	12:10[136]
617	12:7[54]		684	13:14[133]
618	11:36[34]		685	13:14[123]
619	12:36[31]		688	13:14[121]
624	12:7[56]		689	13:14[81]–[82]
625	13:14[122]		692	13:14[121]
627	12:2[83]		708	13:11[72]
628	12:2[89]		709	12:9[13]
629	12:7[14]		711	13:11[74]
630	11:36[18]		712	12:9[8]
631	12:2[139]		715	13:11[73]
632	12:2[142]		728	13:14[192]
633	12:14[95]		765	13:15[30]
634	12:14[79]		778	13:14[157]

WP	KSA	WP	KSA
785	12:9[30]	928	13:11[353]
787	10:8[19]	933	12:9[139]
789	12:2[206]	935	13:23[4]
797	12:2[130]	943	11:35[76]
800	13:14[117]	949	13:11[44]
802	12:9[102]	962	11:34[96]
804	12:10[167]	966	11:27[59]
809	13:14[119]	1011	12:6[25]
810	12:10[60]	1014	12:2[81]
812	13:14[119]	1022	13:11[38]
820	11:37[12]	1040	13:18[1]
842	13:14[61]	1050	13:14[14]
843	12:7[16],	1051	11:41[6]–[7]
	13:14[119]	1052	13:14[89]
846	cf. GS 370	1062	11:36[15]
852	12:10[168]	1063	12:5[54]
864	13:14[182]	1064	11:35[54]–[55]
881	12:10[111]	1065	13:11[94]
883	12:9[119]	1066	13:14[188]
904	13:11[151]	1067	11:38[12]

Index

objectivity, 54, 111–12, 134, 135, 155–59, 157–58, 161
ontological relativity, 4, 55n57, 60, 92, 97, 155–59. *See also* empiricism, holistic; holism
ontology, 4, 7, 19–20, 69–70, 163–64, 241; naturalized, 75–79. *See also* being; interpretation; ontological relativity; perspectivism; thing in itself
ontotheology, 6–7, 217–19, 225–26, 244

Paley, William, 226n28
Papineau, David, 5
Parmenides, 169, 186, 190–93, 195–96, 199. *See also* Eleatics
perception. *See* sense perception
periodization of Nietzsche's corpus, 7–8
perspectives, 38–39, 54, 65, 92n26, 97; affective interpretation and, 111–18; appearance and, 38–39, 154, 156; as cumulative, 121–22; and ordinary human vision, 120–21, 149–50, 163–67; as public system of evaluation, 154–55; as species viewpoint, 119–20.
perspectivism, 3, 4, 8, 105, 109–168, 196, 200–201; antiessentialism and, 163–68; chaos and, 206–7; as doctrine, 109–11; ego-substance and, 122–25; neo-Kantianism and, 118–21, 176–77; object of, 139–63; realism and, 120–21, 148–52, 161–63; subject of, 118–39; visual account, 120–21, 149–50, 163–67. *See also* interpretation
pessimism, 170, 186–87
phenomenalism, 109, 118, 153n93
philosopher-artist, 67–68
Plato, 19, 25, 30, 33, 56n59, 65, 81, 83n17, 86, 87, 91, 120, 162n111, 169, 178, 179, 180. 190, 193, 195–96, 198, 199
Platonic Form, 20, 22, 42, 84–85, 87, 199
Platonism, 20–24, 33, 44, 178, 199
positivism, 19, 30, 43–44, 47, 49, 56, 66, 92n27, 95–96, 170, 243
postmetaphysical position, Nietzsche's, 2, 3, 6–7
postmodernism, Nietzsche and, 1–2
potlatch, 234–35
pragmatism, 24, 30–31, 41–43, 46–48, 81. *See also* truth, pragmatist theory of
Prigogine, Ilya, 210n105, 211n109, 219n10, 222n15, 223n17, 238

progressivism, 226–29
Putnam, Hilary, 97n34, 155, 115n11
Pythagoras, 198n73

Quine, W. V., 2, 5, 35n27, 44n38, 55n57, 93n28, 97n34, 155, 115n11, 137n65, 153n93, 162n111, 214–15n3, 243n76

realism, Nietzsche *vs.*, 48–51, 94–95, 161–63, 197; commonsense, 148, 161; metaphysical, 103, 148–49, 161. *See also* neo-Kantianism, realist
relativism, 3, 53–54, 60–61, 70, 106, 135, 154–55, 159, 172; ontological, 97, 155–56, 159. *See also* ontological relativity
responsibility, 124, 209
ressentiment, 128, 134, 159n105, 233
Richardson, John, 32n22
Ricoeur, Paul, 115n11
Rorty, Richard, 2, 60n65, 155, 114n11, 137n65, 242

Schacht, Richard, ix, 10, 59n62
Schelling, Friedrich, 154n94
Schlechta, Karl, 9n14
Schopenhauer, Arthur, 94, 148, 154n94, 170, 184, 186–89, 192, 193, 195, 221, 239
Schrift, Alan, ix, 57n61, 114n9
science: art and, 63–68, 162; becoming and, 30–31; dogmatism and, 50–51; generalization and, 31, 35–36, 88; morality and, 24–26; naturalism and, 5–6, 215–16; theology and, 5–6, 21–27, 64; truth and, 23–24. *See also* evolution; mechanism; positivism; thermodynamics
self-overcoming, 1, 6, 17–19, 26, 27, 63–65
self-preservation, 30, 89, 102, 138, 228–35
Sellars, Wilfrid, 2
semblance, 32–34, 37–39, 66. *See also* appearance
sense perception, experience, 6, 19–20, 65, 88–91, 93–95, 98, 144, 180, 190–91, 194–95; holistic view, 92–101, 197; knowledge and, 142–43. *See also* empiricism
skepticism, 54, 147–48, 171–75; Nietzsche's rejection of, 99, 176–77. *See also* neo-Kantianism, skeptical
Solomon, Robert, 136n64
soul, 77, 123, 125, 130–32, 132, 182, 184, 236, 240

Text: 10/13 Sabon
Display: Sabon
Composition: G & S Typesetters, Inc.
Printing and binding: Haddon Craftsmen